The Pearl Harbor
Papers

Also by the Authors

Fading Victory: The Diary of Admiral Matome Ugaki—1941–1945 (1991)
    (translated by Masataka Chihaya)
*The Williwaw War: The Arkansas National Guard in the Aleutians
    in World War II* (1992)

With Gordon W. Prange

At Dawn We Slept: The Untold Story of Pearl Harbor (1981)
Miracle at Midway (1982)
Target Tokyo: The Story of the Sorge Spy Ring (1984)
Pearl Harbor: The Verdict of History (1987)
December 7, 1941: The Day the Japanese Attacked Pearl Harbor (1988)
God's Samurai: Lead Pilot at Pearl Harbor (1990)

With J. Michael Wenger

The Way It Was: Pearl Harbor—The Original Photographs (1991)

The Pearl Harbor Papers

INSIDE THE JAPANESE PLANS

EDITED BY Donald M. Goldstein

AND Katherine V. Dillon

 BRASSEY'S (US)

A Maxwell Macmillan Company
WASHINGTON • NEW YORK • LONDON

Brassey's (US)

Editorial Offices	*Order Department*
Brassey's (US)	Brassey's Book Orders
8000 Westpark Drive	c/o Macmillan Publishing Co.
First Floor	100 Front Street, Box 500
McLean, Virginia 22102	Riverside, New Jersey 08075

Brassey's (US) is a Maxwell Macmillan Company. Brassey's books are available at special discounts for bulk purchases for sales promotions, premiums, fund-raising, or educational use through the Special Sales Director, Macmillan Publishing Company, 866 Third Avenue, New York, New York 10022.

   Library of Congress Cataloging-in-Publication Data
The Pearl Harbor papers : inside the Japanese plans / edited by Donald
   M. Goldstein, Katherine V. Dillon
      p. cm.
   Includes index.
   ISBN 0-02-881001-5
   1. Pearl Harbor (Hawaii), Attack on, 1941—Sources.
I. Goldstein, Donald M.   II. Dillon, Katherine V.
D767.92.P397   1993
940.54′26—dc20   93-13514
                                                   CIP

Designed by Jack Meserole
10 9 8 7 6 5 4 3 2 1
PRINTED IN THE UNITED STATES OF AMERICA

CONTENTS

PART III. Pearl Harbor

PART IV. Aftermath

PREFACE

W HEN THE LATE Gordon W. Prange was in Japan as Gen. Douglas MacArthur's historian, he was in a position to obtain interviews and papers that no one else was able to secure. He became acquainted with many ex-officers of the Japanese Navy who had played important roles in Japan's war effort. As soon as these men realized that Prange's persistent questions meant that he wanted to know what had happened, how, and why, and not that he wanted to hang anybody, they cooperated freely. Indeed, many personally prepared these documents for Prange's use. These papers cover a wide gamut of Japanese politics and diplomacy, naval history, strategy and tactics, action aboard carriers and destroyers, and, in particular, the planning, preparation, and execution of the Pearl Harbor attack.

Most Japanese official records of that operation were destroyed at the Battle of Midway in June 1942, and many of the pilots were killed in the course of the war. Thus the documents presented here are doubly valuable, having been written either at the time—such as the diaries—or within a few years of the war's end while memories were still sharp.

Many books about the Pacific War ignore the Japanese point of view. This is especially true of Pearl Harbor, where the emphasis has been on how the Americans could have been caught napping. Prange took into account both sides of the conflict. Familiarity with the Japanese aspect of the problem gives one an entirely new dimension to this ever-fascinating subject. One learns that the Japanese who planned and carried out the attack were neither bungling amateurs nor racially inferior people. They did not need Homer Lea, Hector Bywater, or anyone else to put ideas into their heads. Their success did not depend upon American errors or "conspiracy." Japan's best and brightest were in its Navy at the time, and they devoted months of planning and training to making the Pearl Harbor attack possible.

Reading the Japanese point of view, one readily sees the complexity of the operation and the planning, organization, and coordination that went into the battle plan. This operation was neither simple nor easy. From the Prange documents one gets a sense of the technological progress and of the tremendous problems overcome in the development of torpedo, bomb, and refueling techniques.

A striking point of revisionist literature on the Pearl Harbor attack is the concept that Franklin D. Roosevelt knew about it in advance, maintaining that the United States had broken the Japanese code and was picking up the task force's messages as it crossed the Pacific. Recent revisionists indicate that Winston Churchill knew of the attack, that documents prove that the British had picked up messages being broadcast by the Japanese along the way, but Churchill failed to tell Roosevelt because he wanted to make sure that the Americans would enter the war. These messages are allegedly on file in British archives but are not to be released for some time. Almost all the Prange documents in this volume, from action diaries to after-action reports, however, state positively that the task force never broke radio silence on the outward journey to Hawaii. Hence their messages could not have been intercepted, meaning the charges against Roosevelt and Churchill, if based solely on the concept that the task force broke radio silence, are unfounded.*

Of particular interest to the student of the Pacific War are the monographs prepared by Minoru Genda. He was the tactical genius behind the Pearl Harbor attack, and his documents give an unusually detailed account of what is involved in realizing a daring, unprecedented operation, as well as the workings of a brilliant, original mind. It is important to remember that "Operation Hawaii" trod heavily on the toes of previous naval strategy. In general, Japanese naval officers were firmly battleship-minded and devoted to the strategy of "The Great All-Out Battle," in which the U.S. Navy would be lured across the Pacific, whittled down by submarines on the way, and once in the waters near Japan, soundly defeated. In view of this mind-set, it is most unlikely that the Pearl Harbor plan would ever have left the drawing boards had not Adm. Isoroku Yamamoto, commander in chief of the Combined Fleet, pushed it through.

Some of the studies herein are what Capt. Mitsuo Fuchida, who led the air attack on Pearl Harbor, called "memory documents." At the end of the war, the Japanese armed forces conducted a wholesale destruction of documents. Untold quantities of valuable historical material went up in smoke. During the Occupation, the Military History Section of Headquarters USAFFE (U.S. Army Forces, Far East) attempted to reconstruct events on the basis of the memories of survivors and bits and pieces of other documents. Thus, this particular type of study cannot be adjudged as absolutely, officially correct. There is no reason, however, to question the expertise or good faith of the officers engaged in their preparation, so these "memory documents" are probably reliable within the powers of human recollection.

Most of the documents herein are not available anywhere else. Many have never before been available in English, and indeed, few have been published in Japanese. Our purpose in preparing this book has been to make them readily available to scholars and buffs of the Pacific War. This book allows

---

* Of course, Japanese naval headquarters sent many messages to all fleets during this period using the JN25 code, which the United States had not yet broken. It has been claimed that the British had done so—Eds.

the scholar to review these rare papers without having to go to the library or send for them. Prange was very protective of his sources while preparing his manuscripts, but now that his books have been published we are sure he would want to share them so that they can be used to set the record straight from the Japanese point of view.

This book is divided into four parts. A certain amount of chronological overlapping of material exists, because many of these documents cover both the plans and preparations for the Pearl Harbor attack and its actual performance.

Part I, *Plans and Preparations for the Pearl Harbor Attack,* features the work of Minodu Genda, who as Air Staff officer of the 1st Air Fleet was the foremost planner and architect of the operation. Genda spent many hours with Prange, and his studies of air power were of unique value to Prange in his work. This section also contains the diary of Rear Adm. Giichi Nakahara, who as chief of the Navy Ministry's Personnel Bureau was intimately concerned with the Pearl Harbor preparations. This part also contains extracts from the diaries and papers of Shigeshi Uchida and Sadamu Sanagi, both of whom were in the Operations Section, Naval General Staff, in 1941. Part I closes with a "memory document"—the "General Outline of the Orders and Plans" of the attack.

Part II, *Letters of Adm. Isoroku Yamamoto,* contains a brief sampling of his correspondence. Some of these letters are of inestimable historical importance; others are full of human interest. With the exception of Adm. Heihachiro Togo, hero of the Russo-Japanese War, no naval figure is more honored in Japan than Yamamoto. He conceived the Pearl Harbor operation and pushed it through to final acceptance.

Part III, *Pearl Harbor,* covers the actual attack. It opens with extracts from an important book, *Rengo Kantai,* by Ryunosuke Kusaka, who was chief of staff of the 1st Air Fleet. An invaluable view of the operational planning and logistics, these extracts outline the operation from its beginning to the task force's return to Japan. As in other documents herein, Kusaka stresses radio silence. He also gives an account of the attack and of the voyage home. Second comes the diary of Sadao Chigusa, who was executive officer of the destroyer *Akigumo.* He provides an excellent, detailed story from a relatively low echelon of the rendezvous at Hitokappu Bay, the voyage to Hawaii, the anxious waiting to learn the results, and the homeward voyage. Perhaps a major feature of this section are the war diaries of the 5th Carrier Division, 1st Destroyer Division, and 3d Battleship Division for December 1941. These diaries are important, not only because they tell what happened from the Japanese point of view, but also because they clearly indicate that the task force maintained radio silence throughout the outgoing voyage. They also show each day's latitude and longitude, so the reader can follow the task force as it proceeded on its way. Next comes a study of the operation prepared at the Yokosuka Naval Air Corps and written approximately in August 1942. This was fairly close to the event, and many of the Pearl Harbor veterans were still alive.

Part IV, *Aftermath,* concludes this book with a detailed report by Masa-taka Chihaya, "An Intimate Look at the Japanese Navy," which summarizes the Japanese Navy's successes and failures, especially the latter, during the war. Here one finds neither whining nor buck-passing, just frank and honest analyses.

The endpapers of this book are copies of an after-action report map, one of the most important recently discovered documents of World War II. Our preliminary research indicates that it was prepared by the leader of the air strike, Comdr. Mitsuo Fuchida, based upon action reports compiled aboard the carrier *Akagi* following the Pearl Harbor attack. Fuchida used this map at an imperial briefing held on 27 December 1941. December 8 is the attack's date in Tokyo time. The original map eventually will be exhibited publicly.

We believe *Pearl Harbor Papers* is the first attempt to put the Japanese story in proper context. The documents herein are primary source material and should be cited as such by any student making use of them. We have made no major changes that would affect the meaning or in any other way compromise the integrity of the material. Our part has been confined to providing minor grammatical corrections, identification where possible of individuals not fully cited, a few explanatory footnotes, and the introduction to each part and to each individual study.

There are no endnotes in this work because the individual documents are their own sources. They are major extracts from the Prange files, and we are happy to make them available to the layman so that he may better understand the war in the Pacific.

We dedicate this book to all those who died in the Pacific War on both sides of the ocean and to all historians who seek the truth.

DONALD M. GOLDSTEIN, PH.D.
Professor of Public and International Affairs
University of Pittsburgh
Pittsburgh, Pennsylvania

KATHERINE V. DILLON
CWO, USAF (Ret.)
Arlington, Virginia

The Pearl Harbor Papers

PART I

Plans and Preparations for the Pearl Harbor Attack

T O UNDERSTAND THE BACKGROUND of the Pearl Harbor attack, one must have a general idea of the organization and psychology of the Japanese Navy. As World War II loomed, that organization was in many respects a foster child of Great Britain. When Japan broke out of its isolation and began to make its way into the modern world, it turned to the Mistress of the Seas for guidance. Until Japanese shipbuilding developed the ability to take over, most of Japan's warships came from British shipyards. Japan sent students to England and imported British teachers. Nor was the United States without influence. Capt. Alfred Thayer Mahan, with his theories of the influence of sea power upon history, was one of the gurus of Japanese naval officers. The Sino-Japanese and the Russo-Japanese wars proved the mettle of the new Navy.

While in the early days the Japanese Navy was happy to learn what the West had to teach, it did not rely mindlessly upon Occidental examples and teachings. Top Japanese naval officers did not need Homer Lea, Hector Bywater, Billy Mitchell, or anyone else to prime their mental pumps; they were quite capable of working out their own strategy. Under the test of time and combat, some of those strategies might prove exceedingly ill conceived, but they were the Japanese Navy's own ideas.

Following the Washington Conference of 1921–22, the Japanese Navy called one of its rare national defense planning seminars and laid down the Empire's naval mission—to secure command of the Western Pacific. From that moment on, the Japanese concentrated on the "Great All-Out Battle" strategy. This concept mesmerized Japanese strategists. As mentioned in our preface, this plan called for luring

1

the U.S. fleet into waters near Japan while Japanese submarines picked off its ships until, by the time it reached the predestined rendezvous, the two fleets would be equal in strength or nearly so. Victory of course would be Japan's. To achieve this objective, Japan built its ships to fight in seas adjacent to the homeland, sacrificing range and heavy armor to achieve speed and firepower. With this in mind, one can appreciate the opposition the Pearl Harbor plan aroused in the naval hierarchy.

The Navy was divided into three parts—the Naval General Staff, the Navy Ministry, and the Combined Fleet under the emperor as commander in chief. Because the Naval General Staff disseminated the imperial orders to the other echelons, that branch could claim pride of place. Chief of the Naval General Staff for most of 1941 was Adm. Osami Nagano, an experienced, genial officer who believed in the battleship and the Great All-Out Battle as firmly as he believed in imperial benevolence. If Yamamoto could not sell him on Operation Hawaii, it would die aborning.

Nor could Yamamoto proceed without at least the tacit approval of the Navy Ministry. Until the advent of the Tojo cabinet on 18 October 1941, the Navy minister was Adm. Koshiro Oikawa. His ministry had charge of procurement and administration of ships and materiel, and it controlled assignment of personnel. Obviously the Navy minister's cooperation was just as essential as that of the Naval General Staff if any operation was to be carried out.

As commander in chief of the Combined Fleet, the third organization of the Japanese Navy, Yamamoto too held a powerful position. In the words of Adm. Soemu Toyoda, the last man to hold that title, ". . . The Commander in Chief of the Combined Fleet, directly subordinate to the Emperor, commanded . . . the Combined Fleet, receiving direction . . . from the Navy Minister in regard to military administration, and instruction from the Chief of the Naval General Staff in operational plans. . . ." Obviously a commander answerable only to the emperor and limited only by "direction" on the one hand and "instruction" on the other is in a position to do pretty much as he pleases.

Where in this picture was the civilian government? It was firmly under the thumb of the military. For the Navy and Army ministers were by law officers on active duty. Very little imagination is required to see how the armed forces were able to pull down a cabinet at will by reassigning the minister or taking him off active duty.

Thus one may well form the opinion—correctly, we believe—that for most if not all of 1941, Japanese-U.S. diplomacy was irrelevant. Any agreement reached between the Foreign Ministry and the State Department would be meaningless unless the Japanese military supported it. And the Japanese military—particularly the Army—was not interested in peace; it was interested in conquest and power.

Inevitably, the diplomatic negotiations between Tokyo and Washington were long and tedious. The United States could not possibly acquiesce to Japan's take-over of Asia. In particular, the brutality of the Japanese occupation of China revolted Americans, and Japan's membership in the Tripartite Pact placed it in the camp of the enemies of freedom. For their part, the Japanese believed they had the right to anything they had the strength to take and, indeed, a divine mandate to rule Asia.

Into this virtually hopeless situation Tokyo sent an honorable, intelligent, and well-disposed ambassador, Adm. Kichisaburo Nomura. Nothing would have pleased him better than to arrange a rapprochement between Japan and the United States, for he was convinced that the friendship and support of the latter would far outweigh any advantages that might accrue to Japan through armed conquest. But the Foreign Ministry kept him on such a short leash that he was probably the most frustrated man in Washington. The dispatch of Saburo Kurusu, a much more experienced diplomat, to assist Nomura, came much too late for his expertise to make any difference, if indeed such had been Tokyo's intention. For by that time, mid-November, plans and preparations for the Pearl Harbor attack were almost complete.

Strategically, in the long run that operation turned out to be a disaster for Japan, but tactically and operationally it was a classic in planning, training, technology and persistence. Plenty of the latter was needed, because the problems involved were many and daunting. The concept flew in the face of the Great All-Out Battle strategy. Thanks to this mind-set, few of Japan's fighting ships could make the round trip to Hawaii without refueling. If this proved impossible, the project would have to be abandoned. Torpedoes did not exist that could run in Pearl Harbor's shallow waters. Could they be modified to do so? Pilots and bombardiers must be trained in special methods requiring cool nerve and pinpoint accuracy. And it would all have to be done in the tightest possible secrecy.

That Operation Hawaii was carried out successfully was due in no small part to the efforts of one man, Comdr. Minoru Genda. Yamamoto had the rank and prestige to force his Pearl Harbor plan on the Naval General Staff, but Genda had the brains, vision, and experience to make it work. He would, of course, be the first to add that, like any major military operation, it was the product of many hands.

An expert naval aviator, Genda was years ahead of his time in his understanding of the potentialities of air power. He served throughout the Pacific War in responsible positions, but considered his work on Operation Hawaii the pinnacle of his naval career. After the Japanese Self-Defense Forces were organized, Genda returned to active duty, this time in the Air Force, and rose to be its chief of staff, with the rank of lieutenant general. Prange liked and respected Genda and had many interviews with him.

The three Genda studies we present in this section are of the utmost historical importance, and they were invaluable source material for Prange. Following them comes the diary of Rear Adm. Giichi Nakahara, who as chief of the Personnel Bureau, Navy Ministry, was actively engaged in pre–Pearl Harbor events. The period covered is August through December 1941. Next come extracts from the diaries and papers of Capt. Shigeshi Uchida and Comdr. Sadamu Sanagi, both of whom in 1941 were members of the prestigious Operations Section of the Naval General Staff. The final document in this section is a reconstruction of the actual orders and plans covering Operation Hawaii. This is one of the "memory documents" mentioned in the preface to this volume, and we believe it to be as reliable as possible under the circumstances.

CHAPTER 1

How the Japanese Task Force Idea Materialized

Minoru Genda
with
Masataka Chihaya

THIS STUDY COVERS a period from 1935 up to the Pearl Harbor training in the autumn of 1941. The main emphasis, however, is upon the evolution of the carrier task force. We see Minoru Genda placing less and less faith in the Great All-Out Battle strategy and, in fact, coming to consider battleships as obsolete. His combat experience in China convinced him that command of the air was "imperative even in a land operation," hence fighters should be used aggressively, and not primarily as escorts. A tour of duty as assistant attaché in the Japanese Embassy in London during the Battle of Britain further solidified this belief.

This essay is particularly interesting for its revelation of Genda's farsightedness and his courage in sticking to his beliefs even in the face of some who thought him crazy. He conceived the idea of the carrier task force as early as 1936. Not until 1941 did his concept become fact and then, as he points out here, not because of his own persuasion but at Yamamoto's behest.

The translation is Masataka Chihaya's, and all times and dates are based on Japanese time.

In retrospect, the idea of the Japanese task force which launched its initial aerial attack upon Pearl Harbor had more strategical significance than the ill-famed attack itself. The attack originated from "hit and run" tactics, but, together with the sinking of two British battleships off Malaya Peninsula by friendly land-based air forces two days later, not only did it eventually bring an end to the much-debated argument of "battleships vs. air force," but it also proved to all of the world's naval strategists that the very task force centering around carriers was the main power of the naval forces.

But the idea was not born overnight. It was only after consistent and strenuous

4

struggles on the part of progressive elements in favor of air supremacy against stubborn and predominant resistance of conservatives who stuck to the old doctrine of gunpower supremacy.

As a matter of fact, in 1936, when I strongly advocated the wisdom of a task force centering around carriers, there were very few supporters even among my colleague fliers, and there was always a feud between me and listeners as I argued the need of it. Even in the middle of 1941, when the same task force which eventually attacked Pearl Harbor was organized, it was a fact that most of the leading admirals and strategists in the Japanese Navy were opposed to the idea. Only because of a strong, unyielding demand by Admiral Isoroku Yamamoto, then C-in-C of the Combined Fleet, who firmly believed that his strategy of launching a surprise aerial attack on Pearl Harbor at the very outset of war could only be made with concentrated air power, was the idea finally materialized.

I was at least one of the early advocates of this task force idea, and ever since had been in the center of the whirlwind which had swirled in the Japanese Navy for several years, until a showdown of the debate was decisively made in early December 1941.

* * *†

Back in 1935 I was transferred to the Naval War College in Tokyo as a student officer to study naval strategy and tactics, after quitting my career as a flier for a while. Originally a fighter pilot, I had the deepest interest in the future of naval aviation, especially in view of the outstanding rapid progress which had just been taking place. A new era of aviation was about to open with the adoption of the all-metal monoplane well streamlined along the line of aerodynamics. A study of naval strategy and tactics for about two years at this important moment, in fact, gave me the best chance of studying the naval strategy and tactics of tomorrow in earnest.

Soon after my entry into the college, I could not help feeling much doubt about the wisdom of the hitherto-cherished doctrine of the Japanese Navy's strategy. Commonly known as *"Zengen Sakusen,"* which meant a successive slashing operation by auxiliary forces before a showdown between capital ships of both sides, it aimed to ambush an oncoming American fleet in the Southwest Pacific with submarine forces, later also with land-based air forces to be deployed on the Marshall, Caroline and Mariana Islands, with the hope of reducing the enemy strength until it was equal to—if possible even less than—ours, before a decisive showdown was made in the waters around the Mariana and Caroline Islands.

The main tricks upon which the Japanese Navy placed much expectation for having its *Zengen Sakusen* work out included: (1) to keep watch upon enemy bases with submarines, shadow enemy fleets as they sortied from bases, and attack them on their way to the west, (2) to launch forestalling attacks upon enemy carriers with our carrier strength and land-based air forces, and finally (3) to further reduce the enemy strength in a night engagement to be launched with our light vessels, including destroyers, the night before a decisive engagement. It was no exaggeration to say that all of the

† *Note:* We do not know whether the asterisks in this translation signify omissions or merely transitions from one subject to another—Eds.

training and studies of the pre-war Japanese Navy were devoted rather fanatically to finding out how to wage a successful decisive engagement and its preceding so-called *Zengen Sakusen*. In fact, few of them were directed any farther.

The reason why forestalling attacks upon enemy carriers were sought, however, was not necessarily because Japanese strategists regarded them as the main striking strength of naval warfare. Though a view of regarding carrier strength as part of the decisive elements in a sea battle was, in general, predominant in the Japanese Navy of those days, even if it did not stem from the realization of the power of air arms, but from regarding them as one means of making up a strength gap in capital ships between the United States and Japan, a ratio of which had been set forth as 10 to 6 by the Washington Armament Limitation Treaty. Everything was established on the basis of battleships first, and of nothing else. The rapid progress in aviation which had just taken place seemed not enough to change this old concept of naval strategy and tactics.

In the annual fleet training of 1935, on not one occasion did aerial torpedoing score a 100% rate of direct hitting, and dive bombing with the Type 94 Carrier Dive Bombers, which had been employed on carriers for the first time, achieved a 30% rate of hits, a figure that could never be obtained by ordinary level bombing. In addition, prototypes of later Type 96 Land-based Medium Bombers and Type 96 Carrier Fighters were displaying their outstanding features.

The more I studied, the more I couldn't help doubting the wisdom of the basic strategical concepts of the Japanese Navy, upon which the long-cherished *Zengen Sakusen* was established. "In view of a surprisingly big improvement in aerial torpedoes and bombs of late, won't they soon be more destructive than gun projectiles?" "With more accuracy as well as the unequalled long range of attacks, will they not soon deprive the leadership in a naval battle away from battleships' gunpower?" "Won't they make battleships useless in future sea battles?"

In the middle of April 1936 our student officers were incidentally requested to submit a work on the theme of a suitable armament of the Japanese Navy for an encounter with the United States.

After elaborate contemplation, I replied as follows: "The main strength of a decisive battle should be air arms, while its auxiliary should be built mostly by submarines. Cruisers and destroyers will be employed as screens of carrier groups, while battleships will be put out of commission and tied up."

The basic concept to support this assertion was obviously a flat denial of the hitherto long-cherished concept of a sea battle, a concept which was built on an idea of waging once and for all a decisive gunfire engagement with battleships as the nucleus of strength. Instead, it aimed at launching a fatal series of aerial attacks upon enemy fleets from carrier groups operating a few hundred miles away from the enemy force, while land-based air forces and submarines were to support them.

In order to materialize this drastic idea, I further proposed that a drastic change should be made in fleet organization as follows:

> Naval power should be mainly divided into the surface force, the land-based air force and the submarine force. The surface force should be built around two air fleets, which in turn should be made up of three carrier divisions, each division consisting of two or three carriers, supported by two cruiser divisions and also two destroyer squadrons.

Naval land-based air forces will be made up with two and more land-based air flotillas which, in turn, will consist of two or three air groups, and each air group will comprise 36 Type 96 land-based medium bombers and the same number of Type 96 carrier fighters.

For this end, too, all battleships will be tied up and new construction of cruisers and destroyers suspended for the time being, while efforts will be concentrated exclusively on constructing carriers and building up air strength.

No wonder my revolutionary proposal was subject to fierce attacks by instructors and colleague student officers, when it was studied in our classroom! Not only was my idea attacked, but even my mental soundness was doubted. Virtually I had no support, and I had to fight back alone.

The strongest opponents in our discussion were career gunnery officers, and those of torpedo and submarine careers were the next. Almost all the instructor and student officers of the aviation career at first stood pat against me, but they gradually began to share my viewpoint.

But I was not alone in the Japanese Navy in advocating air supremacy over the firepower of capital ships. One of its strong advocates at that time was Capt. Takijiro Onishi, who was then Chief of the Education Bureau of the Naval Aeronautics Department, and who later, in 1944, originated the *Kamikaze* attack tactics in a desperate attempt to defend the Philippine Islands and killed himself in expiation when the war ended in Japan's surrender in the summer of 1945. Being an air officer to the core, he advocated a drastic reorganization of naval armament based upon precise calculations. In early June of 1936, he gathered many air-minded officers at the Navy Club in Tokyo to discuss that problem for the purpose of sending the naval authorities a strong recommendation to that effect. But this action initiated by Captain Onishi was frowned upon by the responsible officers of the Navy Department and the Naval General Staff, who then prohibited any such meeting to be held whatever purpose it might have. As a result, a study of this important problem had to be made individually, so that those air power advocates had to struggle further for several years against the predominant advocates of battleships' firepower.

*   *   *

Primitive and powerless as this argument might be, at least it flared up a new development in the Japanese Navy. In the meantime, in July 1937 the so-called Sino-Japanese Incident broke out in the China continent, and I was transferred as a staff officer of the 2nd Combined Air Groups which participated in air operations over Central China with a total of 36 fighters, 36 dive bombers and 36 carrier bombers. During my tenure there, my air force advanced its operations to Nanking, Nanchang, and Hankow in cooperation with the advance of friendly Army forces. My participation in that operation gave me the precious chance of learning actual battle lessons, which proved not to be overlooked in the development of my thinking about the naval air power problem.

What impressed me most among them was that the domination of the air was imperative even in a land operation which was less vulnerable to aerial attack. The domination of the air arm was only grasped and maintained by the supremacy of fighters over the opponent's power, and so heavily was it that it was no exaggeration to say that the outcome of the whole operation depended upon how the struggle for air domination came out.

The most effective and wise way of making use of fighter units was to use them positively in seeking a decisive engagement with enemy fighters in the air. To this end, the use of fighters on other missions such as escorting bombers or surface forces should be limited as much as permissible.

Facts evidently proved that piecemeal attacks couldn't inflict destructive damage; in order to launch effective bombings, a destructive blow should be given in a short while, using a great number of planes at one time. By that time, the Japanese Navy aviation hadn't yet undergone aerial attacks with a great number of planes.

My battle experiences during this incident, though only of short duration, intensified my belief that the very air power should be the main striking power of the naval arm. Early in 1938 I was transferred as an instructor at the Yokosuka Experimental Air Group, and also was instructed to lecture on air strategy and tactics to students of various naval schools there. By that time, the majority of young flying officers shared the view of air power supremacy, but other naval officers still stuck to the old doctrine of battleship supremacy. My lecture on naval air strategy and tactics, emphasizing its supremacy over the surface forces, naturally caused heated debates with student officers as well as instructors of various schools. There were even some occasions on which heated discussions had to be made throughout the lecture hour between me and instructors who attended to hear my lecture. Finally, I was requested to suspend my lecture on naval air strategy and tactics, on the ground that my lecture would spoil the strategical thinking of student officers of various schools.

There was another instance showing how my thoughts on the naval air arm were not accepted by average naval officers. One day in the same year I made a speech to cadets of the Naval Academy at Etajima, and explained to them the naval aviation activities then in progress in the China continent. When I concluded the speech, saying that the reason for making those fliers devote themselves in battle was nothing but the firm belief from top on down that the outcome of the air struggle would decide the fate of a battle, on land or at sea as well, my assertion [was] countered by immediate and fierce opposition. Capt. [Kakuji] Kakuta, who was then superintendent of the academy and later became one of the strong advocates of air power, stood up as soon as my speech ended and declared that so far there had been little proof of air power being decisive in battle. Captain Kakuta, later promoted to Vice Admiral, was appointed the C-in-C of the 1st Air Fleet in 1944. When the Allied Forces came to attack the Marianas in early summer of that year, the land-based air fleet deploying to Saipan and Guam Islands encountered there in vain, and he was also killed on Tinian Island.

Also, what could not be overlooked in connection with the development of my thinking was some influence of the European War upon myself. I stayed in London from March 1939 to September 1940 as an assistant attaché to the Japanese Embassy in London. During my tenure, I witnessed the early stages of the struggle of the European War. One of the lessons I learned was that the domination of the enemy air by mighty fighters was imperative for inflicting a fatal aerial blow upon the opponent. One of the main reasons for the Nazis' failure to give a thorough aerial blow upon the British mainland was their lack of this idea. Their proud Me-109 and He-113 were, after all, interceptors and not suitable for making a long-range challenge for the domination of the air to British Spitfire and Hurricane fighters, which were apparently superior to them in dog-fighting performance. Another impressive lesson I learned was that the Nazis' use of air forces en masse, in one wave or in successive waves, evidently proved very effective in spite of their inferior abilities.

With these precious lessons in mind, I returned to Japan in the fall of 1940. My immediate concern after my return to the homeland was to see how Japanese naval aviation had progressed in the respects mentioned above, as I found myself immediately associated as the air staff officer of the 1st Carrier Division. The carrier division was then made up of the first-class carrier *Kaga* and constituted the main body of the carrier forces of the Combined Fleet under the command of Admiral Isoroku Yamamoto.

Admittedly Japanese naval aviation had made some progress while I was abroad. Upon my return I learned that it was now possible to have up to 36 fighters fight as a group, and Type Zero new fighters, later widely known as "Zeke" fighters in the subsequent battles in the China continent, were available. As to the use of air forces en masse, fleet training of that year proved that an aerial attack en masse, mobilizing up to 150 fighters, dive bombers and torpedo bombers, was possible and so effective was it that the defensive fleet, including intercepting fighters, could hardly cope with it.

But how to concentrate such a large air force in the air was an unsettled problem which needed further exploitation. By that time the predominant view in the Japanese Navy on how to place carriers in the fleet formation was to disperse them at some 50-mile intervals within the formation, in view of the peculiar vulnerability of the carrier itself and also the peculiar features of aircraft. To assemble more than 100 planes in the air which took off from three or four carriers operating separately with some 50 miles or more apart from each other was not an easy task to do, which had to be maintained at all times.

While I contemplated this and that on this issue, it was incidental that I happened to see a newsreel showing four U.S. carriers, two *Lexington* types and the other two *Yorktown* types, at sea making a formation. Whether the U.S. Navy adopted the concentrated disposition of her carriers at that time I don't know, but the scene I happened to see in a newsreel served to make me conclude that the very concentrated formation of carriers was the shortest way of enabling the concentration of a large air force in the air.

While this concentrated use of carriers had other advantage points of facilitating the command of carriers without a danger of breaking radio silence, and also enabling returning planes to land on other carriers in case of their mother ship being damaged, it involved a great danger of exposing the whole strength in the event of its element being discovered by the enemy. But I thought the danger involved could be evaded, if and when all available fighters could be mobilized to intercept oncoming enemy planes as well as with concentrated antiaircraft gunfire.

In fleet training during the earlier months of 1941, the concentrated disposition of carriers was intensively practiced, combining CV *Kaga* of the 1st Carrier Division and CVs *Soryu* and *Hiryu* of the 2nd Carrier Division under one command temporarily only for fleet training. At that time the two carrier divisions belonged to the Second Fleet. This method proved to be very effective, but it was soon found that this way of temporarily combining two carrier divisions instead of placing them under the proper unified command involved some defects, too. The main issues were difficulties involved in selecting an overall commander of the airborne attack force, in making fliers familiar with the tactical intentions of the overall commander and, furthermore important, in maintaining conformity in training of both carrier divisions.

The adoption of the concentrated disposition of carriers thus led to bringing home the necessity of establishing a permanent unified carrier command. There was one more very important factor which motivated the rapid materialization of this request. By that time Admiral Yamamoto intended to launch an aerial blow upon Pearl Harbor with carriers at the very outset of war in the event of the worst case. Though I was not more than a Commander at that time, I knew this as I was trusted to draw up the original plan for Admiral Yamamoto, then C-in-C of the Combined Fleet.

*   *   *

On April 1, 1941, a composite fleet with mostly carriers was organized for the first time in the Japanese Navy, and Vice Adm. Chuichi Nagumo was appointed to be its first commander. Named the First Air Fleet, it consisted on the date of organization of the 1st Carrier Division of CVs *Akagi* and *Kaga* with 4 destroyers and the 2nd Carrier Division of CVs *Soryu* and *Hiryu* with 4 destroyers and the 4th Carrier Division of CVL *Ryujo* with 2 destroyers.

The new commander in chief of the 1st Air Fleet had been a torpedo officer having little experience in aviation. So his chief of staff, Rear Adm. Ryunosuke Kusaka, who had spent most of his naval career in aviation though not a flier, was chosen. The senior staff officer of the new fleet had had no experience in aviation, either. Appointed to be air staff officer of the newly-established air fleet, I virtually was the only person in the fleet headquarters who had had experience in aviation.

This step of organizing the composite air fleet marked an epoch-making progress in the field of naval strategy and tactics of those days, although much was hoped, as later developments proved, in making battleships, cruisers and destroyers its composite units. It was an admitted fact, too, that this revolutionary change in the Japanese fleet organization was not made even with strenuous efforts of our progressive element, but only with the firm belief in favor of air power of Admiral Yamamoto, who was exceedingly farsighted in the change of naval strategy and tactics.

With the organization of this new air fleet, the training of carriers and carrier-borne air forces showed quick improvement. After extensive experimental training, we concluded that the most suitable standard disposition of carrier strength was to have six carriers in two columns, seven kilometers apart, and in each column three carriers lining up with an interval of seven kilometers. On a semi-circle of 10 to 15 kilometers from the center of carriers, two battleships, two heavy cruisers and one destroyer squadron took the position of guarding the carriers. Several trainings in which this concentrated disposition of carrier strength was adopted proved it very effective; the overall commander's intentions could easily be related to his subordinated commanders even during radio silence, carrier-borne planes rapidly launched and concentrated, and planes of a damaged carrier easily recovered on other sister ships. Another advantage point for the concentration of carriers lay in a possible concentration of fighters. It was feared that a carrier striking force inevitably would be encountered by enemy land and carrier-borne planes, if and when it made an aerial blow upon enemy land bases, since it was hardly expected to escape from the eagle eyes of enemy patrol planes.

How to train for a mass aerial attack and how to command it in the air was the hardest problem we had to solve by any means. It was my firm belief, learned from battle lessons in the China Incident and the European War, that a destructive blow could not be inflicted unless mass strength was used in an aerial attack. By that time, the Japanese Navy had seldom had a training with more than 180 carrier-borne planes. Moreover, it was almost impossible for the Japanese Navy at that time to prepare more than 300 experienced units for carrier service. It was apparent that some drastic step should be taken to get a sufficient number of trained fliers to launch an aerial attack on an enemy base at the outset of war—on Pearl Harbor.

But it was hard work for me to tackle indeed. As already mentioned, not only was I the only staff officer in the new air fleet headquarters who had had experience in aviation, but most of the air fleet officers didn't have even a hunch of the idea of the Pearl Harbor attack which was then under contemplation. Only a limited number of flag commanders and staff officers of the air fleet had been informed of the real secret of the plan. Unaware of it, most fliers complained and sometimes showed strong opposition to my unduly strong requests for hard training.

One of the drastic steps then taken, upon which much criticism was naturally focused, was to have commanders of the carrier-borne air force take responsibility for training their respective forces on land as well as commanding them in the air. By that time, the carrier division commander and the carrier skipper had been made responsible for training and maintenance of their respective air forces on land bases as well as on board, before they took off. The new step had one great advantage of making carrier-borne air force commanders train their subordinate forces as they saw fit, but most of the carrier division commanders and carrier skippers were displeased with it, asserting that it broke the chain of command.

The adequacy of the revision was soon justified, however. A good example of how bombing efficiency was improved by this shift of responsibility could well be shown in the improvement achieved by level bombing units. For 1941's first part, fleet training ending in March, the average attack hit rate of level bombing was only about 10%, so low a figure that I, representing the 1st Carrier Division, strongly advocated the wisdom of giving up level bombing for torpedo bombing and dive bombing, and many shared this view. But what made me worry was a fear that our 250-kilogram dive bombing bomb might not penetrate the deck armor plate of U.S. battleships, and thus be unable to inflict a fatal blow upon them.

In a fleet exercise held in June of that year, however, some hope was born when

Akagi's level bombing unit of 27 Type 97 torpedo bombers achieved 11 direct hits out of 27 bombs against the target ship *Settsu* which freely tried to evade. This remarkable mark, especially so in light of the fact that Japanese torpedo bombers of those days were only equipped with a primitive bomb sight, was traced to arduous and painstaking efforts of specialists of pilot and bomb-sighter for level bombing. This made me see a solution to the long-unsettled problem of how to improve level bombing technique.

Thus the idea of bomb lead planes manned by a specially trained pilot and bombardier was born. The lead plane in each squadron led the squadron after entering the bomb run to take a precise aim at the target, while the rest of the bombers followed suit in bombing, seeing the release of the lead plane's bomb. When bombings were actually made on Pearl Harbor on December 8, 1941, this method of bombing paid off very well.

The selection of squadron and group leaders to command the Air Fleet's air force was not an easy task, but the Japanese Navy managed to supply the necessary number of able flying officers to the fleet, mobilizing the whole Navy. Then Cmdr. Mitsuo Fuchida was appointed the overall commander of the carrier air force, and battle-experienced officers of the so-called China Incident were appointed as other leaders. As a matter of fact, no better team could have been selected among the Japanese Navy of that time.

Early in September, two battleships of the 3rd Battleship Division of the *Kirishima* class, 8th Cruiser Division of two *Tone*-class heavy cruisers and the 1st Destroyer Squadron were placed under the operational command of the 1st Air Fleet, thus materializing for the first time the idea of a task force centering around carriers, the very idea which we had long strongly advocated. Together with the final reshuffle of flying personnel taken at about this time, fleet training was vigorously intensified so that the fliers' skill was surprisingly improved.

As the international situation turned worse day after day after September of that year, men of the 1st Air Fleet, especially the fliers, who well realized the grave responsibility they were to bear on their shoulders in the event of war, sensed the gravity of the situation and firmly made up their minds to devote themselves to their mother country. But most of them did not seem to have any hunch of the Pearl Harbor attack idea upon which their main aim of training was actually focused.

As a matter of fact, the progress of the fliers' skill was so remarkable that their skill eventually proved to be the best in the Japanese Navy before and during the war. By the time the final preparations for the Pearl Harbor attack was made in the middle of November 1941, our planners firmly believed that there would be no matched opponent before them. It was a fact that almost all the fliers of the 1st Air Fleet as well as the planners took it for granted that a successful aerial attack could be launched, if and when the fleet could reach the designated aerial attack-launching point about 200 miles due north of Oahu Island without molestation.

CHAPTER 2

Affidavit of Minoru Genda

Genda gave this affidavit to Prange on 15 March 1948. Certain internal references to "the Prosecution" indicate that this was prepared for use in connection with the Far East War Crimes Tribunal.

Here he relates in brief how he came to be involved in the Pearl Harbor planning. Yamamoto had turned his idea over to Onishi who, as we have seen, had been one of the few supporters of Genda's radical air supremacy ideas. Naturally Onishi sent for Genda to provide the necessary expertise. Within ten days, Genda had supplied Onishi with his outline suggestions. In his opinion, "This attack, while extremely difficult, is not impossible."

Genda then touches upon some of the preattack maneuvers and problems he covers in more detail elsewhere.

1. I am Minoru Genda, formerly a captain in the Japanese Navy.

I was appointed Staff Officer of the 1st Air Squadron on 1 November 1940, promoted to commander 15 November 1940. I became Staff Officer of the 1st Air Fleet on 1 April 1941 and remained in that post until the latter part of June 1942.

2. Circumstances leading up to the drawing up of the plan for the attack on Pearl Harbor.

Early in February 1941, when the Flagship, the *Kaga,* was anchored in Ariake Bay (Kyushu), I received a letter from the Chief of Staff of the 11th Air Fleet, Rear Admiral Onishi, with whom I was well acquainted personally, though not under his direct command officially. In this letter he asked me to come to Kanoya at once as he wanted to see me on important business. So I proceeded to Kanoya on the following day and called on Rear Admiral Onishi at the Fleet Headquarters.

He then showed me a private letter which he had received from Vice Admiral Yamamoto, Commander in Chief of the Combined Fleet. The substance of that letter was to the following effect:

> In the event of outbreak of war with the United States, there would be little prospect of our operations succeeding unless, at the very outset, we can deal a crushing blow to the main force of the American Fleet in Hawaiian waters by using the full strength of the 1st and 2nd air Squadrons against it, and thus to preclude the possibility of the American Fleet advancing to take the offensive in the Western Pacific for some time.
>
> And it is my hope that I may be given command of this air attack force, so that I may carry out the operation myself. Please made a study of the operation.

Rear Admiral Onishi said to me, "Please make this study in utmost secrecy, with special attention to the feasibility of the operation, method of execution, and the forces to be used."

I commenced this study upon returning to my ship, and after a week or ten days, I again called on Rear Admiral Onishi and handed him my answer.

What I remember of that answer was the following:

A. Need of maintaining utmost secrecy, so as to prevent any leakage of the plan.

B. Use of sufficient force to put the main force of the American Fleet out of action for at least six months at one blow, i.e., to use all available carriers.

C. To make effect certain, the attack to be made by daylight.

D. If, owing to the extreme difficulty of torpedo attack because of shallow water, use of torpedo is found to hold little prospect of success, emphasis to be placed on dive bombing, and for that reason, the kind and number of planes aboard carriers to be changed as necessity may dictate.

E. Carriers to be selected as primary targets.

F. In short, this attack, while extremely difficult, is not impossible.

With some slight reference to my answer, Rear Admiral Onishi prepared his answer on the basis of his own views and sent it to the Commander in Chief of the Combined Fleet.

At the time of the organization of the 1st Air Fleet in April, the only officers in the Headquarters of the said Fleet who were aware that the Commander in Chief of the Combined Fleet had the idea of an attack on Pearl Harbor in mind were Commander in Chief Vice Admiral Nagumo, Chief of Staff Rear Admiral Kusaka, Senior Staff Officer Commander [Tomatsu] Oishi and myself who was Air Staff Officer.

From then until the early part of September, we did not undertake to draw up any concrete plan.

Early in September, Rear Admiral Kusaka, Chief of Staff, summoned the staff and ordered us to study and draft a plan for this attack, and I was named secretary for this purpose. After working for about a week aboard the *Akagi,* I completed a preliminary plan.

While this preliminary plan was in the main similar to the operational plan that was actually executed, it differed from the latter in the following respects:

A. The point of rendezvous prior to departure for the attack was fixed at Atsukeshi Bay or Matsukai Bay.

B. There was no connection with the advance force (submarines).

C. There was nothing concrete as to time.

D. The air-raid plan was not worked out in detail.

Around the 12th or 13th of September the chart maneuvers of the Combined Fleet were held at the Naval Staff College. The maneuvers relating to the Hawaiian operation, which were carried out separate from the general maneuvers, were for the most part based on the above preliminary plan, the one difference being that it used Hitokappu Bay as the rendezvous point.

I believe that it was on 1 October that Vice Admiral Nagumo summoned to his Flagship the Headquarters personnel of the various Air Squadrons, and commanders, Chief Flying Officers and Squadron Leaders of all the carriers and issued the instruction that this fleet would receive the assignment of air attacking Hawaii in the event of war, the training and study of the fleet thenceforth should be carried out with emphasis on that point. From that time, the flying officers pursued this study with principal attention on torpedo attack until we were confident of its feasibility.

About that time, there was transmitted from the Combined Fleet "the intention of the Central Authorities to take the 2nd Air Squadron and the *Akagi* out of the force that was intended for the attack on Hawaii because of the needs of the southern operations." We, who were assigned to carry out the Hawaiian operation, of course insisted on the need of our full strength and were notified by the Combined Fleet a few days later that our full strength would be left to us.

The last chart maneuvers of the Combined Fleet were held aboard the *Nagato*, in the western part of the Inland Sea in October (about the 3rd), and were carried out on the basis of the 3-carrier plan.

3. Adoption of the plan for attack on Pearl Harbor.

So the Task Force Headquarters, the Senior Staff Officer drafted the Hawaii operational plan (Secret Task Force Order No. 1) toward the end of October and then took it to the Combined Fleet Headquarters for approval.

On 2nd November the whole of the Task Force (with the exception of the fighter force and the 2nd submarine squadron) rendezvoused in Ariake Bay. All unit commanders and above and flying officers were summoned aboard the Flagship *Akagi* where they were told of the duties that would be assigned to our Task Force in the event of war and that, by way of preliminary training, maneuvers would be carried out with Saeki and Sukumo as targets, and the plan for these maneuvers was explained.

These maneuvers were pursued for several days beginning on the 3rd. Upon completion, some of the ships went into port at Kure, the rest to Sasebo, and took on fuel and bombs and made other preparations for battle.

I do not have a clear recollection as to the time when we received the Combined Fleet General Order No. 1, but I believe it was just after we had completed the above maneuvers. The Task Force Order No. 1 was immediately printed, and a part was distributed on 17th November prior to departure from Saeki Bay to the advance force (submarines) and other necessary quarters with, as I recall, the date of issue of the order left blank; the balance were distributed, with the date of issue filled in, after arrival at Hitokappu Bay.

I believe that the part of the Combined Fleet General Order No. 1 pertaining to the Task Force (whether that part had been cut out from the General Order or printed as a separate pamphlet I do not recall) was as follows:

> The Task Force, keeping its movements in utmost secrecy and in accordance with a special order, shall advance into the Hawaii area, and immediately upon commencement of war it shall attack the main force of the American Fleet in the Hawaii area and deal it a mortal blow.
>
> Air attack is scheduled for dawn of X-Day (exact date to be given by a later order). Upon completion of the air attack, the Task Force is to return to Japan.

Should the negotiations with America prove successful, the Task Force is to return at once.

Although the Task Force Order No. 1 was probably the same, in the main as the exhibit submitted in evidence by the Prosecution, I recall that communication and supply plans were attached to it.

The ships of the Task Force, upon completion of preparations, came to Saeki Bay one by one, and by the 16th all had rendezvoused there with the exception of the *Kaga*.

On the 17th the ships left Saeki at intervals in scattered groups and rendezvoused at Hitokappu Bay on the 22nd. The *Kaga* arrived there somewhat later. The Task Force Order No. 3, which was the plan of our attack, was completed at this time and distributed to all the ships together with Order No. 1 on 24th November.

This Order No. 3, I believe, was much the same as that submitted by the Prosecution.

In addition to the above orders, there was issued to the various units an order in the form of verbal instructions from the Chief of Staff pertaining to the measures to be taken under various conditions. Most of this order I drafted myself. Its principal points were the following:

A. If, while proceeding eastward from Hitokappu Bay, the Task Force should encounter American warships, merchantmen or airplanes or neutral merchantmen, it should change direction sharply as soon as discovery is made by the patrol vessel, but advance toward the objective should be continued while maintaining greatest secrecy as to position. If the whole of the Task Force is discovered, turn back as though nothing had happened, but if such discovery is made on X-1 Day or later, resolutely carry out the attack.

B. If no information concerning the American Fleet is received while proceeding toward destination, send the 8th Squadron (*Tone* and *Chikuma*) in advance on X-2 Day or X-3 Day to scout Lahaina Anchorage and Pearl Harbor in the afternoon of X-1 Day and obtain information on the enemy.

C. If all the attendant conditions dictate an assault, dispatch the combat planes of the 2nd attack corps at the same time as those of the 1st attack corps.

Torpedo and bomb attacks are to be carried out while the 81 combat planes maintain control of the air.

All unit commanders and flying officers of the Task Force were summoned aboard the *Akagi* on 24th November for final explanation of the operational plans and consultation, and the start for the attack was made from Hitokappu Bay on the 26th.

CHAPTER 3

Analysis No. 1 of the Pearl Harbor Attack, Operation AI

Minoru Genda

G ENDA PREPARED this two-part analysis for Prange under the date of 12 May 1947. This study is historically important because, as we have noted, Genda, more than any other single individual, was responsible for the plans and preparations, hence the ultimate success, of this operation. Here, then, is the story of the making of the Pearl Harbor attack, written by the man best qualified to do so, at a time when memory was still fresh and detailed.

These two analyses cover some of the material already touched upon in the preceding two studies, but in much greater detail. First and always an airman, and full of bold ideas, Genda suggested to Onishi that they follow up the air attack with a landing on Oahu, to deprive the United States of "her largest and best advanced base"—a project far beyond Japan's capacity at the time in the context of its major operations in the southern areas. He also insisted that the prime targets should be the U.S. carriers and was bitterly disappointed when on 7 December those carriers were at sea.

The problems of training and preparing for a major operation of such secrecy that most of the participants had no idea for what they were making ready were many and difficult, and Genda's account does full justice to the details. The first analysis carries this story up to the rendezvous at Hitokappu Bay.

The second analysis first backtracks to explain how certain technical breakthroughs came about, and Genda gives excellent character sketches of the leaders of the various types of attack. He relates events of the voyage to Hawaii, the raid itself, and the return homeward.

PROGRESS OF THE PEARL HARBOR ATTACK

2 February 1941

After the training was over, the First Carrier Squadron entered Ariake Bay. A little later I received a message from Rear Admiral [Takijiro] Onishi, Chief of Staff of the 11th Air Fleet, saying, "Urgent. Come to our Unit."

The following day I went to the base at Kanoya to visit Rear Admiral Onishi.

After the visit, the Chief of Staff handed me a letter and asked what the meaning was. In studying the letter, I found that it was a letter from Vice Admiral [Isoroku] Yamamoto, Commander-in-Chief of the Combined Fleet to Rear Admiral Minoru [*sic*] Onishi and the contents in brief were as follows:

> In the event that war breaks out between Japan and America, attack the main force of the American Fleet in Pearl Harbor with our main carrier fleet, the First Carrier Division and the Second Carrier Division. It is important that the American Fleet does not go into the western Pacific until the first stage of the operation is over. I am hoping to be allowed to command such an attacking unit by an order from the Emperor. Make an outline of the plans for the operation that I mentioned.

To this Rear Admiral Onishi said, "This sort of thing must be done or else we won't be able to carry out a successful operation. However, at the present time the person in the navy higher-ups who can do this is Commander-in-Chief Yamamoto or Vice Admiral Soemu Toyoda.* The others do not have the power to make such a decision.

"The operation needs absolute secrecy. Study the matter carefully and bring me the answer."

I returned to the carrier fleet the next day and began my careful study during the break hour of my regular duty.

My first impression of this study was as follows: "I† had much confidence in any new ideas but I did not think about this idea. Back in 1935 when I was commanding an air detachment at Yokosuka this same idea was presented at one of our military tactics conferences. Also when I was a student at one of the higher training schools, as I remember, this idea was discussed, too. But since then, all the tacticians gradually began to think about tactics which are common and used often. If I am not careful, I will be thinking that way too."

The more I studied this plan of attack, the more I thought of it; I also realized the difficulty of such a plan.

After about two weeks I brought the answer to Rear Admiral Onishi. The content of the answer to the letter, as I recall, is as follows:

A. This attack must be a perfect surprise attack. And the result of this attack must be such that the main force of the American Fleet will not be able to advance to the western Pacific for a period of at least six months.
B. The main target of the attack must be against the American aircraft carriers and land-based planes.
C. We must use the entire carrier strength that we have.
D. In order to continue the attack by carrier-based planes, we must have sufficient means of supplying the carriers.
E. An attack by torpedoes will be the best, but when it is not possible due to antisubmarine or antitorpedo obstructions in the deeper waters and near harbors, we must use dive bombers for the attack. In that case, we must change the type of planes on the

---

* Toyoda would be chief of the Naval General Staff at the end of the war. It is possible that Genda, or the translator, meant Admiral Osami Nagano, chief of the Naval General Staff at the time of this meeting —Eds.
† A translator's note "(who have failed once)" follows the pronoun. The meaning is not clear—Eds.

carriers. Whether the torpedo attacks be in shallow or deep waters, plans for such attacks must be made.

F. This attack will be difficult but not impossible. The success of this attack lies in the success of the initial attack, therefore, the planning of the attack must be done in strict secrecy.

The message with which I handed the answer to Rear Admiral Onishi was: "It is necessary to follow up this attack on Hawaii with a landing operation. If Hawaii is occupied, America will lose her largest and best advanced base and, furthermore, the command of future operations for us will be very good."

As he received the answer, Rear Admiral Onishi said: "With out present strength, we are not able to take the offensive in both the eastern and southern areas. First, we must destroy the larger part of the American Fleet."

The foregoing was the studied plan of the Hawaii Operation. About this time there were similar plans being considered by Mr. [Cmdr. Akira] Sasaki, a staff officer of the Combined Fleet. However, his plans were aimed at American battleships and I had been constantly insisting that the attack must be aimed at the carriers.

If I remember, the persons who were informed of this problem were the chief members of the staff of the Combined Fleet Headquarters, the chief members of the staff of the Army Headquarters operational bureau, and staff officer [Cmdr. Tomatsu] Oishi of the First Carrier Fleet Headquarters.

So far the thoughts of Commander-in-Chief Yamamoto of the attack against the battleships had not materialized, and I believe that from the tactical point of view he knew well the fact that an attack against the carriers was necessary. At this time the leaders of both Japan and America, the greater part of the navy personnel and the people as a whole had overestimated the power of the battleships because most of their thinking was just wishful thinking. Even the claims of the Japanese people as one-way attackers cannot be understood nor what they would do in the first attack of a battle. I cannot help but think that the American people were filled with the idea that there could hardly be a war against such absurd people.

I continued to make plans for this operation and for its training with the utmost secrecy until about June. However, in the meantime, because the Combined Fleet trained under the old-fashioned Great All-Out Battle method, the air force could not take part in any real tactical maneuvers or training for the operation. Consequently, we regretted the fact that practical training could not be carried out and that our training had to be ended at the halfway point.

The stubbornness of the naval leaders did not help at all and I dare say that this was one of the main reasons that the people of Japan were brought to such a miserable condition as they are today.

If the proposal to convert the navy into the air corps as proposed by some air corps men in 1936 had been adopted, and if the expanded air force were used from that time, the fleet training during 1941 we have been quite different and the result of this war would have been quite different, too. In that same year (1936) when the plans to build the *Yamato* and *Musashi* were laid out, I said that we are building something that is useless—these ships could not stand an attack from the air, that these ships will be just another one of the three great [useless] defenses built by man and the world will laugh in later years. These are:

1. The pyramids.
2. The great wall of China.
3. The *Yamato* and *Musashi*.

However, at that time I was just a student with no influence at all to do anything.

Well, around May there was a meeting of the Navy* Headquarters Operations Section and the Pearl Harbor operation was studied. The persons present at that meeting, I think, were [Cmdr. Shigenori] Kami, [Cmdr. Sadamu] Sanagi, [Cmdr. Tatsukichi] Miyo and [Cmdr. Shigeshi] Uchida of the Navy Headquarters; Sasaki of the Combined Fleet; and Oishi and Genda of the First Air Fleet.

Furthermore, in April of the same year the First Carrier Division (the *Akagi, Kaga,* and one destroyer squadron); the Second Carrier Division (the *Soryu, Hiryu,* and one destroyer squadron) and the Fourth Carrier Division (the *Ryujo* and one destroyer) were combined into the First Air Fleet and I was made staff officer to Vice Admiral [Chuichi] Nagumo.

Even in the aforementioned studies on the operations, men of the Combined Fleet adhered to having the main target as the battleships. But I stuck to the aircraft carriers as being the main target. *Kami, staff officer of Navy Headquarters,† supported me in having the aircraft carriers as the main target.* The rest of the men did not have much of an opinion.

From about this time there arose serious criticizing of this problem between Commander-in-Chief of the First Air Fleet [and its] leaders, the chief of staff, the senior staff officer and myself. The Commander-in-Chief, being a pessimistic person, looked at everything as being difficult, especially the problem of the endurance and behavior of the aircraft in flight. The chief of staff and the senior staff officer did not have any clear opinion. I was a progressive-minded person. The feelings of Commander-in-Chief Yamamoto concerning this operation was the feeling of the men flying the aircraft, and he always asked, "What are the feelings of the men?" The men could not express their ideas directly because they were not informed of the plans of the fleet commander and other commanders, but I, being with these men during peacetime, spoke for them, saying that they are willing to do anything that comes.

The training alone must be given to the men without their knowing the purpose of the training. The men were led to train for deep and shallow torpedoing without knowing their fate, which was a little too much, but they did it. With information from the G-3 of Headquarters that both east and west sides of Pearl Harbor and Ford Island were about 40 feet deep, training was started to discharge the torpedoes so as not to go below 33 feet. I am not sure, but I think it was in the southern seas area in Kyushu that dummy torpedoes were discharged from the lowest possible altitude

---

* The translator rendered this word as Army, but these were naval officers —Eds.

† Kami was with the Operations Section of the Naval General Staff, where he was in charge of "war preparation and operational plans "—Eds.

against the *Akagi* and *Kaga* with automatic depth calculating meters. One was good but the other was not. Since that time we had not been able to get any constant results. Some rounds were good, others were not. The rounds shot to go no deeper than 33 feet were about 40% effective.

Around June the training was still done in the old-fashioned way, using only the battleships with no help from the air force. One day I wrote a letter to staff officer Sasaki of the Combined Fleet, saying, "Stop this worthless deployed tactic training. Let the air units practice spot-attacking on land. And if the fleet training calls for air units to participate, arrange for it."

When the senior staff officer of the Combined Fleet saw the letter, I am told that he was quite angry. However, from July, I am not sure whether my letter had anything to do with it, but the air units began to train at land bases.

Finally, not only torpedo bombing was practiced but also dive bombing and low-altitude bombing training were carried out in a real way.

Around September there was a great change in the personnel and also the Fifth Carrier Division (the *Shokaku*, the *Zuikaku*, and one destroyer squadron) was assigned to the fleet.

In order to make clear the concentrated power of the air units for the Pearl Harbor attack and the operation with it, plans for special organizations and training were presented to the higher-ups for opinion, only to receive much opposition from the district and air unit commanders, but later the plans were approved. By "special organizations," I mean that all of the air units of every fleet are to be formed into two large groups with a commander in chief for both groups. Training will be carried out according to the situation of the groups. As for "special training," it is to train for the attack on Pearl Harbor as planned under the organization just mentioned.

From July to September, the aforementioned plans of training and deployment were completed as follows:

TYPE OF PLANES	STATION
Carrier-based attack planes of the 1st CarDiv (level bombers) and (guide planes) of the 1st, 2nd and 5th CarDivs	Kagoshima
Carrier-based attack planes of the 2nd CarDiv	Demizu
Carrier-based bombers of the 1st CarDiv	Miyataka
Carrier-based bombers of the 2nd CarDiv	Kasanohara
Carrier-based attack planes of the 5th CarDiv	Usa
Carrier-based bombers of the 5th CarDiv	Oita
Carrier-based bombers of the 1st and 2nd Fleets	Saeki
Carrier-based fighters of the 5th CarDiv	Omura (later transferred to Oita)

The outline of the training is as follows:

UNIT	SPECIAL TRAINING	GENERAL TRAINING
Carrier-based attack planes of the 1st and 2nd CarDivs:		
Akagi, Kaga—12 planes each	Water-level torpedo attacks	Day and night torpedo attacks on navigating fleet
Soryu, Hiryu—8 planes each *Total* 40 planes		
Akagi, Kaga—15 planes each *Soruy, Hiryu*—10 planes each *Total* 50 planes	Bombardment of the anchored fleet	Daylight torpedo attacks on navigating fleet
Carrier-based attack planes of the 5th CarDiv: *Total* 54 planes	Bombardment of the anchored fleet	Day and night torpedo attacks on navigating fleet
Carrier-based bombers of the 1st and 2nd CarDivs:		
Akagi, Soryu, Hiryu—18 planes each	Bombardment of the anchored fleet	Day and night torpedo attacks on navigating fleet
Kaga—27 planes *Total* 81 planes		
Carrier-based bombers of the 5th CarDiv: *Total* 54 planes	Bombardment of the anchored fleet	Day and night torpedo attacks on the navigating fleet
Carrier-based fighters of the 1st and 2nd CarDivs: *Total* 84 planes	Formation air battle, land strafing, over-water navigation	Same as above.

  The training in shallow and deep torpedo attacks was commanded by Lt. Cmdr. [Shigeharu] Murata, commander of the air unit on the *Akagi,* and an extensive training schedule was carried out. As for approaching the enemy and firing the torpedo, the training unit was well trained, but there was still some lack of assurance as to controlling the missile under water, even up to the beginning of the actual operation.

The result of the level bombing in the yearly maneuvers was not satisfactory. Almost all the attacks from the air on ships afloat were not satisfactory, but during the June maneuvers the air unit on the *Akagi,* led by the lead plane, thrice attacked the very maneuverable target ship *Settsu* with a surprising result of 33 hits out of 100. (The planes attacked in formations of 9 planes from the altitude of about 10,000 feet.) Each unit with lead planes (one lead plane with 9 carrier-based attack planes) was assembled in Kagoshima. The units began a daily systematized training schedule with the target ship *Settsu* as target under the command of Lt. [Izumi] Furukawa, commander of the *Akagi* unit. Soon the units reached a point where they could attack a navigating fleet with confidence. This type of attack was very good, because it could do the work that the dive bombing attack could not.

The carrier-based bomber units of the 1st and 2nd Carrier Divisions continued to progress under normal conditions under the command of Lt. Cmdr. [Takashige] Egusa, commander of the air unit on the *Soryu.*

The carrier-based fighter units of the 1st and 2nd Carrier Divisions continued in various types of training under the command of Lt. Cmdr. [Shigeru] Itaya, commander of the air unit on the *Akagi.* These trainings also progressed normally.

The airplane units of the 5th Carrier Division could not keep up with the 1st and 2nd even to the end because the units were newly organized and were not trained sufficiently.

In the mass change of personnel in September, the Naval Personnel Affairs Section did not know of this plan and assigned the men according to the plans of previous years. Since this was very inconvenient from the standpoint of training and also as far as this plan is concerned, I went to the Personnel Affairs Section and explained that the fleet had special plans. With this, all the skilled personnel were sent to the First and Second Fleets. The necessary commanders were sent to the fleet flagships and to the squadron flagships. Lt. Cmdr. [Mitsuo] Fuchida, commander in chief of the air attack on Pearl Harbor, is a very intimate friend of mine. Because he was my friend and I knew him to be a very able man, I went to the Personnel Affairs Section and had him especially *appointed as commander of the air unit on the Akagi.*

With the situation as it was, the airplane units were prepared and because the old type of fleet training was not carried out too far, the Japanese navy was training in a way that was never equaled in years past. However, the Headquarters of the 2nd Carrier Division and 5th Carrier Division, especially the second, who did not know about this plan, expressed quite a bit of opinions. Rear Adm. [Tamon] Yamaguchi,* who did not understand the plans of the fleet Headquarters, also made comments. Because the ignorance of the battle unit headquarters concerning this plan was a hindrance to the advance of the training, this information was given to the various important leaders of the battle unit Headquarters immediately after the 2nd Carrier Division entered port from the southern French Indo-China operation. After this began the violent advance movement of veteran Rear Admiral Yamaguchi.

In the beginning of September the chief of staff of the First Air Fleet assembled all the leaders and laid out the concrete plans. I was among the men in the group and

* Commander in chief, 2nd Carrier Division—Eds.

for a week after that I was assigned to make the finished plan all by myself in the chief of staff's room without any outside help.

Furthermore, two divisions of the 3rd Battleship Division (the *Haruna** and the *Kirishima*); the 8th Cruiser Division (the *Tone* and the *Chikuma*); about eleven of the newest-type destroyer and the flagship of the 1st Destroyer Squadron were assigned as the forces to be used in the operation by the Combined Fleet. Three submarines and a few of the fastest tankers were also assigned.

The general outline of the plan after a week's study is as follows:

A. Forces to be used

   The complete forces of the 1st Carrier Division, 2nd Carrier Division, 5th Carrier Division, and the necessary forces assigned.

B. Time of attack

   At daybreak of the same day as the beginning of operations.

C. Target of attack

   1. American carrier group

   2. American battleship group

   3. Land-based aircraft

   4. All other ships

D. Method of Attack

   1. Torpedo and dive-bombing attack against the aircraft carriers.

   2. Torpedo and water-level bombing against the battleships.

   3. Strafing and low-level bombing against the land-based aircraft.

E. Route of attack

   The northern, central and southern routes were the three routes considered and there was much difficulty in determining the route to be used.

   The northern route was very good as far as carrying out the plan in secret went, but there was the question of being able to supply the units at sea in the stormy waves of the northern Pacific Ocean because the operation was to begin in the winter season. This was the main reason that Vice Admiral Nagumo always insisted upon taking the southern route. However, my insistence was that from looking back into history for examples of surprise attacks, such as the Battle of the Hiyodori Pass, the Battle of Okehazama, and Napoleon's Battle of the Alps, if we do not take the northern route we will not succeed. With the aid of Rear Admiral Yamaguchi, the Commander-in-Chief understood the reason for taking the northern route. The southern route had very calm waters, the distance was only two thousand miles and it was best from the standpoint of navigation, but the chance of being spotted was too great. Therefore, ninety-nine out of a hundred agreed that a surprise attack was impossible by way of the southern route. The road to the success

* *Hiei* actually participated—Eds.

of the attack was opened because all efforts were restored for taking this difficult way.

In any plan which the people agree to be the most natural and best, the enemy will have the counter-attacking forces prepared. The scarcity of ships navigating in the northern Pacific Ocean in the winter was a great help to us.

There was no special characteristic nor any value in using the central route.

With the foregoing understanding, I made plans to use the northern route.

F. Assembly point before the attack

There was quite a bit of trouble in determining this port to assemble secretly a large fleet and to prepare same for an operation. The ports at the homeland and Hokkaido would not ensure secrecy. Chichi Island was too small and also easy to be spotted by submarines. It was not very close, either. We were hoping to get a port as far north as possible and during the search, we came upon Hitokappu Bay. This bay was chosen for the assembly point.

G. Supplying at sea

Out of the six carriers there were only the two from the 5th Carrier Division and the *Kaga* which were able to cruise to and from Hawaii on their own power. (I am not positive but I think that their cruising speed was 18 knots and their range 8,000 sea miles.) At any rate, because the other three ships could only cruise 60 percent of the distance, there was a need for the carriers to be supplied at sea.

In October, while the map maneuvers were carried out at Tokuyama, the *Kaga* carried out the first experimental trip. We had much confidence in the success of the attack.

H. An assault plan in case the surprise attack does not succeed

There was a necessity to consider this also, and in this case all the fighter planes will be sent out first, then the attack will be carried out after we get command of the air.

At that time we had complete confidence in the strength of the fighter units. We thought that we could easily destroy an enemy fighter unit two or three times the size of ours in one attack. For this reason especially, we put our strength into these formation air battles.

I. The follow-up of the attack

Plans were made for the second attack, but Commander in Chief Nagumo did not approve of them from the beginning. He had the opinion that a continued attack was too much.

J. Searching for the enemy

The search for the point of origin of the American Fleet was left to central intelligence and to the submarine reconnaissance. The reconnaissance of the enemy immediate front was carried out by two Type Zero water-reconnaissance planes.

The foregoing was the basic plan of the Pearl Harbor attack. This was shown to the First Air Fleet Headquarters in September by means of map maneuvers of the Combined Fleet at the Naval Staff College.

This map maneuver was participated in by almost all of the important men in Naval Headquarters and in the various Headquarters of the Combined Fleet, but the maneuvers concerning the Hawaii attack were participated in only by the important men of the Combined Fleet Headquarters, the 1st Air Fleet Headquarters, the 2nd Carrier Division Headquarters, and the men of the 5th Carrier Division Headquarters, in a special room to ensure secrecy.

The results of the war games (the maneuver was carried out twice) were that on the first day an American reconnaissance plane discovered the attacking fleet but the attack was carried out, and that on the second day the surprise attack was successful.

Around this time I sent the staff officer for communications to the Naval Headquarters to investigate the condition of the electric wave radiation of the American aircraft in the Hawaii vicinity and to investigate the number of ships navigating in the waters of the southern Aleutian Islands and their routes in the coming winter. We found the American reconnaissance planes from the Hawaii area were thick in the southern area and very little in the northern area. The number of planes reconnoitering the northern area beyond 2,300 sea miles from Hawaii was very few and again ships in the southern Aleutian Islands were very few. Now all the more we were determined to use the northern route for the attack. The only problems left now were the decisions concerning supplies and ability of the air units.

About this time there was another meeting at the Navy Headquarters in Tokyo concerning the right or wrong of carrying out the Hawaii operation. The men at the meeting were:

NAVAL GENERAL STAFF

Rear Adm. [Shigeru] Fukudome, Chief, First Bureau

Capt. [Sadatoshi] Tomioka, Chief, First Section

Commander Kami, member, First Section

Lieutenant Commander Sanagi

Lieutenant Commander Miyo*

COMBINED FLEET HEADQUARTERS

Rear Adm. [Matome] Ugaki, Chief of Staff

Capt. [Kameto] Kuroshima, Senior Staff Officer

Commander Sasaki, Air Staff Officer

FIRST AIR FLEET HEADQUARTERS

Rear Adm. [Ryunosuke] Kusaka, Chief of Staff

Commander Oishi, Senior Staff Officer

Commander Genda, Air Staff Officer

* Miyo was actually a commander at the time—Eds.

Kuroshima and Genda were determined to carry out the operation; Kusaka and Oishi were rather hesitant; the others had some opinions but not of a very definite nature. As a whole, the atmosphere which prevailed in the meeting was that of the difficulty of carrying out the operation. Rear Admiral Fukudome said that he would find out at the Naval Headquarters in a few days whether this operation will or will not be carried out.

When the staff of the Combined Fleet reported the condition of the result of the meeting to Commander in Chief Yamamoto, they were severely reprimanded with these words: "Do you think that Japan's military operations can be established without carrying out the Hawaii attack? I don't care what you do; I will do it! There is no use holding such a senseless meeting!"

At the end of September, Navy Headquarters in Tokyo had had a model of Oahu Island made and the Combined Fleet had a model of Pearl Harbor. The model of Oahu Island was exact to the minutest detail. Both of these models were given to me and I returned to the *Akagi*.

The situation become so that training had to be carried out in a greater way, but the pilots as a whole, especially the leaders, were not sure of the location of the torpedo targets and the stationary targets such as ships in port and planes on the ground. They were skeptical of the value of these targets, too. Here there was the absolute necessity of giving the meaning and nature of the plan concerning the various specialized trainings. There was a need for the opinions of torpedo specialists, too; therefore, on 2 October the main leaders of each First Air Fleet Headquarters, each ship captain, each aircraft leader and each air unit commander were summoned to the *Akagi*. There, with the models before them, the plan of this attack was explained to the men for the first time. Every man present gave a sigh of assurance, saying, "I never thought the plans were anything like this, but now that I know what's it's all about, I'll give the best I have!"

The great matter that had to be decided here now was the possibility or impossibility of carrying out a torpedo attack, but an agreement was reached that whether we could sink the ships or not, we could operate at close range to the enemy.

Only the commanders of the air units understood the aim in this meeting and they began their actual training.

In the beginning of October there was some talk from the Combined Fleet Headquarters, saying, "From the standpoint of the necessity of the southern operation, the plans of the Navy General Headquarters were to send the *Akagi* and two ships of the 5th Carrier Division. In order to train the ships of the 5th Carrier Division, we are hoping to have the pilots of the 2nd Carrier Division transferred to the 5th Carrier Division."

To this I said, "I am absolutely against using an uncertain force in a battle which will influence the failure or success of our country. If you are not sure about the force to be used, you might as well stop or else make sure of the force. Take one or the other! Another reason that I am against this is because if the pilots of the 2nd Carrier Division were to be transferred to the 5th Carrier Division, that would sever the tie between the men and their commanders, which will be a great danger."

As soon as this talk reached the Headquarters of the First Air Fleet and of the 2nd Carrier Division, Rear Admiral Yamaguchi came to the First Air Fleet Headquarters in a rage, and expressed himself, saying that he was absolutely against such a move, and a big debate was carried out between him and Vice Admiral Nagumo. Rear Admiral Yamaguchi in a very infuriated manner said, "If the pilots of the 2nd Carrier Division are going to be transferred to the 5th Carrier Division, there is nothing for me to do but resign. And again you say that the cruising range of the 2nd Carrier Division is not sufficient. If the 2nd Carrier Division can reach Hawaii, that is good enough. When we run out of fuel, we will just drift. The rest of the units can return without bothering with us."

Both the Commander of the First Air Fleet and the Chief of Staff could only say: "Well, if that is an order from the Naval General Staff, there is nothing we can do about it."

I was in complete agreement with Rear Admiral Yamaguchi's opinion. Ever since this argument, Rear Admiral Yamaguchi seemed to have been a little unhappy.

All during this time the map maneuvers were continued by the Combined Fleet on the flagship *Nagato,* off the coast of Tokuyama. These maneuvers were on a smaller scale than those planned by the Navy General Headquarters. Rear Admiral Yamaguchi was under the command of the commander of the Philippine area aircraft carrier unit in these maneuvers, but he ignored those maneuvers and had "man to man, heart to heart" talks with the Commander-in-Chief of the First Air Fleet and with the Headquarters of the Combined Fleet, saying, "How about sending me to Hawaii?"

Even during the time when these maneuvers were being carried out, there was nothing said about the danger and difficulty of this Hawaii operation. Soon after the map maneuvers were finished, the Commander-in-Chief made a clear expression of this operation, saying, "As long as I am Commander-in-Chief, this Hawaii operation will be carried out under any circumstances. I want each man to know that. And as long as we are carrying out this operation, I want you to understand the methods we will use and the danger we will face because this operation depends on you who are taking part."

After this, no one discussed the problems of this operation.

A few days later there was uneasiness when the number of men to take part in this operation was known. When the decision of the men deciding to take part in all of the operations was received from the Combined Fleet Headquarters, there was much relief.

On the other hand, the aircraft units were continuing violent training morning, noon and night, day after day. The aircraft carriers and two of the ships of the Third Battleship Division and other ships also continued to train for giving supplies at sea.

Because the men as a whole did not know the actual aim of the operation, they imagined many things that could be possible and were very hopeful. They would say, "I wonder where the place will be? Could it be Singapore, or Manila? Guess it couldn't be either of those places because there is no fleet at those places. Surely, it's not Hawaii!"

The training was carried out until the end of October and was completed as follows:

TYPE OF TRAINING	TRAINING COMPLETED
Level bombing (at 8,500 ft.)	13–14 percent
Dive bombing	30–34 percent
Daylight torpedoing	70–80 percent
Nighttime torpedoing	50–75 percent

This training was carried out against a very maneuverable target ship. The torpedo attack training on anchored ships improved up to 3 to 4 hits out of 10.

The submerging of the shallow and deep torpedoes was the only problem we had now. It was about this time that we attached a "fool-proof" fin on the torpedoes.

On 2 November all of the aircraft units excluding the fighter units were assembled at Ariake Bay. All pilots above company grade officers were called to the *Akagi* and this plan was explained. Almost every one was glad that he could take part in this operation and rejoiced, saying, "I was born a boy at the right time!"

The entire carrier fleet and the fleets attached to it (the second section of the 3rd Battleship Division, the 8th Cruiser Division, the flagship of the 1st Destroyer Squadron and eleven destroyers) went to the southeastern waters of Kyushu on 3 and 4 November. The preattack maneuver of the air units attacking Pearl Harbor was carried out with Saeki Bay and Sukumo Bay as the targets.

The maneuvers of the attacking units were neither good nor bad. The reason for this is because the fighter units could not take part in these maneuvers because of the lack of equipment. (There was some equipment to combat the cold of the northern area maneuvers but it was not sufficient.)

After the end of the maneuvers, we examined the results of the bombing and torpedoing of the entire air units and found them to be very poor. (The units that bombed the ships were the only units that came through as planned.) This result was really disheartening.

I flew to the base at Kagoshima with the air units and conferred with all the officers connected with the torpedo units.

At that time the men gathered expressed the opinion that the torpedo units were not the only failure but also that the level bombing was not very good. They said that there was nothing to do except depend on the power of the dive-bombing units, but my request was that the men make another effort to improve. The reason, I thought, for the poor high-level bombing was the "slump" in the men's attitude. "If we can only get a settlement of the torpedo problem, we will be all right." A meeting was held for this purpose.

Two of the opinions of two officers were decided upon to be the final settlements.

1. Attach stabilizer fins on "KAI-2" twice renovated torpedoes. Cut the speed of the plane to 150 knots and release torpedo at approximately 65 feet.

2. Equip the planes with "KAI-1" once-renovated torpedoes. Lower landing gears to cut speed to 100 knots and release torpedo from the altitude at and below 35 feet.

We hoped that one of these two ideas would succeed. If we could not depend on this, our efforts would have been in vain. There were only ten days left before we must assemble at Saeki Bay before going into action.

The aircraft carriers all went into harbor to prepare for action—the 1st Carrier Division to Sasebo and the 2nd and 5th Carrier Divisions to Kure. I left Kagoshima on the 7th for Omura and Sasebo to prepare all preparations for the attack. Various types of preparations were being carried out at Sasebo and air units were completing their training. Around the 10th two [units]* from Kagoshima discharged about ten torpedoes each at the depth of approximately 40 feet. Both were able to shoot the torpedoes over 83% of the expected distance. I also received a wire saying that the horizontal bombing had regained its effectiveness. I thanked God. God does not aid those who do not make any effort or continue in any effort. I felt strongly that help will come to those who heap up efforts and devotion to their work.

After all preparations were completed, various ships of the mobilized unit gathered at Saeki Bay around 13 and 14 November. The final plans were made with the commander in chief of the Combined Fleet. From the 17th each ship began to leave the bay in successions and headed toward Hitokappu Bay. All the unit commanders of the mobilized unit and the pilots, above [company grade] officers, were assembled on the flagship, *Akagi*. Commander-in-Chief Yamamoto of the Combined Fleet came on board the ship and gave instructions concerning every man. The instruction in brief is as follows:

"Our opponent this time is not an easy one. She is of a much higher rating than the enemies Japan has fought until today, and is a much stronger enemy. The enemy lacks nothing. Admiral Kimmel, himself a young man, is said to have gone up to be commander in chief by his ability. He is a man with much courage and 'guts.'†

"The success or failure of the operation of the mobilized unit taking the first step in this battle will influence the success or failure of the entire operation. I'm praying for the best effort from all of us and for our success."

Thus with intervals of a few hours between, the 2nd Carrier Division, 1st Carrier Division and the 5th Carrier Division left Saeki Bay. The line of these ships was a very stirring sight. The plans were made so that the ships would pass the areas west of Tokyo Bay during the night. Every ship cut all radio communications too and headed toward Hitokappu Bay.

When we reached Hitokappu Bay around the 20th and 21st, we saw that there were already several ships in the bay. Within one to two days the entire force of the mobilized unit, the 1st Carrier Division, 2nd Carrier Division, 5th Carrier Division, the second section of the 3rd Battleship Division, the 8th Cruiser Division, the flagship of the 1st Destroyer Squadron, eleven destroyers, three submarines, and six transport ships came steaming through the waves of the northern waters. I wrote up the operation orders of the task force on this trip and had it approved by the commander in chief after I completed it. I am sure that the contents of the opera-

---

* The translator rendered this word as "submarines," an obvious misreading. Two methods of aerial torpedo bombing were being tested at Kagoshima at this time —Eds.

† "The word used here to describe Admiral Kimmel is the word used in olden Japan for the fearless samurai chief who used to 'get his man' "—Trans.

tional orders have already been given; however, I will write some important points of it:

1. The entire fleet will discard the scattered dispersion tactic. Six aircraft carriers will be the nucleus. Group dispersion tactics will be used all the way.

2. Reconnoiter Lahaina Anchorage the night before the date of the attack by means of a submarine, and get a report.

3. Emphasize the importance of the secrecy of the plans during the cruise. Do not have aircraft escort, but for any unexpected need each ship will have six fighters on deck ready for action.

4. Reconnoitering of the immediate front will be carried out by planes from the 8th Cruiser Division. The planes will not only search over Pearl Harbor but also the areas in the near vicinity.

5. In case the following happens, carry out the second phase of attack:
   In case the result of the attack is extremely good or extremely poor.

6. In case no information concerning the American Fleet can be gotten, send the 8th Cruiser Division out two days ahead. The unit will reconnoiter under its own power and acquire information.

7. Depending on the situation, take the southern route as a return route and return by way of the west side of Oahu Island. Search for any surviving American ships and destroy same.

8. In case the American Fleet is in Lahaina Anchorage, attack same, entirely with torpedoes.

9. In case of an assault, send the entire fighter unit to Oahu Island in the first phase, then start the attack after we get the supremacy.

Note: Contents from memory of the answer of Rear Admiral Onishi to Commander-in-Chief Yamamoto:

1. We must make a surprise attack or we will never succeed.

2. We are hoping to use torpedoes as the main weapon, but it is very difficult from the standpoint of skill.

3. In case the foregoing is impossible to carry out, make a bombing attack with lots of bombs smaller than 550 lbs. against the auxiliary fleet group anchored in the northern waters of Ford Island. A fleet without its auxiliaries will lose much of its fighting power.

There was other information discussed in detail, but I can't seem to recall it.

CHAPTER 4

Analysis No. 2 of the Pearl Harbor Attack

Minoru Genda

I am not sure, but I recall that on the morning of 24 November each key man of the headquarters and commanders of each fleet were called together aboard the *Akagi* and the plans of the Hawaii Operation were explained. On the afternoon of the same day, all pilots above company grade officers of each fleet were assembled aboard the *Akagi* and informed of the great operation. After the commanders of each unit were oriented on this operation, each commander explained the plan of attack to his unit.

After the above orientation was finished, we had a farewell meeting in the officers' quarters because we might never meet again.

The accomplishments of the meeting of the leaders on the *Akagi* was held secret and the pilots as a whole were not aware of the actual plans. The plans were told to the men after the fleet left Hitokappu Bay and was heading toward the operational area.

Even in the entire navy, the men who knew about this plan were only the key men of Naval Headquarters and the key men of the headquarters of the Combined Fleet, Second Fleet, and the 11th Air Fleet.

Every airplane unit was carrying out training. If the communication between these units and the carriers was stopped suddenly, there would be danger of suspicion. To avoid this, the carrier-based planes were returned to their carriers as planned, and the land-based units stationed on the western coast carried out "further training" and kept communication with the carriers open.

During the time the fleets began to assemble in Hitokappu Bay until they left the harbor, all mail to the homeland was suppressed.

Here are a few words concerning the preparations and the people responsible in this operation:

1. The improvement of the horizontal bombing.

Our horizontal bombing had been very poor year after year, especially the bombing of moving ships from 10,000 feet. The effectiveness of that bombing could have been said to be zero. During the first part of 1941 (up to the latter part of March) we discussed doing away with horizontal bombing by carrier planes. In the first place, if we used the sights that we were using, we would never make any satisfactory bombing. The only thing that would answer this problem was a new type of sight.

Without any change, however, special training for the horizontal bombing was carried out by the Yokosuka Air Unit. Around April, [CPO Akira] Watanabe and another man (I cannot recall his name)* boarded the *Akagi* and participated in the June bombing maneuvers, making a very good showing with the bombing (the *Settsu* was used as a target ship). There are many basic reasons for this good showing, but I believe that one of the big reasons is that the pilot and the crew of the bomber, who were thought to be of little importance, had trained themselves rigidly for this task. Here, especially, Watanabe had trained rigidly. He serviced his plane as much as he could personally. He personally serviced and repaired the controls and whenever possible he would do his own repairs rather than have the repairman do it. He carefully recorded the amount of fuel left over after each flight, thus he calculated the amount of fuel consumed in different types of flights. In that manner he could go out and return from a mission using the maximum of fuel in the plane.

The feat that Watanabe accomplished in horizontal bombing was a great accomplishment and from that time on, it was said that, even in horizontal bombing, if the right method were used, it could be a success.

With this promising hope, Lt. Izumi Furukawa, who was the commander of a unit on the *Akagi,* was given the responsibility to give special training at Kagoshima. A total of 16 airplanes, three from each carrier of the 1st and 5th Carrier Divisions and two from each carrier of the 2nd Carrier Division, were to be assembled at Kagoshima for this training.

Lieutenant Furukawa was an officer in the reconnaissance group, but he was a man whose interest and deepest desire was to advance the tactics of horizontal bombing. His timely and deep interest in this matter plus rigid training raised the effectiveness of horizontal bombing in the Japanese Navy to a level which never was attained before. The attack on Pearl Harbor was made successful because of the confidence we had in this type of bombing. Later, he was promoted to be the air commander of a land assault unit and became very famous. However, in the latter part of February 1944, when the American Task Force made an air raid on the Marianas for the first time, Lieutenant Furukawa went out at night with a torpedo plane and never returned.

In November 1941 there arose quite a discussion on the accuracy and the effectiveness of these horizontal bombings against the enemy battleships. The leaders of the air units insisted that the altitude of 13,000 feet was necessary to effectively bomb through the deck of the enemy battleships, but the bombardiers opposed because accuracy was lessened at that altitude. For a while this was discussed quite a bit, but finally it was set to be at 10,000 feet as the bombardiers demanded.

The style in which Furukawa carried out the training of pilots was as follows: Until now it was the general understanding that to train anyone or any group of men

---

* CPO Yanosuke Abe—Eds.

for aerial combat, the allowed time, that is, the allowed training period, had to be overdrawn to complete the training. In other words, to have "A" type of training done, "X" number of training hours were required and "Y" number of days or weeks were allowed. However, because it was during the emergency the allotted "Y" number of days or weeks could not be expected. In order to fill this lack of time up, the practice was to move training time, that is, to increase "X," but the results were not very good. The big problem was time.

Furukawa thought up a new method, a method never used before, to solve this problem. For example, until now, the practice was that in the training to take off and to land, the trainees would take off and land, take off and land. This was done five times in the morning and five times in the afternoon. This method was thought to be the best. However, Furukawa said that was too easy, so he would let the trainee and instructor get into a plane with a lunch box and let them train from morning until night, taking off, coming in for a landing, taking off again, over and over again. About halfway through, the instructor and trainee would be so tired and would ask if they could come in for a rest. When Furukawa got such a request, he would order them to stay out longer and train twice as hard. Even in this exhausted state, the trainees learned to handle the plane safely. Furukawa used the method which in years past was used by the instructors of "Kendo," that is, to let the trainee try, try and try a thousand times.

By using this method, Furukawa was able to train his green trainees in one-third of the allotted time which normally took half of the allotted time, and even got into a little of the next training schedule, which was training for torpedo attacks.

If this man could have continued this new way of training, I believe he would have been the foremost leader of Japan's Naval Air Force, but he became one of the spirits to protect our country after he was killed in action in the waters east of the Marianas.

2. Lt. Cmdr. Shigeharu Murata, leader of the torpedo attacks, will be the next person I shall present. (Lieutenant Commander Murata was a graduate of the 58th graduating class from the Naval Academy.)

Japan had put much emphasis on torpedo attacks from the beginning. Whenever there was a lack of strength in a decisive operation of the battleships, these torpedo attacks were carried out. Their training was never lacking. Because the torpedo attacks of the Naval Air Force were used in this capacity, it was only natural that this type of attacking was so stressed and developed. We can say without hesitating that compared with any other method, the torpedo attack was the most effective. It was not unusual to hit a possible against any maneuverable and fast targets. The torpedoes were also used as the most effective means to sink battleships. For these reasons, the torpedo attack was considered the key weapon of the Naval Air Force.

Murata was a pilot of one of the carrier-based attack planes, specializing in torpedo, and he was an authority on torpedo attacks. He is the person who trained the personnel of the torpedo attack units, evaluated the maneuverability of the Type 97 carrier-based attack plane, compiled and organized the necessary information as to the topography and depth of Pearl Harbor and finally made the attack on Pearl Harbor a possibility. The plan of the torpedo attack against Pearl Harbor not only concerned the route and target for the torpedo attack units but also for each attack plane. He compiled every bit of this information himself.

As we saw previously, the deep-water torpedo attack was very difficult until the solution as to the best method was found. The solution was another of Murata's findings through his tenacious efforts.

Murata not only planned the details of the attack but also commanded the actual attack. Almost every leading pilot of the carrier attack unit took part in the attacks under the command of Murata and, needless to say, the results were great.

The success of the torpedo attack which played a great part in the victorious result at Pearl Harbor was mainly due to Murata's efforts. However, after this he led the torpedo attack units of the *Shokaku* in October 1942 in a battle off the coast of San Cristobal (a naval battle in the South Pacific) and gave his life gallantly for his country. From the very beginning, the pilots of the carrier-based torpedo attack unit were among the least complaining and most gallant men in the Japanese Navy. Their planes had no machine gun for self-protection nor did they have much speed or maneuverability to release the torpedoes. There was no other way but to devote their lives to the one torpedo and one armor-piercing bomb each plane carried, and to concentrate only on attacking their targets. This was the special characteristic of these carrier-based attack planes. I am sure that this is the reason that made these pilots as noble as they were.

3. Next on the list is Lt. Comdr. Takashige Egusa (a graduate of the 58th graduating class from the Naval Academy).

The dive bombing attacks by the Type 99 carrier-based dive bombers were carried out normally, but in maneuvers held in March 1941 and thereafter these bombers did not satisfactorily accomplish their missions. After Egusa was appointed commander of the air units on the *Soryu* in September and began directing the training of the carrier-based bombers of the 1st and 2nd Carrier Divisions, the degree of training suddenly went up and results were amazingly good. He was an excellent leader of men and was an ideal pilot because of his scruples and courage. It was he who studied and adopted while at Yokosuka the meter that indicates the angle at which a plane is diving and introduced it to the air units on the carriers. These meters were a means for the great advancement in the method of bombing. Egusa was always studying the tactical actions of the units while in training and there was not a person who was more cautious in all things than he.

His ability to lead the units in flight was indeed god-like. All the commanders of the air units of the 1st and 2nd Carrier Divisions looked up to him and were led by him in complete confidence. I would like to tell an incident here which took place at a much later date. During our attack on Colombo, Egusa led a carrier-based bomber unit to the attack over the Indian Ocean. He had sighted two British cruisers, both 10,000 tons, which were fleeing from the attack. With his group of 53 bombers, he attacked, and that attack was the one that must be recorded in history. He came up on these two ships from the stern and circled to meet them from the bow. The attack took only a few moments and the ships were destroyed. The hits were better than 90%. The training during this time was at its best and it was truly something to admire. And again the fact that not a single plane in the attacking unit was hit shows the expertness of Egusa's leadership ability.

In the Pearl Harbor attack, the plan for the carrier-based bomber units was to especially attack the enemy aircraft carriers, but as none of the carriers were in the harbor at that time, the carrier-based bomber units did not get much publicity as having accomplished a great feat. If the carriers had been in the harbor, or even in the vicinity of the harbor, Egusa's attackers would surely have dealt a great death blow against the enemy's helpless carriers.

Egusa was later assigned as a commander of the Ginga Unit (an air unit of Ginga-type planes) and in June 1944 he was killed in action in the Marianas operation.

Here are some things that I left out in connection with the torpedo attacks.

Along with the planning of an attack against Pearl Harbor, there arose an important question of whether the battleships and aircraft carriers had or had not laid torpedo nets. If they had, our torpedo attack could not have been effective unless some method was found to annul the effectiveness of the nets. The attack units from our carriers would be forced to make horizontal bombings without the use of torpedoes, which would have greatly decreased the results of the entire attack. Again, if the enemy had put up a balloon barrage, our dive bombing attacks would be very difficult, too. All this would have really cut the results of the attack on the harbor. The balloon barrage could have been shot down by the machine guns from the fighters and a dive bombing attack could be carried out, but it was not so with the antitorpedo nets.

There was no definite proof, however, that these nets were laid.

Even though we were not sure if the enemy had laid torpedo nets, we experimented with net cutters in case there were nets. This experiment was entrusted to the Air Technical Depot and to the Yokosuka Air Unit. The experiment proved to be unsatisfactory, because when the net cutter was mounted on the torpedo, the weight was so increased that the torpedo would sink too deep, and it could not accomplish the purpose of hitting the hull of the ships. All this took place during the latter part of October and the beginning of November. Because of this failure of the net cutters, it was decided that we would not use it, but trust our luck and heaven for the best.

If by chance the nets were laid, we had two methods that we could have used:

1. Fly parallel to the net and the ships in row and release the torpedo between the net and ships, hoping that the missile would hit its mark.

2. Have several torpedoes released into the nets, thus destroy the net, then the other planes could release their torpedo through the holes.

These two methods were not impossibilities, but from the technical point of view, they were very difficult. Nevertheless, one must expect to have some difficulty in an attack as large as this.

However, the various conditions of Pearl Harbor at the time of the actual attack were easier than we had imagined.

The main precaution we had to take in the attack against the ships in Pearl Harbor was making sure of hitting the ammunition storage of the ships, because the depth of the harbor was such that even if a bomb would make a leakage and sink the ship, the Americans could repair that hole completely and have the ship ready for action with their large repairing equipment. The torpedo attack and the dive bombing were not good against this. The only way was to get one 1760-lb. armor-piercing bomb into the ammunition storage of each ship, but the accuracy of the bombing attack was not perfect. For this reason, we could not expect too great a success in this attack.

The main purpose for using the horizontal bombing attack in this operation was to neutralize the antiaircraft fire and make the torpedo and dive bombing less hazardous. It was also used because we were not sure of the torpedo and dive bombing attacks as mentioned in the previous paragraph.

We have not written much about the fighter planes so far, but our Navy had a group of excellent fighters, especially in the 1st Carrier Division. Most of the leaders were combat-experienced men from the China Theater. The planes were the Zero-type fighters and every pilot was confident of his plane. We expected to get air superiority over Oahu Island with our 70 fighters as long as the commander of this attack unit did not commit a blunder.

It is true in any warfare, but especially in aerial battle, that absolute power of the fighter planes is the first step in winning a battle. At the beginning of the operation, we had the best of fighter units, but one after another our best pilots were lost, and green, inexperienced men came as replacements. Furthermore, our fighter planes were getting old without new ones and improvements. Finally, we lost air superiority in the Pacific and then the war. Whatever the case, fighter planes play a very important part in an aerial operation.

During their stay in Hitokappu Bay, all the pilots studied the models of Oahu Island and of Pearl Harbor every day on the *Akagi*. Each man studied his own route of approach, his action in the attack, and *how and where he should release the torpedo*. The following results will tell the degree in which each man studied and oriented himself to his task as part of the attacking force.

On the day of the air raid over Oahu Island it was so cloudy that only a small part of the island was seen. But a pilot on the *Akagi* plane could estimate the location of the coast west of Kaneohe by catching sight of a small patch of land off the northern coast of Oahu Island, and could immediately choose the right flying course. And later he said that Oahu Island was just like our model island for practice.

On 26 November [Japan time] all the strength of the Task Force left Hitokappu Bay for the assault and headed straight for the east along the line of 40° longitude north. In this action there was a hot discussion as to whether (1) the forward course should be patrolled or not, and (2) what fleet form should be taken in advancing.

In (1) it came to the conclusion that the probabilities were that patrol planes would be sure to ask the location of the fleet by wireless upon their returning because of losing sight of the fleet in a very poor visibility in the northern Pacific in winter, rather than catching sight of other ships or U.S. patrol planes.

So it was decided that six fighters would be ready on the deck for fighting, patrol in the air being abandoned. Though this was extremely dangerous for the fleet to navigate, it could not be helped, owing to the poor skill of the pilots in general in flying purely by estimate.

In (2), a long formation (◯ ◯ ◯ ◯) was likely to be discovered by patrol planes from Midway and the Aleutian Islands, though they would be less [likely] to be discovered by passing ships; and a broad forma-tion was the opposite. So a comparatively long formation was adopted, taking into account both the convenience of supply and maintenance of fleet formation in a regular shape.

Originally it was scheduled that the submarines were to be kept about 40 or 60 miles ahead of the fleets, but poor visibility made them move around within their sight all the way.

Throughout, navigation was full of hardships owing to poor visibility (dense mist) and rough weather. But we thanked heaven for them, because they reduced the chances of being discovered by the enemy. As for the supply, it was done almost every day if weather permitted. Of course, all the units of the fleet, except the 5th Carrier Division which had a large fuel endurance, had been loaded with drum cans and other cans of oil, even to the living quarters. During the voyage, stress was laid on the economy of fuel; heaving was not done in spite of severe winter and electric lights were reduced to the minimum necessary.

At about the end of November we passed the line of 180°. At that time there came a telegram message that the answer from the United States was so unacceptable to us that the destiny of the diplomatic negotiations threatened to lead to a break; this made us sense that the outbreak of war was inevitable.

During our passage, we received several times information concerning the location of the main strength of the United States Navy from the Naval General Staff and CF.* According to these [messages], the main forces of their battleship forces, excluding aircraft carriers and patrolling forces, were located at Pearl Harbor. The only thing was to push forth the plan—that was our impression at that time. However, what annoyed us to the last was the location of the carriers and patrolling forces which ended in unknown things. One of the reasons for our unsatisfactory attack in its thoroughness and smooth succession was partly due to the doubt about their location.

As we went eastward, the sea became tranquil, but the visibility was as poor as ever.

On the 2nd or 3rd, we received the telegram: "Climb Mt. Niitaka X day 8th December" and we knew that the Japanese had made up their minds. The telegram was dispatched by the Combined Fleet. Until that time we were to sail back, pretending that we were practicing some sort of maneuver.

On the 6th or 7th, we finished our supply in the morning, which was the last one, and sent back the supply ships. Then with the 1st, 2nd, and 5th Carrier Divisions, 3rd Battleship Division, 8th Cruiser Division, and nine destroyers with flagship [CL *Abukuma*] we made up the air raid formation. We went on towards Pearl Harbor southward at the speed of 26 knots an hour. Nothing particular happened up until that time. But I will pick up a few interesting events.

I remember it was on the night of the 5th. There was a telegram message,

---

* The translation reads GF, but we believe this should be CF, i.e., Combined Fleet—Eds.

dispatched by the Special Service Group of the Naval General Staff, that some American submarine(s) was (were) chasing us in the rear. So we took it seriously, and planned patrol actions to be take the next morning. But an hour and a half after that telegram, came another telegram telling us that the sub(s) was (were) heading for Hawaii between the western coast of the U.S. and Hawaii. We were much relieved at this.

Probably at seven in the morning of December [7] (East 135° Line Time) when we sent back our supply ships, all personnel went toward the south with the desperate determination of fighting. The weather turned out to be favorable, and visibility gradually became good. Then we received encouraging telegrams from both the Imperial Headquarters and the Commander-in-Chief of the Combined Fleet to inspire us all.

The one from the Imperial Headquarters was to the effect that the Headquarters was confident of our success in the operation; and the one from the Combined Fleet was that they expected our utmost efforts at the risk of our lives, under the consideration of the importance of the coming war.

A signal was hoisted at the top of the mast telling us "The fate of our Empire solely depends upon the success or failure of this fight. I expect you will do your duty," which is a traditional wording on such occasions by the Commander-in-Chief of the Task Forces Admiral Nagumo.

Sunset is at about half-past one. If we are not to be discovered by sunset, our air raid is sure to succeed about 50 percent. Several hours have passed in a very strained mood, and the sun set. Then we have nothing but a decisive battle at dawn tomorrow.

After sunset, the Commander-in-Chief told me that up until that time the fleet had been brought there safely; from that time it was up to the air forces.

Ten days had passed since we left Hitokappu Bay, and ten months since we participated in this plan. It had to be borne in mind that that one blow at the start of the war would be the most essential one upon which the fate of our Empire depended, as well as dominating in our following operations.

I always felt something heavy on my shoulders. Every precaution was taken. We had been making some little correction to the original plan since we left Hitokappu Bay; on the taking off and receiving of the planes, reconnaissance and patrol, etc.; we made assurance doubly sure. Day and night, or even when I awoke, whether in the Operations Room or in my room, I pictured to myself the situation in which we were, hearing the dashing of waves outside. "Now we are advancing toward Pearl Harbor, not in a dream, but really," or "May God help us," praying. Nothing had been more encouraging in my life than that. I really concentrated all my energy on that. However, there had been many points lacking correctness and preciseness when I look over the past. But at that time I was fully aware of the serious situation, that all depended on that enterprise—the lives of a hundred million people. I had a short nap in the Operations Room for about two hours between eight and ten at night [feeling] something uncertain hover over me. But when I woke up and came up to the bridge, to my wonder, I found myself quite unconcerned about anything, with all worldly thought and chimerical cares such as anticipation of troubles or the keenest desire for our success, absolutely cleared away. I have never experienced such a serene and quiescent mood in my life.

I was absolutely sure of the success of the air raids.

At eight P.M.—"All mechanical hands get up!"—and at ten—"all hands get up!" When I got up to the deck, all the planes were there for the first take-off, shoulder to shoulder for the test work. There had been moderate wind with big swells of the sea; rollings and pitchings of the ship were pretty keenly felt.

We had already received a telegram from the dispatched submarine that the enemy fleet was not at Lahaina, so I had made up my mind to strike nowhere but Pearl Harbor, and all my attention had been concentrated on that. Now it was time for the five special midget submarines which formed the first van of the attacking forces to enter Pearl Harbor. By the way, the account of this most risky enterprise of the midget subs made an enormous impression on the crews of the planes, encouraging them to the fullest extent.

All our fleet had already taken up the deployment formation, since they had left the supply ships in order to welcome any actions without a second of delay. At 0030 eighth, each one plane, O-type sea plane, took off from the cruisers *Tone* and *Chikuma* for the mission of reconnoitering the enemy situations at and around Pearl Harbor and Lahaina. At this, there was a little confusion on board the other ships, taking these two aircraft for enemy planes, but in a minute they proved to be ours and the slight commotion was settled. All the crews of the first and second attack units were to await their turns, after so long a training with many hardships.

Here some tactics that were to be adopted in case the enemy situation should not be available at all will be described briefly:

If no information about the enemy [was available] until 5 December, the following would apply:

"On 5 December, two ships of the 8th Cruiser Division will be sent to Pearl Harbor taking the shortest cut. On the seventh, when they come to 250 miles from Pearl Harbor, the two ships will send forth O-type sea planes for reconnaissance. All the fleet will act according to this certain information; the air raids on the eighth will be carried out."

We had expected a counterattack by the U.S. Navy. We were quite ready for that too. But, in fact, the locations of the U.S. carriers and cruisers were unknown, and there were no counterattacks from the U.S. So we could not have a decisive battle in the air or on the sea.

The withdrawal course of the fleet was as follows, according to the plan:

A. The same course we had come, only in the opposite direction.

B. The course along the line of Hawaii and Midway westward.

C. The course that runs southward through the west of Oahu Island for the Marshall Islands.

If we had taken the third course, we would have been favored with the chance of meeting the U.S. carrier forces at sea, and had a decisive battle in the air. It might have been awfully interesting if that was the case.

The formation at the time of the attack was as follows:

The formation at the time of the attack was as follows:

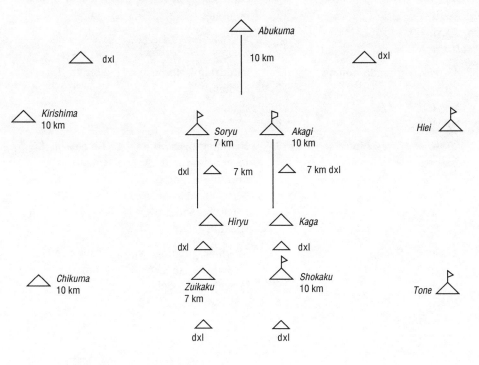

Two notes in Prange's handwriting:

"⊵ flagship of sqdn

⊵ flagship of fleet"

"Note: Location of carriers correct; others not sure."

Since supply went on as scheduled, there had been no problem, but if it had been the opposite—the supply not sufficient or difficult—destroyers were to be dispatched apart from the other ships at time of the supply ships' parting.

As for the flying watch vessel to accompany the carriers, three subs in company of the carriers were to be distributed along the central line that ran amidst the carrier columns. These three subs, at the time of the air raids, were about fifty miles north of Oahu Island for the rescue of airmen.

At half-past one in the morning all the planes from each ship began to take off for the first attack; it was just thirty minutes before sunrise. The formation and military mission were as follows:

The details have already been submitted to the Bombing Survey.

I hope you will refer to it.

Commander in general was Commander Fuchida.

Name of Ship	Kind of Planes	Number	Military Mission	Commander
Akagi	torpedo-bomber[1]	15	battleships—level	Fuchida, Comdr.
Kaga	"	15	bombing	
Soryu	"	10		
Hiryu	"	10		
Akagi	torpedo-bomber[2]	12	battleships—torpedo	Murata, Lt.
Kaga	"	12	bombing	Comdr.
Soryu	"	8		
Hiryu		8		
Shokaku	dive-bomber	27	Bombing over Ford	Takahashi, Lt.
Zuikaku	"	27	Island. Bombing & machine gunning over Wheeler Air Field. Partly bombing over Hickam Field.	Comdr.
Akagi	fighter	9	Machine gunning over	Makiya, Lt.
Kaga	"	9	air fields—Hickam,	Comdr.[3]
Soryu	"	9	Wheeler, Kaneohe,	
Hiryu	"	6	and Bellows in Ford	
Shokaku	"	6	Island.	
Zuikaku	"	6		

[1] The planes were equipped with level-bombing bombs.

[2] The planes were equipped with torpedo attacking bombs.

[3] Leader of the first-wave fighters was Lieutenant Commander Itaya.

The heavy swelling of the waves resulted in severe rolling; in the 1st Carrier Division it was about 7 degrees, in the 2nd, 12–13 degrees, and in the 5th, 15–16 degrees. But the wind was so strong that the takeoff of the planes from the ships was very easy. In fifteen minutes all the planes of the First Attack Group finished the rendezvous over the fleet and headed for Oahu Island.

At about the same time, seaplanes left the ships belonging to the 3rd Battleship Division and 8th Cruiser Division; eight of them were to search for the enemy over 180 miles in radius, and four of them watched for direct defense of the fleet against enemy subs.

After the departure of the First Attack Group, our fleet proceeded southward at 26 knots along the line of 180°, making preparation for the departure of the Second Group. And at three the Second Group began to leave the ships. Its organization was as follows:

Commander in general was Lieutenant Commander [Shigekazu] Shimazaki.

NAME OF SHIP	KIND OF PLANE	NUMBER	MILITARY MISSION	COMMANDER
Akagi	dive bomber	18	Dive-bombing over	Egusa, Lt. Comdr.
Kaga	"	27	battleships and cruisers	
Soryu	"	18		
Hiryu	"	18		
Shokaku	torpedo-bomber	27	Bombing over Kaneohe,	Shimazaki,
Zuikaku	(level bombing)		Hickam, and Ford Air Fields	Lt. Comdr.
Akagi	fighter	9	Attack air fields, get	[Saburo] Shindo,
Kaga	"	9	control of the air	1st Lt.
Soryu	"	9		
Hiryu	"	9		

At three in the morning, the Second Group began to take off the ships, and after finishing their rendezvous they all headed for Oahu Island.

Up until that time we did not meet any enemy patrol planes, so I was confident of our success. But I wanted to know the effect of the power of the explosives used in the attack.

I do not remember the exact time, but perhaps at half-past three or near that time, I received a wireless message "TORA" which meant "I succeeded in surprise attack" from the commander of the First Attack Group. This was the first wireless that had been sent from the units and really it was wirelessed just before the attack.

Then we received wireless from the commander of the torpedo bombing units, "I have attacked the enemy main forces with great effect upon them." Beginning with these, there were numerous messages about the results of the actions. I knew by these that the attacks were a complete success.

After the departure of the Second Group, the fleet took the course of 0° as their sailing standard, but sometimes the course changed to 90° for the sake of the relief of the planes in direct escort of the fleet.

Beginning at half-past five, the returning planes of the First Group were received. For the return of the fighters, it was decided that the torpedo bomber units would lead the fighter units, and the rendezvous point was at ten miles northwest of Oahu Island. As it was supposed that the enemy would try counterattacks against us from the Oahu Island air fields, about thirty fighters were always kept in the air for that, letting the fighters fly up that had been supplied with fuel after landing on the carriers; but our initiative attacks were so effective that there was no counterattack.

What I was worrying about at that time was the location and other information of the U.S. carrier groups and cruisers. If they were found in our hands, since we had made up our minds to have a decisive battle with them at once, both torpedo bombers and dive bombers were fully prepared for the coming fighting, because after the air raids on Hawaii were finished, torpedo bombers were equipped with torpedoes and the dive bombers with ordinary bombs for attacking vessels.

At about nine in the morning, we began to proceed to the north, as soon as the receiving of the Second Attack Group was over, and sent wireless "SENTO-SOKURO" (battle report from the front) No. 1. I remember it was thus: Damages to the enemy: two battleships were sunk, four battleships damaged, four cruisers slightly damaged, many planes were destroyed; our damages are slight.

On 9 December we reconnoitered over the area of 200 miles around the fleet at the point of 600 miles north of Oahu Island, in vain, though we anticipated a decisive battle because of enemy plane activity, with enemy carriers and cruisers, which were supposed to chase us. Refueling was commenced in the evening, and then the fleet returned.

Next day many pictures that were collected from all the ships showed greater results than were expected.

As it was too far from Oahu, and fuel was not sufficient, the Second Attack could not be hoped for.

CHAPTER 5

Diary of Rear Adm. Giichi Nakahara, Extracts, 11 August 1941–1 January 1942

DURING THE PERIOD in question and later, Rear Adm. Giichi Nakahara was chief of the Navy Ministry's Personnel Bureau, hence held a key position in connection with Japan's war effort. It was to Nakahara that in late July 1941 Yamamoto appealed for a moratorium on the usual late-summer personnel changes throughout the Navy. Nakahara could not give him a blanket promise, but he asked for a list of key personnel and promised to cooperate as far as possible. He kept his word, and changes within the 1st Air Fleet and 6th Fleet (submarines) were minimal.

In addition to such usual diary entries as events and opinions, Nakahara jotted down many disjointed words and phrases, apparently as reminders to himself. He also included many statistics, some clear, some quite cryptic. In all cases, we have followed the diary as closely as possible.

There is no indication who made the English translation; however, the single word "Tomioka," in Prange's handwriting, indicates that the diary came to him through his good friend Rear Adm. Sadatoshi Tomioka.

11 August 1941. Since the Japanese occupation of Thailand, the hostile attitude of the U.S. and England against Japan has become very outstanding.

* Military main forces in regard to the concentration of the British Military Forces around Thailand.*

* Entering of "Warspite"[†] into Siam Bay.

* Interview of Roosevelt and Churchill on the Atlantic.

* Freezing of funds and materials, at the same time the winning over of the Dutch East Indies.

* The U.S. supplies the USSR with materials, especially gasoline for aircraft; and it is often reported that those go through Vladivostok over the Pacific.

The Russo-German war seemed at a deadlock for a little time, but lately Germany is announcing considerable war results.

---

* These asterisks seem to have no significance other than to separate items—Eds.
† The quoted English is in the diary—Trans.

```
*  Captured        890,000
                 4,000,000
*  Aircraft          9,000
   Tanks            12,000
```

* Besieging disposition is finished at 100 kilometers southeast of Smolensk.

25 Divisions out of 40 were destroyed at the battle between Kiev and Odessa.

At the same time, a considerable number of British ships were sunk off the British coast.

I cannot but feel that those announcements of war results by Germany is to reveal the fact that Germany wants to show that the Eastern front is not stagnantly defensive facing the severe winter soon to come, although the German attack on the USSR was not through yet.

On the other hand, the British Empire wants positive help from the U.S. Some say that the former intends to take over Norway.

Germany is asking French help and pro-German people in France are increasing.

Rumor is running that Germany asked France to put Tagare into one of the common defense areas against England.

Or it might imply that the preceding paragraph is just a pretext for the U.S. to occupy it.

There is another information telling me that the U.S. is insisting on the claim to Brazil to let Brazil ask Portugal to request common defense of the Azores areas.

Japan, too, is being forced to fight it out to the last on the Pacific; now it is high time to decide on war or peace by external pressure.

SECOND TO FINISH: FIRST (1 OCT)

Defense Unit of the Naval Stations

Oshima Base Force

Maizuru Defense Unit

The 7th Base Force

FIRST (15 OCT)

95

22s

24s

Yokosuka Defense Unit

Kure Defense Unit

Sasebo Defense Unit

Sasebo Special Regiment

SECOND (? NOV)

9B

PROBLEMS CONCERNING THE NAVAL ACADEMY: It is impossible to allot lieutenants (2nd grade) and ensigns for every department, so they will be separated and specialized as soon as they are commissioned.

into ⎰ Air Department
Gunnery, Defense, Communications, Torpedo
Engineering Department
Submarine Department
Electric Department, Construction Office

Students of the Ordinary Course (*futsu-ka-gakusei*) will be divided as before.
Students of the Higher Course will be divided by their specialization.
Lieutenants (1st grade) and Lieutenant Commanders will be specialized.
Rear Admirals—when they reach this rank—
Distribution and harmony of naval schools?
Schools for the students of the Ordinary Course—2nd Group
Students of the Higher Course　　—B system
Gunnery, Torpedo—Mitajiri*
Mechanics, Electricity—Yokosuka

NAVAL STRENGTH NEWLY ORGANIZED FOR 1942 FISCAL YEAR

C in C—13 persons
1F　　　　1S
2F　　　　Taigei
3F　　　　16sf
4F　　　　9ss
5F
6F　　　　2ss (newly-organized one)
1AF　　　6sf
11AF　　　25sf
Southern Detached Fleet　　8B, 9B, 17sf
Combined Fleet　　　　　　25s, 7sf

Arsenals

S ARSENAL (SUB)		G ARSENAL (TORPEDO)	
C in C	Vice Adm.	C in C	Vice Adm.
General Affairs	Rear Adm.	General Affairs	Rear Adm.
Weapon	"	Torpedo Dept.	"
Shipbuilding	"	Steel Plant	"
Machinery	"	Accountant	"

---

* Yamaguchi prefecture—Trans.

† Original Japanese for this word is *shireikan* for a commander in chief in the rank of an admiral; when he is not an admiral he is called just *shirei*—Trans.

S ARSENAL (SUB) *(cont.)*	
Sub Experimental Dept.	"
Accountant	"
Medical Dept.	"

Y ARSENAL (GUNPOWDER)

C in C	Vice Adm.
General Affairs	Rear Adm.
Gunpowder	"
Explosives	"
Accountant	"
Medical Dept.	"

T ARSENAL (MACHINE GUN)

C in C	Vice Adm.
General Affairs	Rear Adm.
Machine gun	"
1st Magazine Plant	"
2nd Magazine Plant	"
Medical Dept.	"
Vice Admiral	5
Rear Admiral	30
Executive Officer	9
Technical Officer	4
Ordnance Officer	5
Construction Officer	1
Engine Construction Officer	1
Accountant Officer	5
Medical Officer	5
	30

G ARSENAL (TORPEDO) *(cont.)*	
Medical Dept.	"

D ARSENAL (ELECTRIC)

C in C	Vice Adm.
General Affairs	Rear Adm.
Electric Dept.	"
Wireless Dept.	"
Air Wireless Dept.	"
Accountant	"
Medical Dept.	"

TOYOKAWA ARSENAL

Navigation weapons

1. NAVY PROMOTIONS AND CHANGES:* To be generally finished at the middle of September or October.

2. MEDICAL OFFICER, 2-YEAR ACTIVE SERVICE:

31/10 — 30/9

Closing of application

* The abovementioned four articles are found on a pasted sheet of paper on the diary; the handwriting is different from that of the diary writer—Trans.

3. 2-YEAR ACTIVE SERVICE: NAVY'S CAPACITY FOR RECEIVING THIS:

Accountant officer	300
Medical officer	400
Technical officer	450

4. LEVY OF NONCOMMISSIONED OFFICERS:

15,000 persons

15 August 1941

INTERNATIONAL SITUATION: There is a proposal to open the Diet Session on 5 September; the end of August or the beginning of September will be a sort of climax; it is a question of money; the Diet will not be called until the end of November.

Freezing of funds—U.S.

How to make use of petty officers?

Material Mobilization.

Stress should be laid on the saving of fuel.

16 August 1941

Chief of the Department	Morinaga, Sato, Iriye
Secretary	Sato
Counsellor	Imaedo, Ide, Nagamura, Yamazaki, Miyauchi, Araki, Samejima, Usui

22 August 1941. Germany has just finished the occupation of the areas west of the Nedoniapro River, captured many ships at the Nikolaiefski Naval Port; Odessa is going to fall. At the same time, Germany has begun to take the offensive in Northern Russia.

Since the interview between the leaders of the U.S. and England on the Atlantic Ocean, the atmosphere is growing to result in the alliance of England, the United States, and Russia. Talks will be held in Moscow at the beginning of September.

The U.S. is carrying on a propaganda actively that she is supporting Russia by supplying the latter with gasoline. Rumors run that oil tankers are headed for Vladivostok. But I wonder if it is true or not.

Another rumor says that they were sent forward to the Persian Gulf.

England and Russia are putting strong pressure upon Iran. But the Shah of Iran will not respond to this.

RUSSO-JAPANESE RELATIONS: Japan will observe neutrality so long as Russia will not threaten Japan. Japan's interest in Sakhalin. Giving up helping Chiang Kai-Shek. An answer from the USSR to Japan seems professedly to be quite satisfactory to us. Our reinforcement of our armed forces in Manchuria does not mean any step against Russia. Concerning this Russia is very understanding, but the question is the Tripartite Agreement.

Interview of the British Premier and the U.S. President—uncertain.

THE U.S. SUPPORTS RUSSIA: It would be better for us to warn the U.S. that the American support of Russia is quite troublesome. Our information Bureau had better be silent.

THAILAND: Since the Japanese occupation of Thailand, Germany is in a different position that has been caused by the relations between Japan, England and the U.S.

It will not be long before Thailand cannot maintain friendship with Japan. The promises that have been made between the two countries will be abandoned by degrees. The Thailand Cabinet is going to be pro-England.

Freezing of funds.

DUTCH EAST INDIES: DEI has refused most of our demands to give us oil.

Repatriation of American people in Japan is now under consideration.

TREATMENT OF THE 5TH PLAN: Ministry Conference will be held at the beginning of September.

Expenses needed for carrying out the program of the 1942 fiscal year—Extraordinary Military Expense.

NAVAL GENERAL STAFF: Extra plan of the 1941 fiscal year will be carried out. Plans and opinions about that are very welcome.

Meeting of the Chiefs of the Economic Bureau and Justice Bureau postponed.

EDUCATION:

Tsukumo, Ohara—3,000 persons
             —70,000 *tsibo* (60 acres)
  1,500 persons—4 classes—total 6,000 persons

PROBLEMS CONCERNING THE MARINE AFFAIRS BOARD:

Mercantile Marine Schools — Navy

Brown coal, heavy oil

Shortage of uniforms for petty officers

Army-Navy Club—between the Ministry of Navy and Army.

25 August 1941. People of the Combined Fleet and Sasebo Naval Station came up to Tokyo and met. Though they had intended to practice necessary training from the point of operation—

1 Oct*	High-speed training
11 Sept	For a week—with new organization
15 Sept	Commissioning of petty officers
1 Oct	By this date the promotions and changes of sailors and enlisted men will be finished (petty officers in September)
	The date may be advanced.
	3S—gunlayer (Warrant officers will receive training in the fleets.)

At the beginning of October—rendezvous

12, 5, 6	western point of the Inland Sea
3	western coast of Kyushu
14F	east of Kyushu
11AF	Formosa, Palau
4F	G area

War-time duty

Battle—its manner will be shown.

* Probably 1 Sept.—Eds.

Each Force will conduct training separately around Kyushu.
During last decade of Oct—

1, 2, category—Training and operation

After these, day battle and night battle of the Combined Fleet.

1AF and 11AF—Early period operation

Fuel—For ten days and nights

Shell

Mexico—Sato
Hainan Island   26th August

STRUCTURE OF THE MARINE AFFAIRS BOARD

Secretariate   1st and 2nd Departments

Administrative Bureau   Three departments 1, 2, 3.
                          Investigation Chambers 1. 2.

Accountant Bureau   1
                      2   Basement
                      3   Civil engines ring
                      4
                      5   Dr. Iso

Hygiene Bureau   1
                   2
                   Tropical Zone, Branch offices

28 August 1941. England and Russia entered Iran and opened battle. Here England could have a connection with Iran through whch the supporting route of the United States to Russia will be completed.

29 August 1941. Iran surrendered to ——.

MEETING OF THE CHIEFS OF THE SECTIONS AND DEPARTMENTS

GUARD OF THE NORTHERN OCEAN

Very satisfactory without any trouble

To withdraw 10 September

Northern Sakhalin—Got 24,000 tons.

Army returned 350,000 tons out of 900,000 tons.
Transportation route of the U.S. to supply Russia with materials for aid—it should be contrived that the route will not be made through the Japan Sea.

CHIEF OF ACCOUNTANT BUREAU: Budget for the 1942 fiscal year—the end of Sept. Meeting 8th.

ARMY MILITARY BILL: Army and Navy in all 700 million yen.

MEDICAL BUREAU: Well-being of dependents of sailors and EM.
Commencement of education—1 Oct.

HAINAN ISLAND: Water—5,000,000 tons in four years.

PETROLEUM: Brown coal oil problems, too smoky.

RICE AND VEGETABLES: Normal crop.

DISCUSSIONS ABOUT THE WAR PREPARATIONS

Air—amounts to 3,000 million, will be reduced to 2,000 million yen.

Ship—3,600 million yen

Air corps—3,600 million yen

Sea, land—5,400 million yen

Ship	800 million yen
Air	1,600 " "
	2,900 " "
	100 " "
	100 " "
	12,000 " "
Preparation for expedition	3,800 " " (for maintenance)
	15,800 " "

11	32		
18	34	23	5.0
19	35	24	4.0
20	23	25	3.5
21	17	26	3.5
22	6		

4,600 million yen

Air   1200 $\begin{cases} 600 & \text{Air} \\ 300 & \text{Fuel} \\ 90 & \text{persons} \end{cases}$

WAR-TIME	1941	1942	1943	1944
Cruiser			A class 2	
Carrier			1	
Destroyer		1	14	11
Submarine		1	18	14
Seaplane tender			1	
Coastal defense		6	19	6
Minelayer			5	9
Minesweeper		14	28	2
Chaser		56	63	1
(?)		6	12	
(?)			3	1
		85	164	44
At present	38	68	31	2
	38	153	195	46 (433)

8th September—Ministry conference.

9th September—Chiefs of the Sections and Bureaus explain.

5 September 1941. War preparation—to be finished at the end of Oct.

9 September 1941. Ministry Conference Plan.

Upkeep expense at the time of completion of 5th plan—4,680 million yen.

Fleet	550	million yen	
Air Fleet	388	"	"
Air Corps	3,000	"	"
Others	750	"	"
Total	4,680	"	"

Fuel			Air 4,200,000 k
Dutch East Indies	3,000,000		
Sakhalin	1,000,000		
Artificial	6,000,000		Navy 1,500,000
	10,000,000		

THE 5TH AND 6TH PLAN: As was proposed by the Naval General Staff. Should be taken a little more

Personnel quota on the land—In proportion to sea power   2–2.6

School

Air Committee Three times as many

Marine War-time 38,000 (20,000 and odds)

Consumption ratio—excluded the killed, wounded.

Naval power in 1947—The 5th plan, list of organization

    2,580,000 tons

    1,300,000 tons

Peace-time   11,476 (3,043)

War-time   14,519   At peace time   13,519 persons

                              (12,500   "   )

Reserved Service officer	800	persons	(*yobi-shikan*)
Reserved officer	200	"	(*yobi-eki*)
Admirals	14,519	"	
Commanders	13,366	"	
Lt. Comdrs*	11,245		
Consumption	1.58% about 1.6% (in calculation)		

THE 5TH PLAN—790 PERSONS

Substitute 2,200 persons

(Now 27%)

C 11.2%

---

* Nakahara listed no captains—Eds.

THE 5TH PLAN

650 (much substitution is contained)

665 (less substitution is contained)

690 (margin—4%)—Students of Submarine School

775–790 persons

Ordinary 100	600
Air and Sub	310
Higher 80%	400
A 15%	80
	1,480

THE 6TH PLAN

Sea	1.3 times
Air	1.5 times
Office	1.3 times
(?)	1.3 times

War 19,000

It will be possible to levy two times as many as above.

11,020	In case the substitute is not obtainable.
830–850	In case the substitute can be obtained.
980–1,000	Students will be organized as those who are in the official quota. (1960)
Substitute officer	In ten years or so substitute officers will be much used.
Air crew—410 persons	—Much consumation is expected.

12 September 1941

Bond—8,700 million yen

Savings—2,000 million yen will remain

Fund—16,000 million yen

    Manchuria 6 times

    China 4 times

Educational year 1/12

13 September 1941. During this week Leningrad was completely besieged by German troops and its fall has come to be a question of time.

During this week two American ships were sunk and one U.S. destroyer was attacked by a German submarine; until this time the U.S. has been very calm, but these events have made the President of the United States issue an order to attack German naval ships and airplanes in the patrol area of the U.S.

Germany has declared it will attack American ships to be found in the German blockaded district.

And then both countries came to show fighting conditions in special zones.

Japan will remain aloof in regard to the declaration of the United States: Lord only knows!

Changes and transference of the fleets were finished on 10 September; it will soon be issued.

17 September 1941. Sinkings of U.S. ships have made the U.S. declare it will attack any ship of any country of the Axis that should be found in the U.S. patrol zones, whether it be a sub or an airplane; hereby the United States and Germany have entered into war substantially.

The German front line surrounding Leningrad has pressed nearer and nearer to the city.

German strength has just crossed the Dnieper and near-Crimea.

19 September 1941

AIR DEFENSE

10m–12——10m–21

Watch communication

Reorganization of Defense Groups

Traffic will be stopped during air defense fighting.

RUSSO-GERMAN WAR: German troops, northern and southern, could have contacted east of Kiev.

Asama—scheduled at the beginning of October.

The problem of carrying out those articles without tax in the canteen.

4, 5   Air

	4		5
Permanent vessel	811		1,080
Special vessel	283		504
Base strength (65 units)	1,117	(132)	3,540
TOTAL	2,211		5,124
Trainer (63)	746	(156)	2,184
TOTAL	2,957		7,308
Personnel			
Pilot: Officer*	1,540		1,010
Pilot: EM	5,000		15,350
Reconnoiter	6,000		16,250
TOTAL	11,000		31,600
Air mechanics (include officer)	13,000		47,500
Weapon	2,100		10,000
GRAND TOTAL	26,100		89,100
Personnel under education			
Airmen	2,000		4,200– 5,700
Air mechanics	1,700		6,200– 8,200
Weapon	300		2,500–16,200
TOTAL	4,000		12,900–30,100

* Pilot officers not included in total—Eds.

Number of planes:

Needed for sea battle	4,543	11,137
To be supplemented during the first year	8,418	17,280

26 September 1941: Germany got four or five hundred thousand captives in the occupation of Kiev. And the operation against Leningrad is under favorable progress; the fall of the city is approaching very rapidly.

England and the United States are inclined to recognize the defeat of the USSR in this war. However, in order to consume the national power of Germany, it is essential to support the Soviet Union and let her oppose as long as she can. This plain idea will drive the two countries into helping the Soviets.

The United States is going to propose a bill to reform the Merchant Marine Ship Armament Neutralization Act, owing to the sinking of U.S. ships as often reported until now.

SPECIAL PROMOTION OF ADMIRALS:

1. Imperial ordinance (number of years in actual service)

Rear Admiral—3 years, Captain—2 years

During war or accident it will be reduced to half

The promotion will be made by his superior or senior officer (above Captain)

2. Special Promotion (Art. 18)*
   With disregard to whether he is above or below admiral
   1) Distinguished service in the face of the enemy.
   2) Those who rendered distinguished service during war or accident, trouble, or became seriously ill during which time owing to wounds at the front.
   3) Those who served with unparalleled distinction and whose deed was announced by the Minister as an example to the whole troops or unit
      Distinguished service
      Conspicuous merits
      Being seriously ill

Art. 21. War-time —— $\begin{cases} \text{Discharge} \\ \text{Reserved} \\ \text{Seriously ill} \end{cases}$

TRADITION: Minimum number of years

Rear Admiral	4 years
Captain	5 years
Commander	4 years

---

* The Japanese for this is *tokubetsu-shinkyu* which means *tokubetsu*—special, *shinkyu*—promotion, but usually the word was cut short to *tokushin*; because the nine heroes of the midget subs at the Hawaiian attack were promoted two ranks, for the first time in Japan. Ensign—Lt. 1st Grade; Lt. 2nd.—Lt. Comdr. Hence the phrase *ni-kaikyu tokushin* which means *ni* —two, *kaikyu*—rank, *tokushin*—special promotion—Trans.

2ND PARAGRAPH, ARTICLE 18.: ITS INTERPRETATION

A. In case of excellent merit in active service

    a. Those who rendered more merit in war than a standard merit stipulated in MERIT STANDARD.

    b. Those who rendered more merit in war than a standard merit stipulated in MERIT STANDARD, and who have served more than half a period necessary to the promotion.

    c. Those who have served well and have passed the term necessary for the promotion.

B. Those who are now in reserved service.

    a. Those who have rendered more merit than standard merit stipulated in MERIT STANDARD.

    b. Those who have rendered more service than a standard merit stipulated in the MERIT STANDARD, and his term of service covers more than six months; but if his service is official business the term will be reduced to one-half.

Airplane accident—promotion
Submarine—underwater
Admiral, Rear

1) Airman, killed—unconditional promotion

2) When seriously ill

30 September 1941. Italian air force attacked a British convoy consisting of a battleship, a carrier, some cruisers and destroyers with the result of sinking several cruisers by torpedoes. This is pretty big news in recent times.

There is a report that German troops have neared Kharkov.

German submarines and torpedo boats have sunk 88 British vessels during the past week.

Moscow talk has begun: England, the U.S. and Soviet.

The Neutrality Act seems to be modified.

2 October 1941. The Moscow talks came to an end, according to which England and the United States will entirely cooperate with each other in aiding the Soviet by sending materials. In that talk Soviet Russia asked England to land on the western coast of Europe, but it was denounced by the British.

Submarine *I-61* sunk at sea off Nago (?).

INTERNAL SITUATION OF JAPAN: People say that the only alternative left for us is to choose war, now that the situation stands thus, and adds that irresoluteness—neither war nor peace—cannot be borne any longer. But, on the other hand, those who have property and assets are likely to stick to life. As the nation has not gone through a severe ordeal since its establishment, it is very difficult to hope that they will devote themselves to unselfish service to their mother country, service to the public good or service to one's job.

6 October 1941

Ministry conference
Policy in war preparation
⎧First to finish
⎨Second to finish —what has been stated already
  ⎧School
  ⎪Fuel
  ⎨Arsenal
  ⎩Military facilities

Total amount 31,000 million yen
          1942 fiscal year   13,900 million yen
            27,100 million yen⎫
            13,200 million yen⎭ to be modified

Assessed amount	Total	10,000	million yen
1942 fiscal year		8,450	″ ″
Ordinary budget		1,500	″ ″
Supplementary budget		50	″ ″
1942		10,000	″ ″
1941			5,000 +1,500 (million yen ?)
War preparation		1,000	
(?)		2,000	
Increase is		3,000	million yen

9 October 1941

MEETING OF THE CHIEFS OF BUREAUS, SECTIONS

Oil tankers of the U.S.

Ships bound for the U.S.
        The *Tatsuta Maru* and two others
        If it is certain, it will be decided around 15 Oct.

Ships bound for Europe
        The *Asama Maru*   20 Oct.   Probably 20th Oct.

Bound for Latin America
        The *Edo Maru* and one other

Raising of railway transportation fee
        For passengers—30%, increased revenue—350 million

Manchuria—Microbe fighting

Sea transportation
        Small motor boat ⅔
        Shipbuilding 300,000 tons

Fuel—

11 October 1941

COMMANDER IN CHIEF OF THE COMBINED FLEET— The Fleet is now under training aiming at 8 Dec.

Although it is to be hoped that the situation would be improving in peace, yet he is quite ready for the worst case. So he need not come up to Tokyo in case the worst turns out. The order to go forward is the order to push forth to the enemy. The most important is this: in relation to the diplomatic situation, the high time to rise in war is one of the most difficult to decide—one may be too late in taking the initiative and the other may be too early. This has a close relationship with the war preparations. In regard to operational affairs and other matters concerning operational preparations, liaison should be kept more closely.

WORK OF FLOATING THE SUNKEN SUB *I-61*:

Putting round wire	about two weeks
Completion of (?)	first decade of Nov.
Wiring works of (?)	a week
Sailing around Karatsu Port	
TORASU (?) works	2 or 3 weeks
Floating	about 15 Dec.

OTHER INFORMATION:

Diving work	When the current is moving, 2 hours
	Underwater work, 10 minutes
Weather ⅔ workable.	

Outside part of the engine room is broken; the problem is how is the keel. The ship will be raised by ropes fixed at five points. The work is very difficult owing to the lack of a big sharan ship (?)*

12 October 1941: Commander in Chief visited those dependents whose heads are officers and warrant officers, and Chief of the Personnel Department those dependents whose heads are EM. Some EM don't hope to live to see their native land again in this expedition, and testaments were written already.

German troops have come as near as 104 kilometers from Moscow. The whole city is in a commotion.

15 October 1941: The German forces are around the city about 96 kilometers from Moscow, and their shells can reach the outside dispositions of the city.

The Japanese Cabinet reached the final point last night. Now we have to choose between war or peace (compromise). But the present Cabinet has no power to take the policy of war or compromise with the U.S.

If Japan should compromise with the United States, the latter would put more and more pressure over the former to the point of the former's surrender. If Japan should surrender to the U.S., the result would be the destruction of the Japanese race spirit. Turning the eye to the Navy, the Navy would be deemed weak and the result would be the loss of the Navy's credit among the people; then it should not even be dreamed to replete the Navy.† On the contrary, the Army will turn their

---

* What Nakahara meant by a "sharan ship" is not clear. Note translator's question mark—Eds.

† The translator's expression "to replete the Navy" is not clear. Perhaps something like "for the Navy to retreat" was meant—Eds.

course to the Chinese continent with the expression of triumph on their faces as if to say "it is only the Army that can support the fatherland." But in case the policy of the Army should fail, Chiang Kai-shek or even Wang Ching-wei may change sides. There will be a more difficult situation. It is now the turning point to turn the nation's eyes to the importance of the ocean from that of the Continent. If we cannot do this, we have to face the decline and fall of the mother country at last. How critical it is now! Its main cause is the deficiency of the people's understanding of the ocean. At the moment when people are going to be wakened up, all is going to be pushed back. What does this mean?

NAVY, STEADY AND KEEP UP YOUR SPIRIT!

16 October 1941: The Cabinet resigned en bloc this afternoon.
    —Disagreement of policy.
    The United States demands that Japan evacuate all armed forces from China; unless Japan does this, adjustment of diplomatic negotiations between Japan and the United States will not improve. (However, the evacuation does not mean that the U.S. accepts Japan's advance toward the Southern areas.)
    What we aim at is to find improvement without evacuation.
    But the Army will not agree with this idea on the grounds that the unity of the Army cannot be preserved if this is put into practice.
    Konoye discussed with the Army with the view to withdraw the forces in China, as if to pay off by installments (to evacuate little by little surreptitiously), but this did not come to terms.
    There are elements in the Army itself that insist on our evacuation or a peaceful solution. Those who insist upon withdrawal say that if everything will be settled wholly by Japan's evacuation, this will be the best policy. But no compromise could have been reached.
    At last Konoye has to determine by himself either peace or war. Konoye consulted with Kido, but nothing was resolved. Then the resignation. This is the hope of all.
    It was decided that the Navy Minister would be Admiral Toyoda.

17 October 1941: According to the man in the street, the Premier will be either General Ugaki, Konoye or [Koki] Hirota, but they have strong and weak points, though they all are not militarily biased.*
    Among those who are on the side of the Army, the candidates were Tojo, Terauchi, and Hata. Some say that to each of them a telegram has been dispatched already.
    Among those on the side of the Navy are Oikawa and Yamamoto, but the Navy will not send either of them to the Cabinet.

---

* The Japanese for this is *gummbu shoku nashi*, which means *Gummbu*—military faction or league; *shoku*—tincture; *Nashi*—no, not, without. At that time the word *gummbu* was one with full antipathy of the public, especially the intellectuals and those who were peace-loving people always accusing the Army by calling the Army by that name. The word was one of the most popular at that time —Trans.

Number of Personnel to Be Levied in 1943

	1 Jan.	1 April	1 May	30 June	1 Sept.
Conscripted	45,678	1,500	—	31,022	—
Enlisted			15,600		15,600

$\frac{1}{1}$ $\frac{1}{2}$ $\frac{1}{3}$ $\frac{1}{4}$ $\frac{1}{5}$ $\frac{1}{6}$ $\frac{1}{7}$ $\frac{1}{8}$ $\frac{1}{9}$ $\frac{1}{10}$ $\frac{1}{11}$ $\frac{1}{12}$

45,678 $\uparrow$ 47,000

$\quad\quad$ | 1,500 $\quad\quad\quad\quad$ $\uparrow$ 31,000 $\uparrow$

$\quad\quad$ $\downarrow$ 15,600 EM $\quad\quad\quad$ | $\quad\quad$ | 16,000

45,000–48,000 . . . 8 months $\quad\quad\quad\quad\quad\quad\quad\quad\quad\quad$ 15,000
17,000–15,000 . . . 4months
$\quad\quad\quad\quad\quad$ 17,000 $\quad\quad$ 48,000 $\quad\quad$ 46,000

$$\frac{45 \times 8^2 + 15 \times 4}{3} = \frac{90 + 15}{3} = \frac{105}{3} = \boxed{35}$$

_____ 35,000 × ½ = 17,000–18,000 _____

$\frac{1}{1}$ $\frac{1}{2}$ $\frac{1}{3}$ $\frac{1}{4}$ $\frac{1}{5}$ $\frac{1}{6}$ $\quad$ $\frac{1}{6}$ $\quad$ $\frac{1}{7}$ $\quad$ $\frac{1}{8}$ $\frac{1}{9}$ $\frac{1}{10}$ $\frac{1}{11}$ $\frac{1}{12}$
(Conscripted 20,000)
_____ $\quad\quad$ 20,000 _____
$\quad\quad$ 2,000
_____ $\quad\quad$ 20,000 _____
$\quad\quad\quad$ 15,000 _____ $\quad\quad\quad$ 15,000 _____

Maximum 40,00–38,000
Minimum 35,000–34,00

The graduates will be:

According to the modified draft   15,000–19,000
According to the original draft   45,000–34,000

EM   265,000—Deficiency-supplying ratio about 40%

1. STANDARD OF THE NUMBER OF THE ENLISTED MEN
   90,000

2. Number of levied personnel   48,000 $\quad$ ⎫
   Those who rejoined their corps   41,000 $\quad$ ⎬ at present
   $\quad\quad\quad\quad\quad\quad\quad\quad\quad\quad\quad\quad\quad\quad\quad$ ⎭

3. AT PRESENT

{Special Marine, Air defense	30,000	
{Others		
25,000 + 15,000 = 40,000		
Marshalls and Carolines	8,000⎫	
China	20,000	
		36,000
Homeland	⎧5,000	
	⎩3,000⎭	

THE 6TH PLAN	{Petty officer	147,000	
	Sailor	289,000	(23,000—air)
	Standard	To be levied	65,000
		Supplementary	78,000
	Special ship	50,000	

THE 5TH PLAN	{Petty officer	112,000	
	Sailor	228,000	
	Standard, to be levied		50,000

19 October 1941: His Majesty approved the transfer of Admiral [Vice Adm. Noboru] Hirata to the Yokosuka Naval Station, and he asked about the relation of Admiral Ozawa with the Army.

21 October 1941

INTERNAL CONDITIONS OF THE HOMELAND (REPORTED BY ITO) The Navy is now left behind and the general situation is that the tables were turned to our disadvantage. The Navy has to stand firm.

MEETING OF THE CHIEFS OF THE BUREAUS AND DEPARTMENTS: Political Affairs—about the National policy that was decided on 3 September. Now the diplomatic relations with the United States are not turning favorably to us or showing any sign of hope. On the other hand, there is an operational disadvantage. Here opinions disagree.

Army 2,100,000⎫
Navy 1,800,000⎭ 3,900,000—hypothesis is to employ them sometime

during November. Preparation has begun concerning the employment of "Second to Finish."

22 October 1941: The United States destroyer *Kearny* was attacked by a German submarine near Iceland. The United States issued an order to arm merchant marine ships. Hereupon the United States and Germany have entered into war without a regular declaration of war between the two countries. But again on the 22nd two American ships (merchant marine) were sunk by attack on the Atlantic Ocean. With these the said two countries became belligerent states.

24 October 1941: The United States has announced that the States has now 4 naval bases under construction in England.

Again it is reported that another American merchant marine ship was sunk on the Atlantic by attack.

The United States made it clear that to transport materials for aiding the USSR through Vladivostok would be stopped. (I wonder if it could be done through Archangel?)

Moscow, Kharkov and Rostov are facing a real crisis.

26 October 1941. The United States Navy Department made a showdown that the transportation route of sending material for the aid of the Soviet was changed to Boston-Archangel course.

Of course, this is the policy of giving offense to Japan as well as to deter Japan's good start together with the freezing of funds in the U.S. Notwithstanding, this will cause a tendency among the Japanese, giving them a sort of optimistic prospect of improving diplomatic relations between the U.S. and Japan, consequently it is feared Japanese resolution may be weakened by such an opinion.

The United States prefers to choose a chronic way of entering into war; the bill of arming merchant marine ships passed the Lower House, and the bill permitting passage into the blockaded area.

In England, on the other hand, there are two elements disputing each other; one is that the British forces should land on the Continent, and the other is to send needed materials to the Soviet Union, for the British Empire is not so strong as to be able to land on the Continent. Anyway, England is still agonizing how to help the USSR in this Russian crisis. Russia has promoted to use the forces in the Asiatic Far East. The crisis is so pressing.

31 October 1941: An American destroyer was sunk off Iceland.

2 November 1941: The U.S. is not yet so excited. The bill allowing U.S. armed merchant marine ships to enter the blockaded areas of England should have been passed, yet the time is not ripe for that, because the armament is not sufficient.

Since the change of the Japanese Cabinet, the Government has been considering the National policy and it was recently decided that the Government will take positive steps in this situation.

It came to this—that some change of political idea is absolutely necessary from the standpoint of armament plans.

3–4 November 1941: Commanders in Chief of the Combined Fleet and Naval Stations were summoned.

Ambassador Kurusu left Japan for the United States by plane via Hong Kong and the Philippines.

7 November 1941

MEETING OF THE CHIEFS OF EACH BUREAU AND DEPARTMENT

Report of the location of ships⎫
                                ⎬ will be stopped.
Report of weather   ⎭

20/11 —9a
20/11 —Special Marine

FINANCIAL BUREAU: SUPPLEMENTARY BUDGET DEMAND

Economizing—100,000,000 yen
Responsibility Payment—28,000,000 yen

A CORRUPTION SCANDAL AT KURE

Inside the Navy	104
Outside the Navy	260
250,000 yen	

 For the use of spies of the Communist International Okada, Lt. 1st grade, Navy (non)

2 Nov.—March of the Veterans in the street—Hamamatsucho Unit—Speech—criticism of the general situation—he was about to make a speech.

OVERSIGHT OF THE CORRUPTION SCANDAL
Cooperation of important members in the Navy based upon

priority-principle
strict keeping of secrets

 Operational directives were sent to the Combined Fleet, CSF, Naval Stations and Naval Ports.

8 November 1941: Dispatch of Ambassador Kurusu will not mean any break or development of the situation.
 Modified American Neutrality Act of the Sailing of the U.S. Armed Merchant Marine Ships through Belligerent Areas—the bill passed the Upper House of the United States.
 American forces in China will be repatriated, it was announced.

10 November 1941: Against the sailing of American armed merchant marine ships through belligerent areas on the sea, Hitler announced that Germany issued [orders] to attack any of them found in those areas for the sake of Germany's self-defense.
 It is reported that some part of the German Forces are being sent back to Germany from the Soviet Union, for such damage has been inflicted upon Russia to the extent of Russia's not being able to stand up again for the time being.
 Which course will the new operation take?
 Another rumor runs that a new order to attack Moscow was issued.

11 November 1941: Meeting concerning the reconstruction of armament.
 According to this, building of big ships will be stopped and in its stead concentration will be put upon building aircraft and submarines.
 Concerning the aircraft, the 5th Plan will be put into effect immediately.
 Concerning the submarines, a total of 107 vessels (including 32 vessels as an addition) will be built by March 1944; during the three years between March 1944 and March 1946 another 160 vessels will be built.

	FLAG SUB.	CRUISER SUB.	TRANS- PORT	MIDDLE SIZE	SMALL SIZE	SUPPLY	TOTAL
Now Dec. 1941	4	18	25	17	0	0	64
Rapid building	3	37	10	36	18	3	107
The 4th Plan	1	13	10				24
In 1940				9	9		18
1.		12		12	9		33
2.	2	12		15		3	32
	7	55	35	53	18	3	171
1944–1946							160
							331

FROM 1944 UNTIL 1947 (MARCH)

Sub A	6	}	
Sub B	41	} 90	
Sub C	42	}	
Transport	14		
Middle size	12	—160	62
Small "	36		
Supply	6		
Special, big	3		

13 November 1941: Interview of Ambassador (Kurusu) has been postponed day by day.*

Thailand could not keep her neutrality and people are crying for their firm stand.

14 November 1941

MEETING OF THE CHIEFS OF EACH BUREAU AND DEPARTMENT:

Accident of the *Kehi Maru*

The military expense of Thailand

The airliner between Timor and—

England and the United States may take steps to prevent it, but we want to put it into practice.

Things are not going well between Amoy and Formosa.

Two times a day between Japan and Formosa, so the Navy will act separately.

Strict keeping of Navy secret—to contrive so as not to leak it before the investigation for the sake of full armament, especially to those who are not related to the affairs.

---

* Actually Kurusu did not reach Washington until 15 November—Eds.

Modification of Air Act.

Concerning the short-wave-searcher—men who handle it—60 K.

About the official papers.

17 November 1941: The president of the U.S. signed [the bill] to arm U.S. merchant marine ships and the plan of escorting British ships. It was decided that the United States will rent bases on the Atlantic to England.

18 November 1941: The First Period Plan will be drafted by 10 December 1941. The Second Period plan will be drafted by the coming March.

The 110 ship will be so constructed that it will be able to be used with middle deck finished by October 1943.

The 237 ship—it is not advantageous to convert it into a merchant marine ship; it should be converted into bengine ship.*

From the beginning of December 1941 until 10 January 1942—11,000 persons.

21 November 1941

MEETING OF THE CHIEFS OF EACH BUREAU AND DEPARTMENT: ARMY— 1,500 MILLION; NAVY—1,000 MILLION. New mines were discovered, joint investigation will be made, at Tsugaru Channel and on the southern part of Korea.

U.S. Marines will be withdrawn; occupation of common settlement.

England reinforced India with her naval power:

Battleships 1–2, cruisers—same.

The *Hikawa Maru*

Naruto $\begin{cases} 23\ \text{Nov.—left port} \\ 29\ \text{Nov.} \end{cases}$

The bill should be proposed as early as possible.

Year-end bonus

4 months — $\begin{cases} 2\ \text{months} & \text{— pw 2.3} \\ 1\ \text{months} \\ 1\ \text{month} \end{cases}$

Ratio to be paid in bond will be high.

Commendation of technicians.

Reported by Kondo:

Radio rocketer is very efficient.

Loss until September this year amounts to 7 million tons.

$$
\begin{array}{r}
18,000,000 \\
7,250,000 \\
3,800,000 \\
\underline{1,500,000} \\
30,550,000
\end{array}
$$

$30,550,000 - 7,000,000 = 23,000,000$ tons

---

* Bengine ship: Nakahara's meaning is not clear—Eds.

Foreign trade exclusively   10,000,000 tons

It is critical when it is below 7,000,000 tons.

Shipbuilding	England	1.5 million⎫	
	The U.S.	1.5 million⎭	3 (increase in a year)

22 November 1941

MAINLY ARMY'S RESPONSIBILITY	NAVAL BASE FORCE UNIT
Hong Kong	Hong Kong
Philippines	Manila, Davao
British Malaya	Singapore, Penang
Sumatra	Sumatra
Java	
British Borneo	
Burma	

MAINLY NAVY'S RESPONSIBILITY

Dutch Borneo
Celebes
Molucca Islands
Small Sunda Islands
New Guinea
Bismarck Islands
Guam

HIGH SHIP CAPTURING OFFICE—IN THE PRIVY COUNCIL

Commander in Chief—Privy Councillor
Councillor, procurator, administrative officer, secretary, clerk
Procurator—Admiral 2 persons
    Naval judiciary might be a councillor (Chief of the Naval Judicial Bureau)

YOKOHAMA SHIP CAPTURING OFFICE

Commander in Chief—Prefecture Governor ranking admiral
    Councillor—Navy officer 2 persons either Captain or Comdr.
    Two persons out of Judicial officer or secretary
    Procurator—1 person out of Judicial officer

SASEBO SHIP CAPTURING OFFICE

Same as above

INVESTIGATION DONE ON 1 NOVEMBER

Active Service	209,403
Cadet	161
Permanent service converted from temporary	41,313 ⎫
Convoked	52,624 ⎭ 93,937
(?) TOTAL	303,501

Items

Naval practice student	22,575
New conscript	6,911
	6,062
Student	124
Others	1,062
Newly promoted	1,262
TOTAL	38,546

Those cannot be supplemented

1944	1943	1944	1945
1 April A 2/5	B 2/5	C 2/5	D 1/5, E 1/5
1 Aug A 2/5	B 1/5, C 1/5	D 215	E 1/5, E 1/5
1 Feb A 1/5, B 1/5	B 1/5, C 1/5	C 1/5, C 1/5	D 1/5, E 1/5

1942		1943	1944	1945	1946	1947
1 June	A 3/5	B 2/5, C 1/5, C 1/5	D 3/5	E 2/5	H 2/5	G 2/5
1 Dec	A 2/5, B 2/5	B 1/5, C 2/5	C 1/5, H 2/5	D 1/5, E 2/5	E 1/5, H 2/5	H 1/5, G 2/5

23 November 1941: Rostov was captured by German troops.

25 November 1941

ARMAMENT CONFERENCE

The *Yamato* two months

11   May 1941

Transportation Order 12%

Armament Examination Conference—about 20 December

27 November 1941: German troops have neared 30 kilometers from Moscow.
A German submarine sank the British cruiser *Condl.*
The President of the United States went on a trip for his recreation when an important conference of the regular month-end one [was scheduled?].

28 November 1941: German troops have approached within 26 kilometers from Moscow.

A British destroyer, one vessel, was sunk by a German submarine.

The United States returned an answer, on record, denouncing the Japanese demands.

29 November 1941: Troops have approached within 20 kilometers from Moscow, and Tula (or Tura) was surrounded by them.

The American answer is very forcing.

1 April 1942	Adm. Koga to be promoted
" " "	Senior Rear Adm. will be promoted
	Half of Admirals (Rear) who served four years or more than that will be promoted.
	Half of Captains who served 6 years or more than that will be promoted.
	Part of Commanders will be promoted.
1 March 1942	Petty officers will be appointed.
1 April 1942	Other special officers will be promoted or appointed.
1 July	Petty officers will be appointed.
1 Nov	"
	Officers, Special Officers to be promoted. Rear Admirals who
" "	served three years or more than that will be promoted; part of Captains who served more than five years will be promoted.

1 December 1941

MEETING OF THE CHIEFS OF BUREAUS AND DEPARTMENTS: The point of the American answer.

1. Respect for the Nine-Power Treaty in Asia.

2. Evacuation of Japanese armed forces from China and French Indo-China (includes Manchuria).

3. Open Door principle of the Chinese Continent, equality of trade and commerce.

4. Trade and commerce under barter system.

5. Parting from the Axis Party.
   Etc.

Eight articles in all; but, in short, it is not unthinkable to dispose of the China Incident and to establish the Greater Far Asiatic Co-Prosperity Sphere, and that the United States does not recognize the independence of Japan; now it is high time for Japan to decide with resolution.

The Imperial Council—decision.

Professedly, we go with two principles.

4 December 1941: Commander in Chief Admiral Yamamoto sailed out for expedition.

Draft for the New Naval Organization in 1947

Combined Fleet	2 Sqd, Bx2, destx6	3 Sqd, Bx2
1F	2 Sqd, Bx4, Destx6	3 Sqd, Bx2
	4 Sqd, Bx2	11 Sqd, Cx2 (*Kaga*)
P + 2	12 Sqd, C$_2$x 2	1 Sqd, LCx1, DesDivx4
	3 DesSqd, LCx1 DesDivx4	5 Air Sqd, Carrier (*Hosho*) x 2, destx2
2F	5 Sqd, BCx4, Destx4	6 Sqd, C (A class)x2
	7 Sqd, Cx2 (*Tone*, or B)	8 Sqd, C (*Takao*)x4
P + 2	9 Sqd, Cx4 (*Mogami* class)	10 Sqd, Cx3
	2 DesSqd, LCx1, DesDivx4	4 DesSqd, LCx1, DesDivx4
	Taigei	
3F	13 Sqd, C (*Myoko* or *Yubari*)x2	16 Sqd, *Kawanami* Classx2
	5 DesSqd, LCx1, DesDivx4	10 SubSqd, Subx12
P + 1	11 Air Sqd, Seaplane tenderx3	16 Air Sqd, Special Air Forcex5
	1B, 2B	
4F	17 Sqd, Cx2 (*Aoba*)	18 Sqd, *Itsukushima, Yaeyama,* Minelayersx2
	19 Sqd, Special Cx4	6 DesSq, LCx1, DesDivx4
	8 Sqd, *Isuzu,* Subx9	12 SubSqd, subx12
P + 3	12 Air Sqd, Seaplane Tenderx3	
	3B, 4B, 5B, 6B	
5F	21 Sqd, Cx2, Coast Defender x 2	22 Sqd, Special Cruiser x 1
	23 Sqd, Special Cx1, Seaplane tender x1	24 Sqd, Special Cx2, Seaplane Tenderx1
P + 3	13 Subsqd, *Chogei,* subx9	7 Base Force
6F	C (c class)x1	
	1 SubSqd, *Katori,* subx13	2 SubSqd, subtenderx1, subx13
P + 1	3 SubSqd, *Katori,* subx13	4 SubSqd, subtenderx1, subx13
7F	C (c class) x 1	
	5 SubSqd, subx9	
1AF	1 Air Sqd, *Zuikaku, Shokaku, Taiho,* destroyer x4	
P + 2	2 Air Sqd, *Soryu, Hiryu,* carrier for fighterx1, destroyer x 4	
	3 Air Sqd, *Kaga* class x 2, destroyer x 4	
	4 Air Sqd, aircraft carrier x 3, destroyer x 4	
	6 Air Sqd, __ , __ , __ , destroyer x 4	

	7 Air Sqd, Special Carrier x 3, destroyer x 3
11 AF	21 Air Sqd, __ , __ , __ , Special carrier x 1, 22 Air Sqd, __, __, __, __, Special x 2
	23 Air Sqd, __, __, __, __, Special x 2, 24 Air Sqd __, __, __, Special x 1
12 AF	31 Air Sqd, Yokohama, Shimizu, P, P + 5 Hamanako, Special x 2
	32 Air Sqd, __ , Nanao, Shinji, Special x 2
	33 Air Sqd, Inland Sea, __ , __ , Special x 2
	34 Air Sqd, Western Kyushu, __ , __ .
13 AF	25 Air Sqd, Tainan, Takao, __ , __ , Special x 2
	26 Air Sqd, Chintao, Shanghai, Special x 1
	27 Air Sqd, __ , Special x 2 P, P + 4
14 AF	28 Air Sqd, Palau, Truk, Tinian, Special x 2
	35 Air Sqd, Palau, Saipan, P, P + 4 Special x 1
	36 Air Sqd, To, Po, Special x 1
Attached to the Combined Fleet	9 SubSqd, sub x 9 11 SubSqd, Sub x 9
	25 Sqd, __ , __ , __ .
	26 Sqd, Special Cx4
	8 Air Sqd, Carrier x 2
1 G cg	Combined Communication Corps

Base Force

3F ⎰1 Base Force
   ⎱2 Base Force

                                       ⎧3 Base Force
                              4F ⎪4   ″   ″
                                           ⎨5   ″   ″
                                           ⎩6   ″   ″

Southern Dispatched
  17 Air Sqd., Special x 3
  8 Base Force (11)   5F—7 Base Force
  9   ″   ″

China Area Fleet
  1 China Fleet
  2 China Fleet
  3 China Fleet
  Hainan Guard

Naval Station	Naval Port
Kure	Ominato
Yokosuka	Osaka
Sasebo	Chinkai
Maizuru	Port Arthur
Takao P	
P 5 P 28	Admiral Sub-137

Now I have no concrete plan how the organization in 1946 should be concerning the guard outside the Marshall and Caroline Islands; but I think we will have to allot more strength for the guard of the said areas. And as for the others:

NAVAL PORT

P Southern Pacific, Marshalls, Borneo, Singapore, Celebes, Morotai, Solomons—7 in all

$$P5 + P5 + P28 + P^0 1 + \frac{21}{PI} + \frac{11}{P} + 1 + \frac{\text{Naval Port}}{P6} + P6 + 6\text{—}53$$

Rear Admiral   10 x 4   Ten will come out after promotion
Vice Admiral   7 x 2

OFFICE FOR ENGINEERING & CONSTRUCTION   *Admiral*

Formosa, Philippines, Borneo, Singapore

Total—9   Engineer 3 x 3   promoted Rear Adm. 3 will come out, 15 others will be levied

To ally 70 persons (Executive Department) have to be increased.

```
⎧ Newly established              1
⎪ Special Accountant Department  3
⎨   "    Munitions Department    2
⎪   "    Naval Hospital          3
⎩   "    Engineering Department   2 + 1
```

TO BE ABOLISHED:

Port Arthur Naval Guard	15 Jan 42
" " " Engineering Department	
" " " Hospital	
Hankao, General Affairs	20 Dec 41
" Base Force Unit, Guard	15 Jan 42
Chintao " " " "	15 Jan 42
Amoi (Rear Adm.) Force Unit, Guard	15 Jan 42

THE UNITED STATES

	OFFICER	RANKING OFFICER	WARRANT OFFICER	EM
Actual service	7,487	2,275	2,052	224,511
Retired officer	1,149	261	1,020	(?) 2,962
Total				321,778
Marine				61,685
Actual service		49,766		
Retired officer		11,919		
Higher than warrant officer		3,700		

	1 Jan 39	1 Jan 40	1 Jan 42	1 Jan 43	1 Jan 44	1 Jan 45
Nagano	58–6	59–6	60–6	61–6	62–6	63–6
Yonai	58–10	59–10	60–10	61–10	62–10	63–10

	1 Jan 46	
Nagano	64–6	At the end of June 1946
Yonai	64–10	At the end of Feb 1946

To return Yonai to active duty it is necessary to propose it to the Premier first and then the Premier will ask the Emperor.

His Majesty's sanction

Navy Minister,

   Secret representation to the throne

   His Majesty's sanction

Since our country is facing a real crisis, it can be carried out; it will be justified. And the circumstances under which Admiral Yonai had been placed on the reservist list was of a special category, so this treatment is also all right from that standpoint.

Reasons that Yonai is needing this consideration:

1. Admiral Nagano's health is feared for.

2. The only one who may succeed to Nagano's post will be Admiral Yoshida, whose health will not bear his responsibility from the standpoint of his physical temperament.

3. In case Nagano should stand at a pinch, Yonai, if he remain as he is now, can do nothing, for two reasons:

   a. This sort of official treatment cannot be done so quickly.

   b. He will not be accustomed to current military affairs.

4. So that it is necessary to make him State Councillor beforehand.

Except Yoshida, the only one is Admiral Yamamoto. Yamamoto is now at the Combined Fleet, and he cannot leave the post until at least next May or June.

Koga can succeed Yamamoto at the Combined Fleet.

Admiral Toyoda is most fitted for Commander in Chief of the South Detached Fleet. If Toyoda may leave the post, Admiral Sumiyama will succeed him.

After Koga, the successor will be Admiral Shiosawa or Admiral Hirata. Anyhow, we have to ask them and have answers.

As for the idea of placing Admiral Yonai on the active service list:

1. Admiral Yamamoto and Prince* were OK.

2. But the Army insisted that the Minister should be the one on active duty and to call one back to active duty for that purpose from the reservist list was denounced.

3. So the idea was given up.

---

* Takamatsu?—Trans.

Does this mean that he is against the Tripartite Axis policy? On this point, Admiral Yamamoto too is an opponent of the policy, but he is already on active duty. Then no one can absolutely interfere with this.

12 December 1941: On 10 December 1941 our 6th Submarine Division, after attacking the enemy on Wake Island, received heavy damage from enemy airplanes: one destroyer, *Kisaragi*, was sunk by bombing and some minor damage was given to the Division by machine-gun fire. So the Division retired to Queseline Island.

On the 11th, another air attack was made on the enemy which had lost half of her fighting strength on the previous day. Our 15 planes engaged in air fighting with the result of shooting down 3 enemy planes and losing two of our planes and receiving some damage to another seven.

WAR LESSONS: The abovementioned result tells us that well-protected islands are strong, as our war result shows. As the island is so small, our forces are supposed to land on it during this week. But it is very difficult to wholly destroy such an island though we can easily bombard or bomb those enemy gun dispositions. If such an island is guarded by any submarines, we shall be all the more in a disadvantageous position in carrying out our operation against the island, and at the same time, the occupation of such an island will not be easy if the circumstances were thus that supporting enemy forces are coming there. Accordingly, we have to waste an unexpected amount of our strength in occupying Wake Island.

On the other hand, this reasoning shows the reasonableness of the following operational view: if we put each of the Marshall and the Caroline Islands in such a position that each island can help and support mutually with considerable strength on it, our defense power will be very strong; that is, the dispersion of armed islands have a great fighting power.

If a corner of such dispositioned areas should be taken by the enemy or were to be taken, all the air strength should be concentrated to that point with the intention of enlarging our war results.

14 December 1941: On the strength of our success at Pearl Harbor we should occupy Hawaii now, some people say. It goes without saying that it is the best policy to take Hawaii to decide the future of the Pacific. If we lose a day in occupying the Islands, our operation to capture them will be so much the more difficult. Our experience at Wake Island shows this.

However, if we fail in this, the tables will be turned favorable to the United States again in a minute. So it cannot be done so hastily.

1. The U.S. has yet fairly strong sea power in her hand. And air fighters will be reinforced day after day. Consider how strong they were in defending Wake Island with their fighters!

2. England has yet a predominant sea power. We know how it will be when we are attacked in our rear. Our Malay operation will end in a fiasco, if this should happen.

3. It must be borne in mind that Russia might attack us in our rear.

4. It will be disadvantageous for us to keep and maintain the Hawaiian Islands in our hands after capturing them.

So that it can be thought of and should be well considered to have them, if we have to take into consideration the relations with the United States only. But this is a dangerous idea. We must not take an inch if given an inch.

It is necessary to put the idea into practice after our operational line that runs through Burma, Sumatra, Java, New Guinea and the Solomons is secured for us.

It demands at least three months to acquire this line. Then Hawaii will have been reinforced so that our operation will not go as we want it to.

After all, we have to destroy more of the enemy's sea power and await the chance of our absolute success.

For the time being, the United States will not try her active transocean operation:*

And the U.S. will try to evade war with the USSR, dividing the former's naval power into 60% in the east and 40% in the west (of course the situation will make her concentrate her whole power in one part).

THEN THE CONCLUSIONS WILL BE AS FOLLOWS: The Japanese Navy should decoy out the British fleet and merchant marine ships by attacking them in the Indian Ocean (for India is her treasure-house; so if it is charged by us, England will make desperate efforts in defending her).

And we should try to shake hands with Germany through the Suez Canal.

And on the other hand, we should try to baffle the U.S. intention of making cross-ocean operations by pushing forth our operation in New Guinea and the eastern part of the Pacific Ocean; at the same time we should decoy out the U.S. fleets and destroy them by our submarines and planes of the Combined Fleet.

During this period we should have to send many submarines in order to intercept U.S. supply there as well as to cut off U.S. reinforcements of naval strength there. Thus the rehabilitation of Hawaii will be hindered. (To make use of Japanese.)

18 December 1941: Merits of shallow sinking of aerial torpedoes.

Planes from our subs are reconnoitering around Hawaii.

3 January 1942: Our submarines bombarded Hilo (Hawaiian Islands) and Maui and Kauai Islands. Woodpecker strategy!† Will not this strategy decoy out the enemy?

Our subs chased a U.S. carrier (1) and a cruiser (1) that were coming out of the harbor, but, to our regret, they missed them.

The U.S. has to atone for the failure at Pearl Harbor, and at the same time, the morale in the U.S. Navy had to be maintained and heightened. They have to do both. By what means? Will they attack Wake, the Marshalls, Hokkaido, or Tokyo? They will not come out as far as Tokyo.

---

* *Toyo sakusen* = *to*, across, trans; *yo*, ocean; *sakusen*, operation—Trans.
† *Kitsutsuki sempo* = *kitsutsuki*, woodpecker; *sempo*, strategy, tactics—Trans.

CHAPTER 6

Extracts from Diary and Duty Book of Capt. Shigeshi Uchida

P RANGE HELD three important interviews in 1951 with Uchida. To the second of these interviews, on 27 April 1951, Uchida brought with him extracts from his diary and duty book for 1941. These extracts were translated by Comdr. Masataka Chihaya, Prange's friend and colleague, who was present at the Uchida interviews as translator. At this interview, Uchida amplified his diary and papers. It is not clear whether he did so orally or whether he submitted further written notes. So that the reader may have full information, we have included this additional material in parentheses.

In 1941, Uchida, then a commander, was a member of the Operations Section, First Bureau, Naval General Staff. This section was responsible for naval planning, and an assignment thereto testified to an officer's quality and potential. A table dated 10 April 1941 that Uchida submitted reveals that during this early period he was responsible for "operations against U.S. and Dutch, matters concerning operational data and maps, and administrative matters." By 22 November 1941 his duties were "Philippines operations and Dutch operations. Communication raiding operations and operations against Soviet Russia."

DIARY EXTRACTS

11 January 1941. Drafted up the detail plan of the "H" Operation (i.e., Dutch Operation).

6 and 7 February 1941. Had a conference with staffs of the Operation Section of the Army General Staff on the Southern Operations.

24 February 1941. At 0550 left Yokohama for Saipan on board a flying boat of the Nippon Air Lines. Arrived in Saipan at 1630 and contacted the 5th Base Force.

25 February 1941. Left Saipan at 0755 and arrived in Palau at 1430. Made contact with the 3rd Base Force.

28 February 1941. At 0640 left Palau and arrived in Deli at 1520.

3 March 1941. Left Deli at 0630 arriving Palau at 1523.

5 March 1941. Arrived Saipan at 1456.

7 March 1941. Returned back Yokohama at 1530.

9 April 1941. Left Tokyo for Sasebo.

10 April 1941. Arrived Sasebo. Inspected vessels of the 1st Base Force. Had a conference with Staffs of the Sasebo Naval Station.

14 April 1941. Rear Admiral Fukudome reported to become the Chief of the Bureau.

3 July 1941. Left Tokyo by plane to inform the Second China Expeditionary Fleet of the outline of occupying French Indo-China. Arrived in Taihoku.

4 July 1941. In the morning reached the *Ashigara,* the flagship, and briefed the C-in-C and others on the central Army and Navy agreement and the operational outline to be followed.

7 July 1941. Entered Canton aboard *Ashigara.*

8 July 1941. The central Army and Navy agreement was concluded.

9 July 1941. Left Canton by plane arriving Taihoku in the evening.

19 July 1941. Returned back Tokyo.

28 July 1941. Advance forces landed Natran without events.

29 July 1941. The main force reached Cape St. Jacques. With the occupation of southern French Indo-China, tense arguments began to be heard.

28 and 29 July 1941. Our Army advanced in southern part of Indo-China. The U.S. freezing of Japanese assets caused the Japanese to give up the idea of going north and put all energies into the rich southern regions. In view of the above circumstances the outbreak of the war should be 15 October, i.e., the Japanese would expect the commencement day of war to be 15 October.

14 August 1941. Participated in the table-top maneuver of the Army General Staff pertaining to the Southern Operations.

15 August 1941. Same as the 14th.

23 August 1941. Army's table-top maneuver of the Southern Operations was held in the Army General Staff. Attended it representing the Navy and explained the Navy operations to Tojo, War Minister; Muto, Chief of the Military Affairs Bureau; and others.

29 August 1941. In the afternoon an operational conference was held at the *Suikosha* between both operational sections of the Army and Navy General Staffs. The Army's war preparations were chiefly discussed.

6 September 1941. A lunch party was given in the name of the Chief of the Naval General Staff to those staffs of the NGS [Naval General Staff] who attended the table-top maneuvers, and also to members of the Army's Operational Section. It was held in the *Suikosha.*

1 October 1941. A table-top maneuver of the Army General Staff was held at the Army War College and I attended it. In this maneuver also participated those who were slated to become staff officers of each army of the Southern Army.

6 October 1941. Members of the Army Section came to confer with us on a draft of the central agreement which had been concluded in the table-top maneuvers of the Army War College.

7 October 1941. The outline draft of the Army and Navy central agreement was completed.

15 October 1941. The Chief of Staff of the First Air Fleet came to the NGS and requested again that all ships of that fleet be used in the P.H. [Pearl Harbor] operation.

17 October 1941. The Third Konoye Cabinet resigned and General Tojo was asked to form a new cabinet.

18 October 1941. Drafted a Naval General Staff order and directive.

28 October 1941. From yesterday a liaison conference has been held between the Cabinet and the High Command, but a decision has not yet been made to the national policy.

29 October 1941. The Chief of the 1st Section and Comdr. [Yugi] Yamamoto went down to the Combined Fleet headquarters and informally informed them [of] the operational principle, order, directive and the central Army and Navy agreement.

1 November 1941. The Liaison Conference between the Cabinet and the High Command reached a conclusion to go to war with the U.S. by 0100 on the 2nd.

10 November 1941. At the Army General Staff, had a conference for table-top maneuvers in the presence of the Emperor and also had a preliminary exercise for it.

14 November 1941. From 0900 had a preliminary exercise of the table-top maneuvers in the presence of the Emperor in the Imperial Palace with all participants including the Chief of the Army and Navy General Staffs.

15 November 1941. From 1300 the table-top maneuvers of the Southern Operations was held in the Imperial Palace in the presence of the Emperor. It ended at 1600.

The Emperor asked the Chief of the Naval General Staff what steps were to be taken in case of our convoys en route being attacked by the main force of the British Fleet, and also the Chief of the Army General Staff what steps were to be taken to a Chinese offensive toward French Indo-China and to a landing of the British forces on our occupied areas.

24 November 1941. Prince Takamatsu* became a member of the Operations Section.

25 November 1941. From today all operational forces are to leave for the designated stand-by points. We, too, are kept on the strain.

26 November 1941. From today half of the Operations Section are to stay in the *Suikosha* to stand by. Miwa, a staff officer of the Combined Fleet, came up to confer

---

* Comdr. HIH Prince Nobuhito Takamatsu was a younger brother of Emperor Hirohito—Eds.

with us. He came to tell us that the Combined Fleet saw no need of changing a plan of the battleship group which the NGS thought should be reconsidered in view of keeping alert against the British Fleet.

27 November 1941. Our staying in the *Suikosha* was suspended lest it cause too much attention to us and reveal our real intention.

30 November 1941. Received a report that two U.S. minesweepers headed north ten miles east of Boko Islands.

1 December 1941. In the afternoon the Imperial Conference was held in which a decision was made to go to war. After the conference ended, the Emperor asked both heads of the Army and Navy General Staffs to stay and told them that, since this war bears the most important thing, the Army and Navy should do their best in cooperating closely. The Army Chief of Staff, representing both services, swore that the Emperor's will would be complied with to the utmost.

In the afternoon today a report came in that three big U.S. planes went southeast of the southernmost cape of Formosa.

5 December 1941. A Japanese patrol plane sighted five enemy submarines near Palau Island.

8 December 1941. At 0325 came in a flash of *Tora, Tora, Tora!* which meant "A surprise attack made." With this news all members became wild with joy. In the morning a toast was drunk for the success of P.H. operation.

9 December 1941. It seems that one more enemy battleship was sunk last night by our midget submarines.

15 December 1941. Left Tokyo accompanying the Chief of the Section for the Combined Fleet.

16 December 1941. In the morning arrived at *Nagato* and held a conference. When we were going to leave the ship, we were asked by the C-in-C to bring with us handwritings by those boys of the Special Attack Force to submit to His Majesty's inspection.

26 December 1941. In the morning the C-in-C of the First Air Fleet reported to the General Staff. Comdr. [Mitsuo] Fuchida and Lt. Comdr. [Shigekazu] Shimazaki were honored to be received in audience by the Emperor. A dinner party was given to them by the Chief of the General Staff at *Suikosha*. I also attended it.

31 December 1941. The senior staff officer and air staff officer of the First Air Fleet were invited to a luncheon party at *Kojimachi Saryo*.

DUTY BOOK EXTRACTS

As of 15 November 1940, appointed as a staff officer of the Naval General Staff and reported to the new assignment on the 25th. Principal assignments: operations against the U.S. and Dutch matters pertaining to operational data, maps and history. In view of the imminent world situation, I was asked to draft up a detailed plan as soon as possible. I was told at that time that I would be transferred to the Combined Fleet headquarters in the event of a war. Also I was told to make a thorough study into operational plans against the U.S. as much as possible.

December 1940. No big changes. Studied operational plans against the U.S. and Dutch, and began drafting its basic plans.

January 1941. A draft of a detailed operational plan against the U.S. completed.

July 1941. A detailed operational plan against the U.S. completed and I took an additional job of helping prepare operations against Soviet Russia which had been taken by Lt. Comdr. Kacho.

Early August 1941. It was decided that preparations be made so as to go to war on 15 November of this year.

7 August 1941. The senior staff officer and torpedo staff officer of the Combined Fleet came up to Tokyo to discuss with us the P.H. air strike, operations against the Philippines and Russia.

(8 August 1941. Since July, war conditions between Russia and Germany not so progressive. Russian resistance good. So Japan could not begin operations in Siberia against Russia in 1941. It could be foreseen that there would be no chance for such an operation.) [According to Uchida, the Army planned to hit Russia in case she bent under the German attack. But by August 1941, the Japanese began to doubt whether the Germans could do it. The idea in Japanese military circles, especially the Army was: If England should fall, there would be an advance to the south; if Russia should falter, there would be an advance in the north.]

15 August 1941. The Second Step of War Preparations was started. Early August the senior staff officer of the Combined Fleet and others came up to Tokyo to confer with us. On the 15th I discussed with the senior staff officer of the Second Fleet operations against the Philippines. On 14 and 15 of this month a war game for the Southern Operations was held in the Army General Staff. Yamamoto, Miyo, Kacho and I attended it.

19 August 1941. In the afternoon the air staff officers of the Combined Fleet [Sasaki] and the First Air Fleet [Genda], and the senior staff officer of the 11th Air Fleet [Capt. Chihaya Takahashi], gathered in the operational room to discuss general matters (i.e., the overall air operations). [This of course included the Southern Operations and Pearl Harbor.]

20 August 1941.
    a. General Situation. Again, there are doubts about the ability of the Germans to bring Russia to her knees.
    b. Nomura's work progressing hopefully.
    c. To complete the Southern Operations, the Army needs five (5) divisions. The Navy must expedite the commencement of the war.

23 August 1941. At the Army General Staff a war game was held aiming to explain operations to the War Minister, Chief of Military Affairs Bureau and other key

members of the War Ministry. Representing the Navy, I alone attended it and explained the naval operations. It commenced at 1300 and ended at 1830.

29 August 1941. In the afternoon a conference was held at the *Suikosha* between both operations sections of the Army and Navy General Staffs. Mostly the Army's preparations for the Southern Operations were discussed.

3 September 1941. A liaison conference between the Government and the High Command was held in which it was reported a decision was reached so as to exert preparations with a determination of not avoiding a war. A part of the Army's mobilization is expected to be started from the middle of this month.

3–5 September 1941. A war game for the Southern Operations was held (in the Operations Section of) the Naval General Staff (between a Blue and a Red team for review of the Southern Operations).

BLUE FORCE

NGS represented by Comdr. Kami.

Combined Fleet and others by Comdr. Yamamoto.

2nd and 3rd Fleets by Comdr. Uchida.

Southern Expeditional Fleet by Lt. Comdr. Kacho.

Air Forces by Miyo.

RED FORCE

British forces represented by Comdr. Matsunaga.

Dutch forces by Comdr. Tonaki.

U.S. forces by Comdr. Muchaku.

Air Forces by Comdr. Kanamoto.

8–10 September 1941. A war game of the communication raiding operations (to protect commerce) was held at the Naval Staff College by the NGS and the Navy Ministry combined.

20 September 1941. Since the 11th, the Combined Fleet's war games were held at the Naval Staff College until today, based upon the draft of the operational plan which was made by the NGS. Almost every morning and afternoon I attended. In the result-studying meeting, the ability to supply air strength, especially fighters, became the main issue. (Japan's industrial capacity to do the job was raised in this discussion. The oil-carrying ability of the destroyers was seriously considered. It was decided to carry oil drums.) [In the September war games, Uchida recommended that the attack come on a Sunday.]

4 October 1941. From the 1st until today a war game was held at the Army War College by the Army General Staff. Those who were slated to become staff officers of each Army of the Southern Army conducted the war game. (Commander Yamamoto and I) attended it (to represent the Navy's point of view). The main issue was a landing operation upon the east coast of Malaya.

10 October 1941.

　　a. A telegram came from Nomura that there is little hope to get concessions from the U.S.

　　b. Many grave doubts whether it would be possible to reach an agreement with the U.S. The Navy Minister by this time was becoming quite doubtful.

11–13 October 1941. A war game was held at the Combined Fleet headquarters (*aboard Nagato*). (Here again it was discussed that the First Air Fleet wanted to use their total air strength to carry out the P.H. attack.)

16 October 1941. The Konoye Cabinet resigned.

17 October 1941. General Tojo was ordered to form a new cabinet. As a result of the *Nagato* table maneuvers, Chief of Staff of the First Air Fleet went up to Tokyo and requested again that the whole strength of the First Air Fleet be used in the P.H. operation.

　　Combined Fleet headquarters also requested to change the date of the Malaya landing. The idea of making a landing on Malay on "X" day was not adequate, they asserted. As a result, the Naval General Staff made negotiations with the Army General Staff, but the latter did not consent.

21 October 1941. The NGS's orders and directives to be sent out prior to the outbreak of war were discussed and decided. They were all drafted by me. It is expected that we are going to go to war on 8 December.* The operational plan of this coming war was completed.

28 October 1941. The national policy has not been decided. The Emperor ordered a study of the present situation from the very beginning, cleaning the slate. (The shipping problem was thought to be the most serious question at the time.)

2 November 1941. It is said that the liaison conference between the Government and the High Command, after several days' discussions, by midnight of 1 November has reached the decision that Japan will go to war.

　　On 28 and 29 October, the chief of the section and Comdr. Yamamoto went down to the flagship of the Combined Fleet off Saeki Bay to inform them of the NGS's orders and directives and operational principles, central agreement between the Army and the Navy.

8 November 1941. Effective 5 November, NGS Orders Nos. 1, 2 and 3, and Directives Nos. 1, 2 and 3 were issued. Also effective 6 November an order to start the Second Step for war preparations was issued. From 8 to 10 November the central agreement between the Army and Navy was made at the Army War College.

12–16 November 1941. Agreements between naval commanders and Army commanders were concluded at Iwakuni Air Base.

15 November 1941. From 1300 to 1545 a war game was held (in the Imperial Palace) in the presence of the Emperor. Those present were:

---

* This statement is important as revealing that X-Day had been decided as 8 December Tokyo time, as early as 21 October—Eds.

ARMY

[Gen. Gen] Sugiyama, Chief of the Army General Staff
Vice Chief of the Army General Staff
[Lt. Gen. Shin'ichi] Tanaka, Chief of the First Bureau
[Col. Takushiro] Hattori, Chief of the Second Section
[Col. Kumao] Imoto
[Col. Keiji] Takase
Prince [Tsuneyoshi] Takeda

NAVY:

[Adm. Osami] Nagano, Chief of the Naval General Staff
[Rear Adm. Seiichi] Ito, Vice Chief
[Rear Adm. Shigeru] Fukudome, Chief of the First Bureau
[Capt. Sadatoshi] Tomioka, Chief of the 1st Section
[Comdr. Sadamu] Sanagi
[Comdr. Shigeshi] Uchida
[Lt. Comdr. Hironobu] Kacho

BYSTANDERS:

Chief Aide de Camp
War and Navy Ministers
Field Marshals
[Prince Kotohito] Kanin and [Prince Morimasa] Nashimoto
Fleet Admiral [Prince Hiroyasu] Fushimi

21 November 1941. Operational orders and directives were issued to Fleets and the Inner Perimeter forces (Naval Base Forces).

24 November 1941. 3rd Submarine Squadron left the Marshall Islands for Hawaii.

26 November 1941. The Task Force centering around the First Air Fleet left Hitokappu Bay heading for Hawaii.

1 December 1941. The Imperial Conference was held and a decision was made to go to war. After the conference ended, the Emperor pointedly asked the Chief of both the Army and Navy General Staffs to say, and told them that, since the fate of the Empire depends upon this coming war, the Army and Navy in close cooperation should exert their utmost efforts. Then, the Chief of the Army General Staff, representing both services, assured him that they would comply with his will.

2 December 1941. It was reported that three U.S. planes were seen off the southern tip of Formosa.

An order was issued that "X" Day was established as 8 December.

3 December 1941. A report came in to the effect that one *Prince of Wales* battleship has entered Singapore harbor.

4 December 1941. In the afternoon patrol planes sighted U.S. submarines 50 and 150 (miles) west of Palau Island.

5 December 1941. In the morning our patrol planes sighted five submerged submarines 5 miles northeast of and 50 miles northwest of Palau Island. It was reported that the U.S. Army ordered all fighters (aircraft) to be alert on 15 minutes' notice.

6 December 1941. In the evening a report came that our convoy of the Malay Force was sighted by a large-type British plane south of Saigon from 1345 to about 1500. The Malay Force commander then ordered the air force to shoot it down, but so far, it seems, that plane has not yet been shot down. I stayed in the NGS the night of the 6th. That decision to shoot down tracking planes seems a little bit premature.

7 December 1941. At 1020 our army plane shot down a British plane tracking our Malay invasion force. All members of the section stayed in the NGS the night of the 7th [except Prince Takamatsu and Marquis Katcho]. (News also came in that at Wake Island 12 aircraft were on the land airdrome and 6 flying boats were also at Wake.)

8 December 1941. At 0330 a message "Surprise attack made, time 0322" came in. Prior to this, past 0200, a report came in that the Advance Force of the Malaya Force entered the landing berth at 0045 and began landing at 0130.

At 0320 the operation against Hong Kong commenced.

Due to thick fog, our planes at Formosa did not take off until 0900.

At 0045 Clark Field ordered its base to place all fighters on 15 minutes' notice alert.

At 0537 MacKay Radio at Manila broadcast that Manila was bombed.

At 0535 came a report that Singapore was bombed with good results.

At 0415 the U.S. Asiatic Fleet ordered "alert."

At 0430 the U.S. Secretary of the Navy ordered U.S. Navy forces to fight the Japanese forces.

At 0800 came a report that Guam was attacked.

At 0820 a radio calling for sweeping of magnetic mines was intercepted. Our midget submarines seem to have entered Pearl Harbor.

At 0842 Davao was bombed.

At 0300*, according to radio interception, the enemy mistook six transports west of Barber's Point for Japanese ships and gave orders to sink them. How they were put in confusion could be seen.

At 1430. According to the Buenos Aires reports, the *West Virginia* was sunk and *Oklahoma* was burning.

At 1705 the C-in-C of the U.S. Pacific Fleet gave orders in a plain language message to cease firing on aircraft.

---

* As Uchida recorded that Fuchida's message of *Tora, Tora, Tora!* (surprise achieved) was received at 0330, obviously this time notation of 0300 is incorrect. Possibly it was a typographical error in the translation. We believe it should have been 1300—Eds.

At about 1930 a brief action report came in from the Task Force. It said: Two battleships—they seem to be *West Virginia* and *Oklahoma*—were sunk and four other battleships severely damaged, and four cruisers also greatly damaged. In addition, one carrier seems to be sunk off Honolulu.

At 1850 the half section of the 7th Destroyer Division bombarded Midway Island and destroyed oil tanks and hangers. Enemy counter-firing was met but without damage.

We were all wild with joy receiving such big news on the first day of the war. Today's weather was fine and warm, as if it foreshadows the future of the war.

CHAPTER 7

Extracts from Diary and Papers of Comdr. Sadamu Sanagi

S ANAGI WAS an experienced air officer. He had served in Washington as assistant naval attaché and had traveled widely in Europe when studying aviation. He had been air staff officer of the Combined Fleet and, at the time of Pearl Harbor, was a member of the Operations Section of the Naval General Staff.

While it is not indicated on the document from which we worked, we are quite sure it was one of several studies that Chihaya prepared for Prange. All times cited herein are Japanese time.

10th Feb. 1949

SUBJECT: Matters concerning the P.H. Operation extracted from diaries, memos and notes of Mr. Sadamu Sanagi. (Comdr. N. G. S. in Dec. 1941; no Japanese name given on his diary.)

During the war, Mr. Sanagi wrote diaries, memos and notes which still remain. In the entry covering from the latter part of 1941 to the early part of 1942, there were considerable articles concerning the P.H. operation, although they were very fragmental. The following are the extracts from them, of which the first one covering the discussion on the P.H. attack in September is most interesting:

1. THE CONFERENCE TO STUDY THE P.H. OPERATION

A. Although he did not mention the date, the following entry was found:

The Chief of Staff, 1st Air Fleet, stated that (1) to achieve surprise would be an absolutely important factor in such kind of operations; (2) a destroyer squadron composed of sixteen destroyers would be preferable—if possible, the 4th, 16th, 17th and 18th Destroyer Divisions, desirable: (3) the Sixth Fleet should be placed under the command of the Task Force.

He further stated that (1) what he most wanted to be informed of were the exact distance of the enemy scouting radius and the location of the enemy ships together with the situation of the harbor; (2) torpedo-attacking in the area south of Ford Island would be impossible, and finally (3) the speed limit of 280 knots of the "Zero fighter" should be lifted.

Then the 8th Cruiser Division Commander requested that three-man seaplanes should be assigned to the Division.

B. Also, he wrote that on 24 September the Chiefs of Staff, senior staff officers and air operation staff officer of the Combined Fleet and the 1st Air Fleet further discussed the problem with the Chief of the First Bureau, Chief of the First Section, and other key staff officers of the First Section at General Staff Headquarters.

The essence of their discussion was as follows:

CHIEF OF STAFF, 1ST AIR FLEET:

The operation would be possible tactically, but very difficult from the strategical and political points of view. In order to make it possible, there would be no other way but to launch a surprise attack upon the enemy. I wonder, however, whether the enemy could be surprised by political measures. On the other hand, our naval strength for the southern operation is not sufficient. I think, therefore, from the viewpoint of the general situation, it would be better to concentrate our efforts first upon the southern operation.

COMMANDER [SHIGENORI] KAMI:

It can be admitted that tactically the operation might be possible, as maintaining round-the-clock patrol in all directions is very difficult. Moreover, our expected damages would not be great. On the other hand, the following points should be taken into consideration: (1) Refueling of the fleet would be difficult; (2) serious damages could not be inflicted by bombing and, even though they were damaged, they would be repaired by use of the Navy Yard; (3) there are many probabilities in the northern course to be discovered.

AIR OPERATIONS STAFF OFFICER, 1ST AIR FLEET:

In the event of the American fleet being in Lahaina anchorage, eight battleships would be sunk by torpedo attacks alone. Even when the effectiveness reduction in battlefields is kept in mind, at least four to six battleships can be sunk. Against carriers, fifty-four dive bombers can be spared, with an expected result of three carriers knocked out. Another eighty-one dive bombers must be reserved for launching air attacks upon air bases. In case level bombing is carried out instead of torpedo attacks, either five battleships or two or three battleships and three carriers can be sunk.

SENIOR STAFF OFFICER, 1ST AIR FLEET:

In case the enemy scouting limit is not more than three hundred miles, it is easy to select the course, but it is awfully difficult in case of more than four hundred miles. Refueling on sea with more than eleven-meters-per-second wind becomes difficult even to destroyers. The ships other than destroyers can manage to operate, if they could receive one refueling on their way.

AIR OPERATIONS STAFF OFFICER, 1ST AIR FLEET:

The operation has possibilities of success from the standpoint of the air forces; crews of the 1st and 2nd Carrier Divisions have firm confidence of their success.

It is requested that air forces which remain in the homeland pretend that carriers are still training there.

AIR OPERATIONS STAFF OFFICER, COMBINED FLEET:

The operation would be better given up, in the event the southern course has to be adopted after all. Discussions would never cease with regard to a surprise attack; I recommend it would be better to make up our minds to do it.

CHIEF OF THE FIRST BUREAU:

It is desired that X day be fixed around 20 November. In my opinion a successful surprise attack seems difficult, because it is too late now to conduct political measures so as to make the operation easy. The most essential matter is to secure the southern area as soon as possible at any cost. At the same time we must make preparations for Soviet Russia, too.

CHIEF OF STAFF, COMBINED FLEET:

Can't the general situation be better developed by launching an attack upon "X"* even though the P.H. operation is postponed a month?

CHIEF OF THE FIRST BUREAU:

From the political standpoint it seems probable that the American fleet stations in Pearl Harbor, but there are more probabilities that they are in their homeland waters for operational preparations.

2. DIARY

26 Nov. 1941. At 0600 the Task Force secretly left Hitokappu Bay. In the Operations Room the weather chart covering the Pacific, including the Far East and America, was hung on the wall, and twice a day aerologists from the Hydrographic Office were to be in the room to study weather conditions for the Task Force, to which necessary weather information was to be sent. From today on, a duty staff officer was to remain in the Operations Room all day long, and half of the staff officers of the First Section were to stay in the *Suikosha* (Navy Club) at night.

27 November. The press reported that the United States delivered a message to our side yesterday. A low pressure area which has hung over near the Task Force is rapidly moving to the north; fine weather seems likely to continue for a few days.

29 November. The enclosed orders (only to be opened by another order) of the Imperial General Headquarters Order directing the date of opening the war were delivered to representatives of all Naval Stations and Minor Naval Stations.

30 November. In spite of its being Sunday, Prime Minister Tojo was summoned in audience by the Emperor from 1600 to 1700. Then, the Chief of the Naval General Staff and Navy Minister were also summoned.

1 December. At 1400 a conference was held in audience with the Emperor. The Imperial Order directing use of armed strength was issued.

---

* The translator noted here: "Code name unidentified, but most likely P.H." However, from the context it is obvious that a site other than Pearl Harbor is meant. This could be any one of Japan's initial targets, possibly the Philippines —Eds.

2 December. The *Tatsuta-Maru* left Yokohama heading for North America. Thirty-five foreign evacuees were on board.

3 December. Admiral Yamamoto, Commander-in-Chief of the Combined Fleet, was summoned to audience by the Emperor, representing all navy commanders.

4 December. Admiral Yamamoto left the official residence of the Navy Minister, receiving hearty send-offs from Vice Admiral [Tomoshige] Samejima; Aide-de-Camp to the Emperor Captain Hosoya; Aide to Prince Fushimi; the Navy Minister, the Chief of the Naval General Staff, members of the Military Council, Chiefs of Bureaus of the Navy Ministry and General Staff, staff officers of the First Section of the General Staff and Prince Takamatsu.

Hawaii area: Shore leaves of American sailors as usual. Reports from the Consul-General in Honolulu covering ships' locations in Pearl Harbor came successively from 2nd December. No particular change.

The Fourteenth Naval District Commandant dispatched an urgent message at about noon (local time). It might be that drifting oil from our submarines was discovered.

6 December. A Consul-General's report which had not come since 2nd December came again. Relaxed, but no carrier is in the harbor.

No particular change was observed in the enemy radio traffic activities; the enemy in the Hawaii areas seemed quiet, without any knowledge of our intention. Although the Fourteenth Naval Commandant dispatched an urgent message on the 4th, no change was observed there.

A Liaison Conference was held with regard to the time of dispatching the ultimatum to the United States of America.

7 December. A Consul-General report; in the harbor, nine battleships, but neither a carrier nor a heavy cruiser.

8 December. Every nerve had been concentrated to receive messages. It was not until 0330 that messages began to come in. Wild joy burst out with the news of "Tora Tora . . ." and "successful surprise attack." Relaxed receiving the news of "bombed the enemy main strength with good results" and "torpedoed enemy heavy cruisers; heavy damage inflicted."

How the enemy was surprised can be easily imagined by such a Task Force's message as saying that they were encountered by enemy defense gunfire only after the torpedo attacks. The enemy in the Hawaii area had been completely surprised at about 0730 on Sunday morning. The following messages received suffice to indicate how they were surprised:

"Wipe out magnetic mines and mooring mines in the East Loch."

Attacks by midget submarines might be successful.

Every message was sent in plain code.

Mistaking four American merchant ships sailing southwest of Barbers Point as Japanese transport convoys, the C-in-C of the American Pacific Fleet so informed all forces. It seems likely that the enemy made attacks upon them.

By 0900 the enemy seemed to have detected our carriers by means of radio-direction-finding instruments to the north.

Our air force, together with the submarine force, achieved a great success unprecedented in history by the Pearl Harbor attack. About 400 planes, of which 120 were fighters, 160 dive bombers and 120 torpedo-attacking planes, inflicted the following damage upon the enemy:

Two battleships sunk, four battleships seriously damaged and about four cruisers seriously damaged.

(All above-mentioned figures sure.)

Additionally, a great many enemy planes were destroyed.

Our losses: 30 planes.

The surprise air attack coupled with submarine attacks by the midget submarines solely contributed to this successful attack, which could only be done by the Imperial Navy. This success is owing to the Imperial Navy's hard training for more than twenty years. Our navy had made this hard training only for this one day. So excited to hear of this success today!

Nothing could hold back our Imperial Navy which had kept silent for a long time. But once it arose, it never hesitated to dare to do the most difficult thing on this earth. Oh, how powerful is the Imperial Navy!

10 December. At 1330 the *Enterprise* with a heavy cruiser was observed sailing at 20 knots with course of 60 in the channel east of Oahu Island. Other submarines of the 1st Submarine Squadron began to chase them.

CHAPTER 8

Pearl Harbor Operations: General Outline of Orders and Plans

T HIS IS ONE of many such studies prepared in the Military History Section of Headquarters, U.S. Army Forces, Far East (USAFFE) in Tokyo over a period of several years following the end of the war. Obviously this document was the work of the Japanese ex-naval officers employed in the History Section. Unfortunately no explanatory note is included herein as to whether this study was originally made in Japanese or in English. The Japanese Navy conducted a wholesale destruction of documents, including the originals of these, shortly before the end of the war. Thus, as explained in this document's Foreword, these were "reconstructed from personal notes and memory." We believe the results to be as reliable as possible under the circumstances. Please note that following the cover sheet the first page, the Foreword, is numbered iii, and the next, the Table of Contents, is numbered vii; therefore, somewhere may exist other explanatory pages.

To the best of our knowledge, these studies were never published, the copy included herein being a reproduced copy of a typewritten manuscript.

[COVER SHEET]

Japanese Monograph No. 97

PEARL HARBOR OPERATIONS:

General Outline of Orders and Plans

Prepared by
Military History Section
Headquarters, Army Forces Far East

Distributed by
Office of the Chief of Military History
Department of the Army

(1953)

[Page ii missing; page iii:]

FOREWORD

This monograph is a collection of pertinent Navy Orders and Directives, Combined Fleet Orders, and Carrier Striking Task Force Orders concerning the Pearl Harbor operation. Since all copies of these orders were destroyed prior to the end of the war, they have been reconstructed from personal notes and memory.

In editing, explanatory footnotes were added when deemed necessary.

19 February 1953

[Pages iv–vi are missing; page vii:]

TABLE OF CONTENTS

[Page 1:]

Navy Order No. 1

5 November 1941

Order to: Yamamoto, C in C, Combined Fleet

1. In view of the great possibility of being compelled to go to war against the United States, Great Britain and the Netherlands in the cause of self-existence and self-defense, Japan has decided to complete various operational preparations within the first ten days of December.

2. The Commander-in-Chief of the Combined Fleet will make the necessary operational preparations.

3. The details of the operation shall be directed by the Chief of the Naval General Staff.

> By Imperial Order
> Chief of the Naval General Staff
> Nagano, Osami

Navy Directive No. 1

> 5 November 1941

Directive to: Yamamoto, C in C, Combined Fleet

1. The Combined Fleet will advance necessary forces at a suitable time to their preparatory points to stand by for the start of operations in the event of unavoidable hostilities against America.

[*Page 2:*]

Great Britain and the Netherlands, in the first ten days of December.[1]

2. During the above-mentioned advance, strict watch will be kept against unexpected attacks.

3. The operational policy against America, Great Britain, and the Netherlands, in case of hostilities, is scheduled as cited in the separate volume.[2]

> Chief of the Naval General Staff
> Nagano, Osami

Note:

Combined Fleet Operations Order No. 1 issued on 5 November 1941 and titled "Preparations for War and Commencement of Hostilities" was an 89-page volume covering all phases of war preparations. In general this order stated the following:

---

1. Preparatory Points

Carrier Striking Task Force	Hitokappu Bau
Philippine Invasion Force	Bako (Formosa)
Malay Invasion Force	Cam Ranh Bay
Main Body, Southern Force	Samah (Hainan Island)
Submarine Force	Kwajalein

2. All copies of "The Separate Volume" were destroyed prior to the end of the war. Attached as appendix I is a reconstructed version prepared from personal notes and memory by Capt. T. Ohmae, former Chief, Plans Section, Naval General Staff.

[*Page 3:*]

A. The Empire is expecting war to break out with the United States, Great Britain and the Netherlands. When the decision is made to complete all operational preparations, orders will be issued establishing the approximate date (Y Day) for commencement of hostilities and announcing "First Preparations for War."

When these orders are issued, the forces will act as follows:

(1) All fleets and forces, without special orders, will organize and complete battle preparations for operations in accordance with "the Allocation of Forces for First Period Operations of First Phase Operations." When directed by respective commanding officers, they will proceed at a proper time to the pre-operation rendezvous points and wait in readiness.

(2) All forces will be on strict look-out for unexpected attacks by the U.S., British, and Netherlands forces.

(3) The commanding officers of various forces may carry out such secret reconnaissance as is necessary for the operations.

[*Page 4:*]

Combined Fleet Operations Order No. 2

7 November 1941

Order to: Combined Fleet

First Preparations for War
Y Day 8 December.[3]

C in C, Combined Fleet
Yamamoto, Isoroku

[*Page 5:*]

Navy Order No. 5

21 November 1941

Order to: Yamamoto, C in C, Combined Fleet

1. The Commander-in-Chief of the Combined Fleet will dispatch at an appropriate time the necessary forces for the execution of operations to positions of readiness.[4]

---

3. This order was issued by C in C, Combined Fleet, after he had received verbal notification from Chief, Naval General Staff, that 8 December had been tentatively selected as "Y" Day.

4. So-called positions of readiness were designated operational sea areas. They were as follows:

Southern Force (2nd, 3rd and Southern Expeditionary Fleets)	South China Sea (Elements in Western Caroline Area)
South Seas Force (4th Fleet)	Inner South Seas Area
Northern Force (5th Fleet)	Kurile Area
Submarine Force (6th Fleet)	Hawaiian Sea Area
Carrier Striking Task Force (1st Air Fleet)	Hawaiian Sea Area
Commerce Destruction Force	Indian Ocean
Land Based Air Force (11th Air Fleet)	Formosa, French Indo-China and Palau

2. The Commander-in-Chief of the Combined Fleet is empowered to use force in self-defense in case his fleet is challenged by American, British or Dutch forces during the process of carrying out military preparations.

3. The details concerned will be directed by the Chief of the Naval General Staff.[5]

> By Imperial Order
> Chief of the Naval General Staff
> Nagano Osami

[*Page 6:*]

Navy Directive No. 5

21 November 1941

Directive to: Yamamoto, C in C, Combined Fleet

1. The Commander-in-Chief of the Combined Fleet will immediately assemble and call back the operational units if the Japanese-American negotiation is successful.

2. The exercise of military authority cited in the Imperial General Headquarters Navy Order No. 5 will be effected in the event the American, British, or Dutch naval forces invade our territorial waters and carry out reconnaissance, or approach our territorial waters and their move is recognized to be threatening, or an aggressive act is taken to endanger us even beyond our territorial waters.

> Chief of the Naval General Staff
> Nagano, Osami

[*Page 7:*]

Carrier Striking Task Force Operations Order No. 1[6]

23 November 1941

To: Carrier Striking Task Force

1. The Carrier Striking Task Force will proceed to the Hawaiian Area with utmost secrecy and, at the outbreak of the war, will launch a resolute surprise attack on and deal a fatal blow to the enemy fleet in the Hawaiian Area. The initial air attack is scheduled at 0330 hours, X Day. Upon completion of the air attacks, the Task Force will immediately withdraw and return to Japan and, after taking on new supplies, take its position for Second Period Operations. In the event that, during this operation, an enemy fleet attempts to

---

5. On the same day C in C, Combined Fleet, issued the necessary orders for dispatch of forces to the designated operational sea areas. Time of departure was left to the discretion of respective force commanders.

6. General outline.

[*Page 8:*]

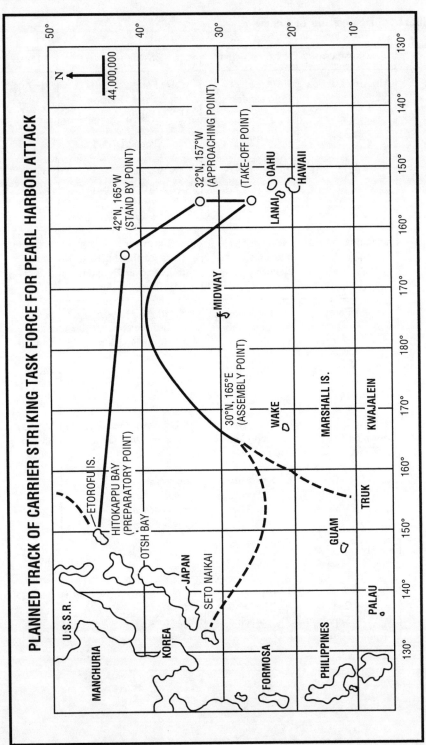

[*Page 9:*]

Chart 1   Disposition of Forces

	CLASSIFICATION		COMMANDER	STRENGTH	DUTIES

TASK FORCE	Air Attack Force		1st Air Fleet Commander	*1st Air Fleet*
				  1st Carrier Division
				  CV *Akagi*
				  CV *Kaga*
				  2nd Carrier Division
				  CV *Hiryu*
				  CV *Soryu*
				  5th Carrier Division
				  CV *Zuikaku*
				  CV *Shokaku*
					Air Attacks

	Screening		1st Destroyer Squadron Commander	17th Destroyer Division
				  (*Nagara* flagship)
				18th Destroyer Division
				  (*Akigumo* flagship)
					Screening and Escort

	Support Force		3rd Battleship Division Commander	3rd Battleship Division (less the second section) 8th Cruiser Division	Screening and Support
	Patrol unit		2nd Submarine Division Commander	I-17 (flagship) I-21 I-23	Patrol
	Midway Bombardment Unit		7th Destroyer Division Commander	7th Destroyer Division (less the 2nd Section)	Midway Air Base Attack
	Supply force	1st Supply Unit	*Kyokuto Maru* Commander	*Kenyo Maru* *Kyokuto Maru* *Kokuyo Maru* *Shinkoku Maru*	Supply
		Kyokuto Maru Commander			
		2nd Supply Unit	*Toho Maru* Inspector	*Toho Maru* *Toei Maru* *Nippon Maru*	

intercept our force or a powerful enemy force is encountered and there is danger of attack, the Task Force will launch a counterattack.

2. The disposition of Force will be as shown on Chart 1.

3. The Operation of Each Force.

   a. General

   While exercising strict antiaircraft and antisubmarine measures and making every effort to conceal its position and movements, the entire force (except the Midway Bombardment Unit) in accordance with special orders will depart as a group from Hitokappu Bay at a speed of 12–14 knots. The force refueling en route whenever possible will arrive at the standby point (42 N, 165 W). In the event bad weather prevents refueling en route to the standby point, the screening unit will be

[*Page 10:*]

ordered to return to the home base. Subsequent to the issuance of the order designating X Day (the day of the outbreak of hostilities), the force will proceed to the approaching point (32 N, 157 W).

[*Page 11:*]

Around 0700 hours, X-1 Day the Task Force will turn southward at high speed (approximately 24 knots) from the vicinity of the approaching point. It will arrive at the take-off point (200 nautical miles north of the enemy fleet anchorage) at 0100 hours X Day (0530 Honolulu time) and commit the entire air strength to attack the enemy fleet and important airfields on Oahu.

Upon completion of the air attacks, the Task Force will assemble the aircraft, skirt 800 nautical miles north of Midway, return about X + 15 Day to the western part of the Inland Sea via the assembly point (30 N, 165 E) and prepare for Second Period Operations. In the event of a fuel shortage the Task Force will proceed to Truk via the assembly point.

The force may skirt near Midway in the event that consideration of an enemy counter-attack is unnecessary due to successful air attacks or if such action is necessitated by fuel shortage.

In this event, the 5th Carrier Division with the support of the *Kirishima* from the 3rd Battleship Division will leave the Task Force on the night of X Day or the early morning of X + 1 Day and carry out air attacks on Midway in the early morning of X + 2 Day.

If a powerful enemy force intercepts our return route, the Task Force will break through the Hawaiian Islands area southward and proceed to the Marshall Islands.

   b. Patrol unit

   The patrol unit will accompany the main force. In the event the screening unit is returned to the home base, the patrol unit

[*Page 12:*]

will screen the advance of the main force and the launching and the landing of aircraft. After the air attacks, the patrol unit will station itself between the flank of the main force and the enemy. In the event of an enemy fleet sortie, the patrol unit will shadow the enemy and in a favorable situation attack him.

c. The Midway Bombardment Unit
The Midway Bombardment Unit will depart from Tokyo Bay around X-6 Day and, after refueling, secretly approach Midway. It will arrive on the night of X Day and shell the air base. The unit will then withdraw and, after refueling, return to the western part of the Inland Sea. The oiler *Shiriya* will accompany the bombardment unit on this mission and will be responsible for the refueling operation.

d. Supply Force
The supply force will accompany the main force to the approaching point, carrying out refuelings, separate from the main force, skirt 800 nautical miles north of Midway, return to the assembly point by 0800 hours, X + 6 Day, and stand by.

4. The Task Force may suspend operations en route to the Hawaiian area and return to Hitokappu Bay, Hokkaido or Mutsu Bay, depending upon the situation.

Commander
Carrier Striking Task Force
Nagumo, Chuichi

[*Page 13:*]

Carrier Striking Task Force Operations Order No. 3[7]

23 November 1941

To: Carrier Striking Task Force

The Hawaiian operations air attack plan has been decided as follows:

1. The Operation of the Air Attack Forces
The force will be 700 nautical miles due north of point Z (set at the western extremity of the Island of Lanai) at 0600 hours X-1 Day and advance on a course of 180 degrees from 0700 hours X-1 Day at an increased speed of 24 knots.

Air attacks will be carried out by launching the first attack units 230 nautical miles due north of Z point at 0130 hours X Day, and the second attack unit at 200 nautical miles due north of Z point at 0245 hours.

After the launching of the second attack units is completed, the task force will withdraw northward at a speed of about 24 knots. The first attack units are scheduled to return between 0530 and 0600 hours and the second attack units are scheduled to return between 0645 and 0715 hours.

---

7.   General outline.

Immediately after the return of the first and second attack units, preparations for the next attack will be completed. At this time, carrier attack planes capable of carrying torpedoes will be armed with such as long as the supply lasts.

[*Page 14:*]

If the destruction of enemy land-based air strength progresses favorably, repeated attacks will be made immediately and thus decisive results will be achieved.

In the event that a powerful enemy surface fleet appears, it will be attacked.

2. Organization of the Air Attack Units
(see Chart 2)

3. Targets

a. The First Attack Units
The targets for the first group will be limited to about four battleships and four aircraft carriers; the order of targets will be battleships and then aircraft carriers.

The second group will attack the enemy land-based air strength according to the following assignment:

The 15 Attack Unit   Hangars and aircraft on Ford Island
The 16 Attack Unit   Hangars and aircraft on Wheeler Field

The targets of Fighter Combat Units will be enemy aircraft in the air and on the ground.

b. The Second Attack Units
The first group will attack the enemy air bases according to the following assignment:

The 5 Attack Unit   Aircraft and hangars on Kaneohe, Ford Island and
                       Barbers Point.
The 6 Attack Unit   Hangars and aircraft on Hickam Field.

The targets for the second group will be limited to four

[*Page 15:*]

or five enemy aircraft carriers. If the number of targets is insufficient, they will select targets in the order of cruisers and battleships.

The Fighter Combat Units will attack the enemy aircraft in the air and on the ground.

4. Attack Procedure

a. The First Attack Units

(1) With the element of surprise as the principle, attacks will be carried out by the torpedo unit and bomber unit of the First Group, and then the Second Group.

Chart 2   Organization of the Air Attack Units

1ST ATTACK UNITS	CO Commander Fuchida
1st Group	CO do
1st Attack Unit	CO do
15 Kates each fitted with a 800-kg Armor Piercing Bomb for level (high-altitude) bombing	
2nd Attack Unit	CO Lt. Comdr. Hashiguchi
15 Kates—Same bombs as 1st Attack Unit	
3rd Attack Unit	CO Lt. Abe
10 Kates—Same bombs as 1st Attack Unit	
4th Attack Unit	CO Lt. Comdr. Kusumi
10 Kates—Same bombs as 1st Attack Unit	
1st Torpedo Attack Unit	CO Lt. Comdr. Murata
12 Kates each fitted with an Aerial Torpedo, Mark 91	
2nd Torpedo Attack Unit	CO Lt. Kitajima
12 Kates—Same torpedoes as 1st Torpedo Attack Unit	
3rd Torpedo Attack Unit	CO Lt. Nagai
8 Kates—Same torpedoes as 1st Torpedo Attack Unit	
4th Torpedo Attack Unit	CO Lt. Matsumura
8 Kates—Same torpedoes as 1st Torpedo Attack Unit	
2nd Group	CO Lt. Comdr. Takahashi
15th Attack Unit	CO do
27 Vals each fitted with a 250-kg Anti-ground (general-purpose) bomb for dive bombing	
16th Attack Unit	CO Lt. Sakamoto
27 Vals—Same bomb as 15th Attack Unit	
3rd Group	CO Lt. Comdr. Itaya
1st Fighter Combat Unit	CO do
9 Zekes for air control and strafing	
2nd Fighter Combat Unit	CO Lt. Shiga
9 Zekes—Same mission	
3rd Fighter Combat Unit	CO Lt. Suganami
9 Zekes—Same mission	
4th Fighter Combat Unit	CO Lt. Okajima
6 Zekes—Same mission	
5th Fighter Combat Unit	CO Lt. Sato*
6 Zekes—Same mission	
6th Fighter Combat Unit	CO Lt. Kaneko*
6 Zekes—Same mission	
2nd Attack Units	
1st Group	CO Lt. Comdr. Shimazaki
6th Attack Unit	CO do

* The Japanese Navy's study of lessons learned shows Kaneko in command of the 5th and Sato in command of the 6th. See p. 300—Eds.

Chart 2   Organization of the Air Attack Units (continued)

27 Kates, each fitted with a 250-kg Anti-ground (general-purpose)
bomb and six 60-kg Ordinary bombs for level (high-altitude) bombing
5th Attack Unit   CO Lt. Ichihara
    27 Kates—Same bombs as 6th
Attack Unit

[Page 16:]

2nd Group	CO Lt. Comdr. Egusa
13th Attack Unit	CO do
18 Vals each fitted with a 250-kg Ordinary bomb for dive bombing	
14th Attack Unit	CO Lt. Kobayashi
18 Vals—Same bombs as 13th Attack Unit	
11th Attack Unit	CO Lt. Chihaya
18 Vals—Same bombs as 13th Attack Unit	
12th Attack Unit	CO Lt. Makino
27 Vals—Same bombs as 13th Attack Unit	
3rd Group	CO Lt. Shindo
1st Fighter Combat Unit	CO do
9 Zekes for air control and strafing	
2nd Fighter Combat Unit	CO Lt. Nikaido
9 Zekes—Same mission	
3rd Fighter Combat Unit	CO Lt. Iida
9 Zekes—Same mission	
4th Fighter Combat Unit	CO Lt. Kumano*
9 Zekes—Same mission	

[Page 17:]

(2) During the initial phase of the attack, the Fighter Combat Units will, in one formation, storm the enemy skies about the same time as the First Group, and contact and destroy chiefly the enemy interceptor planes.

   In the event that no enemy aircraft are encountered in the air, the units will immediately shift to the strafing of parked aircraft as follows:

1st and 2nd Fighter Combat Units:	Ford Island and Hickam Field
3rd and 4th Fighter Combat Units:	Wheeler Field and Barbers Point
5th and 6th Fighter Combat Units:	Kaneohe

(3) In the event that the advantage of surprise attack cannot be expected due to strict enemy security, the

---

* The Japanese Navy study of lessons learned shows Lt. Nono in command of the 4th Fighter Unit. This is probably correct. See p. 301—Eds.

[*Page 18:*]

approach and attack will be made in the order of the Fighter Combat Units, Dive Bombing Units, Horizontal Bombing Units and the Torpedo Attacking Units.

b. The Second Attack Units

All units will storm the enemy skies almost simultaneously and launch the attacks.

Although the general outline of the operations of the Fighter Combat Units corresponds to that of the First Attack Units, the strafing will be carried out according to the following in case there are no enemy aircraft in the air.

1st and 2nd Fighter Combat Units: Ford Island and Hickam Field
3rd and 4th Fighter Combat Units: Wheeler Field and Kaneohe

c. The general outline of attack in the event that enemy aircraft carriers and the main body of the U.S. Fleet are in anchorages outside Pearl Harbor are:

(1) The organization and targets are the same as mentioned above. The First Attack Units of the First Group, however, will increase the number of torpedo bombers as much as possible.

(2) Escorted by the Fighter Combat Units, the Air Attack Units will proceed in a group and attack the designated targets in the order of the enemy fleet anchorages and the Island of Oahu. If attacks on

[*Page 19:*]

the enemy fleet anchorages progress favorably, however, the Fighter Combat Units and the 2nd Group of the First Air Attack Unit will immediately proceed to the Island of Oahu. Upon completion of the attacks, the anchorage attack unit will return directly to the carriers.

d. Rendezvous for Return to Carriers

(1) The rendezvous point will be 20 nautical miles at 340 degrees from the western extremity (Kaena Point) of the Island of Oahu. The rendezvous altitude will be 1,000 meters. (If this vicinity is covered with clouds, it will be below the cloud ceiling.)

(2) The Attack Units will wait at the rendezvous point for about 30 minutes and return to their carriers, after being joined by the Fighter Combat Units.

(3) While returning to carriers, the Fighter Combat Unit will become the rear guards for the whole unit and intercept any enemy pursuit.

5. Reconnaissance

a. Pre-operation Encounters

Pre-operation reconnaissance will not be carried out unless otherwise ordered.

[*Page 20:*]

    b. Immediate Pre-attack Reconnaissance

Two reconnaissance seaplanes of the 8th Cruiser Division will take off at 0030 hours, X Day, secretly reconnoiter Pearl Harbor and Lahaina Anchorage and report the presence of the enemy fleet (chiefly carriers and the main body of the fleet).

    c. Scouting Patrol

The reconnaissance seaplanes of the 8th Cruiser Division will take off at 0300 hours and will carry out an extensive search of the waters between the enemy and the friendly forces and the waters adjacent to the two channels situated to the east and west of the Island of Oahu. They will observe and report the presence and activities of the enemy sortie force and enemy aircraft on counter-attack missions.

    d. Before returning to its carrier, after the attack, an element of fighters designated by the Fighter Combat Unit Commander will fly as low and as fast as circumstances permit and observe and determine the extent of damage inflicted upon the enemy aircraft and ships.

        Air Security Disposition No. 1 Method B will be followed from one hour before sunrise until 45 minutes after sunset on the day of the air attack.[8]

                        Commander
                        Carrier Striking Task Force
                        Nagumo, Chuichi

[*Page 21:*]

Combined Fleet, Operations Order No. 5 (General Outline)

25 November 1941

Order to: Carrier Striking Task Force

    The Carrier Striking Task Force will immediately complete taking on supplies and depart with utmost secrecy from Hitokappu Bay on 26 November and advance to the standby point (42 N, 170 W) by the evening of 3 December.

                        Commander-in-Chief, Combined Fleet
                        Yamamoto, Isoroku

[*Page 22:*]

Navy Order No. 9

1 December 1941

Order to: Yamamoto, C in C, Combined Fleet

    1. Japan has decided to open hostilities against the United States, Great Britain, and the Netherlands early in December.

---

8.   This Security Disposition called for combat air cover over the carriers.

2. The Commander-in-Chief of the Combined Fleet will smash the enemy fleets and air forces in the Orient and at the same time will intercept and annihilate enemy fleets should they come to attack us.

3. The Commander-in-Chief of the Combined Fleet will occupy immediately the key bases of the United States, Great Britain, and the Netherlands in East Asia in close cooperation with the Commander-in-Chief of the Southern Army and will capture and secure the key areas of the southern regions.

4. The Commander-in-Chief of the Combined Fleet will cooperate with the operations of the China Area Fleet, if necessary.

5. The time of the start of operations based on the aforementioned items will be made known later.

6. The Chief of the Naval General Staff will issue instructions concerning particulars.

By Imperial Order
Chief of the Naval General Staff
Nagano, Osami

[*Page 23:*]

Navy Directive No. 9

1 December 1941

Directive to: Yamamoto, C in C, Combined Fleet

Operations of the Combined Fleet against American [sic], England and Holland will be conducted in accordance with the Separate Volume, Imperial Navy's Course of Action in Operations against United States, Great Britain and the Netherlands.

Chief of the Naval General Staff
Nagano, Osami

[*Page 24:*]

Navy Order No. 12

2 December 1941

Order to: Yamamoto, C in C, Combined Fleet

1. As of 8 December the Commander-in-Chief of the Combined Fleet will start military operations in accordance with Imperial General Headquarters Navy Order No. 9.

2. Military operations will be launched against the Netherlands at an opportune time after attacking the United States and Great Britain.

By Imperial Order
Chief of the Naval General Staff
Nagano, Osami

[*Page 25:*]

Verbal Directive of the Chief of the Naval General Staff

2 December 1941

Verbal Directive to: Yamamoto, Commander-in-Chief, Combined Fleet (in Tokyo at the time)

Should it appear certain that Japanese-American negotiations will reach an amicable settlement prior to the commencement of hostilities, it is understood that all elements of the Combined Fleet are to be assembled and returned to their bases in accordance with separate orders.

> Chief of the Naval General Staff
> Nagano, Osami

Combined Fleet Telegraphic Operations Order No. 021730

(Date and time of dispatch)

8th December designated as X Day.

> Commander-in-Chief, Combined Fleet
> Yamamoto, Isoroku

[*Page 26 was not included in original; page 27:*]

APPENDIX I

Imperial Navy's Course of Action in Operations Against United States, Great Britain, and the Netherlands

(Attached to Navy Directives No. 1 and No. 9)

I. Outline of Operations

Continue control over China Coast and Yangtze River.

Quickly destroy enemy fleet and air power in East Asia.

Occupy and hold strategic points in Southern Area.

Destroy enemy fleet.

Consolidate strength to hold out for a long time and destroy enemy's will to fight.

II. Combined Fleet Course of Action

(a) The First Phase of Operations

1. With the forces of the Second Fleet, Third Fleet, First Expeditionary Fleet and Eleventh Air Fleet as a nucleus destroy enemy fleets and air forces in the Philippines, British Malay, and Netherlands Indies. In cooperation with the Army, take the initiative in attacks on air forces and fleets in the Philippines and Malaya. Push forward our bases by landing advance troops. Then with main body of invasion forces occupy the Philippines and Malaya.

In early stages of operations, first occupy British Borneo and then as quickly as possible occupy Dutch Borneo, Celebes and Southern Sumatra. The above to be followed by occupation of Molucca Islands and Timor. Established air bases in all of

[Page 28:]

the above-mentioned places. Utilize the air bases for subjugation of Java and then occupy Java. After capture of Singapore, occupy northern Sumatra and then at an opportune time commence operations in Burma. Cut supply routes to China.

2. Forces of the Fourth Fleet.
Patrol, maintain surface communications, and defend the South Sea Islands. Capture Wake. At opportune time attack and destroy enemy advance bases in the South Pacific Area. In cooperation with Army capture Guam and then at an opportune time Bismarck Area.

3. Forces of the Fifth Fleet.
Patrol the area east of the home islands. Make preparations against surprise attacks by enemy. Make reconnaissance of Aleutians and defend Bonin Islands. Maintain surface communications. Be on guard against Soviet Russia.

4. Forces of the Sixth Fleet. (Submarines)
Make reconnaissance of American Fleet in Hawaii and West Coast areas and, by surprise attacks on shipping, destroy lines of communications.

5. Forces of First Air Fleet. (Carriers)
Hawaiian attack. Thereafter support Fourth Fleet operations and assist in capture of Southern areas.

6. Main Body of Combined Fleet.
Support operations in general. Operate according to the situation.

[Page 29:]

7. Part of Combined Fleet. (24th Commercial Destruction Unit)
Destroy enemy lines of communication in the Pacific and Indian Oceans.

(b) Second Phase of Operations.

1. Forces of Sixth Fleet. (Submarines)
Make reconnaissance and surprise attacks on main forces of enemy fleet. Destroy enemy surface communications in cooperation with a part of Combined Fleet. At opportune time make surprise attacks on enemy advanced bases.

2. Forces of First and Eleventh Air Fleets. (Carriers and Land-Based Air Forces)

Search for and attack enemy forces. Destroy enemy advanced bases.

3. Forces of Third Fleet, First Expeditionary Fleet and Other Forces as Necessary.

Defend occupied key areas in Southern area. Operate patrols, maintain surface communications, search for and destroy enemy shipping in Southern Area, attack and destroy enemy advanced bases on our perimeter.

4. Forces of Fourth Fleet.

Defend and patrol points in South Seas Islands and Bismarcks. Maintain surface communications. Search for and attack enemy shipping. Make surprise attacks and destroy enemy bases on our perimeter.

[*Page 30:*]

5. Forces of Fifth Fleet

Defend Bonin Islands and patrol area to north of those islands and east of home islands. Maintain surface communications. Search for and attack enemy fleet should it appear in the area. Attack and destroy enemy bases in the Aleutians.

6. Part of Combined Fleet. (24th Commercial Destruction Unit)

Destroy enemy surface communications in Pacific and Indian Oceans.

7. Main Body of Combined Fleet.

Support all operations. Operate as required.

8. In case of attack by strong American Force.

A part of the Sixth Fleet will maintain contact with the enemy. Reduce enemy strength by air and submarine attacks. At suitable opportunity assemble major portion of Combined Fleet and destroy enemy.

9. In case of attack by strong British Force.

By movement the Third Fleet, Fourth Fleet, First Expeditionary Fleet, Air Force, and Submarine Squadrons will maintain contact with enemy force and destroy it by concerted attacks. The main body of Combined Fleet, depending upon the strength, movement and location of American Fleet, will also be used in destruction of the British Fleet.

10. The important places to be defended among the points which were to be occupied were as follows:

[*Page 31:*]

Manila*, Hong Kong, Davao, Singapore, Batavia, Surabaya* Tarakan, Balikpapan, Mendao, Makasser, Ambon, Penang, Rabaul. (Asterisk indicates advanced bases.)

III. China Area Fleet Operations
Continue operations against China. Cooperate with the Army in destruction of United States and British forces in China. Second China Fleet cooperate with Army in capture of Hong Kong and destruction of enemy forces there. Maintain surface communications along China coast. Prevent enemy from using China coast. Cooperate with Combined Fleet and Army in operations. (Escort of surface transport and defense of assembly points.)

IV. Operations of Naval District and Auxiliary Naval Station Forces
Defend assigned areas. Maintain surface communications in assigned areas. Cooperate with Combined Fleet and China Area Fleet in operations affecting assigned areas.

PART II

Letters of Adm. Isoroku Yamamoto

EXCEPTING ONLY Adm. Heihachiro Togo, hero of the Russo-Japanese War, no naval figure is more honored in Japan than Yamamoto. He graduated from the Naval Academy at Etajima in 1904, just in time to participate in the Russo-Japanese War and lose two fingers from his left hand. He moved up steadily in his chosen career. In 1919 the Navy sent him, then a lieutenant commander, to the United States to study at Harvard. Becoming a captain in December 1924, he became executive officer at Kasumigaura, Japan's Pensacola. Thus began his close association with naval aviation.

Next came a two-year assignment to Washington as naval attaché. Not long thereafter, he went to the London Naval Conference as a delegate. Back in Japan, he commanded the 1st Carrier Division, then was sent back to London, this time to head the delegation. After his return came two high-level desk jobs at the Navy Ministry, including that of vice minister, in which capacity his opposition to Japan's joining the Axis outraged the jingoists. Then came his culminating post as commander in chief of the Combined Fleet.

Yamamoto possessed to an unusual degree two of the most desirable characteristics of a high commander—the ability to win the hearts as well as the fierce loyalty of his subordinates, and the ability to project a reassuring image of dependability. The Japanese had the feeling that while Yamamoto was at the helm, somehow everything would come out right. That is why his death on 18 April 1943 was such a national shock and cause for grief.

This section comprises a group of Yamamoto's letters and a magazine article that also contains some of his correspondence. While these letters cover dates both before and during the war, we have chosen to offer them as a unit because of the well-defined picture of the man they present. Indeed, this sampling is so revealing that a reader who knew little about him but his name could gather from it a fairly good idea of the kind of man who wrote them.

111

We meet the tough-minded strategist who insisted upon his Pearl Harbor project in the face of all opposition, the realist who disapproved of Japan's ties with Germany and Italy and who took a dim view of the politicians in charge of Japan's government. He realized that Japan's early successes were due in no small measure to Allied mistakes, and as the war progressed the Allies would make fewer and fewer.

Chihaya prepared for Prange the document headed "Two Letters." Both of the letters underline Yamamoto's impatience and pessimism with the national trend toward war.

The magazine article revealed a long-standing love affair between Yamamoto and a geisha named Chiyoko Kawai. After Yamamoto's death, the Navy ordered her to burn his letters, but she saved a few. These demonstrate a softer side of the admiral's character than appears in his semi-official correspondence with his naval friends.

CHAPTER 9

Letters from Yamamoto

O F THIS GROUP, we especially direct the reader's attention to Yamamoto's letters of 7 January 1941 to Oikawa and of 24 October 1941 to Vice Adm. Shigetaro Shimada. The historical importance of these documents can scarcely be exaggerated. In the first, Yamamoto frankly expressed to the then-Navy minister his skepticism about traditional strategy and training. He pointed out the embarrassing fact that in no past maneuvers had the Japanese Navy won "an overwhelming victory," that the maneuvers were usually suspended for "fear that our Navy might be dragged into gradual defeat." Thus he believed that the only chance was for Japan "to fiercely attack and destroy the U.S. main fleet at the outset of the war. . . ." He then outlined an operational plan for use against Pearl Harbor. Realizing the enormous risk involved, he wanted to lead the task force himself, for he was not the sort to ask of his men what he was not willing to face himself. To this end, he was prepared to give up the command of the Combined Fleet. His remarks about considering himself not fully qualified for that post might be chalked up to courteous Oriental self-criticism; however, it is a fact that he had little high-level command experience before being selected to head the fleet.

His letter to Shimada begins disconcertingly by commiserating with him on his recent appointment as Navy minister. Yamamoto did not hesitate to term the idea of war against the United States, Britain, and China, and possibly the Soviet Union, as "risky and illogical." He hoped peace was still possible, but feared matters had reached the point where "the only thing that can save the situation is the Imperial decision." Again he asked to be relieved as commander in chief in favor of his old friend Adm. Mitsumasa Yonai.

Amid the hectic days following Pearl Harbor, Yamamoto took the time to write to the student son of an old friend. In those days the courage and sacrifice of the midget submariners at Pearl Harbor impressed him deeply. As if to prove he was no superman, he succumbed to the propaganda that they had sunk a battleship, a myth widely circulated and believed in Japan.

His brief letters to Rear Admiral Hori and Mr. Enomoto again express his disgust and alarm at the situation into which Japan seemed to be racing. He found himself in the strange position of carrying out his duties "entirely against my private opinion."

LETTER FROM YAMAMOTO TO VICE ADM. SHIGETARO SHIMADA

Sukumo [Shikoku]
4 September [presumably 1939]

Dear Shimada:

I received your letter with thanks, and am grateful for your message of congratulations.*

Conscious of my poor qualifications for so responsible a post, I feel lost to find myself suddenly promoted to the Combined Fleet. Had this been a part of a periodic personnel shift, this post would have been yours as a matter of course. But the policy this time seems to have been to confine the scope of the shuffle to the minimum; and it seems that you are already slated to succeed [Admiral Koshiro] Oikawa some time between December and April. While that may mean that you will again be asked to undertake the bothersome task of disposing of various difficult problems that arise, maybe that, too, stems from the machinations of Ribbentrop† and Hitler.

In that connection, I shudder as I think of the problem of Japan's relations with Germany and Italy in the face of the tremendous changes now taking place in Europe.

I look forward to seeing you when my ships next visit your station.

With compliments and appreciation,

Yours cordially,
Isoroku

4 November 1940

Dear Mr. Mitsuari Takamura,

Many thanks for your letter. I am glad to hear that you are well in this beautiful autumn season. Also I thank you for your congratulatory telegram on the naval review. Owing to the preparation for war, only an element of the fleet participated in the naval review, so that it was not such a big one. Notwithstanding, the press wrote it up in headlines; this made me feel somewhat irritated.

When I think of what situation the Empire is now facing, I have no time to be impressed by such an honor as the naval review. I feel now that there is no other way but to devote every effort for completion of the preparations for war.

This moment is the critical time upon which the fate of the country depends. This is not because I fear the military strength of the United States and Great Britain, but because there is no able man among the authorities and also I fear such a crisis as this might be an unprecedented one. How dangerous the future of the Empire would be!

I can't help exclusively relying upon the Emperor's virtue and God's help. However, I feel that there is no other choice for me, who am taking the present

---

* On his appointment as C-in-C of the Combined Fleet—Trans.
† Joachim von Ribbentrop, German Foreign Minister—Eds.

position at this most critical moment, but to make every possible effort I can, while keeping in mind the following poem by the Emperor Meiji:

> Even though too much for me the burden be
> I won't care because it is for the sake of
> the country and the people.

I wish good health to you and your family, taking good care of yourselves.

Sincerely yours,
Isoroku Yamamoto

(CORDIALLY REQUEST THAT YOUR MINISTER ALONE READ THIS.)
(IT IS ALSO REQUESTED THAT THIS LETTER BE BURNED AFTER READING.)

7 January 1941
Aboard *Nagato*
Isoroku Yamamoto

To Navy Minister Koshiro Oikawa

Opinions on War Preparations

Although a precise outlook on the international situation is hard for anyone to make, it is needless to say that now the time has come for the Navy, especially the Combined Fleet, to devote itself seriously to war preparations, training and operational plans with a firm determination that a conflict with the U.S. and Great Britain is inevitable.

Therefore, I dare say here generally what I have had in my mind, to which your kind consideration is cordially invited. (This generally corresponds to what I verbally said to you roughly late in last November.)

1. WAR PREPARATIONS: Views on war preparations of the Combined Fleet have already been conveyed to the central authorities in Tokyo, and I believe the central authorities have been exerting the utmost efforts for their completion.

As the aforementioned request covers general major points alone, however, I think more detailed requests will be made when a real war is sure to come. Preparations are required to be made by all means will be marked as such, to which your special consideration is cordially invited. Especially, in view of the fact that satisfaction can never be attained in air strength, whether aircraft or personnel, your special encouragement is kindly requested to promote their production whenever opportunities arise.

2. TRAINING: Most of the training that has so far been planned and carried out deal with normal and fundamental circumstances, under which each unit is assigned a mission with the "*yogei sakusen*" as its main aim. Needless to say, the utmost efforts should be made to master it, as by so doing sufficient capabilities will be made so as to meet requirements needed in varied scenes of an engagement and a battle.

Considering a case in which this country goes to war with the U.S. and Great Britain as a practical problem, however, I think there may be no such case happening throughout the whole period of an expected war as all of the Combined Fleet closing in an enemy force, deploy, engage in a gunnery and torpedo duel, and finally charge into the enemy force in as gallant a way as possible. On the other hand, there may be cases in which various problems that have been somehow neglected in peace-time training in spite of their importance actually happen. In view of the current situation, therefore, I think earnest studies should be made of those problems.

Even when aforementioned normal and fundamental training is carried out, instead of being engrossed in overall tactical movements lacking precise consideration, unremitting studies should be made as to whether his fleet, squadron, division and ship display its fighting power to the utmost degree in every phase of maneuvers. (It will be an effective way for that end to let deviate shell firing and actual torpedo firing be included in every maneuver, and designate units at random during the maneuver to practice this training.)

If either of the British and Italian Fleets, which encountered in the Mediterranean Sea last year, had been fully trained from peace time to rouse up in the fighting spirit of "attacking enemy whenever it is sighted" and accustomed to a sudden firing, there ought not to have been a case in which none was sunk on either side in spite of the fact that the duel took place for 25 minutes. It should be regarded as a blunder that could not be allowed in our Navy.

3. OPERATIONAL POLICY: Studies on operational policy, too, have so far been based on one big *"yogei sakusen"* to be fought in a formal way. Review of numerous maneuvers held in the past, however, shows that the Japanese Navy has never won an overwhelming victory even once; they used to be suspended under such a situation that, if by letting things take their own course, there was much fear that our Navy might be dragged into gradual defeat.

It might be of some use only when collecting reference materials for determining whether we should go to war or not, but it should not be repeated by all means if and when a decision is made to go to war.

The most important thing we have to do first of all in a war with the U.S., I firmly believe, is to fiercely attack and destroy the U.S. main fleet at the outset of the war, so that the morale of the U.S. Navy and her people goes down to such an extent that it cannot be recovered.

Only then shall we be able to secure an invincible stand in key positions in East Asia, thus being able to establish and keep the East Asia Co-Prosperity Sphere.

Well then, what policy should we take to accomplish this?

4. OPERATIONAL PLAN THAT SHOULD BE ADOPTED AT THE OUTSET OF WAR: We learned many lessons in the Russo-Japanese War. Among them, those concerning the outset of war are as follows:

a. Japan had a chance to launch a surprise attack upon the enemy main force at the outset of war.

b. The morale of our destroyer force at the outset of war was not necessarily high (there being exceptions) and their skill was insufficient. This was most regrettable, about which serious reflection should be made.

c. Both the planning and execution of the blockade operation were insufficient.

In view of these successes and failures in the Russo-Japanese War, we should do our very best at the outset of a war with the U.S., and we should have a firm determination of deciding the fate of the war on its first day.

The outline of the operational plan is as follows:

a. In case of the majority of the enemy main force being in Pearl Harbor, to attack it thoroughly with our air force, and to blockade the harbor.

b. In case they are staying outside of the harbor, too, to apply the same attack method as the above.

The strength to be used in the aforementioned operation and their assignments:

a. 1st and 2nd Carrier Divisions (2nd Carrier Division alone in an unavoidable case) to launch a forced or surprise attack with all of their air strength, risking themselves on a moonlit night or at dawn.

b. One destroyer squadron to rescue survivors of carriers sunken by an enemy counterattack.

c. One submarine squadron to attack the enemy fleeing in confusion after closing in on Pearl Harbor (or other anchorages), and, if possible, to attack them at the entrance of Pearl Harbor so that the entrance may be blocked by sunken ships.

d. Supply force to assign several tankers with the force for refueling at sea.
 In case the enemy main force comes out from Hawaii before our attack and keeps on coming at us, to encounter it with all of our decisive force and destroy it in one stroke.

It is not easy to succeed in either case, but I believe we could be favored by God's blessing when all officers and men who take part in this operation have a firm determination of devoting themselves to their task, even sacrificing themselves.

The above is an operation with the U.S. main force as a main target, and an operation of launching a forestalling and surprise attack on enemy air forces in the Philippines and Singapore should definitely be made almost at the same time of launching attacks on Hawaii. However, if and when the U.S. main force is destroyed, I think, those untrained forces deploying in those southern districts will lose morale to such an extent that they could hardly be of much use in actual bitter fighting.

On the other hand, when we take a defensive stand toward the east and await the enemy coming on out of fear that such an operation against Hawaii is too risky, we cannot rule out the possibility that the enemy would dare to launch an attack upon our homeland to burn our capital city and other cities.

If such happens, our Navy will be subject to fierce attacks by the public, even when we succeed in the southern operation. It is evidently clear that such a development will result in lowering the morale of the nation to such an extent that it cannot be recovered. (It is not a laughing matter at all to recall how much confusion our nation was thrown into when the Russian fleet appeared in the Pacific in the Russo-Japanese War.)

I sincerely desire to be appointed C-in-C of an air fleet to attack Pearl Harbor so that I may personally command that attack force.

I firmly believe that there is a more suitable man to command the normal operations of the Grand Combined Fleet after that operation, as I previously stated my view verbally to your Minister.

Sincerely hoping that you will pass a clear judgment on my request to shift me to that post, so that I may be able to devote myself exclusively to my last duty to our country, I remain,*

Yours very sincerely,

LETTER FROM YAMAMOTO TO SHIMADA, WHO HAD RECENTLY BECOME NAVY MINISTER

24 October 1941

My dear Shimada:

Many thanks for the rare present which you kindly entrusted to the Adjutant of the Southern Expeditionary Fleet.

You have my sincere sympathy, as I can appreciate how complex must be the problems that are yours now in the wake of the recent important political change. I therefore consider myself extremely fortunate in being able to devote myself exclusively to the affairs of the fleet.

On the basis of the numerous chart exercises and table maneuvers that were held since last year, I have come to the conclusion that however smoothly the southern operations may progress, we are bound to suffer considerable losses in heavy cruisers and lesser types by the time the operations are completed under pressure; and in aircraft, we will probably expend two-thirds of its strength every day (and even of the remaining one-third, hardly any will be left in sound shape). The resulting situation, I am afraid, will find the Navy's strength stretched beyond the limit of its capacity. And in view of our very poor ability to replenish our air force, it will be virtually impossible for the Navy to meet the needs of the major sea operation that is likely to follow. After much study, therefore, I have come to the opinion that the only way is to have a powerful air force strike deep at the enemy's heart at the very beginning of the war and thus to deal a blow, material and moral, from which it will not be able to recover for some time.

Judging from Admiral Kimmel's† character and the recent trend of thought in the American Navy, it does not appear to be likely that the American Navy will necessarily confine itself to the strategy of a steady frontal offensive. And when I think what the strength of our homeland defense will be while the southern operations are in progress, I cannot but be truly apprehensive. Even if the southern

---

* This letter was published in the December 1964 issue of the Japanese Navy Officers' Association *Bulletin*. Chihaya gave the translation to Prange on 17 December 1963. It bears a note in Prange's handwriting: "This letter was written in Yamamoto's own hand with a Japanese brush. The only letter of Yamamoto kept secret until now."—Eds.

† Admiral Husband E. Kimmel, then C-in-C of the U.S. Fleet—Eds.

operations should develop to our advantage, I dread to think what our public (most of them being shallow-minded) will say of the Navy, if, in the course of these operations, enemy planes should suddenly raid Tokyo and Osaka and inflict even slight damage. We need only recall what happened at the time of the Russo-Japanese War.

I have recently heard that there are some elements in the General Staff who argue that since the air operation to be carried out immediately upon the outbreak of war was after all nothing more than a secondary operation in which the chance of success was about fifty-fifty, the use of the entire air force in such a venture was to risky to merit consideration.

But even more risky and illogical, it seems to me, is the idea of going to war against America, Britain and China following four years of exhausting operations in China and with the possibility of fighting Russia also having to be kept in mind and having, moreover, to sustain ourselves unassisted for ten years or more in a protracted war over an area several times more vast than the European war theater. If, in the face of such odds, we decide to go to war—or rather, are forced to do so by the trend of events—I, as the authority responsible for the fleet, can see little hope of success in any ordinary strategy. Indeed, I would feel compelled to resort to the combined strategies of *Okehazama, Hiyodorigoe,* and *Kawanaka-jima.**

These matters the senior staff officer of my fleet explained to the responsible authorities in Tokyo when he was there recently and obtained their approval, but there seem to be some who have misgivings as to my character and ability as supreme commander. The fact is that I do not think myself qualified for the post of C-in-C of the Grand Fleet; and besides, there is no time to think of one's own interests in a time of such national emergency as the present. That is why (late in November of 1940) I asked the Chief of the General Staff and Navy Minister Oikawa to give this post to Admiral Yonai.† Please dispose of the various problems from the broad point of view and having regard to what I have set forth above.

N.B. 1. Last November I recommended that in the event of the Combined Fleet and the First Fleet being separated, Admiral Yonai should be given command of the Combined Fleet by all means, for I would be satisfied to take over the First Fleet. (Such a move, moreover, would pave the way for Admiral Yonai's eventual elevation to the post of Chief of the General Staff, which step I also recommended.)

Admiral Oikawa agreed with me. And the Prince,‡ too, consented to the idea of having Admiral Yonai returned to active service for a post on the Supreme War Council or as his own successor; but the Combined Fleet, he said, must be commanded by Yamamoto.

---

* Those are the names of famous battles in Japanese history in which the warriors Nobunaga, Yoshitsune and Kenshin defeated their opponents by surprise attacks —Trans.

† Admiral Mitsumasa Yonai, at the time retired from active duty. Yamamoto had served as his vice minister when Yonai was Navy Minister, and the two men entertained a deep mutual admiration —Eds.

‡ In November 1940 the chief of the Naval General Staff was a member of the Imperial family, Prince Fushimi —Eds.

2. When, at the time of the revisions of operational plans for the Combined Fleet, I caused air operations in the initial stage of the war to be included therein, the state of my mind was that this operation was so difficult and dangerous that we must be prepared to risk complete annihilation. (At the time I was also thinking of having one carrier division jump into the fray accompanied by one destroyer squadron.) And if the air force should not be daring enough to undertake this operation, I was resolved to ask for the command of the Air Fleet and to carry out the operation myself with the forces which would then be under my direct command. In such event, too, I thought that Admiral Yonai would have to be asked to take over the Combined Fleet.

Since I have formulated the above plan as a last resort because, owing to my lack of adequate experience and ability, I have no confidence in a safe and steady frontal offensive, I shall be only too glad to be relieved whenever a qualified successor is available.

War with America and Britain should still be avoidable when the overall situation is taken into consideration, and every effort should of course be made to that end. But I wonder whether Japan, having been driven into the present situation, has the courage and strength necessary to make such a change of attitude now. I fear with trepidation that the only thing that can save the situation now is the Imperial decision.

With best wishes for your good health,

> Yours cordially,
> Isoroku Yamamoto

> 19 December 1941

Dear Admiral Sankichi Takahashi:

It was my great honor to have been given your excellency's congratulatory letter upon our early victory in the war. But I think much could not have been done unless the traditional spirit of the Imperial Navy, which my preceding Commanders-in-Chief, including your excellency, had long built up, was fully displayed to save our country's crisis. I think I owe you very much in this respect.

The plan of launching a surprise attack on Pearl Harbor at the outset of a war to give a fatal blow on the enemy fleet was decided in December of last year, when the fleet strategy was revised. Since then, everything possible had been studied or tried to make it possible. Especially in the Nagumo force, which actually undertook the attack, those concerned from Nagumo down to the men exerted themselves to make the plan possible; it was not before the fall that aerial torpedoing in shallow waters of only 10-odd meters was made possible with the great help of the technicians concerned, and it was also only in last August and September that the technique of horizontal bombing had been improved so that one hit might be expected from nine attacking bombers. Until then, it had made little progress from the days when your excellency took command of a carrier division.

What made me worry more than anything, however, was the fact that the time of our going to war was called off by one month, a fact which pressed me with intensified fear that refueling in the northern route, the only possible route to take, would no longer be possible to determine the fate of the operation.

As it turned out, however, I should say we were blessed by the War God, since a wide high pressure zone, the last one appearing in that district in this year, prevailed in the district extending as long as 2,000 miles. It was the first such phenomenon since 1938, which enabled refueling at sea. (Though a detailed report on this point is not yet available, I conclude as above.)

Such good luck, together with negligence on the part of the arrogant enemy, enabled us to launch a successful surprise attack. Especially of note is the fact that the actual hit rate of aerial torpedoing and bombing was upped 50 percent compared with that of training. I can't help but conclude that such an achievement was beyond the reach of human beings, and the loyal fliers must have been inspired by the soul of the Emperor, who graciously worried about the outcome of this attempt. I am deeply impressed by this development.

Some of the above apparently should be classified as "confidential," but I dared to write them, believing that you must be glad to hear them, as your excellency, once as C-in-C of the Combined Fleet and also as CO of a carrier division, exerted yourself to improve the skill of our Navy to the present level.

I cannot understand, from the viewpoint of common sense, not to speak of the strategic point of view, why the British Fleet made such a movement. Such a tragic fate ought to have been theirs, since they either made light of our strength and ability or lacked ability to make a correct strategic judgment.

Be that as it may, least expected was the fact that 51 medium land-bombers launched a successful attack on a fully-protected enemy fleet without any help from a surface force or fighters, and sustained a minor loss of only three bombers, and even those were shot down after releasing a torpedo. I believe this fact should be taken into serious consideration in planning future war preparations.

On the other hand, I don't think it is time to tell the full account of the midget submarines which penetrated the harbor, but at least it is certain that a radio dispatch saying "successful surprise attack" was received from one of them and also that a battleship was sunk at a time when there was no aerial attack. When thinking of the fact that those daring young men, including young officers who had graduated from the Naval Academy only less than one year before, penetrated an enemy base in spite of darkness and accomplished such a success, I think I should not say such a big word that the youngsters in these days are not a match to. . . . This is another point in which I was deeply impressed by this operation.

I well realize that it will be long before we reach a successful conclusion of the war and there are numerous difficulties lying ahead of us. But, as mentioned, the burning spirit and the skill of those young officers and others are worthy of appreciation and respect. Therefore, I am now thinking that we may be able to meet His Majesty's wish when we exert ourselves to fulfill our mission.

Thanking you again for your kind letter, I am also asking you to teach me anything you happen to think of in the future. Hoping you take good care of yourself in the cold winter, I remain,

> Yours very sincerely,
> Isoroku Yamamoto

22 December 1941

My dear Yoshiki Takamura

Thank you for your letter. That we could defeat the enemy at the outbreak of the war was because they were unguarded and also they made light of us. "Danger comes soonest when it is despised" and "don't despise a small enemy" are really important matters. I think they can be applied not only to wars but to routine matters.

I hope you study hard, taking good care of yourself.

Good-bye,
Isoroku Yamamoto

April 1942

Dear Mitsuari Takamura

Gladly I received your letters of 25 March and 4 April. With regard to your request of 25 March, I made several writings which were sent to you on about 3 April. (In order not to reveal the location of fleets, mail is to be dealt with in post offices on board ships where they are kept about five days and then sent to post offices on land.)

Please accept my congratulations of your second son, Yoshiki-kun, having entered the Fisheries School with top grades. I hope he will make a big success in the future.

With completion of the Philippines operation, the First Phase Operation is to be generally finished as far as the Navy is concerned. From now on, it will be hard to achieve such a big success as the public expects. Depending upon commencement and outcome of the air operation in the northern area, I think we would face a considerably difficult situation.

The past operations were bright, but it can be said that we achieved such a success because the enemy we met was weak. The subsequent operations will be serious, in which both sides will fight in earnest. Having fully realized our real strength, the enemy will not make mistakes, therefore the situation will be very serious.

I moved my headquarters to the *Yamato* in February. The name of the *Yamato* may be known to the public, but in order not to cause too much attention my address is set as "Combined Fleet Headquarters, c/o Kure Post Office." You may use the name of the *Yamato* instead of the *Nagato*. (Mail addressed to the *Nagato* reaches our hands without fail.)

The *Yamato*'s characteristics being military top secret, she is off limits to visitors. At first glance, she looks little different from the *Nagato* class, but their real fighting strength might not be decided unless they participate in a real engagement. Her fighting strength is supposed to be about two to five times that of the *Nagato*.

I suppose that with little snow remaining, you have a pleasant season full of bright spring all over your place. Wishing good health to your family,

Isoroku Yamamoto

P.S. I am feeling funny, having been informed my answers failed to reach you. I do not think I have been rather lazy in sending letters to you. Somebody said that it might be because someone is taking Yamamoto's letters as amulets. If so, this is quite a trouble for me. By the way, I tell you I was never angry with you.

Toward the end of December 1942

Dear Mitsuari Takamura

Thank you for your letter of 25 November. It is a year since the war broke out. It seems to me that there are some who are weary of war, while the majority can't be in real earnest. If that should be a groundless fear on my part, nothing would please me more.

Since support of the family is, as you wrote in your letter, a very important mission assigned to those of the nation who are not engaged at the battle front, I would like to ask you to concentrate your whole mind upon support of your big family rather than seeking such business as carrying cargo at Guadalcanal Island.

Although it might be necessary to mobilize all men able to work so as to let them work more effectively, it cannot be done unless those who think themselves experts by devoting themselves to speeches and movements—whom I blame as not being in earnest—try to ponder on completely and reform themselves in their minds and abilities. I therefore hope you will devote yourself to accomplishing your big job as the boss of your family.

It seems likely that even Hokkaido will be often subjected to rains of bombs next year and some of the preparations and training for such an eventuality are hard on old persons, women and children.

I wish good luck to your family,

Isoroku Yamamoto

CHAPTER 10

Two Letters Written by Admiral Yamamoto That Were Considered Sufficient to Indicate His Personal Character* (12 March 1947)

A LETTER FOR REAR ADM. TEIKICHI HORI, WHO HAD BEEN ONE OF ADMIRAL YAMAMOTO'S INTIMATE FRIENDS, DATED 11 OCTOBER 1941:

Many thanks for your kindness which you gave me at the time of my departure. I have received your letter which you sent to me from Ofuna.

1. I beg your favor of looking after my dependents.

2. It seems to me that the situation has already reached its critical point. It would be lamentable indeed for us to give up all hope, presuming this situation as a fact of "God's will be done." However, it would be nonsense so late now to accuse somebodies of the responsibilities of leading Japan into this situation.

In Japan today, the circumstance seems to be such that only the Emperor pays his utmost concerns about the situation, and also that he would be the only and the last man who could check the tide. But even his decision, if made, would be difficult to be effective in present Japan. I cannot but help thinking so.

3. My present situation is very strange. Because I have been assigned the mission, entirely against my private opinion, and also I am expected to do my best. Alas, maybe, this is my fate.

4. Although from the beginning of this year grave accidents succeeded one after another, owing to not serious errors, I have managed to tide over those difficulties.

---

* I got these letters from some sources that are going to introduce these letters in the Military Tribunal for the Far East as documents for the defense side. I was requested not to reveal these letters beforehand before they would be introduced in the Military Tribunal for the Far East. So that it is desirable that you would take this situation into your consideration —Trans.

A LETTER FOR MR. SHIGEHARU ENOMOTO, WHO HAD BEEN A
SECRETARY OF THE NAVY DEPARTMENT FOR MANY YEARS, DATED
17 FEBRUARY 1941:

I agree with your opinion concerning how to get into a war. But it is a problem, to what extent those persons who were so beside themselves with joy, making out such a thing as the Tri-partite Pact, would stick to their own opinions in the hour of need.

To me there is a smell of changing the present post; however, it causes me some confusion in calculating which is better for me, either to attempt to improve the naval organization in Tokyo or to continue to make the fleet as in the pink as ever.

I expect to be in Tokyo by the latter part of April if anything does not hamper me.

It is still so cold that I hope you will take care of yourself. Many thanks for your kindness.

(End)

CHAPTER 11

"Admiral Yamamoto's Sweetheart"

T HIS ARTICLE, subtitled "The War God Was a Human Being, Too," appeared in the *Weekly Asahi*'s issue of 18 April 1954—the eleventh anniversary of Yamamoto's death. According to Masataka Chihaya, who translated the article for Prange, it "caused a sensation in Japan." He sent along a few clippings from Japanese-language newspapers that gave some reactions. They seem to have been divided into three schools of thought: First, as the subtitle indicated, some found it touching to discover that the revered Yamamoto had an emotional side to his life; second, there was resentment that Miss Kawai had gone public and thus cast a shadow over the "beautiful memory" of the admiral; third, sympathy for Mrs. Yamamoto, who had had to go to work to support her family and who now had the humiliation of having her husband's infidelity exposed to all Japan.

The article makes clear that Yamamoto made no effort to keep his association with Miss Kawai secret from his close naval associates, and indeed that they treated her with courtesy and a certain respect. All judgments aside, we believe that Yamamoto is so central to the Japanese side of the Pacific War, and especially to Pearl Harbor and Midway, that anything that sheds a little light on his personality and mentality is worth knowing.

Chihaya not only translated the article, he visited Miss Kawai to check it out with her. As the reader will see, there was one incident that she denied.

There is a Japanese-style restaurant named *Seseragi* (which means in Japanese a stream current) not far away from the bustling district at Numazu city in Shizuoka Prefecture. Every early morning and night voices chanting Buddhist sutras are heard from that house. A good-looking hostess of that house is praying for the late Admiral Isoroku Yamamoto in front of his picture and mortuary tablet. She is Chiyoko Kawai, aged 51, who once lived to love the late admiral.

The late Admiral Yamamoto's sweetheart was once a geisha girl from the Shimbashi circle in Tokyo. Born in 1903 in Nagoya City, she had tasted the bitterness of life in her younger days. She even gave herself up to become a concubine, but no sense of love occurred between them. When she was 25 years old, her parents died in succession, which was such a shock that she tried suicide, but in vain. Finally she settled down to living as a geisha girl from the Shimbashi circle in Tokyo.

In the summer of 1933 she attended a party held at a Japanese restaurant named *Kinsui* in Tsukiji in Tokyo. At a guest seat of the party sat a cropped-headed man in a slightly worn-out black and white striped suit. Though he did not drink sake at all, he chatted cheerfully with nearby persons. When he tried to lift the lid of the soup bowl in front of him, he could not do so in spite of his efforts.

Chiyoko, who was serving beside him, happened to notice that his index and long fingers of his left hand were lost from their roots. Surprised in noticing it, she approached him and suggested that she help him. With cool, sharp eyes, the man refused her help, saying, "I don't want help for my own business," and lifted the lid by himself. Chiyoko thought him a disgusting fellow. The man was Rear Adm. Isoroku Yamamoto, then 51 years old, who was then commanding officer of the 1st Carrier Division.

About one year thereafter . . . in June of 1934 Yamamoto was transferred to the Naval General Staff to become a member of the Preparatory Committee for the Naval Armament Limitations Treaty. He was slated to be a delegate to its preparatory negotiations to be held in London.

One evening Chiyoko happened to see that man at a certain party. Though in uniform, he was undoubtedly the same man whom she saw about one year before. When she told him that she had seen him before, he bluntly said, "I have seldom been here; I don't remember you." Even when she told him about the lid of a soup bowl, his response was as abrupt as before, saying only, "I scarcely remember such an event or you either." Chiyoko thought what a hard-to-handle man he was.

A couple of days later Chiyoko met Yamamoto again. Next to Yamamoto sat Zengo Yoshida, who was Yamamoto's classmate and later became Navy Minister. Yoshida happened to ask Chiyoko whether she liked cheese. When she replied, "Yes, very much," Yamamoto said, "Well, I'll treat you. Please come to the Imperial Hotel at noon tomorrow." "I have hardly ever heard this man say such a thing," Yoshida said, making a joke of it. "You must go."

Though she scarcely believed that Yamamoto's remark was more than a mere joke, she went to the Imperial Hotel the next day, only to find that the admiral was there waiting for her in the dining room. Soon a cocktail and a dish full of cheese were served, but nothing else. Yamamoto did not drink a cocktail at all. Without many words, Chiyoko and Yamamoto ate cheese and departed.

Yamamoto came to sympathize with Chiyoko after he heard about her life from Yoshida and from Kiyoshi Hasegawa, then the Navy Vice Minister, both of whom were acquainted with Chiyoko. Unblessed in his family life, he himself, too, was a lonely man in various respects. As such, he had been a misogynist in some respects. But since the cheese treat both of them had suddenly become intimate, and by 20 September, when Yamamoto left the homeland for London, Yamamoto had changed from calling her Umeryu (her geisha name) to Ume-chan, and finally to Chiyoko.

On 12 February 1935 Yamamoto returned to the homeland. Complicated was the mind of this man who returned home after vainly resisting limitation of strength, parity of strength and abolishment of offensive strength, including carrier strength, in the preliminary negotiations.

Public opinion was insistent upon abolishing both the Washington and London Conferences. In some respect, his dispatch as a delegate to the conference was nothing but a formal step, so his arduous efforts in the conference appeared to have ended in his own game without an opponent. Toward the end of 1934, while he was still in London, Japan's intention of withdrawing from the treaty was announced.

About three months after he returned home, Isoroku Yamamoto, now promoted to the rank of Vice Admiral, sent the following letter to Chiyoko:

> When I went to London, I was fired with high spirits and determination to hold myself responsible for the fate of the country. Besides, my passion burned with the excitement of seeing the rapid development of my intimacy with you.
>
> But, seeing that even some persons in the Navy, not to speak of the general public, were gradually showing a much too indifferent attitude toward the London conference for which I exerted myself so much, I couldn't help feeling very unpleasant, as it seemed to me I was being used just as an instrument. At the same time, being conscious of my worthlessness, I couldn't help feeling lonely.
>
> Contrary to my previous feeling to console you for your lonely life, I am now inclined to be embraced in your arms. But I am ashamed to show you weakness as an individual, and well realizing that such would betray your trust in me, I merely feel very lonely.
>
> As I am now writing to you of such a feeling for the first time, please keep this only in your mind.

Yamamoto keenly felt that only elder seniors, intimate friends and Chiyoko greeted him back home with the same attitude as at the time of his departure from the homeland.

His letter to Chiyoko in September read as follows: "Last night I had a dream. I myself cannot understand why I did so. In the dream I drove with you at the coast of Nice in South Europe. I thought how wonderful it would be if it were true."

In his writings there was no hero or war god at all, only a fresh feeling rare for his age of over fifty.

In August 1939 Isoroku Yamamoto was appointed the Combined Fleet Commander in Chief, and in November of the following year promoted to the rank of full admiral. In the meantime, Chiyoko discarded her career of geisha girl and managed a Japanese-style restaurant by the name of *Umenoshima*. She also bought a small house in Shiba to receive Yamamoto in her own house.

In late November 1941 when the international relationship between the United States and Japan was tense, Yamamoto, then on board the flagship *Nagato* as the Combined Fleet Commander in Chief, asked Chiyoko to come down to Miyajima. The couple spent a good time in strolling the tranquil surroundings of the island. Occasionally fawns came close to them and belled "kwu kwu." It was a quiet stay of two days on the island.

Several days later Yamamoto unexpectedly came up to Tokyo on 1 December and spent the busiest time in official business until he left there for his ship on the 4th. Even in his busy time, however, he did not forget to visit her.

In the afternoon of the 4th, they went out to take a walk on the Ginza. Yamamoto, who was very fond of flowers, bought a bouquet of roses at Senbikiya, a famed florist on the Ginza, and gave it to Chiyoko. When he came to see her, he used to bring a bouquet with him.*

But Yamamoto left Tokyo for his ship, leaving behind his words, "Watch for the time when the petals of these flowers fall." In his letter sent from the *Nagato* on 5 December he wrote to Chiyoko:

> As my trip this time was only a three-days stay, and I kept myself so busy that I couldn't have leisure time with you and, besides, I couldn't stay with you even a single night, to my regret. I want you to forgive me. Even so, I think I was lucky to see you even for a short while every day during my stay there. Although I wanted to leave your place in a quiet state of mind, it was my regret, too, that we could not go even to Owaricho in the Ginza.
>
> Have the roses blossomed out completely? By the time when the petals of those flowers fall, what will happen? Please take good care of yourself, and send my best regards to all. Send me your picture as soon as possible. Good-bye.

It was on 7 December that petals of the roses placed on her mirror stand fell. Chiyoko, who learned of Japan's going to war by the radio broadcast on the morning of the 8th, was reminded of Yamamoto's words when he left Tokyo.

In a letter sent to Chiyoko on 28 December, when people throughout Japan were wild with the success of the Pearl Harbor attack, the following portion can be seen: "Many letters from various persons are pouring into my place, but I am longing only for letters from you night and day. Have you already sent me your picture?"

In a letter dated 8 January, he wrote as follows:

> Thank you for your letters of 30 December and 1 January. Since your letter of the 30th stated that it was 10 feet long† I actually measured it to find out that it was about eight inches short of the mentioned length. So I thought I had better ask you to write me about that length more, when your letter of 1 January reached me to make me so happy that I said *kwu kwu* (bell of fawn).

In January, four letters, dated the 8th, 12th, 19th and 27th respectively were sent to Chiyoko.

On 19 March, Chiyoko was attacked with pleurisy and ordered to keep herself absolutely quiet. At one time she was so bad that she had to be supported by oxygen. On 18 April, when Tokyo was first air raided, she wrote on the entry of her diary as follows: "Helped in my hard-labored breathing and got up in spite of myself. Abandoned by doctors, there is no other way but to leave myself in the hand of destiny. Sad indeed."

On 10 May the Combined Fleet returned to Kure. Yamamoto immediately gave her a long-distance call. "Repeatedly called up from Kure," she wrote in her diary, "but hardly spoke by telephone due to much coughing. Only lost patience with tears coming up endlessly."

---

* This episode was denied by Chiyoko, when the translator checked it up with her in April 1954 — Trans.

† Some Japanese letter paper is rolled, so it can be measured by the length when written in letters — Trans.

In the entry of the 13th, she wrote, "Left for Kure by a night train, firmly resolving in my mind to reach there even at the risk of my own life. In spite of the worries of a nurse, I, with little physical strength to get up on a bed, was helped to board a train."

At 1600 of the 14th, she arrived at Kure. At the station platform she was welcomed by Yamamoto in plain clothes, disguised with glasses and mask.*[3] He put Chiyoko, now slim and light, on his back and walked through the station to *jinrikisha.*†

In the day's entry she wrote, "At the Kure station my darling awaited me. I was wild with joy. My trip there was well worth while. My thrilling body was carried in his arms and then taken to *Kikukawa* hotel by car. Having difficulties in breathing, I had repeatedly been given injections, and it was only with this pain that I could be there. Now I feel I wouldn't regret to die."

In the next day's entry after she left his place, she wrote. "I hated to bid farewell to you at that station. I wished I could get off the train and remain beside you. When the train started to move, I hated to loose our firmly held hands. Though I was so weak that I could not hold your hand strongly, you were very, very strong in holding my hands. Please take me as far as we could go together, holding my hands."

But the couple's hands would never be held together again. Shortly before the sortie for Midway, his letter of 27 May was sent to Chiyoko from his flagship *Yamato,* which read:

> How Chiyoko felt on the way back home after coming to see me with all the stamina your weak body could muster, I can easily imagine. But your spiritual strength in overcoming illness day by day is amazing indeed.
>
> I will exert myself to fulfill my last duty for the country, as well as for Chiyoko who is fighting all evils in my behalf. Now I wish, if I could, to desert everything in the world to live alone with you. I will make an early sortie in the morning of the 29th to command the whole fleet at sea for about three weeks, though I expect that there probably wouldn't be much fun.
>
> As tonight is the night of the naval anniversary day,‡ there will be a celebration from now, so I say good-bye to you. Take good care of yourself.
>
> > I don't know how many times I have called Chiyoko today
> > With hot kisses on your lovely picture
> > Thus today has passed, too.§

Night of 27 May

The Midway Sea Battle fought in early June ended in a disastrous defeat for Yamamoto.

---

* Probably a *masuku,* a mask-like device many Japanese wore at times over their noses and mouths to ward off infection or to avoid spreading colds —Eds.

† When the translator interviewed Chiyoko in late April 1954, she confirmed this fact —Trans.

‡ 27 May was the anniversary of the battle of Tsushima in the Russo-Japanese War, celebrated annually as Japan's Navy Day —Eds.

§ In Japanese, this is a brief poem. Yamamoto enjoyed writing such short verses and a number of them have survived —Eds.

As it is said that the secrecy of the operations and movements seems to have been leaked out to the public and foreign countries, sending enclosed letters from the fleet has been suspended for the time being. That's why I sent a brief note written on a card to you the other day. I suppose you have thought it strange, wondering what happened to me. (21 June)

Yamamoto's letter of 2 April 1943, which also enclosed a clipping of his hair cut on board the flagship *Yamato*, was brought to Chiyoko's place. It was a letter written just before he left for the inspection tour of the southern front two months after the fall of Guadalcanal Island. As a matter of fact, it turned out to be his last letter to Chiyoko.

Your letters of 27 and 28 March reached me yesterday, 1 April. Thank you very much for your treatment of my Chief of Staff, [Shigeru] Fujii, Watanabe, Kanaoka and Sanagi,* though I hated to bother you so much. All of them were very pleased and one after another they told me about your house and *Yamaguchi*.† Their stories made me feel that I myself had returned home for a while and enjoyed a visit with Chiyoko.

Fujii told me with admiration that you were a very thoughtful woman as you treated him well in spite of his bad manners of coming to your house very late after drinking, and moreover you left the room thoughtfully when he began to talk about official matters with Kanaoka. So I told him that you were the very one to whom I admitted I could not make lead as well as to the Emperor, and asked him whether he was agreeable with my view or not. Then he admitted he gave in, no matter how proud I was of you, and all of us laughed joyfully. I was very happy indeed.

As I told you, I am now in excellent condition with the blood pressure equivalent to persons in their thirties. The numb portion of my hands was a very small part of the fingertip of the third and little fingers of my right hand, though very slight, but it has been completely cured after I was given forty injections of vitamins B and C combined by the fleet chief doctor. (Though I told them that it had not been completely cured.) So I want you to get rid of worry about it.

And I am going to the front line tomorrow, though for a short while. The Chief of Staff, Kuroshima and Watanabe will accompany me. Such being the case, I want you to understand that I am not going to write to you for about two weeks. I will go in high spirits since I have heard about you. The coming 4 April is my birthday. I am delighted to be going to launch attacks upon the enemy a little bit.

Also enclosed in the envelope was the following Japanese poem written by him:

If I think of you as ordinary passion dictates,
Could I have had a dream of only you every night?

Imperial General Headquarters announced at 1500 on 21 May 1943 as follows: "Combined Fleet Commander-in-Chief Isoroku Yamamoto engaged with the enemy on 18 April 1943, while commanding the overall operations at the front line, and was killed in action on board a plane."

When he died, he was sixty. Chiyoko was informed of this sad news the day before the announcement was made, and wrote in that day's entry as follows:

* These were members of Yamamoto's staff —Eds.
† A famed Japanese drinking place —Trans.

May 20. The face of Mr. Hori,* whom I had known well, looked somewhat stiff this morning, and I listened to him with a tense feeling pressing upon me. His words! "I am very sorry to tell this sad and unexpected news . . ." What a big surprise to hear of the death of Isoroko Yamamoto! I was shocked and couldn't do anything, even look up to Mr. Hori's face. Everything is finished. His death sent me into bottomless sorrow.

May 21. I ought to have resumed readiness of mind, but in vain. I thought I had better confirm his death by listening to the radio news at 1500 hours by myself. Couldn't I believe Mr. Hori's words? No, I don't want to believe it. How wretched this woman's mind is!

May 22. My heart still trembled a great deal so I couldn't feel rested at all. I felt I was abandoned by everything in the world.

May 23. His remains were said to make a sad return to the homeland today. I had waited for this day with oppressing sorrow, but had no courage to get out of the house and welcome his remains. After other people went out of the house to welcome his voiceless return on a street, I opened the windows of the upstairs room with a remaining maid and I called to his soul at the window, saying in mind, "Your soul, please don't go anywhere and come down here where Chiyoko is waiting for you." The soul of my darling must have returned to my place, I believed. He must have been tired out.

May 24. I went to the *Suikosha*† as the general public was allowed today to burn incense in front of his remains. When I proceeded to the altar, I felt my hands and legs go cold and numb, but managed to be able to pray in front of his remains with all my effort.

At night, Commander Watanabe‡ came to see me. When he told me about things as much as possible, his face was pale with deep sorrow. He told me that, as he carried the ashes of that late admiral past near my home, he unconsciously lifted up the small box of ashes. I could appreciate his feelings.

June 1. Another sorrow depressed me further, when Mr. Hori came and took away with him all the letters sent from my darling.

June 5. State Funeral. The night passed quietly in bottomless sorrow. Tonight will remain fresh in my mind forever as the saddest memory of my life.

June 30. The month of June has passed in sorrow, and I feel I have to flight against the misunderstanding and cold treatment of the public.

What, then, did she mean by "misunderstanding and cold treatment of the public?"

On 4 June, the day before the State Funeral of the late admiral, out of the numerous letters sent from the late admiral to Chiyoko for the past ten years, which piled up as high as one cubic foot, those letters since 1941 were brought to the Navy Ministry by Mr. Hori. About one year later, they were returned to her again by Mr. Hori, but she was given instruction of the Navy Ministry to burn all of them. Leaving aside 19 letters, which contained many reminiscences to her, all of the remaining were burnt to ashes. The flames and purple smoke arising from the burning letters still remain fresh in her mind.

But this was not the only persecution she suffered before and after the State Funeral. A certain naval officer called her to the Navy Ministry and demanded that

---

* Rear Adm. Teikichi Hori, a close friend of Yamamoto—Eds.

† The Navy Club—Trans.

‡ Comdr. Yasuji Watanabe of Yamamoto's staff was a prime favorite of the admiral, and it was only fitting that Watanabe be given the sad honor of conveying Yamamoto's ashes —Eds.

she commit suicide by the time of the State Funeral. Some of those who knew her also suggested that she do so. Their request was based upon their desire that no relationship with a woman should be found around the newly-erected God of War.

More than once Chiyoko, too, thought of killing herself, after being informed of the death of her darling. She wanted to do so because of her deep love for her beloved admiral. There were nights when she could not sleep at all, only gazing at the ceiling of her bedroom. She also tried to get medicine to use in killing herself from a doctor acquaintance, but in vain.

In March 1944, she rented her house to Captain Watanabe, who was once a staff officer of the late admiral, and evacuated to a sanatorium at Shizuura of Numazu City. The sanatorium was a villa of the late Eizo Shimizu, and a portion was utilized as a naval installation. Giving a helping hand to the Shimizu family, Chiyoko met the day of Japan's defeat, but her life since then was not an easy one.

After the war, Chiyoko, who had been very fond of writing, lost even the will to continue writing her diary. All that remained to her was a strong will to live in the hard life. Thanks to mild climate, her health had been recovered, so she settled there after building a Japanese-style restaurant about four years ago with the money she had saved in Tokyo.

"It might have been rather fortunate for Yamamoto to be killed in action in that manner," Chiyoko said quietly, "if considering a possibility that he might have lived till the end of the war and been hanged as a war criminal. So I no longer feel sorrow. I am now thinking about living strongly, keeping beloved Yamamoto's memories in my mind." Choked with tears, Chiyoko thus read her old diary which was full of her reminiscences of the late Admiral Isoroku Yamamoto.

PART III

Pearl Harbor

OF PARTICULAR interest in this section are the war diaries of the 1st Destroyer Squadron, the 3rd Battleship Division, and the 5th Carrier Division. It is most regrettable that the diaries of the 1st and 2nd Carrier Divisions are not available, but these were lost when the carriers *Akagi, Kaga, Soryu,* and *Hiryu* sank at Midway. The existing diaries are especially valuable, being contemporary records untainted by hindsight.

The diary of the 1st Destroyer Squadron is maddeningly sparse. Like most ships' logs, it seems almost studiedly devoid of any item of human interest. However, it includes a complete record of all messages received aboard the flagship, the CL *Abukuma*. It is significant that those from the homeland came by telegram, those from within the task force by signal—another indication, if more were needed, that the task force maintained complete radio silence on its voyage to Hawaii.

The diary of the 5th Carrier Division is more detailed, as was only to be expected, because its aircraft took an active part in the operation. This organization also lists the messages received and shows that all originating in the task force went by signal. It closes with a listing of the exact position as of noon each day, thus leaving an exact record of the task force's course from 1 through 31 December 1941.

The 3rd Battleship Division's diary is the most interesting, for whoever kept it was not afraid to let his enthusiasm break through the straitjacket of official form, and it gives a good narrative account of events. This it follows with a day-to-day account of position, weather, training, and refueling from 1 to 24 December when the division arrived at Hashirajima. Notable is the comment: "The absolute radio silence of the task force did not leak anything."

The human touches missing in the war diaries are amply provided by Admiral Kusaka's book, *Rengo Kantai* (Combined Fleet). We have no doubt of its reliability, for it was written while war memories were fresh, and Kusaka was a man of the highest integrity who would scorn to embroider. His account of the planning, training, and execution of the operation dovetails with the accounts of others such as Genda. Prange interviewed Kusaka many times, considered him a close friend and a very reliable source. Like others involved, Kusaka stressed the maintenance of total radio silence on the outward voyage and, indeed, was worried when they had to break it briefly on the way home. Also of especial historical interest is his defense of the decision to return to Japan immediately after the attack as planned and not to launch another strike or search for the American carriers.

Another account of the adventure full of human interest is the Chigusa diary. Here was an officer at a much lower level of command than Kusaka, yet the two had many points in common, such as their strict devotion to duty, their concern for the welfare of their men, and their determination to keep the eastward course "a secret to everyone but God." The essay concerning the role of the submarines in the Pearl Harbor plan was prepared by an experienced submariner, Capt. Tatsuwaka Shibuya, and we know of no better account. Of particular historical interest is the study of Operation Hawaii that the Japanese Navy prepared in the summer of 1942.

CHAPTER 12

Rengo Kantai (Combined Fleet), Extracts

Ryunosuke Kusaka

V ICE ADM. RYUNOSUKE KUSAKA had a long and distinguished career in
the Imperial Japanese Navy. After the usual training assignments as a
junior officer, he specialized in gunnery and served aboard the battleships and destroyers. With his appointment to the staff at Kasumigaura Air
Corps in late 1926, his career took another turn, and he became closely
associated with naval aviation, although he never became a pilot. In 1936, as
a captain, he skippered the light carrier *Hosho,* and after two important staff
assignments became captain of the carrier *Akagi* in 1936. One year later he
was promoted to rear admiral and served successively as commander of the
4th Combined Air Corps and of the 24th Air Squadron.

When the 1st Air Fleet was formed on 15 April 1941, Kusaka was the
logical choice for its chief of staff. From that experience came this excellent
account of the attack on Pearl Harbor. After the Japanese disaster at Midway,
he served throughout the war in key positions including chief of staff of the
Combined Fleet. On 1 May 1944 he became a vice admiral.

Just as from Genda's accounts one receives a clear picture of the operational planning for Pearl Harbor, from Kusaka one sees the problems of
command and logistics. He stresses the overriding importance of intelligence
concerning the American fleet and installations in Hawaii and emphasizes that
without refueling the operation could not have taken place. He also underlines
the necessity for the strictest security, with total radio silence. As a minor
point, it is interesting to note that Kusaka, aboard a large carrier, found the
voyage out fairly calm, while the diary of Chigusa, aboard a destroyer,
records a rough voyage. These reminiscences were first published by the
Mainichi Shimbum in April 1952.

Part I. Surprise Attack or Sneak Attack?
———————————— Pearl Harbor Attack ————————————

CHAPTER I. STEALTHILY PLANNED
SINCE TEN MONTHS BEFORE.

Air Force's Skill Very Much Improved

In early October 1941, when the relationship between Japan and the United States was being intensified day by day, I took a hurried trip on board a carrier bomber from Kanoya in Kyushu to Tokyo. By that time the secret plan of the Pearl Harbor attack had already been decided in our Japanese Navy to meet an emergency. My main business in going to Tokyo was to make the final settlement with the central authorities on the air force to be used in this plan, and also to urge them to place eight oilers under the command of the 1st Air Fleet as early as possible. . . .

In mid-April of that year, the 1st Air Fleet was inaugurated for the first time in the Japanese Navy, and I was appointed its first chief of staff. . . .

The inauguration of the 1st Air Fleet indicated one step which the naval authorities wanted to materialize after realizing the importance of the air forces in operations, and also it was one of the steps that were taken to cope with the imminent crisis between two countries. By that time carrier divisions consisting of two carriers as the nucleus had been placed under the command of the Combined Fleet and participated in peace-time training as one operational unit. . . .

Fateful Booklet Shown

One day soon after I was appointed chief of staff of the 1st Air Fleet, I paid a visit to Rear Adm. Shigeru Fukudome at his office in the Imperial General Headquarters. He was then the Chief of its First Bureau. He was one class senior to me at Etajima. When I met him, he pushed a booklet on his desk toward me as if throwing it at me, and asked me to read it. On its cover I read the title "Pearl Harbor Attack Plan," but its contents mostly consisted of information gathered about Pearl Harbor. When I told him that "this is considerably precise information on the enemy situation, but we cannot launch an operation with this plan alone, because it is not an operational plan," he replied bluntly, "I want you to materialize it by your hand." He seemed to me to have something very important firmly in his mind.

Originally it was the annual procedure of the Imperial Headquarters to draw up the annual operational plan for that year to submit it to the Imperial decision. The general outline of the Japanese operations against the United States thus decided called for the initial invasion of the Philippines and the simultaneous landing on Guam Island to consolidate the defense of the South Mandated Islands, thus establishing the defense patrol networks with those islands as key points in order to have the show-down once and for all after inducing the main strength of the American transocean armada deep in the near waters of our homeland . . . Such a plan as launching an aerial attack upon Pearl Harbor at the outset of war had never been contemplated before.

On the other hand, my own idea was to employ all the strength of the carrier forces first in the Philippines operation, while the whole strength of the land-based air forces should be thrown into the Malaya operation. Borneo and Java were to be occupied next, thus finishing the first-stage operations in the war. The second-stage operations should be started after tightening the belt. My plan therefore was in preference of ignoring the U.S. fleet in Pearl Harbor at the outset of the war.

First, Too Risky an Operation

First, the Pearl Harbor attack was considered too risky an operation. Unless the enemy could be attacked unprepared, the operation had little chance of success, since it aimed to plunge deep into the heart of the enemy, sailing as far as 3,000 miles from the homeland in order to decide the fate of the war once and for all. For that end the absolute necessity was to keep up its security. The difficulties involved were beyond imagination, as it dared to accomplish what others considered impossible. Moreover, the participants in the operation were the cream of the Japanese Navy, a powerful force which consisted of six carriers, two battleships, three cruisers, nine destroyers, three submarines and eight oilers. . . . But I thought that it should be called too risky to stake the fate of this country on this battle alone. . . .

Unyielding Determination of Admiral Yamamoto

The small booklet which Rear Admiral Fukudome showed me seemed to have been made by Comdr. Minoru Genda, then staff officer of the 1st Air Fleet, on the suggestion of Rear Adm. Takijiro Onishi, who was one of the officers most trusted by Admiral Yamamoto at that time as the chief of staff of the 11th Air Fleet, but I don't know about it in detail. But I realized later that by the time I was shown that booklet Admiral Yamamoto had already made up his mind about the matter. . . .

Since then I discussed this matter several times with Rear Admiral Onishi who was the ringleader of this operation. Although one class senior to me at Etajima, he was one of my closest intimate friends. Later, I further discussed this subject with him who gradually came to listen to my views, and finally came to share my view.

Of course, for that I obtained the advance approval of my direct superior, Vice Adm. Chuichi Nagumo, and Rear Admiral Onishi that of Vice Adm. Nishizo Tsukahara who was then the CinC of the 11th Air Fleet. One day both Onishi and I visited Admiral Yamamoto on board his flagship and expressed our frank view on the subject. The admiral, accompanied by his chief of staff, Rear Adm. Matome Ugaki and one or two staff officers, listened to us almost in silence. He only said, half-jokingly, "Don't talk of gambling so much, although I am very fond of playing cards and *shogi.*" Finally he said only that "what you gentlemen urged has a good reason for it," and he did not say anything after that. Apparently he had already made up his mind very firmly. When I was about to leave his flagship, the admiral unusually came up to the gangway to see me off, and said, patting my shoulder, "What you recommended was quite understandable, but, Kusaka, the Pearl Harbor attack plan is what I have resolved to carry out at any cost as the supreme commander. So please do the best you can to materialize it from now on. And I will place all the details of the plan in your hand," he further said, adding that what he said to me should be relayed to Admiral Nagumo.

His faithfulness was quite noticeable in his appearance. At that moment I swore deep in my mind to do the best I could for this commander. "Admiral, from now on I won't say anything against this plan. I swear to do my utmost to materialize the admiral's idea," I swore to him, and returned to the *Akagi*.

As seen in the above instance, Admiral Yamamoto seemed to have already firmly made up his mind about this matter, but it seemed to me that the Imperial General Headquarters did not show serious consideration at first toward this problem. But it seemed that he even threatened to resign from his post if his plan was not accepted, and also that he even wished to be the carrier task force commander, one degree lower in rank than his current position, in order to take direct command of the operation, leaving his post of CinC of the Combined Fleet to Admiral Yonai.

When I received the booklet in question from Rear Admiral Fukudome, I thought that it was anyway a big problem. Naturally the 1st Air Fleet should be its main strength in such an operation. Anyway, the plan should be seriously studied and training should also be made in accordance with the plan. Immediately upon returning to our ship, I reported it to Nagumo commander in chief, and also sent for Commander Oishi, the senior staff officer, and Commander Genda, the air staff officer, to study the plan. The latter officer, however, pretended that he was informed of it for the first time.

To Attack Unprepared Points

As to how to accomplish the objective of the Pearl Harbor attack plan, I thought at that time that the imperative was to attack the enemy unprepared. To that end, first of all the secrecy of the operation should be secured. The second problem was to enable refueling at sea as planned, and the third one was concerned with the strength to be employed in the operation. What was more necessary than that was to get enemy information continuously.

To give a fatal blow to the enemy's main strength at the outset of the war could raise the morale of the whole friendly forces, while on the other hand [be] extremely discouraging to the morale of the enemy. In addition, a great advantage could be achieved by removing an enemy threat toward our Southern operations from the flank.

But its materialization was very hard to be done indeed. In order to launch a surprise attack upon the enemy, it was first of all essential to have a force of great strength cross as far as 3,000 miles unnoticed. However great the Pacific was, nobody could assure that the task force would not meet on its way and attack any ships of any nationality. Its danger would increase greatly as the force neared Hawaii. Since U.S. aerial patrol by flying boats extending 600 miles from their bases was expected even in peace-time, it had to be regarded as the most difficult task of all difficulties to launch a surprise attack without being noticed beforehand. But this impossible thing had to be made possible by any means.

After making an extensive study of all passages of ships all over the Pacific for the past ten years or more, the course was selected to pass through the line near 40 degrees North Latitude that any ships had never passed before, aiming to reach the point about 800 miles due north of the Hawaiian Islands. This course ran through the area outside the enemy patrol supposed to be 600 miles from Hawaii and the Aleutian Islands. Taking advantage of the darkness of night and high speed, the force was to make a high-speed run from the point 800 miles north of Hawaii within 200 miles of that island where attack planes would be launched. The above was the outline of the tentative operational plan we mapped out.

Success or Failure Depends on Refueling at Sea

But there was one difficult point for the materialization of the plan. As foul weather was prevalent in this route in winter, the days available for refueling at sea accordingly could not be expected to be more than 10% at most, although it was one of the reasons for selecting this route to make a surprise attack possible. As a matter of fact, the feasibility of refueling at sea in this season of the year constituted the most important factor in determining whether this operation could be made or not.

As the Japanese Navy originally aimed to have a showdown once and for all after inducing the enemy into the near sea of our homeland, it rather placed more emphasis on high speed than on radius of action. Such being the case, it was more than a hard task for most Japanese vessels to cross 3,000 miles to fight and then return the same distance. Among them, those that could manage to do so were only two carriers, *Shokaku* and *Zuikaku,* and even they had a good deal to fear, if and when fighting was prolonged considerably. For such as *Soryu* and *Hiryu,* both carriers, as well as a light cruiser and destroyers, such a task was utterly impossible. Moreover, unlike an ordinary fleet's tactical movements, carrier fleets of those days needed a relative wind of 14 to 15 meters per second in order to allow heavily-loaded bombers and torpedo bombers to take off from them. This meant that they had to run at high speed for their planes to take off when there was no wind, which in turn required a great consumption of fuel. Therefore, whether refueling at sea could be available or not constituted the determining factor for this operation.

The next problem was concerned with the amount of strength to be used in this operation. In view of the nature of this operation demanding the infliction of a fatal blow with one strike, it was essential to destroy the enemy army and navy's planes estimated to be 500 to 1,000 stationed on several bases on Oahu Island before they got into the air, to say nothing of the enemy fleet, the main objective, thus grasping command of the air in our hand to permit torpedo bombers and level and dive bombers to attack freely. To this end, a total of about 350 to 360 planes of the 1st Air Fleet's six carriers combined was the minimum requirement.

The last and most important problem concerned was how to get enemy information. Originally, the past information had made it plain that the U.S. Pacific Fleet was either in Lahaina anchorage, Pearl Harbor or in waters south of Oahu Island participating in training. It was also known that they used to come back to Pearl Harbor on Sunday for rest in most cases. It was needless to say, however, that to confirm their whereabouts just prior to the actual attack was the most essential thing to be done by any means.

In addition, there were a lot of problems to be solved, which included: how to pilot torpedo bombers into the shallow water torpedo attack in an area where they had to aim at targets at an awfully low altitude as soon as they got over the bay after flying through tall stacks and buildings hedging the narrow bay, how to accomplish the shallow water torpedoing as well as necessary improvement of equipment, how to bomb vessels mooring on the inside row and how to torpedo battleships protected by defense nets.

Relieved from Delusion by Religious Meditation and Swordsmanship

Since it was the first time for me to be responsible for planning and guiding such an important operation, assisting Nagumo commander in chief, I wanted to have some spiritual backbone. After contemplation, I happened to be reminded of *Kinshicho-Oken,* a form of sword play of the Goten of Muto school of swordsmanship, which I had learned from my childhood. This form was to press the foe holding a sword over this head with the thought of *Kinshicho* spreading its wings over the whole sky and strike down the foe with one stroke, and then resume the original form of holding the sword over his head again. Apart from the reasonableness, I firmly believed this was the very tactics which I should take.

Strictest Security Measures

In order to make a surprise attack possible, the most essential thing was to secure the secrecy of the plan. Originally, therefore, the number of persons who were informed of this plan was strictly limited; only important operation staff officers of the Combined Fleet, five or six concerned staff officers of the 1st Air Fleet, the members of the Operations Section of the General Staff and one or two staffs of the Navy Department including the Navy Minister were informed of the plan, and any other big brass of the General Staff, Fleet and Navy Department were not informed of the plan at all.

In September, a map maneuver was held in the Naval Staff College in Tokyo to study the operational plan of the Combined Fleet with Japan's going to war with Great Britain and the U.S. as its main subject. In this maneuver, the scene of the Pearl Harbor attack was separated from the others and conducted separately, so that even commanders in chief and their staffs were not aware of this plan. As a matter of fact, even those officers and men of the task force which participated in this operation were not informed of this plan before they were informed of it at Hitokappu Bay by the enclosed letter of order.

Since this plan was revealed to very limited persons, there often arose cases in which we met some trouble. Aside from the problem pertaining to refueling at sea, each participating ship had to be loaded with fuel as much as possible, taking into account some chance of adverse weather in which refueling at sea was not available. In order to increase the load capacity of fuel, I intended to overload fuel in vacant spaces of ships, a space where anything was forbidden to be loaded by regulation enforced by the Navy Minister, and urged members of the Military Affairs Bureau of the Navy Department to get permission for it. But they were very stubborn, and asked me, "Kusaka chief of staff, why are you demanding such a thing so much?" "Depending upon a situation," I replied, "even equipment will have to be abandoned without permission of the authorities in case of war. For the same reasoning, we will have to load water or fuel in such a space as is vacant, in which anything is forbidden by the authorities to be loaded." And, with the help of an intelligent officer of that section of the Navy Department, who could see something in the air, my request was finally approved.

We were also bothered by a suspicion of why only the Task Force was preparing winter coats and heavy clothing for cold weather, while other forces were busy making preparations for hot weather. But somehow we could get through it too.

In a fleet headquarters were assigned the fleet engineer, the fleet paymaster officer and the fleet medical officers, but they were usually kept from important operational conferences, as they had little direct connection with the operation. However, as I believed we needed their skills in such an important operation as this one, I confided the secret of the plan after calling them in separately and asked their cooperation with the plan, breaking with the past customary procedure. This served to contribute to securing secrecy from this angle too.

Hitokappu Bay Picked as Rendezvous Point

Where the whole fleet should be assembled constituted another problem to be solved, although the course was selected to pass through near 40 degrees North Latitude. Naval bases were considered undesirable, since those places were apt to induce others' attention. Ominato was not desirable either, though there was considerable difference in the degree. What happened to come to mind was Hitokappu Bay in Etorofu Island. Though this bay was one of the key points for the Navy, it did not draw much attention to itself.

When I was a Lieutenant Commander, I had been there for a couple of days as a base personnel officer at the time when seaplanes of the Kasumigaura Air Group underwent slight maneuvering in the Kurile Islands. So I was pretty well aware of that bay. As it was an open bay facing the Pacific, it could not be a good anchorage with swells coming in in summer time, but it was a quiet and wide anchorage preventing the northwest wind, so wide that it could accommodate a large fleet.

Of course it was considered extremely unwise in such a crucial moment to let a large fleet get into there in a gorgeous manner. It was therefore arranged to disperse the fleet for a while into their respective bases and other suitable ports, and get them together at the designated date after bringing them up from those ports through separate and individual courses. I also planned to have land air bases and other ships transmit a great deal of false wireless signals so as to pretend that the Task Force was still in Bungo Strait and its vicinity as before.

It was needless to say that the strictest radio silence was ordered to be maintained in every ship of the Task Force. To keep radio silence was easy to say, but not so easy to maintain.

One or two days before the arrival of the fleet at the designated assembly point of Hitokappu Bay, the *Kunajiri,* a gunboat, was dispatched there to suspend all communications through the Yona Post Office. At the same time, all vessels coming in and going out of the bay were held up for a while after explaining the situation to them.

The most difficult problem in carrying out the operation was how to refuel battleships and carriers at sea. In spite of long studies, it had been an unsettled problem in the Japanese Navy. But, by having an oiler approach a large ship instead of the latter making an approach to the former, this long-unsettled problem was easily solved. And this, I thought with gratitude, was attributable to my hard experience at the times when I was skipper of a ship.

Both Genda's and Fuchida's Painstaking Efforts

Genda staff officer, who took charge of planning and drawing operational plans and operational orders as the responsible officer for the Pearl Harbor attack plan, was one of the ablest officers in the Japanese Navy, particularly in the naval aviation circle, and had exerted himself for six months to materialize the plan. In late August, Cmdr. Mitsuo Fuchida, who was then a staff officer of the 3rd Carrier Division and also a wing commander of the *Akagi* when I was skipper of that ship, was called back to the *Akagi,* and we informally appointed him the overall commander of the Task Force's whole air groups to let him take the entire responsibility for training the air-borne forces, so as to make him fully display his ability. Both commanders were of the same class and intimate friends. Genda's ability to plan and Fuchida's to carry out things were well matched indeed. I tried to accept their recommendations as far as I could, and quietly kept my eyes on what they were doing.

By that time, the carrier-borne air force had been placed under command of the skipper of the carrier in the Japanese Navy. Such administrative matters as personal affairs, training, not to say operational matters, were under the jurisdiction of the skipper's command. Above them, there were carrier division commanders. It was, therefore, understandable that skippers and carrier division commanders felt disgusted when the whole carrier-born air groups were placed under the command of Fuchida out of their commands.

Usually carrier skippers and carrier division commanders were sharp and somewhat stubborn, maintaining their own views. Among them, Rear Adm. Tamon Yamaguchi, then the 2nd Carrier Division commander, was well known in the Japanese Navy as one of the ablest admirals. He little hesitated in making strongly-worded recommendations to either his superior commander in chief or staffs of the fleet. He used to blow up staffs of the fleet and then me who was the chief of staff of the fleet. Even arrogant Genda sometimes came to ask my help, but fortunately he [Yamaguchi] was one class senior to me at Etajima and a classmate at the Naval Staff College, so that I could maintain an intimate relationship with him privately. This served to be helpful in various respects.

Particular Training at Kagoshima Bay

What I wished most was to have both Genda and Fuchida freely display their ability as they wished. In the air force there was no objection at all due to their personalities. The operational plan was informally related to Commander Fuchida by Commander Genda. Fuchida also related it to one or two subordinates whom he trusted, but to others not at all.

The overall training of the air force on which much importance was placed was started in late August after the arrival of Fuchida to his new post, so there was not much time left before the designated date of going to war which was set forth as December. In order to meet the requirement for the peculiar topography of Pearl Harbor special training to some extent was unavoidable.

Torpedo bombers stationed at Kagoshima base were instructed to practice such stunt-like flights as to line up over Shiroyama, sharply lower their altitude skimming treetops in a valley from the Iwasakidani, then make a sharp turn to the seashore, whence the altitude was further lowered to 20 meters so as to release a torpedo immediately. This reckless training not only startled citizens of Kagoshima city, but even the participating flying crews, as they could not see why such training was required.

In the middle of September and thereabouts, a precise model of Oahu Island about six feet square was sent down to the *Akagi* from the Imperial General Staff, and installed in my room on board the ship. Genda was keeping himself awfully busy, contemplating before that model, inspecting training at land bases, going to naval yards to push the installation of a tail fin on torpedoes for use in shallow-water torpedoing, and sometimes going to Tokyo to get replenishment of flyers.

In late September, the 5th Carrier Division, consisting of the newly-built crack carriers *Shokaku* and *Zuikaku,* was placed under the command of the 1st Air Fleet. Rear Adm. Chuichi Hara, who was appointed its commander, was a classmate of mine at the Naval Staff College. He was a well-known torpedo officer in the Japanese Navy.

Task Force Boosting Strength Born into the World

In the meantime, the sands were running out very quickly. As to the number of tankers to be used in the operation, the Imperial General Staff tentatively decided to place six or eight 10,000-ton-class tankers under the command of the 1st Air Fleet, but the plan had not been easily materialized even as December was approaching, so I began to worry. Modification works were necessary for those newly-assigned tankers, and what was more important was to let them have one or two chances of refueling training before their sortie for the operation.

On the other hand, the Imperial General Staff insisted that, because of the agreement with the Army, the number of carriers to be used in the operation could not exceed four, so stubbornly as to indicate that the Operation Section would resign if this was not accepted. Under these circumstances, I was regarded as crazy by those members of the central authorities who did not know the reason, and also as a stubborn fellow by those who knew its reason.

But tankers were assigned to the fleet by and by, which relieved me a good deal. However, the problem of carriers could not be solved so easily. Considering that, in case of our request for six carriers being rejected, there would be no other way but to exclude the 2nd Carrier Division under the command of Rear Admiral Yamaguchi from the plan, I was about to persuade him to accept my informal plan when he, as expected, did not show any sign of consent to my suggestion. On the contrary, he immediately rushed to Nagumo's place and protested it strongly. Finally he could be persuaded, however.

By any means, the strength was insufficient, so this time I myself went to see Admiral Yamamoto and said, "Commander in Chief, didn't you assure me that the details of this plan would be placed under my command, and efforts would be made as much as possible to meet my requirements for the operation?" As a result of requests like this, it was finally decided that six carriers be allocated to the Task Force.

On the other hand, various training at sea of the Task Force could not be neglected. In several training exercises at sea of the whole Task Force, the fleet headquarters alone supposed the Pearl Harbor attack without being noticed to train the overall strength of the whole fleet. Both carriers *Shokaku* and *Zuikaku* of the newly-organized 5th Carrier Division were quickly trained to their strength. As the end of October closed in, the Task Force whose combined strength could be boosted all over the world had thus been trained.

Though inexperienced in aviation, Admiral Nagumo had long been trained in the service of destroyers and destroyer squadrons since his young era. His long experience as a unit commander and his dauntless character like a spirited horse had by that time made him a good admiral rich in humanity. Under him were Gunichi Mikawa,* Chuichi Hara, Tamon Yamaguchi and Sentaro Omori, all being of the rank of Rear Admiral, each of whom was an able naval officer of the Japanese Navy.

In addition, about thirty submarines belonging to the 6th Fleet were placed under the operational command of the Task Force commander. Their assigned missions included to confirm the enemy situation before the commencement of an aerial attack and to catch and attack enemy vessels which might come out of the harbor after the attack was launched, in addition to the grave mission of sending midget submarines deep into the harbor.

Midget Submarine Crews

Among those submarines, five took a midget submarine each on board. It was not an easy task to make a long voyage of 3,000 miles submerging at daytime and only surfacing at night, but a more difficult task was that assigned to those young boys of the midget submarines, to whom our deepest admiration should be paid. Surely even the slightest chance of survival could hardly be seen in their assigned mission. There might be torpedo-defense nets extended along vessels, patrol boats with eagle eyes at the entrance of the bay and mind barriers laid, all of which had to be overcome to penetrate into the bay to destroy enemy vessels at one blow. When I thought of the unsophisticated spirit of those young boys, originally I thought that the spearhead of the attack would better be made by those midget submarines. But it was decided that the initial attack be made by the air forces, lest an untimely attack by midget submarines would spoil this grave operation.

---

* Mikawa was a vice admiral —Eds.

Topographically, the entrance of Pearl Harbor was so narrow that it was hard for a submarine with low view to observe clearly the enemy situation in the harbor. So it was arranged that the enemy situation in the harbor just prior to the attack be determined by *Tone*'s and *Chikuma*'s seaplanes, and the Lahaina anchorage, which could be searched from outside the anchorage, be scrutinized by a submarine in order to get negative information on the enemy situation. Most of those submarines left the homeland bases on or around 18 November. On the other hand, current information on the enemy sent from the spot had been arranged in the Imperial General Staff, which broadcast it successively to our force.

Situation Tense—8th Designated

On 18 October, the Tojo Cabinet was formed with a result that the relationship between this country and the United States was put on the verge of an immediate touch-off. The Pearl Harbor attack plan was officially authorized by the Imperial Staff on 3 November, and the day of attack was designated as 8 December by the order issued on 7 November. Even so, the Japanese Government was continuing its efforts to seek a settlement of the issue at stake by dispatching Ambassador Kurusu to the States on 5 November.

After we left Hitokappu Bay on 26 November, there still remained a slight hope of a peaceful settlement, so that we had to expect at any moment a telegram of ''Compromise reached stop Task Force requested to put about stop'' coming in. If we happened to fail to receive this important instruction, what the hell would happen? Such a thought made me tremble all the way.

CHAPTER II. SORTIE OF TASK FORCE

Farewell Handshakes at a Dirty Drinking Place

In the night of 17 November 1941, the *Akagi,* flagship of the Task Force, left Saeki-Wan in Kyushu for Hitokappu Bay stealthily without a single send-off.

Several days before that, the final briefing conference with commanders and important staff officers of each unit of the Combined Fleet was held at the Iwakuni Air Group. After the conference, a farewell party was held at a dirty Japanese drinking place in the vicinity of the base. With some reason, we of the 1st Air Fleet left there early. Ugaki chief of staff of the Combined Fleet said specifically to me, ''I trust you to do your best. Good luck,'' and tightly gripped my hand. Though his voice was low, its strength stirred up my mind.

In the afternoon of the 16th, the day before the departure, I received a letter from my home in Osaka, which was sent by an old caretaker of my home by the name of Tanekichi Akanuma. He was an old former Navy 1st Class Petty Officer, and he and his wife had long taken care of my old mother. In his letter to me, he wrote that he had dreamed that our Navy's submarines made a surprise attack on Pearl Harbor and all returned safely after attaining a great success. A trivial matter though it might be, I was privately pleased with it, as I felt that I had been given a hint of a bright prospect for the forthcoming operation.

Taking a detour course and making training on the way, the *Akagi* entered

Hitokappu Bay on the 21st. After the arrival, we were advised by the gunboat *Kunajiri,* which had been dispatched there to maintain security and also for guard duty, that every arrangement had been completed. Several vessels had already been in the designated anchorage. With the arrival of the *Kaga* on the 22nd as the last, over thirty men-of-war completed their assemblage at the lonely northern place. They were as follows:

TASK FORCE UNDER THE COMMAND OF CINC, 1ST AIR FLEET.

Aerial Attack Force under direct command of Vice Admiral Nagumo

1st Carrier Division (*Akagi* and *Kaga*)

2nd Carrier Division (*Soryu* and *Hiryu*)

5th Carrier Division (*Shokaku* and *Zuikaku*)

Guard Force commanded by Rear Adm. Sentaro Omori, 1st Des. Sqd. commander

CL *Abukuma*

DDs *Urakaze, Asakaze,** *Tanikaze, Hamakaze, Kasumi, Arare, Kagero, Shiranuhi,* and *Akigumo*

Support Force commanded by Vice Adm. Gunichi Mikawa, 3d BB Div. commander

BBs *Hiei* and *Kirishima*

CAs *Tone* and *Chikuma*

Patrol Force commanded by Capt. Kijiro Imaizumi, 2nd Sub. Div. commander

SSs *I-19, I-21,* and *I-23*

Midway Destruction Force commanded by Capt. Yozin Konishi, 7th Des. Div. commander

DDs *Akebono*† and *Ushio*

Supply Force commanded by skipper of the *Kyokuto Maru*

1st Tanker Train (*Kyokuto Maru, Kenyo Maru, Kokuyo Maru, Shinkoku Maru, Akebono Maru*)

2nd Tanker Train (*Toho Maru, Toei Maru, Nihon Maru*‡)

On 5 November, the Imperial General Headquarters Navy Order No. 1 was issued to Admiral Yamamoto, CinC of the Combined Fleet, the gist of which read as follows:

---

* Should be Isokaze—Eds.

† Should be *Sazanami.* The tanker *Shiriya* was also a part of the Midway unit —Eds.

‡ Usually rendered *Nippon Maru*—Eds.

5 November 1941

To: CinC Combined Fleet Isoroku Yamamoto
Via: Chief of Naval General Staff Osami Nagano
By Imperial Order

1. In view of a great fear that she will be compelled to go to war with the United States, Great Britain and the Netherlands for her self-existence and self-defense, this Empire has decided to complete every operational preparation with early December as its goal.

2. Commander in Chief Combined Fleet will carry out the necessary operational preparations.

3. Detailed instructions will be given by the Chief of the Naval General Staff.

Operational Plan Given to Whole Fleet at Hitokappu Bay

In accordance with this Imperial Operational Order, the CinC of the Combined Fleet issued his operational order, which included the following pertaining to the Task Force:

1. The Task Force will launch a surprise attack at the outset of war upon the U.S. Pacific Fleet supposed to be in Hawaiian waters, and destroy it.

2. The Task Force will reach the designated stand-by point for the operation in advance.

3. The date of starting the operation is tentatively set forth as 8 December 1941.

The Task Force then drew up its own operational order, which was given for the first time to the whole force at Hitokappu Bay. Except to those who participated in its planning, it was indeed a big surprise to all officers and men of the force. To them everything in the past now became clear and their morale rose greatly.

On the 23rd, the last operational briefing was held with skippers and commanding officers, and detailed explanation of the plan was given. After the free-talking in detail, Nagumo commander in chief said, "Since we entered the Japanese Navy, we have exerted ourselves for many years just to meet this day of the coming big operation. No greater honor could we have as warriors. But many difficulties still lie ahead on our long way through cold and foul weather until 8 December. From the bottom of my heart I want you to pay the utmost care and also maintain your good health until that time."

After that I, as the chief of staff, detailed various problems which should be taken care of with careful attention during the action. After the conference ended, all attendees drank up with *kachikuri* and *surume* to the success of the operation, and toasted the Emperor after shouting "*Banzai!*" three times.

Aside from this briefing, another conference was held with all flying officers of the force who were to participate in the aerial attack. Young boys as most of them were, their joy was beyond description. Because of heavy waves which had raged since the middle of the conference, skippers and commanders managed to go back to their respective vessels, but those flying officers who had to remain on the flagship longer were unable to do so. Most of them stayed on board the *Akagi* that night.

Perception as Clear as the Moon

I still had various problems upon which to contemplate. Among them were what to do should the first blow fail to end the enemy, contrary to the original planning, and what to do if we were discovered by the enemy before launching the attack. In the latter case, it was tentatively decided to repeat forced attacks, but actually it was a problem of how many times attacks ought to be repeated. As a matter of fact, there was no other way but to repeat forced attacks again and again until the final objective was achieved. How many times attacks should be repeated depended upon the actual conditions prevailing and could not be determined beforehand, I concluded. Anyway, I made up my mind that the attack should be carried out as swiftly as a demon flashing by and also it should be withdrawn as fast as the passing wind.

After the attack there were some people who criticized why the Task Force did not remain on the scene a little longer to seek out enemy carriers more extensively and also why it did not destroy naval yards and heavy oil fuel tanks, but it was because of the aforementioned reasons.

What should be done if any merchant ship was met on the way? Immediately send the inspection team to prohibit the use of wireless signals and keep watch on her. If and when she had already sent a wireless, there would be nothing to save the situation. What steps should be taken, if and when a powerful enemy fleet was met before the attack? Were it after the formal attack order was given with the Cabinet decision of going to war already being made, the chance would develop to destroy it. On the other hand, were it before the issuance of the attack order, what should be done? Although some said in the conference half in joke that a salute gun should better be exchanged, it was indeed a serious matter to me. When I reached my own conclusion after contemplating this and that, I felt no desire in my mind, as if a clear moon were coming out of clouds. But to Admiral Nagumo, on whose shoulders the grave responsibility of safeguarding the fate of the Empire depended, it would be a much harder task to be solved.

Worries of Admiral Nagumo

At 0800 on 26 November 1941, the Task Force weighed anchor for its glorious mission. Heavy winds and waves which had prevailed since several days before became quiet. Only the still-remaining white tails of waves crashed alongside the vessels.

The island mountains were already covered by white snow, and a chilly morning wind in the northern waters was felt through our overcoats. Three submarines which were to patrol 200 miles ahead of the main force sailed ahead of the others. One of them lagged about 30 minutes, as she got wire tangled in one of her screws. Each vessel moved out of the anchorage into the open sea according to the designated fleet formation. While we were gazing at the mountains of the island with a thought of the last sight of them, they finally dropped out of sight under the horizon.

Each vessel kept on the alert position. Gunmen, lookout-men and underwater sound detectors were watchful at their positions on a shift basis. Several fighters alerted for emergency were kept on the deck of each carrier. It was prohibited to throw any trash and bilge into the water. All transmitters were sealed, and all hands were ordered to keep away from any key of the machine. All attention was focused to catch broadcasts from the Imperial General Staff and the *Nagato,* the flagship of the Combined Fleet, as well as from Honolulu.

"Chief of Staff," Nagumo commander in chief asked me, "what do you think about the forthcoming operation? I now think that I have accepted too big a task. It seems to me that I had better have refused it, having taken a stronger attitude. Although we have sailed out already, I wonder if it will be successful." No wonder he had such an apprehension about the future as the supreme commander responsible for the whole operation. "Don't worry, sir," I replied, "I am sure it will come out well." "You are an optimist. I can't help envying your character," the admiral said.

Various criticisms have been heard about Admiral Nagumo, but I think he was after all one of our good superior officers. Though he was dauntless like a spirited horse as mentioned elsewhere, he had another side of being cautious and also rich in humanity.

I once accompanied him in climbing up to Lake Onami at Mt. Kirishima. At that time I was so fat that I could not go with the same pace as he, and he repeatedly stopped on the way to wait for me, and kindly consoled me.

His ability to command units, the smartness to grasp a tactical opportunity and hold to a bold decision once he made up his mind were what we subordinates had to learn from him. That he had little experience in aviation might hamper him a great deal from fully displaying his ability. It does not hit the nail on the head if we said some criticizing words taking up one or two errors or based upon hearsay.

The economical speed of 14 knots was maintained during the cruise. All possible steps were taken to economize on fuel; electric lamps and baths were saved as much as possible.

The commander in chief, chief of staff, skipper and navigation officer rested in their own small rooms near the bridge with their uniforms on all the while even when they slept. Gunmen and machinegun-men stayed beside their positions under makeshift shelters. Rear Adm. Sentaro Omori, then the 1st Des. Sqd. commander, never left the bridge except to go to the latrine; at night he slept on a folding canvas bed placed on the bridge. Of course, blackout was maintained on all vessels at night. Follow-up ships only followed the white kick-out wave of the preceding ship.

Fortunately the sea turned out to be very calm, so quiet, as seldom seen in the past statistics for many years, that refueling at sea was available at any time we wished. As we had already been using oil-tank oil after consuming the oil stored outside of tanks, refueling was made piecemeal whenever available times were found. As refueling was repeated, the necessary time was reduced and the refueling speed could be raised. The fleet speed which had to be reduced to 9 knots in early refueling could be raised to 12 knots.

What concerned us most during refueling was a possible enemy attack by submarines. Particular attention should be directed against them. While refueling, an oiler and the supplied vessel were connected with pipe lines, so that specific cautions should be made to get them loose at any moment. Moreover, refueling works in raging cold weather were painstaking ones indeed.

Since skippers and crews of oilers were veterans who had grown up at sea for many years, they were able to master refueling works and others in a comparatively short period of training, but a difficult problem for them was to maintain formation at night without any lamps. Vessels that had been in formation in the evening often became lost to sight in the following morning. In peace-time they could be gotten in touch with by wireless, but that method could not be utilized because of radio silence.

After the war I was often asked by many experts as well as street strategists why it was not planned at that time to land two or three army divisions. But, in view of the many problems we confronted in the early stage as seen above accompanied by only eight oilers, it would be evidently clear that it was far from an easy task, to go 3,000 miles in the face of a watchful enemy with a great convoy of 50 to 100 vessels.

Favored by unexpectedly good weather, calm days continued, but we were sometimes bothered by unseasonable fog, too.

Enemy Information Came in Successively

What I worried about most at this stage was never to fail to receive reports on the enemy situation, as well as a possible instruction to pull back the fleet in case of a peaceful settlement being reached between the United States and Japan. As for the latter, I could get rid of worry about it somehow, as every vessel was instructed to dial in that wave channel. But, as for the former, there as no other way but to avail ourselves of enemy information all the time, and also to pray God that the enemy fleet wouldn't move to any other places at the time of our attack. Fortunately, however, thanks to the extensive and minute arrangements conducted by the Imperial General Headquarters, we could avail ourselves of the enemy situation successively. Major messages received since 2 December, when the decision to go to war was given, were as follows:

Received 0017, 3 December
"A" Information (issued 2200 2 December by I.G.S.)
Activities in Pearl Harbor as of 0800, 28 November:
Departed: 2 BB (*Oklahoma* and *Nevada*), 1 CV (*Enterprise*),
2 CA, 12 DD
Arrived: 5 BB, 3 CA, 3 CL, 12 DD, 1 seaplane-tender.
Ships making port today are those which departed 22 November.
Ships in port on afternoon of 28 November estimated as follows:
6 BB (2 *Maryland* class, 2 *California* class, 2 *Pennsylvania* class)
1 CV (*Lexington*)
9 CA (5 *San Francisco* class, 3 *Chicago* class, *Salt Lake City*)
5 CL (4 *Honolulu* class and *Omaha*)

Received 0035, 4 December
"A" Information (issued 2300, 3 December by I.G.S.)
    Ships in Pearl Harbor on afternoon of 29 November:
        District A (between Naval Yard and Ford Island)
            KT (docks northwest of Naval Yard): *Pennsylvania* and
                Arizona
            FV (mooring pillars): *California, Tennessee, Maryland*
                and *West Virginia*
            KS (naval yard repair dock): CA *Portland*
            In docks: 2 CA and 1 DD
            Elsewhere: 4 SS, 1 DD tender, 2 patrol boats, 2
                oilers, 2 repair ships and 1 minesweeper
        District B (northwest area of Ford island)
            FV (mooring pillars): *Lexington*
            Elsewhere: *Utah* (target ship), 1 CA (*San Francisco* class), 2 CL
                (*Omaha* class), 3 gunboats
        District C (East Loch)
            3 CA, 2 CL (*Honolulu* class), 17 DD, 2 DD tenders
        District D (Middle Loch)
            12 minesweepers
        District E (West Loch)
            No ships
    No changes observed by afternoon of 2 December. So far they do not seem
    to have been alerted. Shore leaves as usual.

Received 0420, 5 December
"A" Information (issued 2030, 4 December by I.G.S.)
    Air patrols in the vicinity of Pearl Harbor unknown, but so far no indica-
    tions of sea patrol flight being conducted. It seems that occasional patrols
    are being made to Palmyra, Johnston and Midway Islands.

Received 1036, 7 December
  "A" Information (issued 2200, 6 December by I.G.S.)
    Activities in Pearl Harbor on the morning of 5 December:
        Arrived: *Oklahoma* and *Nevada,* which have been out of the harbor
            for eight days.

        Departed: *Lexington* and five heavy cruisers
    Ships in harbor as of 1800, 5 Dec.:
        8 BB, 3 CL, 16 DD

        In docks: 4 CL (*Honolulu* class), 5 DD

Received 1900, 7 December
"A" Information (issued 1700, 7 December by I.G.S.)
    No balloons.
    No torpedo-defense nets deployed around battleships.
    No indications observed from enemy radio activity that ocean patrol flights
    are being made in Hawaiian area.

Lexington left harbor yesterday (5 December, local time) and recovered planes.

Enterprise is also thought to be operating at sea with her planes on board.

Received 2050, 7 December

"A" Information (issued 1800, 7 December by I.G.S.)

Utah and a seaplane tender entered harbor in the evening of 5 December. (They had left harbor on 4 December.)

Ships in harbor as of 6 Dec.:

9 BB, 3 CL, 3 seaplane tenders and 17 DD

In docks: 4 CL, 3 DD

All carriers and cruisers are at sea.

No special indications observed on the fleet.

Oahu is quiet and no blackout maintained.

Imperial General Staff is fully convinced of success.

Message of "Climb Mt. Niitaka"

For some time since the departure from the homeland, we could learn the domestic situation by broadcasts from the homeland. The so-called Hull note and the resultant international situation between the United States and Japan intensifying the gathering storm over the Pacific could generally be made known, but we couldn't learn anything about the developments of the Cabinet meeting, so that our fleet stealthily made its way to the east having a slight apprehension about the future.

As we neared Hawaii, the Honolulu broadcasts gradually came to be heard clearly, finally letting us listen to them as clearly as if we were there. Those intelligence reports on the enemy situation in Pearl Harbor sent from the Imperial General Staff increased their importance as we approached the target. Finally on 1 December we were given a telegram of "it was decided to go to war," which was soon followed by the code telegram of "Climb Mt. Niitaka" issued by the commander in chief of the Combined Fleet. The latter one meant that "the date of going to war was decided as the 8th. The attack would be made as planned." When we were given this telegram, we felt the apprehension that had made us worry so long disappear suddenly. I felt then that my mind was as clear as the autumn moon in the sky.

Late in the night of 3 December, as I recall, there came from the Imperial General Staff a telegram saying that "enemy sub telegram is detected in the vicinity of your force." Lest the whole enterprise be ruined at this stage, the whole fleet was alerted and also asked whether or not an enemy telegram was intercepted. Although some reported the direction of the telegram coming in, there was none who reported its existence in the vicinity of the fleet. Even so, as we could not get rid of some apprehension about it, we changed our course to the southeast direction earlier than scheduled.

CHAPTER 3. U.S. PACIFIC FLEET ANNIHILATED

After Fully Refueling, Rushed Down to Pearl Harbor

On 6 December, the last refueling at sea was made to the fleet. At first refueling was given to *Soryu* and *Hiryu* of the 2nd Carrier Division, and a light cruiser and destroyers of the 1st Destroyer Squadron, all of which had not sufficient fuel tank capacity. By this time, each of them, especially the destroyers, had been well trained in refueling at sea, to such an extent that they regarded it just like routine business.

After refueling on this day was finished, three oilers, *Toho Maru, Toei Maru* and *Nihon Maru* of the 2nd Tanker Train departed from us and headed for the designated rendezvous point. When we saw them hoisting signals and their crews lined up on their sides waving caps as they went away from us, we felt from the bottom of our hearts very grateful for their hard efforts.

In the early morning of the 7th, the commander in chief of the Combined Fleet relayed to us the Imperial Rescript given to him, which read:

> On the eve of declaring war, we trust you to take command of the Combined Fleet. As we see it, the responsibility assigned to the Combined Fleet is so grave that the rise and fall of the Empire depends upon what it is going to accomplish. We trust you to fulfill our trust in you by displaying the long-trained ability of the fleet, thus destroying the enemy and demonstrating its brilliant deed throughout the whole world.

"Z" Flag Hoisted Up Akagi's Mast

On the following day, the 7th, refueling was also continued. Five oilers, *Kyokuto Maru, Kenyo Maru, Kokuyo Maru, Shinkoku Maru,* and *Akebono Maru,* belonging to the 1st Tanker Train, refueled battleships, carriers and cruisers as well as those light vessels which were refueled the last day. Refueling works which were started in the early morning ended by noon of that day, and five tankers were instructed to depart the fleet and head for the pre-arranged rendezvous point on the way after the attack.

After they departed, the combat force, now free from the slow-speed oilers, raised its speed to 24 knots to rush down due south to Pearl Harbor. Its point was about 600 miles due north to Hawaii.

It was at this moment that a flag was raised atop the mast of the *Akagi,* flagship of Nagumo commander in chief. Lo! It was the very flag signal of "Z" which was hoisted atop the mast of Admiral Togo's flagship some thirty years before at the time of the Japan Sea Battle. It read: "The rise or fall of the Empire depends upon this battle; everyone will do his duty with utmost efforts."

The historic scene, upon the outcome of which the fate of the mother country depended, was now to open. Sensing the grave responsibility assigned to them, and also anticipating the bold enterprise to be carried out early the next morning, all hands were fired up in their blood.

On the flush deck of the carriers, 400 planes in all were readied for the next morning's sortie after painstaking, minute preparations made by the maintenance crew for the past several days. Bombers were loaded with torpedoes and bombs.

In the evening of the 7th, a report came in from *I-72* Submarine belonging to the Submarine Force, saying that "U.S. Fleet is not in Lahaina anchorage." Together with information sent from the Imperial General Staff, this enabled us to conclude that most of the U.S. Pacific Fleet was in Pearl Harbor. The absence of their carriers in port, however, was our only concern and also regretted. But I thought that indecision at this moment considering this and that would only result in blunting the cutting effect of a sword swung down from overhead. Then I made up my mind to concentrate all striking power upon enemy vessels in Pearl Harbor. This meant that I rejected all other ideas including sharing elements of the air forces to search the vicinity to seek out enemy carriers.

Fuchida's Minute Attack Plan

As stated elsewhere, this operation was planned by Genda and executed by Fuchida, both forming a good combination. Especially painstaking were the efforts of Commander Fuchida, who personally led the air force at its van into the most dangerous mission. What he exerted himself most with was his plan of attack, the organization of which force is seen below:

First Wave led by Commander Fuchida
    4 Level Bomber Squadrons led by Commander Fuchida
        50 type 97 carrier torpedo bombers *

        Targets: battleships
    4 Torpedo Bomber Squadrons led by Lieutenant Commander Murata
        40 type 97 carrier torpedo bombers

        Targets: battleships and carriers
    2 Dive Bomber Squadrons led by Lieutenant Commander Takahashi
        54 type 99 dive bombers

        Targets: Wheeler, Hickam and Ford bases
    6 Fighter Squadrons led by Lieutenant Commander Itaya
        45 "Zero" Fighters

        Targets: enemy planes in the air and on the ground.

Second Wave led by Lieutenant Commander Shimazaki
    2 Level Bomber Squadrons led by Lieutenant Commander Shimazaki
        54 type 97 carrier torpedo bombers

        Targets: Kaneohe, Hickam and Ford bases
    4 Dive Bomber Squadrons led by Lieutenant Commander Egusa
        81 type 99 dive bombers

        Targets: carriers and cruisers
    4 Fighter Squadrons led by Lieutenant Shindo
        36 "Zero" Fighters

        Targets: enemy planes in the air and on the ground

---

* Fuchida led the horizontal bombers, not torpedo bombers, in addition to being overall commander — Eds.

The reason for dividing the air attack force into two waves was the fact that all planes could not be launched in one wave due to the space and the take-off range of the carriers. All of the unit leaders were handpicked, crack fliers. Among them, Lt. Cmdr. Shigekazu Shimazaki, who was slated to command the second wave, was a squadron commander on board the *Akagi* when I was the skipper of that ship. At that time, I advised him several times to send in an application for the entrance examination of the Naval Staff College, but he never consented, saying that he was not a type of man for that College. Far from being eloquent, he was little more than a naïve person, but he was highly respected by his subordinates, and, in fact, nothing was too hard for him to accomplish. While he was clever with careful considerations, he also had another side, being open-minded too. In any respect, he was far from a bold but reckless leader. At that time he was a wing leader on board the *Shokaku,* but he was the most suitable man to lead the second wave.

As to the planning and execution of the attack, Mr. Fuchida's book entitled "True Story of the Pearl Harbor Attack" detailed them pretty well, but the outline of its planning will be repeated here, too.

The operational objective of this attack was, as instructed by an order of the superior command, to destroy the U.S. Pacific Fleet once and for all. What I thought about it was, as related elsewhere, to cut it down with one stroke of a big sword to be swung from overhead.

What Commander Fuchida thought first was whether or not a surprise attack could be made. As a sequence of attacks in case a surprise attack could be made, he intended to give a fatal blow to enemy battleships and carriers with torpedoing before they could make an effective encounter, immediately followed by high-level bombing upon the inside row battleships, and then destroy heavy cruisers and others with dive bombing, while simultaneously destroying enemy key bases and antiaircraft gun batteries on the ground, thus facilitating the attack of the second wave.

On the other hand, in case a surprise attack could not be made, he planned to send dive bombers and fighters first into the scene so as to open the way for torpedo bombers and level bombers. In this case, enemy encounters of course were expected in the attack of the second wave, so that it was arranged to direct the attack of the second wave to those battleships, carriers and others undestroyed by the attack of the first wave, while completely destroying important enemy air bases, thus making it unable to launch a counterattack upon our Task Force.

What then concerned Commander Fuchida most was to judge instantly on board his plane which type of attack, i.e., a surprise one or a forced one, should be made. Incoming courses of each unit were selected to pass over the mountain area in the east, in order to evade being discovered by the enemy prior to the attack as well as out of consideration for enemy AA gunfire. But, depending upon the wind direction and strength which had much to do with bombing, those courses were to be changed accordingly. In addition, such minute considerations as expected fire flame, smoke from the first wave attacks which might hamper the subsequent attacks, were taken into consideration in planning the attack plan.

All of the crews, not just the fliers, paid their most careful attention and efforts to maintain their health. In the early mornings, all hands were seen on the flight deck practicing physical drills more eagerly than before. Admiral Nagumo and other staff officers of the headquarters also participated in the drill. As the most important flight training for the fliers could not be made, they spent time in preparing their equipment, familiarizing themselves with the model of Oahu and training in identification of U.S. vessels by using their models. Now the commander and all hands were only waiting for the time to go to war, but still minute instructions had to be sent out one after the other as we thought of another concern.

Sped Straight Down to Pearl Harbor

On the afternoon of the 7th, the last order for the bold operation to be carried out early the next morning was issued to the Task Force. Since the departure from Hitokappu Bay it was indeed a painstaking ten or so days fearing enemy submarines and planes. By that time we had already learnt the enemy situation in Pearl Harbor through intelligence reports sent from the Imperial General Staff, and also confirmed the nonexistence of the enemy main force in Lahaina anchorage by the report of our submarine. What remained ahead of us was only to rush straight to Pearl Harbor.

Admiral Nagumo's order for the attack was as follows:

1. Summing up the enemy situation, it seems that enemy strength in the Hawaiian area consists of eight battleships, two carriers, about ten heavy and six light cruisers. More than half of them seem to be in Pearl Harbor and the remaining are most likely in the training area south of Maui; they are not likely to be in Lahaina.

2. Unless an unforeseen situation develops tonight, our attack on vessels will be launched on Pearl Harbor.

3. So far there is no indication that the enemy has been alerted.

Around this time, the following orders were also given to the respective air units:

To: First Wave's Level Bombing Units

1. Based upon "A" Information, the bombing targets of the level bombing units will be four battleships (*Tennessee, California, Maryland* and *West Virginia*) mooring pillars of District A. They will be selected from the north in accordance with the number of the attack units.

2. When there arises need to designate the target upon a change of the situation, they will be designated in the order from the leading attack unit according to the designated number order.

To: Second Wave Units

1. In the Second Wave's Order revisions will be made as follows:
   a. The course after take-off will be 175 degrees.

   b. Form the preparatory formation for the charge at a point 30 miles, bearing 30 degrees from Kahuku Point.

   c. The first group will proceed south 15 miles north of Kaneohe and hence the charge will be made.

Also successively enemy information came in from the Imperial General Staff, among which was:

The painting and camouflage of U.S. warships is as follows:

1. Battleships, carriers and cruisers are painted in dark grey, blacker than those of Japanese.

2. White pattern of wave is painted in the fore part of carriers and cruisers.

3. Upper parts of the mast are painted in white, and upper yards are pulled down. There are some which have their upper yards cut down.

4. There are some which have fake stack and have their stacks so painted as to seem slender.

While the fleet headquarters was finding itself busy in sending and receiving signals and telegrams, I sat in silence and contemplated this and that, only waiting for the time to come.

All Planes Sortied Through Morning Clouds

At dawn, still so dark that black and white could barely be distinguished, planes lined up on the flight deck started the warming-up of engines before the sortie. There arose the roaring sound of propellers. Weaving through planes lined up wingtip to wingtip, maintenance crews were busy with their work. In the flying crew waiting room, already more than a dozen fliers were seen in complete flying kit with a map board hanging on their breasts. All of them seemed to be happy. On the bridge, two or three staff officers were seen busy making preparations before the take-off of planes, checking the wind direction, consulting the wind meter or seeking the position of the ship on a chart.

The moon of 19 days' age was seen and disappeared in intermittent clouds which covered the whole sky. A considerable east wind blew in presenting an adequate condition for the take-off of planes. Due to the long swell peculiar to the south sea, the ship rolled and pitched a good deal; occasionally the ship listed to about 15 degrees to one side, which made us worry a bit. In peace-time training, it was considered pretty difficult for even trained fliers to take off loaded bombers from carriers when their rolling reached about 10 degrees to one side.

About the time day was ready to dawn and the horizon dimly seen, vessels of the Task Force were seen making way in a gorgeous formation. On the carrier flight decks planes were lined up in immediate ready for take-off. Signals of completing preparations successively came in from each carrier.

All flying crews of the *Akagi* were given the last order and minute instruction in the waiting room by the skipper and air officer. Admiral Nagumo also gave the last encouraging message to them. After that, they ran away to their own planes.

When I observed all of those young fliers joyfully running away as in the usual training without any seriousness, I was rather surprised.

Then a flag signal "Take Off" was hoisted atop *Akagi*'s mast. All vessels of the force simultaneously turned their heads against the wind direction and increased their speed. First fighters, then dive bombers and other bombers in that order revved up engines and took off one after another. Even a good deal of rolling which occasionally reached 15 degrees could not be an obstacle to them. All the planes took off from their respective carriers without any fear at all in a short while.

Each carrier sent in a report of "Take Off completed" successively. An order calling for making preparations for the second wave attack was then issued, and maintenance crews busily ran here and there on the flight deck. It was at 0130 of 8 December Tokyo Time, and the point was 230 miles due north of Pearl Harbor.

The dawn had already come on the sea. Planes which took off in the air circled over the fleet once and then twice, and disappeared into clouds far away to the south. About one hour and fifteen minutes later, planes of the second wave took off and followed the first wave. In spite of a great deal of pitching which had been feared, even a single plane did not fail to take off.

I who watched them take off at the bridge was filled with deep emotion and couldn't help feeling my blood boil up.

"Tora" Which Rejoiced the Whole Navy

As I sat in front of the maps in the operations room expecting to hear reconnaissance reports from *Tone*'s and *Chikuma*'s seaplanes which had been dispatched about thirty minutes before, the first report from *Chikuma*'s plane came in. It read: "The enemy fleet is not in Lahaina anchorage." Soon another came in stating, "Cloud ceiling over the enemy fleet, 1,700 meters. Its density, scale 7. 0308," which was soon followed by "the enemy fleet is in Pearl Harbor. 0308." How pleased we were to receive this report! Instinctively Admiral Nagumo and all of his staff officers looked at each other and could not suppress their smiles. The only thing remaining was to await the result of the attack.

A pre-arranged word for a successful surprise attack made was a single word "Tora," the very word which all attention—not only of the Task Force but also the Malaya Invasion Force, the Philippine Force to the south, the flagship in Hiroshima Bay and the Imperial General Staff in Tokyo—were focused to catch.

Soon a telegram sent from the dive bomber leader to his planes just before the attack saying "wind direction, bearing 70, and wind strength, 10 meters" was intercepted. It was soon followed by a telegram order from the overall commander's plane notifying all planes "to launch attacks."

Sensing that they were now going to launch an attack at last, everyone in the operations room held their breath. At 0310 the long-awaited "tora" was received. At that moment, I was at the bridge with Admiral Nagumo directing actions of the force after launching all planes, and could not suppress tears coming down my cheeks. Without any words I firmly grasped Admiral Nagumo's hand.

Each plane which had kept radio silence by that time began to tap keys. An order of "charge" sent from each leader plane was successively intercepted. Then followed: "Torpedoed enemy battleships. Serious damage inflicted. 0335." "Bombed Hickam at Ford Island. 0340." "Bombed enemy battleships. Position, Pearl Harbor. 0340." "Torpedoed enemy heavy cruiser with serious damage inflicted. 0335." "3 hangars and 50 planes on the ground set on fire. 0345." "After torpedoing, counter fire was met. 0357." "There are many flying boats at Ford Island base. 0405."

After a pause for a while, telegrams sent from planes of the second wave were received. "All force, charge. 0423." "Three enemy planes sighted." "Bombed an enemy heavy cruiser with serious damage inflicted." "Two enemy battleships left Pearl Harbor." "Bombed Kaneohe field with great damage inflicted. 0455." "Bombed Hickam field with serious damage inflicted. 0440." "Bombed Ford Island with minor damage inflicted. 0446." "No enemy planes sighted in the air."

In the meantime, the Task Force had made its way to the south forming a compact formation so as to display concentrated AA gunfire as well as placing interceptors over the force in preparation to meet oncoming enemy planes. In order to facilitate the receiving of returned planes, the force neared a point 190 miles due north of Pearl Harbor.

A carrier force should avoid an excessive approach to an enemy land base. At that time it was considered the limit to approach within 200 miles from an enemy base. Carrier-borne planes were just like kids to their carriers. Even a single plane of those that had achieved a brilliant success should not be compelled to make a forced landing at sea on its way back from the attack. Among them, there might be wounded crewmen, and some planes that were finding difficulties in continuing flight. Some might be at a loss, after losing their way back to their mother carriers. It should be the heart of a parent to make a further approach of even 5 or 10 miles, even at some risk. In addition, Admiral Nagumo ordered submarines to stay on the scene for a while to rescue planes which might be forced to make a forced landing as much as they could afford.

The same was in the mind of the air force overall commander after the attack. Commander Fuchida, without any cover, remained in the sky over Pearl Harbor until he became the last man to leave there. It might be because he intended to confirm the result of the attack made by his force, and also because he wished to see the last of the young boys who perished in their first fighting. Besides, it was because he wanted to assemble as many fighters missing their way back to the mother carriers as possible to take them back to the mother carriers safely.

Such a touching telegram reflecting the feeling between parent and children as below was often intercepted, too: "Shot down one enemy flying boat shadowing us." "There is fear that an enemy flying boat is shadowing us."

The aforementioned telegram of "tora" was received not only by the Combined Fleet, but also by the Imperial General Staff. Submarines of the Submarine Force also intercepted it. Eagerness was seen in support of the Task Force by various departments of the Navy.

Gone with the Wind Without Zanshin

At about 0630 black points appeared far to the south one after another. Our planes were returning, repeating a wave movement in accordance with the identification rule. There were some that flew in a formation, and also some that flew individually. The flight deck became conspicuously busier.

The Task Force swung into the wind direction and increased its speed with remarkable white waves kicked out. Planes appeared to land on the deck, while circling over their own carriers.

Those planes which were not in imminent order for landing flew over an area ahead of the force to protect it from enemy submarines. Ignoring the pitching and rolling, they landed on the deck safely one after another. As soon as they stopped, maintenance crews in side pockets ran to them in order to get them to the proper position.

Then Commander Fuchida's plane landed on the deck. He was immediately called to the bridge to report his account of the fighting on the day. Nothing was more regrettable than the fact that we could not get two enemy carriers, but from the standpoint of the damage inflicted upon the enemy, the attack was considered to have almost achieved its original aim.

The objective of this operation was to protect the flank and back of the Southern Force. So what the Task Force had to meet were a mere one or two enemies. That's why a long-trained sword was swung down under minute planning after making up our mind to swing it once and for all. Inasmuch as its objective was almost accomplished, I concluded that we should not remain on the scene and also should not be distracted to the game achieved indefinitely. So I made up my mind to make an immediate withdrawal.

As to this decision of making the withdrawal, various criticisms were heard later. They included that Admiral Yamamoto was displeased to have missed the enemy carriers; why heavy cruisers and other light vessels were not annihilated; why dock yards and oil tanks were not destroyed and also that there wouldn't have been the Doolittle air raid upon Tokyo had the enemy carriers, the main fighting strength, been sought out thoroughly and destroyed. But I dare say that all of them were nothing but afterthoughts of poor strategists.

Without hesitation, I recommended to Admiral Nagumo to make withdrawal. Necessary steps were immediately taken, and the following two telegrams were sent to the CinC of the Combined Fleet: "Will retire via the first course, but the course will be changed to pass 'L' point (35°N, 160°E). Time, 0600," "Two enemy battleships instantly sunk, four seriously damaged and approximately four cruisers also seriously damaged. The foregoing results are surely made. Many planes destroyed. Our losses of planes are slight."

After sending them, radio silence was again maintained, and the force made its way north like the wind, maintaining strict alert and headed for "F" point (37°N, 160°W) where the 1st Tanker Train was waiting for us. In the meantime, on each carrier a minute examination was conducted against the claimed result of attacks, gathering the returned fliers. Its results were successively sent to the *Akagi*. The brief battle reports of each carrier were shown as below:

AKAGI

1. Level bombing units: four hits were inflicted on battleships. Due to clouds, the bomb spread of the 3rd squadron could not be observed, but it was estimated that they also made a hit.
2. Torpedo bombing units: 11 hits of torpedoes were given to three battleships.
3. Dive bombing units: Though most bombs dropped could not be observed due to smoke caused by big fires nearby, hits were given to battleships, while one hit was inflicted on a cruiser of *Omaha* class. Later, strafed Barbers Point Field, giving serious damage.

4. Fighter units: Shot down three planes (one B-17, one transport plane and one training plane). Out of approximately 30 planes which were parked outside at Hickam Field, about 23 were set on fire and the remaining seriously damaged. Out of about 40 planes at Barbers Point Field, about 30 were either set on fire or destroyed.

Our losses: 1 fighter and 4 dive bombers missing. One was dead on board a torpedo bomber.

KAGA

1. Torpedo bombing units: Four hits each were given to *Arizona* and *Tennessee*.
2. Level bombing units: One hit was given to the fore part of *Arizona,* two to *California* and one to the fore turret of *Maryland* (a fierce explosion occurred). The bomb spread of another squadron could not be seen because of clouds, but believed to make hit.
3. Dive bombing units: Most bombs could not be observed due to resultant smoke from nearby fire and also bomb smoke of the preceding plane, most of them were believed to make hits on *California* and two other battleships. Two enemy planes were shot down in dog fighting, while one was set on fire by strafing.
4. Fighter units: Many set on fire by strafing on parked planes on air fields.

Our losses: 4 fighters, 6 dive bombers and 5 carrier bombers missing. One seriously wounded and three slightly wounded. Besides, 3 fighters, 18 dive bombers and 7 carrier bombers were holed.

2ND CARRIER DIVISION (*SORYU* AND *HIRYU* COMBINED)

1. Torpedo bombing units: 6 torpedoes hit a battleship with basket type mast, while three hit another battleship which sank instantly. Two more scored hits on a battleship. All of them were seriously damaged. A heavy cruiser hit by three torpedoes.
2. Level bombing units: The first bomb hit on a battleship which sank instantly. Two hits scored on another battleship causing a big explosion. In addition, six hits were recorded on three battleships and five on a heavy cruiser.
3. Dive bombing units: Five hits were given on two light cruisers, and one on a destroyer in dock.
4. Fighter units: In cooperation with dive bombing units, 20 grounded planes at Wheeler Field set on fire, and four hangars there destroyed and set on fire. At Barbers Point, 60 planes on the ground set on fire, while 10 were also set on fire at Kaneohe Field. Besides, four enemy planes (light bombers) and one flying boat set on fire.

Our losses: 3 fighters and 4 dive bombers missing. 20 fighters, 23 dive bombers and 3 torpedo bombers got holed.

5TH CARRIER DIVISION (*SHOKAKU* AND *ZUIKAKU* COMBINED)

1. Two hangars for flying boats and one for four-engined planes on Ford Island were set on fire, though another one was hit by two bombs but not set on fire. At Kaneohe about 50 flying boats were set on fire and one hangar on fire too. At Wheeler four out of five hangars set on fire, and two bombs hit on another one which failed to catch fire. At Bellows, out of 30 planes three were set on fire, while seven hangars on fire at Hickam. In addition, three planes shot down.

Our losses: one dive bomber failed to return.

As these reports were made just after the attack, some points were duplicated.

CHAPTER 4. RETURNING TO HOMELAND

Thinking of 30 Planes Which Failed to Return

The return course was decided to pass a little bit south of the course taken on the way to the attack, trying to get out of the supposed enemy air patrol area as soon as possible. Of course, radio silence was maintained. It had to be taken into account that enemy submarines would try their best to ambush us on our way back home. Also enemy carriers which were considered to be two and had escaped from our attack on Pearl Harbor might come to follow us with the remaining cruisers. If and when an enemy was met, a battle had to be launched under the conditions prevailing at the moment. Various hardships and difficulties had to be expected on the way back of 3,000 miles. Since our existence had been known to them, we could never relax.

Every day a strict alert was maintained, flying patrol planes. Information on the enemy situation as successively sent in from the Combined Fleet as well as the Imperial General Staff. They were

"Enemy flying boats at Midway considered to be three or six will arrive in Pearl Harbor at 1330 hours today."

"The enemy issued an order calling for being no trouble at all . . . as patrol planes are going to leave Pearl Harbor at 2100. They may be reconnaissance planes or planes moving to Midway."

"Radio-direction-finders suspect what seems to be a heavy cruiser at a point 600 miles north of Pearl Harbor at 1800."

"U.S. vessels in Hawaiian district suspected by radio-direction-finders on the 9th: (1) the flagship of a submarine group, 200 miles, bearing 310° from P.H. at 1600, (2) call-sign 557Z (which could be suspected to be a carrier), 17°N, 175°W at 1700, (3) the flagship of a minelayer squadron in the vicinity of P.H. at 1900 and (4) other radio directions were almost suspected in the vicinity of P.H., so that there is no indication of a major force moving a great distance."

The above information made us conclude that the enemy was not coming after us. On the 9th, as originally scheduled, the *Abukuma* and one destroyer were sent ahead of the force to facilitate the rendezvous with the supply force in order to refuel at "F" point. The rest of the force sped north generally maintaining the course of 330°.

At about 2100 hours of the 9th, rendezvous with the supply force was successfully made and refueling was started. But no relaxation could be allowed, though such a moment after the long-strained time was apt to induce a relaxation of tension. When we thought of 30-odd unreturned planes, after successfully making contact with the supply force, we couldn't help feeling sorry for them.

They Didn't Know the Way to Treat Heroes

Around this time, the following telegram order was sent to us by the Combined Fleet: "On the way back, the Task Force will, as far as the situation permits, launch an air raid on Midway and strive to completely destroy it so as to render it inoperable."

As it was an order, it had to be carried out under any circumstances. So we drew up our plan to carry out the assigned mission, and necessary orders were issued to our force accordingly. But I myself felt anger in my heart about it, not just that its idea interested me little.

The idea of the plan, as envisaged by those staffs who safely sat in Hiroshima Bay contemplating things only on their desks, was to touch off vulnerable Midway by way of the success just achieved. A war is fought by force of circumstances. To attack Midway with the whole strength of the Task Force, the morale of which has reached its peak after the great success, was anything but a big matter, but I felt anger about the unthoughtful minds of those who planned this order.

A lion is said to use his full strength to attack even a rabbit. No matter how small an enemy it might be, some extent of plan should be drawn up and preparations made accordingly. But the prevailing circumstances at that time did not necessarily warrant the necessity of attacking that tiny island, and, moreover, even if an attack were made it would have been of no use, just like attacking mere land.

Also from the standpoint of emotional feeling, such an order was just like requesting a *sumo* wrestler who beat down a *sumo* champion to get a radish on his way back from his victorious ring. Instead, it was essential to pay attention so as to protect the way back of the Task Force, which was now seething with the great success, and rein in the mind of those who were showing more eagerness. This should be the mental preparation of the superior headquarters which commands various crack units under its control.

Since then, Midway was an ominous direction to me. But I never even dreamed that that tiny island would later become the tomb of the Combined Fleet.

Later, Combined Fleet headquarters gave up its intention toward Midway.

As only the outline of the result of the Pearl Harbor attack was reported immediately after the attack, there was some argument even among the Task Force headquarters advocating the wisdom of sending back the detailed battle report before the opening of the Diet session in December, for the purpose of informing the nation of the detailed account of the attack. But I opposed it and strove to maintain strict radio silence as before in order to conceal the whereabouts of the Task Force.

According to U.S. radio broadcasts, it appeared that they were rushing the air defense of both the east and west coasts and also showing a great deal of confusion with a sharp drop of the stock market and zooming-up of commodity prices. I thought at that time that the fact that the whereabouts of our forces was not known to them somewhat contributed to their confusion, though it might be a selfish view of the picture.

It was not necessarily that the main strength of the Combined Fleet sat idle all the time in Hiroshima Bay protected by torpedo-defense nets. According to telegrams received, it seemed that they sortied toward the northeastern area of Marcus Island to support the withdrawal of the Task Force. Their intention could well be appreciated, but their action was reflected as a half-measure in the eyes of those who fought at the front.

Telegrams reporting the enemy situation successively came in, too. They were:

1. In Hawaiian and Midway districts, the enemy is continuing air patrols as before and exerting themselves in asking defense preparations.
2. Hawaiian district is being strictly alerted against submarines, but our submarines are keeping watch, except some of them.
3. Early morning of the 10th the *Lexington* and two heavy cruisers (which had made port after the air raid) left P.H. and are heading to the west coast. Some of our submarines are following them.
4. On the 10th our air force sank British *Prince of Wales* and *Repulse,* thus annihilating main British battleships in the Far East.
5. Landing operations on the Philippines and Malaya Peninsula were successfully carried out, while invasion operations of Wake Island and Guam are under way.
6. Enemy submarines seem to be operating in the Nanpo Islands and Formosa. "Radio-direction-findings suspect what seems to be a flying-boat-tender at a point 150 miles, bearing 120° from Wake Island at 1830 of the 11th. According to radio intelligence, regular air patrols have been extended to the south of Oahu Island since 0500 of 12 December. According to the cross-bearing of radio directions, it is certain that code-sign KA56 (estimated to be a carrier) was in the vicinity of 90 miles, eastnortheast of Wake Island in the morning of the 12th."

Based upon various situations as well as the abovementioned information, it was judged that enemy submarines would ambush us along the Nanpo Islands, with an element off Tokyo Bay and another element in Bungo Strait.

Cooperate in Invasion of Wake Island

Around the 14th, the Fourth Fleet stationing at Truk at that time was confronted with a good deal of difficulties in the invasion of Wake Island, so that the Combined Fleet sent us an operational order calling for cooperation with that operation.

Unlike the case of the Midway attack, we could not stand still observing the hardships of the friendly force, though it seemed to be a makeshift idea. Moreover, as the Combined Fleet and the Fourth Fleet envisaged an intention of carrying out the invasion of the Bismarck Islands in an immediate succession, it was decided to pour in the full strength of the Task Force in the occupation operation.

And this operation should not be a rash one of rendering help by way of going back to the homeland. It was then decided to change the whole plan of the Task Force's going back to the homeland and hurriedly make port in Truk, where a detailed briefing with the Fourth Fleet would be made to carry out the operation after thoughtful planning. But those fleets which did not appreciate the actual situation the Task Force was confronting sent in such long negotiating telegrams as to compel us to send back telegrams against our will. I was extremely embarrassed by them and forced to send back telegrams breaking the restriction.

At that time, the Task Force was making its way to the west towards Bungo Strait at a point about 1,500 miles east of Tokyo. Subsequently, however, due to the postponement of the Bismarck operation, this plan was again revised, and it was decided to employ a part of the Task Force in the Wake invasion operation, while the rest of the force would make their way back to the homeland.

On 16 December, the 8th Cruiser Division, 2nd Carrier Division accompanied by DD *Tanikaze* and *Urakaze* departed from the others to cooperate with the invasion of Wake Island.

As the *Akagi* had sent a good many telegrams with regard to these problems, our position, course and speed must have been suspected by the enemy. Accordingly, I thought that more enemy submarines would come to gather ahead of us.

As expected, the Imperial General Staff sent in the following information: "From 2330 of the 15th to 0200 of the 16th a total of 14 enemy submarines were detected in the Far East district. They were: (1) ten of them between bearing 50° tp 68° from Chichijima, (2) one in the direction of 18° from Truk, (3) one each in the directions of 87°, 107° and 123° from Ushiomisaki."

So I made up my mind to make a great detour to avoid this submarine group. Since our position must have been known to the enemy, by way of breaking radio silence, it was further decided to send the detailed account of the Pearl Harbor attack, even in such a manner as sending it back in several separate covers with adequate intervals to enable the enemy to pick up our position. But as soon as the final cover of that telegram was sent back, the course of our force was swung south to head for Uracas Island, and its speed increased.

At the same time, the anti-sub alert was intensified, and the course was selected to pass the Nanpo Islands to the west from the northern end of the Kazan Islands. The Combined Fleet headquarters also seemed to worry about the situation, so it dispatched two destroyer divisions under its direct command to sweep enemy submarines in the north of the Chichijima Islands.

Best Time in My Life

Though another big course change was to be made at 1800 of the 17th, it seemed that our force had entered into enemy-submarine-infested area since 1000 hours in the morning, and enemy sub periscopes had begun to appear in close distances from the Task Force, keeping me awfully busy. Orders for emergency evasive movements of the fleet and zigzag movements had to be taken care of by the fleet chief of staff. In the meantime, planes and destroyers had repeated bombing and depth-charges, and two enemy submarines were surely sunk. Especially, one submarine which was half submerging was hit by a bomb just after her periscope and went down with her bow up. It was rather good luck for us to meet enemy submarines before the course change and successfully pass through their line of position.

Such being the case, various commands of the Navy tried to render their help to the Task Force. The Yokosuka Naval Base sent down as many planes and light vessels as it could afford to sweep enemy subs in the northern area of Chichijima. So did the Kure Naval Base which was responsible for Bungo Strait. Even the Fourth Fleet in Truk ordered the Saipan Defense Unit under its command to take care of anti-sub alert near the Ogasawara Islands.

Seeing such help given to our force, our dissatisfaction towards the Combined Fleet operational measures disappeared, and we were thankful from the bottom of our hearts for the hearty cooperation of our friendly forces. Without meeting enemy submarines any more since then, the main body of the Task Force arrived in the entrance of Bungo Strait at about 1300 hours on the 23rd. All of the passing vessels hoisted flag signals and lowered their ensigns to pay their respects to our success and send their congratulations on our safe return. It was, in fact, the best time in my life.

What was regretted at that time was that two or three men were lost in refueling at sea around the 12th, due to a heavy weather raged by a strong wind of more than 20 meters per second in the vicinity of 40°N.

As there was a suspicion at that time that one enemy sub entered the Inland Sea, the Combined Fleet as well as the Kure Naval Station were fussing about it. Therefore, even though our force entered the Inland Sea, an anti-sub alert formation had to be kept until we reached the Combined Fleet anchorage in Hiroshima Bay.

We were heartily welcomed by everyone. After Admiral Nagumo's reporting to Admiral Yamamoto was over, Admiral Yamamoto came over to the *Akagi* to congratulate the efforts of the Task Force, and so did Admiral Nagano who came down from Tokyo.

We were also informed that His Majesty wished to hear the account of the attack directly from participants of the attack. And the chief of staff of the Combined Fleet suggested that I "go up to Tokyo," first because it was not the formal return from the war, and second, because he was not completely agreeable for the commander-in-chief of a fleet to leave his flagship at that moment. But I replied that such formality was out of place, and no person was more qualified than Admiral Nagumo as far as the overall matters of the Task Force was concerned, and also than Fuchida and Shimazaki as far as the air raid itself was concerned. And I had them go up to Tokyo.

CHAPTER 13

Conquer the Pacific Ocean Aboard Destroyer *Akigumo*: War Diary of the Hawaiian Battle

Rear Adm. Sadao Chigusa (Ret.)
Japanese Maritime Self-Defense Force

T HE AUTHOR of this diary, Rear Adm. Sadao Chigusa,* wrote this manuscript in English, of which he had an excellent command, so our editorial tasks have been minimal. Before the full diary came into Prange's
hands, Chigusa had given him extracts during two interviews, held on 18 and
22 November 1964. These extracts were very useful in preparing *At Dawn We
Slept,* giving as they did a vivid picture of the events as they happened,
recorded by an intelligent, conscientious officer.

This full diary as amplified by Admiral Chigusa, gives a fascinating
account of the wartime cruise of a destroyer, in sharp contrast with the
experience of those aboard the major vessels such as carriers and battleships.
For example, the rolling seas that were little more than a nuisance to the latter
were a real nightmare for the light destroyer. The diary also reveals the
day-to-day activities of a destroyer's executive officer as performed by an
officer who loved his ship, had the welfare of the crew always in the forefront
of his mind, and knew his business thoroughly.

The text of the full diary is in standard print. What Chigusa called his "old
diary" is indented. Material in brackets represents information and comments
that Chigusa interpolated during his interviews with Prange.

Dates and hours cited are in Tokyo time.

PREFACE

Thinking back, it is now over thirty years since I departed Hitokappu Bay on
Etorofu Island on board the very new Japanese destroyer *Akigumo* at the end of
November, 1941 over a Pacific ocean of raging waves for the great surprise attack
on Pearl Harbor.

---

* Chigusa gives his own career brief herein —Eds.

A part of my diary of the Battle has already been introduced to the public through the book *Tora Tora Tora* describing the attack on Pearl Harbor.* My old diary which made up my record of the campaign is now very difficult to read, even to my wife and children. For the sake of my wife and children, and in response to my friends' advice, I decided to complete my old diary. This is thus my real diary of the Hawaiian Battle and the Japanese attack on Pearl Harbor across a Pacific Ocean of raging waves on board the destroyer *Akigumo*.

At that time my rank in the Japanese Imperial Navy was Lieutenant Commander, and my position on the *Akigumo* was Chief Ordnance Officer and Executive Officer. Such being the case, if the captain of a ship is the father of the family, the executive officer should be the mother of the family. You may thus understand that I joined in the Battle as the mother of the *Akigumo* crew and therefore this diary is the record of the mother of the *Akigumo*.

In writing this book of my diary in English, Mr. A. L. Burridge, President of Sterling International Pacific, and Cmdr. J. S. Viccellio, USN, Assistant Naval Attaché in Tokyo, helped me very much in editing my manuscript, and I would now like to express my sincere gratitude to them.

September 1974
RADM Sadao Chigusa (Ret.)

TABLE OF CONTENTS

---

* This book, an amplification of Prange's *Reader's Digest* article of the same name, was printed in Japan, in Japanese —Eds.

1. THE BOOK *TORA TORA TORA* AND MY FRIENDS

The Reader's Digest Company issued a book *Tora Tora Tora* covering the Hawaiian Battle which was written by Dr. Gordon W. Prange, Professor, University of Maryland, and translated into Japanese in October of 1966. Dr. Prange quoted from some part of my diary in about twenty points in his book. He was greatly interested in my old wartime diary. One of my friends who had read *Tora Tora Tora* told me that he eagerly sought my views as to how our great Task Force reached its destination near Hawaii so safely, and he added that he would like to know the whole situation surrounding the extensive navigation of over 8,000 sea miles. "The success of the Hawaiian Battle was also a matter of our concern, but I was much more concerned over the safety of our Great Fleet as it made this voyage over the raging waves of the Pacific Ocean. I also wondered how the Fleet could make its round-trip cruise between Hawaii and Japan safely."

By his expression, I understood that he had several specific questions concerning the success of this operation as follows:

1. After leaving the mainland of Japan, how could the big Task Force composed of so many ships (over 20 such as battleships and aircraft carriers) gather secretly at Hitokappu Bay, the departure point for Hawaii?

2. When and where did we get the order for the Hawaiian Battle? And when did we know that we would attack Pearl Harbor on 8 December (Japan time)?

3. Why was our Fleet of such great size not detected by enemy patrol planes on the voyage of 4,000 nautical miles to Hawaii? Also, did we not meet any enemy ships or other ships of neutral powers? What formation did our fleet take during the voyage?

4. How did we supply oil to the *Akigumo* which required resupply so often during the voyage of one month, although it was less necessary for the larger ships?

5. What quantity of water did the *Akigumo* carry? Was it necessary to resupply water during our voyage? How long did raw fresh foods such as vegetables and fruits last?

6. In what detail were we aware of the disposition of the U.S. Fleet at Pearl Harbor?

7. Did we receive damage to the ship since we did not experience a U.S. counterattack?

8. How did our crew spend their days during the long voyage?

Also from my American friends, I used to receive the following questions:

1. Why did you not attempt a landing operation to occupy Pearl Harbor after the successful attack?

2. Why did your air forces not attack Pearl Harbor again following the first attack?

Such questions as the above have never been completely answered, though they have repeatedly been asked by my friends. I can easily understand why they have such questions, because all of them are very reasonable. However, the facts behind such questions can only be understood by the sailors who were in our Task Force.

As the great success of the attack on Pearl Harbor has been reviewed in many books and the movie *Tora Tora Tora,* many people have become familiar with some of the facts. However, there are still some who are interested in knowing how our fleet reached its destination and returned to Japan without damage after the attack on Pearl Harbor. This operation has been largely unknown and, as far as I know, not revealed to the public as yet.

As I have stated, the *Akigumo* belonged to this Task Force and her main mission was to escort one of the aircraft carriers. I was on board this destroyer serving as her executive officer as well as chief ordnance officer. My rank was Lieutenant Commander at that time. At last I have now decided to open all of my diary to public view, although it is not a complete record of the Fleet. It will be my pleasure, if it helps to lend understanding to the great voyage. My diary described how my destroyer cut through the high seas of the Pacific Ocean. I hope that it will provide some of the answers to the questions which have been asked for so long.

My diary was written in two separate parts, that is, the first part was a record of our movement from Kure Base to Hitokappu Bay by way of Saeki Bay (Oita Prefecture). The second part was my record of the voyage to Pearl Harbor from Hitokappu Bay and return.

My old diary, written as "My recollection of the attack on Pearl Harbor," has a foreword on its first page which stated:

> The destroyer *Akigumo* was built at the Urage Dock Yard in Yokosuka and commissioned on 27 September 1941. The *Akigumo* was admitted into the 5th Aircraft Carrier Squadron, which consisted of the carriers *Shokaku* and *Zuikaku,* as soon as she was delivered to the Imperial Japanese Navy.
>
> During her break-in training off the coast of Kyushu, the 5th Aircraft Carrier Squadron was attached to the Task Forces for the *Daitoa Senso* (Great East Asia War), and its operation was thus recorded in my diary. That meant the *Akigumo* was especially selected for the attacking force on Pearl Harbor.* This was the greatest honor for me!
>
> This diary was also a record of proof that the very new destroyer *Akigumo* could conquer the raging billows of the Pacific Ocean on her very first campaign.

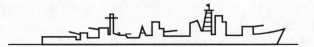

What was the *Akigumo*? I would introduce you to the principal features of the *Akigumo* with her size and capacities:

---

* Chigusa evidently wrote this foreword after the fact, because he informed Prange that he did not know about Pearl Harbor until his destroyer reached Hitokappu Bay —Eds.

Displacement:	2,520 Tons
Length:	117^m (384-¾ feet)
Width:	10.7^m (35 feet)
Draft:	3.76^m (12-⅓ feet)
Machinery:	Three Kampon boilers
	Two shafts
	Geared Turbines
	S.H.P. 52,000—35 Knots
Bunkers & radius:	Oil 600 tons
	5,700 M—14 Knots
Armament:	Six 5-inch/50 cal. D.P. (3 x 2)
	Four 25-mm (2 x 2) Machine guns
	Eight 24-inch T.T. (2 x 4)
Water tank:	44 tons
Complement:	228

2. WAR CLOUDS HANG OVER JAPAN!

It was a time when I felt very cold as the war clouds hung over Japan, like the cold wind of a late autumn, or rather, of an early winter, in November 1941. The Great Fleet of the Japanese Imperial Navy had continued her severe training day and night, thus providing her motto: "Monday, Monday, Tuesday, Wednesday, Thursday, Friday and Friday," meaning no days off in a week of work. Especially right after our great mock exercise attacking Kagoshima Bay in Kyushu as our supposed objective (of course I didn't know what place Kagoshima Bay was supposed to represent at that time, but I knew later it was Pearl Harbor). Our fleet put a stop to its training in mid-November and all ships belonging to the fleet hurriedly returned from the training area to their mother ports, or near the Naval Base to prepare for real war.

Oil tanks were filled and even drums of oil were loaded on board my ship. Our ammunition magazines were filled with ball cartridges. At the same time drinking water and food were loaded and fresh vegetables covered the open deck. These were the preparations for a long voyage.

My ship, the *Akigumo,* made haste to complete her preparations for war at the Kure Naval Base. All necessities for war had been fully loaded. Things which were thought to be unnecessary were transferred ashore to be stored in the warehouses of our Supply Depots. Even the paintings, writings and hangings in our wardroom and the vases which had been filled with flowers every day were sent ashore. Our wardroom had been turned into a very bare room. The *Akigumo* had completed her preparations and at any time was ready to leave the Kure Naval Base.

It was now the pleasant festival day of *Shichi-go-san* (7-5-3) which is a festival for boys of 3 and 5 years old and girls of 3 and 7 years old, observed since olden times on 15 November. However, it was a lonely scene in town, as our crew could not observe the beautiful dresses of the children for their festival just before such a serious affair as war. At that time I had two children who were very close to the ages for *Shichi-go-san.* One daughter, Kimiko, was four years old and one son, Masao, was two years old. They had been innocently living in Yokosuka City near the Naval Base with their mother, not knowing that their father's ship was preparing for war at Kure Naval Base. It goes without saying that I could not find enough time to go to Yokosuka to see my family and it was too strained a situation to take a vacation.

It was also the same day on which the crew enjoyed their final *Hangen Joriku* (a half of the crew were granted shore leave alternately) on 15 November. It was generally known by all the crew that the next day's sailing would be a serious affair, and not for the usual training exercise.

With the permission of the Commanding Officer, I had gone ashore, finally. At that time my parents in their old age lived at Gion-Cho in Hiroshima City, worrying about their two sons serving in the Military Forces. My younger brother had gone to the front in China as a Japanese Army officer. After deep consideration, I had made up my mind to say my final good-bye to my parents. I could go back to my parents without notice, plodding my way on foot for about two hours in the night. I was always pleased to meet my parents, who were very vigorous even though more wrinkled in old age. This time I could enjoy one last sound sleep with my old father and mother.*

3. FROM KURE NAVAL BASE TO HITOKAPPU BAY

The *Akigumo* left Kure Naval Base for Saeki Bay in Oita Prefecture, Kyushu, where our Fleet had temporarily gathered in full force. From there our fleet had broken up into groups of two or three and proceeded to sail to Hitokappu Bay in small units.

16 NOVEMBER (SUNDAY).

Fine weather on a clear autumn day.

My parents came to the Furuichi-bashi Station of a local train line to see me off. I parted from my father and mother with lingering steps, feeling secretly that this might be the last farewell to my parents. On the other hand, my parents should have decided in their own minds to let me join in battle sooner or later.

1022. Left Furuichi-bashi Station and changed to a train at Hiroshima Station for the Kure Line. Returned to my ship, the *Akigumo*, at 1230 with great joy that I had met my parents.

I fortunately received a little parcel, mailed by Fumiko, my wife, which contained winter clothing which arrived just before our departure. After we had loaded the remainder of the stores we must have for our trip, the preparations for our departure were finished.

1735. At last the *Akigumo* left Kure Base for Saeki Bay. When we passed Ujina Port at the southern extremity of Hiroshima City, I looked over the misty sky toward my home and sank into deep thoughts of my parents. I was temporarily overcome with homesickness.

I soon became absorbed in fire training against airplanes, after receiving the order, "Take Stations!" We performed a speed trial at 14 kts at night by illuminating the shore

---

* It was probably on this occasion that Chigusa spoke to his parents about his diary, saying: "This is a family treasure, do not show it to others. If I die, please burn it."—Eds.

mile post when we passed off Okurokami Island, located to the southwest of Miyajima Island. (Later on I learned that this speed of 14 kts was the speed we would hold all the way to Pearl Harbor.)

My ship steamed ahead toward the west on the calm surface of the Inland Sea while I was watch officer on duty on the bridge in the dead of night from 2200 to midnight.

17 NOVEMBER (MONDAY).

0230. In a calm and still dark night the *Akigumo* dropped anchor at her berth at Saeki Bay in Oita Prefecture. At dawn it was fine weather on a clear autumn day with no wind. I felt that the panoramic view of the Fleet which had now gathered here since last evening spread before my eyes was really heroic and even beautiful.

Morning: I made a report of the first step in preparation for war as we had done at the Kure Base.

1215. All the crew gathered on the forward deck on order, and received the following address and instructions from the Commanding Officer, Cmdr. Terumichi Arimoto, which touched our hearts: "Please do your best to do your duties well, as we go forward to Hitokappu Bay by squadrons. War clouds are quickly gathering."

1300. A meeting for the chief ordnance officers of all destroyers under the auspices of Lt. Cmdr. Mikami, who was the ordnance staff officer of the Torpedo Squadron on board the cruiser *Abukuma,* our flagship. I had now made up my mind to be able to cope with whatever challenges the battle would have.

In the evening we had training in antiaircraft fire and finished it very smoothly as our training progressed.

This time, when all ships had gathered together at Saeki Bay, they were under Vice Adm. Chuichi Nagumo's command. And then a great task force which had as its mission attack by airplanes was hereupon composed with especially picked ships both in name and reality.

All ships had secretly weighed anchor at once in the very early morning and then left Saeki Bay by twos and threes for Hitokappu Bay where the next meeting of the Fleet would take place. The Bay of Hitokappu was virgin soil to me, and the reason we went to the Bay was kept secret from all crews at that time. We could only guess at the purpose. We started our movement to the north in great expectation that something most serious was awaiting us. On our northern cruise, training in oil supply from a tanker and antiaircraft fire was preponderantly emphasized.

18 NOVEMBER (TUESDAY).

0200. All ships of the Fleet began to weigh anchor and left Saeki Bay in high spirits in a chilly wind. The *Akigumo* left the Bay as rear guard of the destroyer squadron.

0700. We had our first training ball firing against aircraft off Ashizuri Point in Shikoku Island. I had been nervously anticipating the firing, because I had had only two experiences in live firing since the *Akigumo* had been commissioned the previous September.

I should note that it used to take at least a half year for composite shooting practice to assure normal shooting with firm confidence. As the *Akigumo* engaged in this Battle after only two months' practice, I can easily understand why I wrote in my diary of my worry, in spite of doing our best in our training.

Very fine weather and a good day for shooting. A seaplane belonging to the cruiser *Abukuma,* the flagship of Torpedo Squadron, is pulling a target for our firing. Finally a target plane comes close to our ship, but our bullets cannot be discharged. Moreover there are many dud shells, so it is very difficult for me to confirm the explosive point at which the shells are expected.

At the first shooting at the target on the first pass, I couldn't fire all shells planned for the shooting and retained one shell. At the second shooting on the second pass of the target, I could hardly fire all shells planned including the one shell remaining from the first pass. I couldn't confirm or see the explosive point of our shells because there were many dud shells, also. Machine-gun firing was smoothly operated as all bullets were fired under the best conditions.

Tracing Course Chart for Destroyer *Akigumo*

From: Saeki Bay
To: Hitokappu Bay
True Lap   1,215 Sea Miles

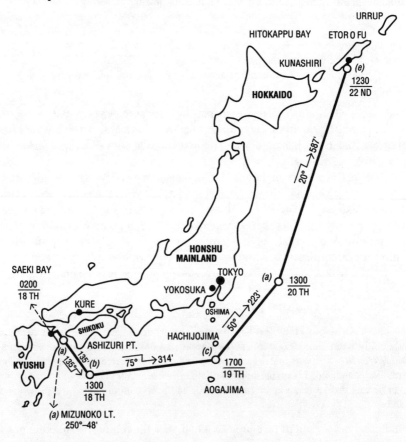

1000. We had fire training for a range finder for one hour.

1300. Made the first formation for alert steaming in which the flagship *Abukuma* was escorted by destroyers, and the *Akigumo* was located at the left side and to the rear of the *Abukuma.* Our course is 75°.

[Chigusa sketched this formation for Prange showing ship positions as follows:

DD   DD   DD   DD
                    Abukuma

        DD   DD

        DD *Akigumo*
        Tanker   ]

Afternoon. The *Akigumo* was supplied 10^T oil from the *Nippon Maru* (a tanker) using the "alongside" method on the starboard. It took a long time owing to our lack of familiarity with the operation.

What is the "alongside" method of oil supply?

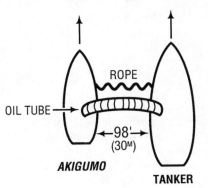

In the "alongside" method oil was supplied from a tanker to the *Akigumo* through a tube, as a tanker and the *Akigumo* sailed side by side in the same direction and at the same speed.

After completing our regular duties each afternoon, we would have gymnastics followed by marching songs that we would sing. I took the lead in our singing with such a loud voice in my ardent wish to buttress our military morale that I finally lost my voice.

Toward evening the wind rose slightly.

Evening. Oil supply was practiced and we practiced it very carefully.

19 NOVEMBER (WEDNESDAY).

Morning. We finished our training for oil supply very smoothly.

About noon. To our left we watched Hachijojima and Miyakejima Islands go out of sight. We were reluctant to part from our islands. It is warm from a south wind.

1700. Our course is changed north to 50°. The oil supply training scheduled at night is cancelled, because it took a long time to supply one of the other ships.

20 NOVEMBER (THURSDAY).

0800. The alarm for "General Quarters" suddenly rang through the ship.* All the crew went to their combat stations. A composite assault exercise by our Torpedo Squadron is launched against the groups of tankers as targets.

0930. As soon as we finished our assault exercise, we had oil supply training using the "astern" method with the *Nippon Maru.*

Oil supply by the "astern" method:

A tanker tows the *Akigumo* and supplies oil to her through an oil hose, with both ships maintaining the same speed and course.

---

* Chigusa informed Prange that the Japanese used a trumpet and bell as well for "General Quarters"— Eds.

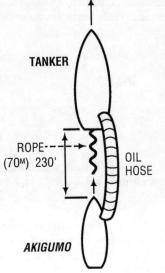

TANKER

ROPE- - -
(70ᴹ) 230'

OIL
HOSE

AKIGUMO

The training is prolonged due to the slow operation of the *Nippon Maru*, but it was completed at 1300. [Chigusa later commented that this exercise took much too long, due to insufficient training.]

The *Akigumo*'s location at noon is 100 miles east of Tokyo. Just past noon the wind changed to the north and the temperature fell gradually. I began to feel cold.

1300. We changed our course to 20° and were headed straight for Hitokappu Bay.

Afternoon. We instituted protection against the cold. (This meant we treated against the cold those parts of our weapons which were apt to have functional troubles due to cold or icy weather.)

High waves at night. The wind is blowing at over 10 meters a second (20 kts). I dug out a heavy coat to wear and lost no time putting on both a muffler and a woolen jacket which my wife, Fumiko, mailed to me to help against the cold weather we anticipated. [Mrs. Chigusa had knit these two garments.]

21 NOVEMBER (FRIDAY).

0800. On the order "General Quarters," all the crew quickly took combat stations. We again had a composite assault exercise against the tanker groups as our targets. I made every effort to do fire training during this exercise. [They did no actual shooting. This exercise was called *Hosen Kyoren*, i.e., no shooting.]

The temperature went down to 8°C (46°F). The wind is now weak and the sea calm. As our ship goes further north, the temperature falls minute by minute.

0930. We had oil supply training.

Afternoon. Ammunition supply training was held which included paymasters and hospital orderlies.

1830. We had night oil supply training. As training advances, oil supply is done smoothly step by step. There is an especially biting cold at night, so I take my night duty on the bridge wearing two pair of socks, one of which was a heavy white wool pair made by my wife, which I wore over the other.

22 NOVEMBER (SATURDAY).

It was fortunate for me that the temperature did not fall below 8°C (46°F) since I was on the bridge wearing just enough clothing against the cold last midnight. During my watch last night, I could dimly see the shadows of the carriers *Zuikaku* and *Shokaku*, belonging to the 5th Aircraft Carrier Squadron which was going north with us on course to the left of the *Akigumo*.

We don't have any schedule for oil supply today, owing to our arrival at Hitokappu Bay.

Morning. We had trial firing for four light machine guns (MK 96), but the movement was not good due to congealing of lubricant. [Real ammunition was used.] This might be caused by the low temperature which suddenly fell to 4°C (39°F). I barely finished my firing by using a special cold-resistant oil. I had an experience that taught me that normal oil should be prohibited in extremely cold areas.

At first Shikotan Island came into view on our port side and next the high mountains of Kunashiri and Etorofu covered with white snow appeared clearly in sight. Sailors on the bridge were remarking on Mt. Berumarube, all covered with pure white snow, rising high in the sky. It is unique that the spelling of "BE RU MA RU BE" has the same pronunciation when spelled backwards.

Afternoon. The wind is northwest at 10ᵐ (20 kts.) The cold has increased and I must protect my face from the cold with a winter cloth, supplied by the Government.

1420. A second live firing practice against aircraft was held. The *Akigumo* and the target plane are passing each other, so the target is approaching us rapidly. I smoothly shot two live shells from each gun with alternate firing method. At last I gained confidence in firing myself.

1535. My ship, *Akigumo,* at last dropped anchor at Hitokappu Bay. I gave a sigh of relief to safely reach the last meeting place of the Task Force. Before long, not only I but all our crew were surprised to hear radio news from our mainland which resounded throughout the ship, and enjoyed having such contact even here at the Chishima Islands (Kuriles).

The *Akigumo* was appointed the air defense watch ship today at Hitokappu Bay, so we applied the Fourth duty station in which one fourth of our crew is on duty all day to detect the enemy's air force.

Today, I really enjoyed playing a game of Bridge for a short time after supper. To my great joy, I also won two cans of pineapple as the prize for the winners of our game. My team, with Lt. Hashiguchi, Chief Torpedo Officer, won a great victory against the other team of Lt. Comdr. Mochida, Chief Engineering Officer, and Lt.jg. Yoshimura, Chief Medical Officer.

I also felt refreshed after being able to shave my face, as this is the first chance to do so since our departure from Saeki Bay.

On the other hand, turning my eyes to the surface of Hitokappu Bay, it is really encouraging to see all the ships of our Task Force steam in one after another and gather in full force by evening. It is a high-spirited group dominating the northern sea with these crack ships of the Imperial Navy.

Vice Admiral Nagumo, Commander-in-Chief of our fleet, sought to avoid public notice. In order to keep our presence secret, we selected a dark night to weigh anchor at Saeki Bay, and broke up our movement to Hitokappu Bay by going up to the northern sea in twos and threes, so it looked like training trips of each small group. Under such a plan, all ships of our force could gather successfully and secretly in full force today. At the same time, the Fleet had done its best to keep silence covering ship movements and preventing external wireless monitoring of our radio at Hitokappu Bay or en route to this Bay from Kure Naval Base. We were plunged into an uncanny silence like the calm before a storm. I say now that it was a fact that even the Imperial Navy's people, except our Task Force's people, didn't know where the Great Fleet of the Task Force was. It was really a great puzzle at that time.

Thinking back to the above, I am sure that the secrecy of our movements made it possible to come stealthily across the Pacific Ocean to the sea adjacent to Hawaii.

As for my ship, the *Akigumo,* my diary clearly tells me that we attached great importance to both training in oil supply at sea, for which we did our best every day and night, and in antiaircraft firing on the way from Saeki Bay to Hitokappu Bay. We knew that the success or failure of the attack on Pearl Harbor depended upon whether our Task Force could arrive safely and secretly at its destination within attack range of Pearl Harbor by our airplanes.

It was absolutely impossible to make a long voyage with such a small ship as a destroyer if she could not get enough oil from a tanker at sea several times. We can understand now how seriously oil supply was considered. As I have already stated, the *Akigumo* had only 600 tons of oil in full tanks and her cruising radius was limited to 5,700 sea miles at a speed of 14 kts.

As for antiaircraft fire training, I must say that we expected to meet the enemy's airplanes first. We might have an attack by their airplanes before we could launch an attack on Pearl Harbor. Also, if we did attack Pearl Harbor, they should give us a counterattack without fail, and we could avoid it by no means. Accordingly, I can tell you from this consideration that it was no wonder we had concentrated training in antiaircraft firing.

4. OUR STAY AT HITOKAPPU BAY

We were on the alert in very cold Hitokappu Bay for three days before our departure for Pearl Harbor in the early morning of 26 November 1941.

23 NOVEMBER (SUNDAY).

I took the duty of chief watch officer from 0600 to 0800.

0805. Gathering on the upper deck in line, we performed the ceremony of worshipping from a distance the *Niiname-Sai* (Harvest Festival) and silence prevailed over the ship upon hearing the sound of the bugle playing *Kimigayo,* our National Anthem. On worshipping the southern sky in the distance, I pledged my loyalty and patriotism from my heart. [This was an annual festival celebrated throughout Japan when the Emperor in his palace was to eat the first bowl of rice from the new harvest. The ceremony aboard ship was called *Yohai Shiki.* As Chigusa described it to Prange, this was to pay respects to the Emperor and Empress. Everyone turned toward Tokyo and saluted. This included every ship in the task force and every ship in the Imperial Navy wherever it might be. Aboard the destroyer and the others the trumpet sounded on every ship, and everyone stood at attention. At exactly 0800 signal flags went up and at 0805 the ceremony began on the dot.]

It was very cold with a driving powdery snow all morning. After the ceremony Commander Arimoto, our Commanding Officer, visited the flagship for an address of instruction by Vice Admiral Nagumo, Fleet Commander-in-Chief.

No work due to the celebration today. All the crew took baths in the morning. Washing was permitted which was one week since we had last bathed. [Chigusa later explained that Japanese ships at that time did not have showers. This had been his first bath in a week, and he thought it might well be a month before he had another chance.]

A destroyer had only a small quantity of water in her tanks and we used it mostly for drinking. Therefore, we could not have a bath during our voyage. Not only during our voyage, but during our stay at the Naval Base, we couldn't have a bath every day except on such occasions as when we got water while mooring alongside a wharf or pier. A full tank of water for the *Akigumo* was 44 tons, so we were limited to using 1.5 tons of water a day for the whole voyage, without any resupply while on the way. We used water mostly for cooking, washing our faces every morning, washing our hands after work, and to disinfect our hands before meals.

Afternoon. We had oil supply to fill our tanks while at anchor by coming alongside the tanker *Toho Maru* today.

After supply Commander Arimoto, our Commanding Officer, explained [to the staff officers] the great operational plan for the battle against the U.S.A., and I made up my mind that "An opportunity certainly offers itself."

When I lost myself in thought at that time, the Hawaiian Battle gave me some sad thoughts because this battle would attack Hawaii where my elder brother was then living. But I would surely fight as well as I could without any change of my mind, forgetting my thoughts of my brother, because this battle would be for my Emperor and my country. [Chigusa's brother was Takeo Nishimura, an American citizen, working in a hotel in Honolulu at the time. Chigusa's birth name was Nishimura, Chigusa his adopted name.]

We were permitted to drink *sake* and also to have amusements for all the crew. All the sailors really indulged in these final pleasures in their confined rooms aboard the ship which was now rolling in the long swells coming from the mouth of the Bay.

It was usually permitted to drink *sake* on board ship in the Imperial Navy, but the privilege was limited in both quantity and time. It was no exception to permit drinking and to enjoy relaxation today, because today was a National Holiday. As I recall, there was a harmonious atmosphere throughout the ship as the sweet sound of a *Shakuhachi* (bamboo flute) came from some of the sailors' quarters.

2200. I patrolled throughout the ship to see that the sailors were sleeping. I found a few of the sailors talking a lot of hot air under the influence of *sake,* and I rebuked them, telling them to go to their beds.

Today all the crew were pleased to be told that our bonuses for the trip would be 200% of each salary. [This meant two months' pay over and above the regular salary.]

2300. I went to bed, after my final security patrol. Very cold.

24 NOVEMBER (MONDAY).

A strong wind came from the mouth of the Bay, blowing 16^m a second (32 kts). We extended anchor cables to 12 *Setsu* (1 *Setsu* = 25 m) for stormy weather. The water was 38^m in depth. The rolling of the ship was 10°–15° by the billow, surged over from the mouth of the Bay.

In the morning after the Commanding Officer gave his instruction for the coming battle, I minutely explained the matters for this operation that demanded the special attention of all the crew. [This was when the skipper told the entire crew about the Pearl Harbor attack. Chigusa's instructions concerned such items as: keep the ship dark; do not throw anything overboard; take care of their health; be alert. It would be a cold, rough voyage; they should expect this and do their best.]

This afternoon we spent in "Mantlet Operations" and all the crew engaged in it in earnest. ("Mantlet" means to make a bulletproof casing with our hammocks and rigging for the bridge, main weapons and other important places.)

In the evening we had a meeting about our campaign, but it was very cold and raining outside.

25 NOVEMBER (TUESDAY).

The wind changed to the north, but we had steady rolling on our ship without letup due to large waves.

Morning. We made haste to complete our mantlet following yesterday's operation.

1330. I visited the cruiser *Abukuma,* the flagship of our Torpedo Squadron, to hear an address of instruction by Rear Adm. [Sentaro] Omori, Commander of the Squadron, and this was followed by meetings for every division under the appropriate staff officers. [As Chigusa recalls, Omori gave a general pep talk, speaking of the great importance of the Pearl Harbor operation, etc.] (The destroyer *Akigumo* was a member of the 1st Torpedo Squadron, according to the organization of the Task Force.)

We had been alert all day long today, as the *Akigumo* was the watch ship to keep a lookout for the enemy's airplanes from morning till night as the final duty ship at Hitokappu Bay. It was very cold, so I prepared more protection against the cold by putting floss silk inside my socks and wearing the vest made by my mother.

Tomorrow morning at last we will sortie for Pearl Harbor. I entrusted our final letters gathered from all the crew to the *Toyomitsu Maru,* a special provisions ship that will remain at Hitokappu Bay until the attack on Pearl Harbor. Among the letters from the crew were two letters of my own for my wife, Fumiko, and my parents.

All the crew were pleased to have warm noodles at their midnight supper. I had nothing to look back on with regret, because we had had enough study and discussion of this campaign today. The war preparation of my ship was completed, and moreover I had left my will for my wife and parents.

What might you think is for the Japanese a very important and traditional thing in war which I secretly took out from my drawer late that night? It was a stomach band of *Senninbari* which my mother had elaborately made for me. (*Senninbari* means "one thousand needles" in Japanese, that is, one thousand people made a knot each using a needle with red thread on a white cloth to wish a sailor good luck in war.) [In peacetime the Japanese Navy officer did not wear his *Senninbari;* he wore it only when he went to war or engaged in battle.] Expressing my last gratitude for my mother's affection, I wound it tightly around my body. And I strongly made a fresh determination not to fall short of the expectation and the prayers of many people, one thousand of whom I didn't even know as faces, but they had kindly given one stitch to my *Senninbari.*

Therefore, the real preparations had now been finished, and at 2230 I took my last sleep at Hitokappu Bay without any anxiety.

We stayed at Hitokappu Bay only four nights and five days, but it had really developed deep meanings. First of all, we received our first order to attack Pearl Harbor, and all the crew could now well understand the Hawaiian campaign. Hitokappu Bay was a world of isolation for the Task Force and had no relationship with outside people. And, finally, all the crew developed an enthusiastic determination to fight against the U.S. Navy.

I believe that Vice Admiral Nagumo, Commander of the Task Force, brought about the complete dedication and understanding of each Squadron's Commander, the Commanding Officers of each ship, and each Commander of an Air Attack Squadron while his flagship was in Hitokappu Bay.

We all sent our final letters home which were written there. I am sure the great part of those letters were last wills to be left under the special care of the provisions ship which remained at Hitokappu Bay. We wrote our last letters assuming that we would not come back alive, and of course I expected as much. As none of the crew thought they could come back safely but rather would go down with their ship off Hawaii in the greatest and most desperate battle in our history, it was no wonder that each man felt it necessary to leave his will.

I wrote my own farewell message to my wife and parents. To my father and mother I gave thanks for their affection and care all my life. I wrote my will with tears to Fumiko, my wife. I thanked her for her love and our life together. I delegated the care of our two children to her hands and, as if at my deathbed, asked her to take good care of them even after her husband passed away. I will never in my life forget my feelings as I gave my eternal farewell to my wife in a letter in which I also enclosed a small snipping of my hair as a keepsake.

The ship to which these wills were entrusted did not leave Hitokappu Bay until after the successful attack on Pearl Harbor, so my family received my letters after hearing the report of our great victory at Hawaii, saving them much anguish. Of course my parents in Hiroshima and my wife in Yokosuka were most pleased at hearing the news. I believe my parents and my wife read my will with a smile instead of tears as they looked back upon how ready I had been to die.

As I recomposed this diary, absorbed in old recollections of 33 years ago, my wife left her seat and carefully brought to me a very old envelope from her chest of drawers. She opened it quietly and showed me the small lock of hair which I had sent her at that time.

I have grown my hair long since the war, but I kept it closecropped when I served in the Imperial Navy. I used to have my hair cut every week to keep it short, and the hair my wife showed me was less than one millimeter long, and colored *Gomashio* (salt and sesames in Japanese), which means gray-haired, since I had been slightly gray-haired since I was a young boy. I was not a little surprised and my eyes were moist with tears of thanks, knowing that in spite of my good health now, my wife had carefully kept this lock of hair until today. My wife returned the hair to its secret place, and whether she doesn't want to forget her hard times of those days, or whether she is thus providing for any accident I might encounter even in peacetime, I am not sure.

5. EN ROUTE TO PEARL HARBOR

Not only my ship, the *Akigumo,* but our whole Fleet wanted to keep their course toward the east a secret to everyone except God. We continued our secret voyage for the 12 days before "X" Day (the attack day) with such care that I could hardly suppress my uneasy feelings and prayed to God that we would not be detected by the U.S. Navy.

26 NOVEMBER (WEDNESDAY).

We were in a raging snow storm when we woke up this morning, and I felt the biting cold and the strain of our determined sally.

0600. At last we left Hitokappu Bay for Hawaii to attack Pearl Harbor, seeing Mt. Berumarube disappear behind us.

0630. On passing the mouth of the Bay, trial firing of a shell at the right gun of No. 1 turret was made toward a cliff, and the results were very good. The shell exploded on the target, emitting volumes of dreadful brown smoke, making a roaring sound. As a result of this firing, I found no problems in our procedures and gained confidence in myself as Chief Ordnance Officer.

A northwest wind of 5–6 m/second (10–12 kts) blew, and it was very cold with occasional gusts of driving snow. A big roll of 20° to each side continued due to large swells on the rough sea. But the *Akigumo* continued to head east at a smart speed of 14 kts.

The sally of our great fleet was really a majestic sight. It was no wonder, however, since it was composed of the first-line ships of the Imperial Navy, all especially selected for this crucial mission.

27 NOVEMBER (THURSDAY).

0600. The *Akigumo* was supplied 30 tons of oil from the *Toho Maru* (a tanker) by the "alongside" method. It took about 45 minutes for the operation. I felt concern often during the oil supply operation because of the large waves and a 5–7 m (10–14 kts) northwest wind. Today we have very fine weather, but still encounter large swells. The maximum roll is 30° to each side.

Our midnight supper was *Shiruko,* which is a soup of sweetened bean jelly. We served it before our supper, because preparations for supper were delayed this evening.

28 NOVEMBER (FRIDAY).

0430. Reveille.
0500. Oil was supplied to the *Akigumo* by the "astern" method from the *Toho Maru.*
The wind changed to the south and blew a little stronger, reaching 12^m–15^m/second (24–30 kts). Swells have now decreased.
1030. Lunch.
1420. Supper.
I felt like all we did was eat meals, because lunch and supper was the only time we looked at a clock. (We used Japanese local time throughout this campaign.)

We received the following information from Imperial Headquarters as we more carefully continued our course toward the east under the intense attention of the watch officers and sailors on the bridge: "Two Soviet merchant ships left the west coast of the U.S.A. and are taking a course in the northern Pacific toward the west on the 12th and 13th of this month. You might have an opportunity to meet them today or tomorrow." [This meant to avoid these ships.]

Our midnight supper was coffee with cakes. [Cake and coffee were rare; generally the snack was noodles.]

29 NOVEMBER (SATURDAY).

Swells became calm as we steamed east on a comparatively calm sea with small rolls of 10 degrees to each side.

This morning we received oil from the *Toho Maru* by the "astern" method. Beyond our expectations, we finished the operation without the least difficulty.

We received news of the breakdown of diplomatic negotiations with the U.S.A. as well as information that British battleships were loitering about the Indian Ocean.

We were now occasionally caught in a dense fog peculiar to the north Pacific Ocean.

I shaved for the first time in five days.

You can appreciate that it was more or less a calm day, because it is difficult to shave in stormy weather.

30 NOVEMBER (SUNDAY).

At last we spend the last day of November today.

Owing to a dense fog last night, we were continuously alert all night to the safety of our navigation. We kept sharp watch with our searchlight playing as well as posting a bright shop lamp to warn any ship approaching too closely.

In normal times, we generally navigated on foggy seas as follows: At first we blew our siren to call the attention of other ships. Next we illuminated the front and rear of our ship with a searchlight, and last, we pulled a fog target astern so that the following ship would know our location. However, in this case we must be completely quiet, preceding our attack on Pearl Harbor, since there was no telling when we might meet the enemy's ships or airplanes. In this case, we could only do our best to keep fleet formation by illumination, even if we were blinded by fog and had a short range of vision.

Since leaving Hitokappu Bay, we were continuously strained and tested by nature which confronted us with such obstacles as severe cold, big rolls and dense fog like last night. As day dawned, the fog gradually cleared. A south wind blows at 12 m–13 m (24–26 kts), but waves are rough and high. Our ship is rolling at 15° to each side which continues all day long. Today, when oil was being supplied by the "astern" method from the *Toho Maru*, the mooring rope between the ships parted due to the severe rolling. On this occasion I was operating the ship. It was an immense relief to find no one injured, as I stood drenched with the cold sweat of embarrassment. I tried again to receive oil by putting us in tow, but we were compelled to stop the operation owing to darkness when the work became too difficult.

I felt "stuffy" and found I was affected by a cold, in spite of being armed with an outfit protecting me against cold. When I used a *Kairo* (pocket warmer) sent to me by my wife directly on my abdomen I felt very hot, and at the same time became aware of being slightly burnt.

Coffee with sweet bread, especially made by our cooks, was served for midnight supper.

Today, for a short time before *Junken,* I enjoyed playing Bridge in our wardroom. I enjoyed this little diversion. (*Junken* in the Imperial Navy was a patrol throughout the ship performed by the executive officer to assure security every night after all the crew had gone to their beds.) When I could finish the *Junken* peacefully the ominous day was past.

I was very sorry that something concerned the Commanding Officer today and I think this might be due to the failure of our oil supply to be on schedule. I went to bed suffering, feeling that the responsibility lies with me.

Our Task Force is silently continuing eastward at 14 kts.

The *Akigumo* received an order to escort the *Toho Maru* and devoted herself to guarding the tanker all night.

As I already explained, there were the "alongside" and the "astern" methods for oil supply on the ocean. It is easily understood that the alongside method is easier than the astern method from the facts of our experience.

Oil was supplied to the *Akigumo* 18 times during the one-month voyage from Saeki Bay (Oita Prefecture in Kyushu) to Hawaii via Hitokappu Bay and its return home. Fourteen times it was done using the alongside method and only four times using the astern method. The alongside method is much easier than the astern method, especially in rough weather. Only three tines were we refueled at night and each time of course it was with the alongside method. You can clearly understand how seriously we took a view of the oil supply, and how often it was operated almost every day even at night, so far as circumstances allowed. I would like to fully explain this matter of oil supply later.

1 DECEMBER (MONDAY).

A south wind of 12 m or 13 m (24 kts or 26 kts) was blowing. The maximum roll reached 35° to each side.

At last, only one week remains to "X" Day (the day scheduled for the attack). The *Akigumo* is steaming eastward rapidly with a wild sound from her screw propeller.

We received a signal from the *Akagi*, flagship of our Task Force. This was an order from Vice Admiral Nagumo calling for caution, as follows: "Our fleet just passed the 160° longitude (180° E) and has entered the sphere of air patrols from Kiska and Midway, so please take strict precautions against the enemy's patrol planes."

At this time I heard someone talking in our wardroom: "What an awful experience it will be for Japanese residents in Hawaii after our air raid there." My elder brother was living in Honolulu at that time, so I worried uncommonly about this problem after hearing these words. However, I again made up my mind to do my best in war, because I fought for my Emperor and my country. Thus I did not excuse myself from dashing to Hawaii in spite of the effect my act might have on a dear one.

0600. We had an oil supply operation by the alongside method from *Toho Maru*. It took about 40 minutes to supply us with 40 T oil.

All the crew were very happy to receive the balance of their special allowance for navigation (sea pay) today.

I decided to serve *Shiruko* (red bean soup with rice-cake in it) for their midnight supper, which everyone would welcome.

It has now been one week under continuously severe secrecy every day, earnestly observing silence without wireless, since leaving Hitokappu Bay. So as not to be found by the enemy, to take more easily and accept the challenge of a raid by the enemy and to provide a tanker location convenient for supplying the destroyers, we followed a special formation. All the ships of our Fleet did their best to keep an assigned position relative to the flagship, *Akagi*, which was the Task Force guide. All steamed toward the east for Hawaii on the same course and at the same speed.

The change to daytime formation from night formation began automatically one hour before sunup without an order. All ships did their best to rapidly assume their regular cruising position in the formation. We shifted in the same way going to night formation from daytime, starting a half hour before sunset.

formation to shorten the distance between destroyers in the front row as follows:

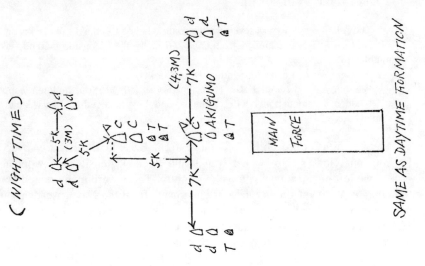

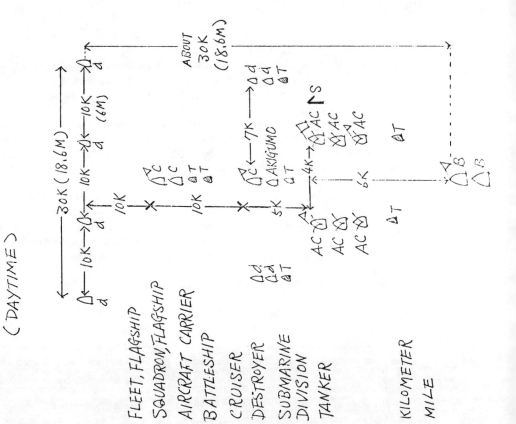

□: FLEET, FLAGSHIP

∧: SQUADRON, FLAGSHIP

AC: AIRCRAFT CARRIER

B: BATTLESHIP

C: CRUISER

d: DESTROYER

S: SUBMARINE DIVISION

T: TANKER

K: KILOMETER

M: MILE

2 DECEMBER (TUESDAY).

The roll of our ship was severe with a south wind of 13 m or 14 m (26 kts or 28 kts). Oil of 28 T was supplied from *Toho Maru* by the alongside method, taking 28 minutes to complete.

At night we had a strong wind of 18 m (35 kts).

We enjoyed a piece of *Yokan* (sweetened bean jelly) for our midnight supper.

I had a dream that my wife, Fumiko, and I were together, but we had moved somewhere.

Navy families were obliged to move from Base to Base nearly every year. Packing our clothes into wicker trunks and kitchen utensils into wooden apple boxes, we left our residences, traveling lightly. There were many rented houses in the cities near Naval Bases, and our classmates from the Naval Academy used to help us in our search for a house, settling our residence problem as if it was his own affair. I now recall that our frequent moves kept us very busy, but on the other hand we enjoyed the frequent changes.

3 DECEMBER (WEDNESDAY).

A strong south wind at 18 m (35 kts). The field of vision is short owing to heavy drizzle we occasionally encountered.

At last the matter which I had so eagerly looked forward to occurred today. This was a signal from the flagship to report the issuance of an Imperial Command saying "X day is decided for the 8th." All the crew were in high spirits to know that the decision for "X" Day was now made.

The greatest degree of roll today reached 47° to one side, which was the largest roll since leaving Hitokappu Bay, and of course I hadn't experienced anything like it ever before. Severe rolling like this was a fight and trial against nature, which was a real task for a small ship like our destroyer. All dishes placed on the table for our lunch were thrown to the floor, and rolled about here and there.

Osushi (special rice seasoned with vinegar) was our supper, but not of very good flavor. However, this was no wonder, with such stormy weather. Hard biscuits which we had as emergency food were all that was served for our midnight supper. [This was *kaumenpo,* a special biscuit the size of a U.S. bun, made of flour. Chigusa explained that with the great pitching and rolling of the vessel the cooks could not prepare the warmed type of snack.]

I again had a dream of my wife, Fumiko, and my children.

4 DECEMBER (THURSDAY).

A south wind of 18m–19m (35 kts–37 kts). Occasional rain. Dark clouds were hanging over the sea and our difficult navigation under strong wind was obliged to continue. We suffered from large rolls of 45° to one side again and our oil supply operation was cancelled.

0400. As soon as we changed course to 145°, some pitching commenced, and we noticed that the water-hammer became very strong. On the other hand, it now became warm from the rising temperature as our ship moved to the south.

Information on the enemy's fleet in Hawaii was frequently broadcast to us by wireless.

The morale of all the crew became higher and higher.

Rice-curry was our lunch, and we had three pieces of *Onigiri* for our supper. [A sort of rice ball they could grasp in their hands and eat without chopsticks, this was served because of the rolling and pitching of the ship.] However, two of them were enough for me. I ate *Onigiri* with my fingers on the bridge.

At dusk the wind fell below 10 m (20 kts) and the sea became fairly calm. But swells still remained.

I served *Shiruko* for midnight supper again.

I had a dream again in which I enjoyed life with my family.

5 DECEMBER (FRIDAY).

After a long interval, the sea became calm.

1000. The wind of 5 m (10 kts) changed to the northeast. A swell still remained, but I should say that the sea was calm. Occasional rain.

We were supplied 95 T oil from the *Toho Maru* and it took 35 minutes for the operation. During the oil supply operation we got a signal "to be gifts" from *Toho Maru*. We threw a rope from my bridge to the *Toho Maru*. The gifts from the Captain of *Toho Maru* to the Commanding Officer of the *Akigumo* were American cigarettes which we received by a rope ferry. It is really surprising that the cigarettes are American made, this is a curious gift. This gift represented the encouragement of the Captain of the *Toho Maru*.

The temperature rose and the thermometer showed 14°C (57°F). Taking off my overcoat at last, I was relieved of this burden.

After a long time I got my hair cut and shaved in the afternoon. I really felt well and refreshed.

Our midnight supper was doughnuts, especially made by our cook.

A professional barber is assigned to each large ship, above cruiser size, as a military-attached civilian, but not to destroyers such as our ship. Therefore, our crewmen took turns cutting each other's hair. Usually some sailor would politely offer to cut each officer's hair. We had many sailors who were good barbers and I was always thankful for their help in keeping my hair cut neatly.

6 DECEMBER (SATURDAY).

From this morning we had a southwest wind blowing over 10 m (20 kts), and it increased strongly in the evening to about 15 m or 16 m (30 kts or 32 kts) bringing us very high waves.

0230. 10 T oil was supplied by the tanker, *Nippon Maru*, which took a half hour.

0700. The 2nd Supply Division (consisting of three tankers, the *Toho Maru, Toei Maru* and *Nippon Maru* and the destroyer *Arare* which escorted the Supply Division, parted from our Task Force and Fleet line to go west to point "L" to make preparations to supply oil to the Fleet on its return from Hawaii.

Point "L" was located at 35° N and 160° E nearly at the midpoint between Midway and Yokosuka. On our first schedule, our ship was expected to have an oil supply on the return trip at point "L."

All the crew of the *Toho Maru* which had followed the *Akigumo* up to today stood side by side in orderly rows in *Togenreishiki* (Manning the side). I could see them clearly as they stood waving their caps to pray for our success, really unwilling to part from our Task Force. At the same time I could see a flag signal on the yardarm of the *Toho Maru* which meant "We hope for your courageous and glorious success." All our crew were deeply moved by this farewell message.

0800. We had trial shooting of our machine guns, firing 4 bullets each, which was smoothly performed. This morning we completed equipping our mantlet with our hammocks.

We served *Shiruko* with bread to the sailors for lunch and the officers had *Gomoku-meshi* (variety rice). [This was very good food. It was rice with much fish and vegetables put in to give flavor to the rice. Chigusa pointed out that with the battle coming on shortly everyone was given more of a better variety of food.]

At last, tomorrow we go straight to the south and boldly head for Pearl Harbor. Hereafter we will be close to the enemy's territory. We must take more strict precautions against enemy surveillance.

During daytime: the second station (a half of our crew on duty). During nighttime: the third station (one third of our crew on duty).

I felt dullness in my head, because I now had a slight cold. I caught cold as it became warmer last night. But it was of no great concern to me.

What we called a "hammock mantlet" protected each important point, such as the following, from the enemy's bullets:

Mantlet location	Number of hammocks required (pcs)
On the canopy of the bridge	32
Searchlight controller	12
Rear steering room and Direction Search Instrument room	13
Searchlight	12

Even after a heavy rain and the seawater spray from a stormy weather encountered for ten days, no water had penetrated our hammock mantlets.

7 December (Sunday).

The wind is 9 m (18 kts), and the sea a little calmer.

0200. We received 20 T oil from the tanker *Kokuyo Maru,* which is the last supply before we attack Pearl Harbor. It took about half an hour to complete.

0400. The 1st Supply Division consisting of four tankers, the *Kenyo Maru, Kyokuto Maru, Kokuyo Maru* and *Shinkoku Maru* and the destroyer *Kasumi,* which was an escort ship for the tankers, made up one group turned aside, parting from our main Task Force. A little to our right and ahead of us, the *Shinkoku Maru* turned and disappeared, fluttering her signal flags meaning, "The best of luck to you!" I silently offered thanks for their efforts in supplying oil to us every day.

0700. The time has come. As soon as we received orders, "Course 180° and Speed 20 kts" from the flagship, the *Akagi,* we immediately increased our speed to begin our dash true south to Pearl Harbor. Our large white waves together with those of the other consort ships of the Fleet marked our path and put us in high spirits. The wind fortunately changed from the northwest to the north. It was now just a fair breeze of about 10 m (20 kts). I should feel that even God was now with us. But strong swells still remain on the surface.

0710. The signals flags "D-G" were gallantly hoisted high on the mast of the flagship, the *Akagi,* meaning: "The fate of the Japanese Empire will depend upon the issue of this battle, so please everyone exert yourself to the utmost." This no doubt was the direct order and instruction of Vice Admiral Nagumo, Commander-in-Chief of the Fleet Task Force. Were there any sailors not excited over the honor, as a member of the Task Force, of receiving this order? I have heard many times of that order given by the "Z" flag from Admiral Togo in the Japan Sea Battle against Russia in 1905. Now I have actually received the same order myself.

Following this we received an encouraging address from Admiral Yamamoto, Commander-in-Chief of the Great Fleet: "The fate of the Empire rests on this campaign. Please do all in your power so as to carry out your duties." We also had the gracious Imperial Rescript which was transmitted by the Commander-in-Chief of the Great Fleet through wireless. These messages were transmitted to all the crew of my ship by our Commanding Officer.

Our morale grew higher every moment as our fleet was on the enemy's line to the south. We completed all remaining preparations for war and battle which had not been completed in the morning. On receiving the order "Be well dressed," we changed to clean uniforms for battle. After that, both my ship and myself had completed our preparations for attack against the enemy at any time.

Conforming to the spirit of our old chivalry, when we fight a battle against our enemy we change to clean and proper clothing for combat. . . .

If I think quietly today, this was the last day which we could call peace time. I wanted to give some last pleasure to the crew on this calm day of peace, and also as their present when entering the land of promise where they will live in eternity from tomorrow.

Very seriously I asked the crew, "What food do you want to eat?" Of course I would like to give them the best of any food we had stocked, because food was about the only thing available that would give enjoyment to our crew at that time.

"Please, *Ohagi!*" was the unanimous answer. Thus I had them served very sweet *Ohagi* made by our cooks, and I added to their lunch the two raw apples for each sailor which had been reserved for this day.

The request for *Ohagi* from the sailors was according to my expectations, and the necessary materials for *Ohagi*—sugar and red beans—had been reserved for this special service today, though we had many times served *Shiruko* and cakes (which also required sugar and red beans) for our midnight supper.

At that time all daily necessities were distributed under the control of our Government in Japan. It was very difficult to get sugar, not only at home, but even on board a naval ship. Every Japanese hungered for sweets and sailors were no exception.

It was exactly at lunch time on the day previous to combat that we concluded that we would all die. When driven to bay, we human beings become children again, don't we? A sailor is of course human. The delighted, smiling faces of the sailors as their cheeks puffed out with *Ohagi* still linger in my mind. Even now I cannot forget that scene. Although it was a small kindness to serve *Ohagi* with two apples, I was extremely glad and felt a deep satisfaction being able to do this for the crew.

Today we received a wireless from Japan that reported the movement of the enemy, and we were in high spirits to know that there were enough targets for attack in Pearl Harbor.

The 7th, 1800:

From *Dai-Kai Daiichi-Bucho* (Chief of the First Navy Division, Imperial Headquarters):

(1) U.S. Naval ships in Pearl Harbor on the 6th (local time):

Battleships	9
Light Cruisers	3
Seaplane Carriers	3
Destroyers	17

(2) Berthed ships:

Light Cruisers	4
Destroyers	2

(3) All Heavy Cruisers and Aircraft Carriers are under way.

I had felt very uneasy throughout the day, fearing that our enemy might observe our fleet dashing toward the south to Pearl Harbor, because today is really the last day before our combat. Our fleet continues on its bold dash throughout the night to close in upon Pearl Harbor bravely in rapid formation.

6. "X" DAY (THE DAY OF THE ATTACK ON PEARL HARBOR)

It was for this day that our Task Force consisting of over 20 naval ships made a forced cruise of over 4,000 sea miles in the northern Pacific Ocean under difficult navigation conditions and stormy weather for 12 days, since leaving Hitokappu Bay early on 26 November.

Today would be "X" day. This is the very day we wage war against the U.S.A. and Great Britain, at the moment that we attack Pearl Harbor. About 350 airplanes of all air forces of our Task Force would simultaneously take to the air at daybreak and head for Pearl Harbor. And at last the War would begin.

8 DECEMBER (MONDAY) / 7 DECEMBER (SUNDAY) IN HAWAII BY THE DATE LINE.

Now we are in the very day to which we have been looking forward so eagerly. That is, the long-cherished "X" day for the outbreak of war now offers itself.

0030 (0530 in Hawaii). As soon as all the crew jumped out of their beds on the order to "Get up," they went hurriedly to their combat quarters. The bow of my ship was covered with splashes from waves raised by the strong east wind of 14 m–15 m (29 kts–30 kts)

0100 (0600 in Hawaii). We could hear the sounds of the propellers as trial runs were made by the planes on board aircraft carriers. They had begun their preparations for their sally against Pearl Harbor.

0130 (0630 in Hawaii). Just before dawn all planes on the flight decks of our carriers began launching one by one. This was a gallant scene, launching the first group of the air attack force. We felt rather confident seeing the planes flying to their rendezvous points, passing close to the *Akigumo* one after another. All our crew waved to the planes as they were flying past our upper deck, giving them our prayers "Do it as a favor to us" by waving our caps at them. I noticed that I was waving my cap vigorously and unconsciously from my position on the bridge. By and by the first group launched and joined in a formation of 183 planes, and they soon disappeared into the southern sky.

0245 (0745 in Hawaii). The second group of 167 attack planes started their launch one by one. I could clearly see a torpedo that seemed very heavy carried by a torpedo plane, passing close to my ship. I saw all the planes off, earnestly wishing them "The best of luck." Especially I must pray "Good luck" to Lt. Comdr. [Shigeharu] Murata, Commander of the Torpedo Plane Wing, because he was in my class at the Naval Academy.* Furthermore, Lt. Comdr. [Takashige] Egusa, who had an important responsibility as Commander of the Wing of [dive] bombers, was also my classmate and I must pray to God for his success.

Turning my eyes to the sky, in the distance a group would go into formation and vanish one after another in the southern sky. Since it had now come to this, the reports of news from our planes would be the only thing to which I could now look forward.

The first news came from one of our patrol planes. "No ships of the enemy's fleet are in Lahaina berth, but eleven capital ships are in Pearl Harbor." The above was the first report from our own airplanes.

All our crew were so anxious to hear from our attacking force that they stood without moving an inch, glaring into the southern sky.

News of the enemy's ships in Pearl Harbor had already been sent to our Task Force several times from Japan, but we welcomed it today, knowing that there would be a lot of the U.S. battleships in Pearl Harbor.

This news was sent by a patrol seaplane from the cruiser *Tone* which had been continuing her patrol since 0030 (0530 in Hawaii) before the launching of our attack force. There had been no other information which would surely confirm the state of our enemy fleet with such confidence.

0335 (0835 in Hawaii). The first battle report from our air attack force to come in was by code *"Tora Tora Tora."* "Succeeded in our surprise attack. Our raid direction was 60°. Attacked the main force with torpedoes. Had a great effect."

Following this a second message came from the bomber group: "Bombed the enemy's main force. It has been quite successful."

0355 (0855 in Hawaii). We received the following wireless: "We have received the

---

* Chigusa was mistaken in this. There were no torpedo planes in the second wave. Murata was indeed their leader, but they took off in the first wave —Eds.

enemy's defensive gunfire." News of the attack on each enemy air base from each air group flew into our fleet one after another.

Although I was always stationed at the "top" (as we used to call the fire control tower) in this period and it was ready for firing at any moment, since we expected to receive a counterattack by the U.S. Air Force without doubt, I couldn't see even one plane of the enemy's counterattack. I was really surprised by this and I had such a strange feeling, thinking "How simple war really is!"

0830 (1330 in Hawaii). As soon as we had accommodated all the planes that returned to their mother ships, our Task Force headed straight north at a high speed of 26 kts. (This is the highest speed we reached in this operation.) A heavy spray covered the bow as we increased our speed due to the high waves and swells.

1030 (1530 in Hawaii). On the interception of a cipher, one of our submarines reported the enemy's wireless message that was given to all ships from the flagship of the Pacific Fleet, USN: "The signal direction looks like an enemy carrier is positioned in the true north." I wondered if the enemy would now detect the location of our fleet.

In the evening I knew by the news from Japan that today's war results had already been reported in Japan as follows: "Two battleships were sunk. Four battleships and four heavy cruisers were seriously damaged. A lot of airplanes were destroyed." Following the above, we had news of our Navy in the South Seas and the Philippines area that put all the crew in high spirits.

The *Akigumo* escorted the aircraft carrier *Zuikaku* all day long today. I was glad that planes of the *Zuikaku* could return safely to their mother ship without loss of a single plane, in response to our prayers. However, 13 of them (58 airplanes from *Zuikaku* were engaged in the battle) had barely made their way homeward, having received damage from enemy bullets.

On recalling that time, how vexing it was to wait impatiently for a report from the attacking air force! I had never experienced such anxiety as waiting for news like this.

If the first report from the attacking force would be "Failure of the surprise attack," it is not difficult to imagine how much difficulty our ships would experience and how much misery they would suffer. Truly, we assumed that on this occasion our air force would suffer heavy damage without fail.

Secondly, of course our fleet not only couldn't avoid a big air raid by U.S. air forces, but also the U.S. Fleet in great force would sortie against us from Pearl Harbor. Consequently, a great sea battle between our Fleet and the American Fleet would inevitably occur.

Moreover, all our crew had made up their minds to give themselves up for lost and that they should have been counterattacked by the enemy's airplanes without fail, even if we would succeed in our surprise attack. So we continuously expected the enemy's counterattack by airplanes and battleships.

You can understand my serious concern that we absolutely could not avoid a fight against the enemy's planes from the order Commander Arimoto, Commanding Officer, gave me as Chief Ordnance Officer on that day. At the moment the last airplane disappeared from sight in the southern sky, the vigorous voice of our skipper on the bridge reached me at the "top" (fire control tower) through a voice tube, saying, *"Hojutsu-cho!* Please load guns with shot right now, because the enemy's planes should come to attack us without fail." This was the only order I received from the Commanding Officer; however, this order was deeply serious and meant the following: "The enemy's planes will surely come to our ship, so we must shoot them down as soon as possible by taking the offensive. And even a few seconds to load a gun is unacceptable."

Of course I answered, "Yes, certainly, sir," and made preparations against the enemy in my mind such as loading the guns, but actually I did not load them. Of course it is evident that against a target on the surface of the water such as a ship I can shoot quickly as soon as I confirm the target, if I had loaded the guns in advance. But the method used to shoot airplanes is a little different than this, so we do not load our guns in advance.

The reason comes from the use of time fuses for antiaircraft shells. We cannot set the requisite time to the fuse until we confirm our target visually. The fuse will explode depending on the time set. However, when firing against a ship on the surface of the water, we generally use an impact fuse which will explode instantly upon impact instead of a time fuse, so it is possible to load our guns in advance in such cases.

Needless to say, Commander Arimoto, my experienced skipper, understood the use of time fuses. Nevertheless, the fact that my skipper gave me this order speaks for our expectation of an inevitable raid sooner or later by the enemy's planes. The serious voice of my skipper on that occasion still lingers in my ears and I'll never forget it. A gun was the only weapon that could stand against the enemy's airplanes, so it was no wonder that the crew trusted this gun with their faith.

Now, even though I emphasize the subject, I regret that I cannot fully express the tenseness of the situation at that time. On thinking back, there was no room for doubt that it was a critical moment that determined whether we would beat the enemy or be beaten by him. So even when our planes were returning to their mother ships, we used to welcome them with some suspicion that they might be enemy planes.

Anyhow, owing to the great success of the surprise attack, we had neither a counterattack by their planes nor their ships against our expectation. And, sweeping away our feelings, the *Akigumo* and all the other ships of our fleet could safely leave this theater of war for our motherland.

Was it a "Mystery"? Or was it "Good luck"? Certainly, I cannot help clasping my hands in prayer to express my gratitude for the grace of Heaven and the help of God. I felt that I had a narrow escape from death, now that I am safely through the present battle. In exchange for my great joy I think of my elder brother in Honolulu and feel a little uneasy about him. How much is he suffering? What kind of retaliation is he to receive?

7. THE RETURN TO KURE NAVAL BASE

Although we had made brilliant achievements at Pearl Harbor on "X" Day, we had exposed the existence of our fleet to the U.S. Navy. However, we must now return home whether we like it or not and must pass through the severe security watch to escape the enemy's pursuit. Furthermore, we must continue to fight desperately against the raging billows left after the passing of a typhoon. So, burning with an ardent wish to set foot again on our motherland, our Fleet started on its way home.

9 DECEMBER (TUESDAY).

Patrols over a wide area by our airplanes were continued from early morning, but not a sign of the enemy was to be seen. On a course of 330°, we continued north at a speed of 26 kts throughout today.

In spite of the rough sea, three patrol planes somehow made a forced "ditch." The *Akigumo* went to the rescue of our plane; all the crew were fortunately recovered safely.

In the evening the *Akigumo* met the *Kyokuto Maru,* from which 250 T oil (the largest quantity transferred during this operation) supplied at 12 kts speed in rough swells. It took one and a half hours, so we could scarcely finish the supply working until 2330.

10 DECEMBER (WEDNESDAY).

As we left the battlefield behind us, I felt a bit easy. All of our crew were delighted to hear news of the victory from Japan and to be on the way home without a counter-attack. Today, we experience extreme rolling because of large waves.

As soon as we receive an order to "attack Midway" from Admiral Yamamoto, Commander-in-Chief of the Great Fleet, our Task Force immediately changed course toward Midway.

At night officers in our wardroom were very excited over the welcome news of the sinking of two British battleships, the *Repulse* and the *King George V.**

11 DECEMBER (THURSDAY).

From early morning we experienced large swells against which the *Akigumo* must fight, suffering severe pitching. This bad weather made oil supply impossible for ships of the 8th Cruiser Squadron (cruisers *Tone* and *Chikuma*) and 2nd Aircraft Carrier Squadron (carriers *Soryu* and *Hiryu*) which were expected to have it in the morning.

The information that "Three enemy patrol planes are to assault you" sent us immediately to our combat stations, but we could not see a plane in sight and in a little while we were restored to our former condition.

We suffered terribly from the high waves, large swells, strong wind and severe cold all day long. The wind blew 20m/second (39 kts) at night. As it was difficult to navigate at ordinary speed (14 kts), we reduced our speed to 9 kts, but we still had a stormy voyage.

12 DECEMBER (FRIDAY).

Owing to the storm the front benzine tank was taking water through a storm venti-lating hole. We pumped out about two tons of water with a hand pump with great difficulty. We had the most terrible raging seas with angry waves like mountains and the largest swells we had yet seen. We must continue our stormy voyage ever rougher in spite of reducing our speed to 9 kts frequently.

However, receiving good news of our successive victories, the morale of the crew became more and more elevated and they could face the storm weather with grit, think-ing, "What is this? We must overcome all difficulties."

* Actually *Prince of Wales*—Eds.

The following report of our attack on Pearl Harbor reached my ship by signal from the flagship of our Fleet:

Putting all the general reports from each unit together, the results of our air attack on Pearl Harbor (at the most moderate estimate) and our damage are as follows:

1. SUNK:

4	Battleships. On one ship, the magazine exploded. Others, cut off its hull and capsized or was sunk by a torpedo and bombing planes.
1 or 2	Heavy or light cruisers
1	Oil supply ship

2. SERIOUS DAMAGE OR SUNK WITH A RUMBLE:

2	Battleships
2	Light cruisers
2	Destroyers

3. SLIGHT DAMAGE:

4	Light cruisers

(As for each battleship, damage extent was caused by one torpedo or No. 80 bomb (800 kg).)

4. HANGARS:

Destroyed by fire	16 buildings
Destroyed by bombing and gunfire	222 planes
Shot down	14 planes
Total damaged planes	450 planes

Beside, there are countless planes which are destroyed by gunfire but not burned.

5. OTHER DAMAGE:*

(Includes the planes which made a forced ditching after the attack operation)

9	Fighters
15	Bombers
5	Attack planes

13 DECEMBER (SATURDAY).

Stormy weather continued again throughout today. The south wind changed to a northerly wind of over 15 m (30 kts). Owing to the enormous angry waves rising like mountains over us, we suffered from terrible, big pitchings. We lost sight of even the gigantic figures of our aircraft carrier sailing just 500 meters ahead of my ship. When my ship plunged to the bottom of each wave from the top of it, the bridge was completely enveloped in waves like a diving submarine. The large ships, sailing ahead of us, looked as though they were not suffering so much from the stormy weather. On the contrary, the scene of the *Akigumo,* a small ship of 2,500 T at the mercy of the waves, was just like a leaf as she continued her desperate struggle which was utterly beyond description. It

* These were the Japanese losses —Eds.

took the greatest effort to keep standing on the bridge under the repeatedly rough and difficult sailing.

We passed through the sea area 700 M north of Midway today. We also crossed the date line to the west.

14 DECEMBER (SUNDAY).

The long spell of stormy weather continued today and we again suffered from the raging, angry waves rising over us like mountains. These angry forces of nature were much more fearful than the enemy's fleet at Pearl Harbor, and it was also very trying to my body.

I concluded that it was the true anger of the Pacific Ocean that we suffered during this long spell of stormy weather. I had never experienced such pitching since joining the Navy. This was to be my first and worst such experience. In peacetime we could set a course to avoid a typhoon if possible, but we can't do so now in the face of our enemy. Even if it was pretty unnatural navigation, we dared to make it.

During such severe, stormy weather it is almost impossible to serve a regular course of meals. We cannot avoid having only hard biscuits and occasionally a rice ball with water. We had to fight against the angry waves, hardly eating, refreshing ourselves with water as we clung to the handrail on the bridge. [Chigusa emphasized to Prange that the voyage back to Japan was much rougher than the voyage from Japan to Hawaii.]

> *Afternoon.* It cleared up a little, and at intervals I made sure the condition of "Secure" ("Secure" was Japanese Navy English, meaning to make fast all movable materials with ropes).
>
> The northerly wind is now 13 meters (26 kts). From dusk we had rain again and our field of vision was shortened. From today I let Ensign Wakamatsu, Communications Officer, join the watch officers for the rest of the voyage.
>
> Suddenly we receive a signal from the flagship, *Akagi:* "Take strict precautions against the enemy's submarines. Daytime the Second Station (half of crew on station), and nighttime the Third Station (one-third of the crew on station)."
>
> Our midnight supper was doughnuts, especially made by our cooks. Fresh apples for the officers' meals were exhausted today, but there were still some in stock for the enlisted men. [In the wardroom of a destroyer there was generally only the CO, the Executive, the Engineering Officer, the Gunnery Officer and the Torpedo Officer— sometimes the Communications Officer, but not always.]

You will note the change of our midnight supper to doughnuts from the dry biscuits we always had during stormy weather meant that the weather had now become a little better.

15 DECEMBER (MONDAY).

One week has now passed since the attack on Pearl Harbor. My heart was filled with deep emotion when I became lost in thought of "X" Day.

The wind changed to westerly and the weather turned poor from the morning.

It took about 30 minutes to take on a supply of 150 T oil from the *Shinkoku Maru.* [Delay or not, the general idea was "good old wonderful tanker."] As soon as the oil supply was completed, we turned south without delay at news that "The operation against Wake Island is delayed." For the sake of supporting the capture of Wake Island, our operation against Midway was cancelled.

After a long interval, I now shaved and washed my underwear.

All fresh oranges (tangerines) in stock were exhausted today.

16 December (Tuesday).

The interior of the No. 1 turret was submerged in water on account of the stormy weather lasting all day today. What had I done to deserve such a fate? Indeed, a most unpleasant day continued again today.

Soon the 8th Cruiser Squadron and 2nd Aircraft Carrier Squadron and two destroyers, the *Tanikaze* and the *Urakaze,* were appointed to support the Wake Island Operation. At night, they separated from our Fleet and turned south in haste.

Quietly thinking back over the past few days, it has been just one month since I left Kure Naval Base. I had never experienced such a long voyage as this.

17 December (Wednesday).

It is fine weather today, but a swell still remained.

In the morning we had "General Quarters" upon orders of "Find three enemy submarines," and we carefully took evasive action against the submarines which we never really located.

At night we turned south to a course of 200°.

Canned *Yude-Azuki* (boiled red beans) were served for our midnight supper.

How did the crew spend their days during such a long voyage?

All sailors on duty were on battle stations for two hours each duty period. Off-duty sailors engaged in daily tasks as follows: The daily routine during extended patrol duty:

(1) The hour for rising is usually around sunrise.

(2) Breakfast is taken one hour after rising.

(3) Sweeping is begun 45 minutes after breakfast.

(4) Morning training consists of education at a combat station.

(5) Afternoon routine:
    Gymnastics from one hour after lunch.
    Singing of war songs followed the gymnastics.

(6) The change in methods of patrol disposition inside the ship in day and night battle.

    (a) Change to day battle from night battle: One hour before sunrise sailors on duty change to day battle, and off-duty sailors take their combat quarters after rising and change to day battle.

    (b) Change to night battle from day battle: 30 minutes after sunset, all the crew take to "General Quarters" and change to night battle on the order "Prepare for night battle."

The reasons why we must change disposition from day to night battle are as follows:

For night battle we must prepare illumination weapons (searchlights). And it is necessary that every weapon be prepared for short-distance battle. On the contrary, we expect long-range battle in daytime battle and it is especially necessary to prepare for aircraft firing.

To cope with the above requirements, a change of preparations for day or night battle is enforced every morning and every evening.

18 DECEMBER (THURSDAY).

Fine weather, but there was a slight swell on the sea.

It is now just one month since I left Saeki Bay, Kyushu.

I had an upset stomach, but not so serious that I must be in bed. I wondered if I was poisoned by pork we had for supper last night.

Although air patrols were out all day long, we couldn't detect any movement of the enemy's submarines. So I wondered if we were now out of the submarine area.

Hearing the following radio news from Japan, all the crew were delighted to know of an amendment to the battle damage at Pearl Harbor. "The annihilation of the enemy's fleet."

At dusk we received the following signal from the flagship of the fleet, *Akagi*, and took strict precautions with the Second Station (a half of the crew on station) against submarines: "One enemy submarine is heading north, so there will be an opportunity to intercept it."

On first consideration for surface firing today, we prepared shells 60% for surface and 40% for air at the side of our turrets.

Of course we had prepared our shells mainly for air on the day of the attack on Pearl Harbor.

19 DECEMBER (FRIDAY).

Very fine today. We had a slight swell with a northerly wind of 10–13 meters (20–26 kts).

A scouting plane from Japan came just over our fleet. Watching the airplane I felt, at last, close to our motherland. A few planes launched from the *Zuikaku* escorted the scouting plane, as if saying "Thanks for the welcome."

We received the following signal from the flagship, *Akagi:* "The fleet will pass through *Bungo Suido* channel on the 23rd for Kure."

The transfer order for Commander Arimoto, our skipper, to be Captain of the destroyer *Kagero* came by signal too, and we knew that the successor was to be Commander Soma, who was a classmate of Commander Arimoto.

Today I had time to see the Battle Report from Vice Admiral Nagumo, Commander of the Task Force:

THE GENERAL BATTLE REPORT OF THE TASK FORCE NO. 1

1400 17 December 1941

(1) Under the illustrious virtue of His Majesty, relying on the Grace of Heaven and the Help of God, our Task Force reached a point 200 M north of Pearl Harbor at

daybreak on the 8th of December. And 361 attack planes, bombers, fighters and sea scouting planes were successfully launched from 0100 in spite of very difficult conditions for launching owing to a roll of 10° caused by a long swell. Then, in the teeth of strong defensive fire and heavy clouds, we carried out the raid on Hawaii on schedule from 0330 to 0500. After finishing the recovery of our airplanes at 0900, the entire force withdrew from the theater toward the NNW as planned. On that day we did not have a counterattack by enemy planes and only were pursued by a few flying boats.

(2) Results:

(Which were confirmed after investigation by photographs and in other ways)

A. Ships:

(a) Sunk:

Battleships		4
Type of the *California* (Sunk by bomb hit)	1	
Type of the *Maryland* and *Arizona* (Hull cut by torpedoes and bombs)	1 each	
Type uncertain (Sunk by torpedoes)	1	
Heavy cruisers (or light cruisers) (Hit by 4 torpedoes and 5 bombs of 250 kg)		2
An oil-supply ship (Hit by 5 bombs of 250 kg)	1	

(b) Heavy damage:

(This meant impossible to repair or very difficult to repair)

Battleships		2
Type of the *California* (Hit by 4 torpedoes and 4 bombs of 250 kg)	1	
Type of the *Maryland* (Hit by 3 bombs of 800 kg, several bombs of 250 kg and conflagration)	1	
Light Cruisers (Hit by a bomb of 250 kg)		2
Destroyers (Hit by a bomb of 250 kg)		2

(c) Small damage:

(This meant possible to repair)

Battleships		2
Type of the *Nevada* (2 direct hits by 800 kg bombs and fire)	1	
Type of the *Nevada* (Hit by a torpedo)	1	
Light cruisers (7 direct hits by 250 kg bomb)		4

B. Airplanes and shore facilities

(a) Shot down   14 planes

(b) Hangars

16 buildings were burnt.

2 buildings were destroyed.

C. Airplanes outside hangars:

Over 220 planes were burnt following machine-gun and bomb attacks. Total estimated planes which were burnt were 450 airplanes, and a number of planes were destroyed by machine guns and bombs.

In addition, the surprise attack of matchless loyalty and valor by our special attack submarine group surely had great results, so I realized that the capital forces of the U.S. Pacific Fleet were annihilated only one hour and a half after the outbreak of war.

(3) Our damage:

Fighters	9
Bombers	15
Attackers	5

These were heroically killed in action by enemy defensive fire.

(4) My opinions:

A. The power of No. 80-5 bombs and mark 91 torpedoes is enormous and sufficient to deal any battleships in existence a mortal blow if hit by 5–6 bombs or the same number of torpedoes.

B. We did not consider reducing our effort in this battle in spite of the terrible defensive fire of the enemy.

The hits scored by No. 80-5 bombs were over 11 among 49 bombs which we used.

The torpedo hits were over 35 out of 40 which we discharged in spite of the shallow sea.

C. The results of aerial combat showed the effect of the enemy's large airplanes was a little less than their official announcements claimed.

For the first time in a long time we enjoyed a Bridge game in the wardroom after supper.

We had very nice cakes as a surprise for our midnight supper especially made by our cooks.

I could now expect a calm voyage, so I took off my *Sennin-Bari* bellyband with thanks for my safety.

The thermometer showed 23°C (73°F) and it became a little warmer. I changed into a spring uniform.

We dismantled the hammock mantlets today and our ship was restored to its original state.

20 DECEMBER (SATURDAY).

Today it was fine weather with a fair wind of 10 meters (20 kts). As we were still going south, it became warmer and in the morning it was nearly 23°C–24°C (73°F–75°F).

1130. Changed course to 270° with a speed of 18 kts.

In the morning I completed my records of this battle.

The thermometer in our wardroom showed 31°C (88°F) at lunch time, so we were dripping with sweat and very hot. Even on the bridge it showed 28°C (83°F).

Afternoon: We met and passed a Japanese bonito fishing boat, hoisting a *Hinomaru* flag (Japanese national flag) and we welcomed each other with a wave of our hands.

I served fresh apples we had reserved to all the crew for their supper. These apples were finally the last, because they were exhausted today. I had kept them as long as I could by giving fresh fruit only a few limited times a week.

Not to mention the natural obstacles, that is, besides the cold, we met a strong wind, high waves and dense fog on our course in the north Pacific Ocean. Out of

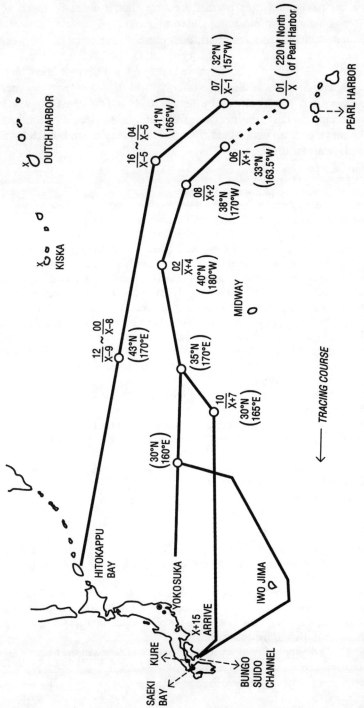

Chart of the Course planned for the Task Force (Hitokappu Bay–Hawaii–Hiroshima Bay) Real distance covered by the *Akigumo*–8,593 NM.

consideration for navigation, this northerly course should never be taken at this season, so it was natural that most ships used to avoid it.

As you can understand from our chart, our course was selected just between the end of the patrol line running from the north at Dutch Harbor to the south at Midway. I think it was wise to select a course at the end of the patrol line which was apt to be neglected. And it was also true that the field of vision from the enemy's patrol planes was often interfered with by heavy clouds and the dense fog which hid our fleet. Such being the case, our fleet was fortunately not detected by the enemy's patrol net. I believe you can understand from this that many natural obstacles affect the course to Hawaii at this season.

21 DECEMBER (SUNDAY).

For these days we have fortunately had fine weather every day and the sea was calm. The temperature was 28°C–20°C (82°F–84°F), so it was still pretty hot.

0900. All destroyers of the 1st Torpedo Squadron met the 2nd Supply Group, and the *Akigumo* began to be supplied oil from the *Nippon Maru*. During this operation, on account of strong waves from the stern and some trouble in the gyrocompass, a slip (a joint metal) of a front rope and an oil tube stretched between the *Akigumo* and the *Nippon Maru* were cut off. In the middle of the supply, after 180 T oil was received, we were obliged to give up the operation. We then started north on a course of 335°.

1430. Our carriers [four—two were at Wake] and battleships stopped their engines for a time and waited for an hour and a half while the operation of pulling a wire (paravane) through the sea against mines was undertaken. In the meantime, we dismantled the ''hammock mantles'' and the equipment against cold, and the *Akigumo* was then restored to its normal condition.*

In the evening the *Akigumo* exchanged missions with the destroyer *Shiranuhi* and joined the screen for the capital ships.

We were a little surprised to receive the following wireless, but later we found that there was no enemy submarine: ''Enemy's submarine is located at the western part of the Inland Sea.''

The date of arrival in our motherland was now only three days off, so we were too excited to play Bridge after our supper.

The *Shiruko* for our midnight supper was extremely delicious.

22 DECEMBER (MONDAY).

Calm sea, but occasionally a drizzling rain owing to the approach of a small low pressure area. The wind blew 5m–10m (10 kts–20 kts) from the north and the temperature was 19°C (66°F).

In the morning all our airplanes were launched from their carriers. They formed groups of several planes each, and each group flew spiritedly westward to the Kanoya Naval Air Base in Kagoshima Prefecture. On the other hand, our fleet was going directly toward the western part of the Inland Sea.

1100. The 2nd Supply Group separated from us and followed the fleet.

We enjoyed playing cards this evening under the really happy atmosphere of our wardroom.

---

* As Chigusa made this same statement on 19 December, it is not clear exactly when *Akigumo* was actually restored to her ''normal condition ''—Eds.

We had very sweet *Kuzumanju* (a steamed bean jam bun made of arrowroot starch) at midnight supper.

At night there was occasionally low visibility, perhaps owing to low pressure.

All the food for our midnight supper was homemade, of course made by our cooks. I was grateful to have good cooks aboard the *Akigumo*. I have thankful feelings for their great efforts. How much they enhanced our spirits with their distinguished services!

23 DECEMBER (TUESDAY).

At last we are in the very day of arrival at our motherland. It was very fine weather after a typhoon had passed. Our fleet was dashing directly to *Bungo Suido* channel at 20 kts.

0730. At first, the Shikoku Mountains came dimly into my view.

0800. Next, Ashizuri Cape, which I was used to seeing, appeared very distinct. And then Okinoshima (a small island at the western end of Kochi Prefecture) came into sight. What a dearly-loved spectacle it was! I felt deeply moved.

0600. All the crew was called to "General Quarters," but before long the station was reduced to *Daini Haibi* (Second Station—half of crew on the station).

0930. "General Quarters" again.

Patrol planes from our mainland bases were dancing in the air over our fleet. On the other hand, our fleet was surrounded two-fold and three-fold by several kinds of patrol ships belonging to the Sayeki Defense Base to escort our fleet carefully.

Following the pilot destroyer, the *Akigumo* entered the Birojima Channel which was swept, towing a "paravane."

We took lunch under "General Quarters."

1300. The *Akigumo* passed through the Hayasui Strait and entered the Inland Sea. It was so calm, the surface was like oil. It was so quiet that I could hardly imagine the stormy weather against which we had continuously engaged in a struggle to the death up to yesterday. But it was just a transient relief, because we must get a call to "General Quarters" and the following information: "The location of an enemy submarine is in the northern area of the Tsurishima Lighthouse at 1000 a.m." (Of course the lighthouse is situated in the Inland Sea, and later we understood that there were no submarines there.)

Taking in the "paravane" at the eastern area of Aoshima Island, the main ships of our fleet came safely into Hiroshima Bay one after another, passing through Tsurishima Channel. Until all the main ships had passed the Channel, our destroyers took precautions to make a screen at their rear.

1840. At last the *Akigumo* cast her anchor at the Hashirajima berth in Hiroshima Bay for only a one-night stop after passing the Tsurishima Channel as the last ship among the protective destroyers. It took a load off my mind. With great relief I could feel refreshed in body and mind and took my first bath in over one month. [As Chigusa remarked to Prange, "After one month, please imagine!"]

Commander Arimoto, Commanding Officer of my ship, made haste to visit *Abukuma,* the flagship of the Torpedo Squadron, to share a *Kanpai* (toast) with Rear Admiral Omori, Commander of the Squadron, on the success of this Hawaiian campaign. [In any case, Japanese naval custom was that just after anchoring the CO always paid his respects and reported to the CO above him.] On the other hand, since our skipper was absent, all officers gathered in the wardroom and drank a toast to our success in the Battle and congratulated each other on their services during the long voyage.

Nothing more deeply impressed me today than the words "Take a load off my mind." I was really filled with joy to have successfully carried out my important mission. I lost no time writing a letter to Fumiko, my wife, who had remained at my house in Yokosuka.

The *Akigumo* was appointed a warning duty ship today, so I went to bed under the Third Station (one-third of the crew on station).

24 DECEMBER (WEDNESDAY).

In the morning all the crew really enjoyed taking a bath again. [In Japan the custom is to take a hot bath in the evening, but here was Chigusa and everyone else taking a hot bath in the morning. It was so good they could not resist it.]

The crew knew the value of water deep in their hearts, because they were obliged to save water, even for washing their faces, every day. But today, we could get enough water at Kure Harbor. It was no wonder that they enjoyed a bath with all the water they wished to use.

My skipper, Commander Arimoto, visited the flagship, *Akagi,* for an address from Vice Admiral Nagumo, Commander-in-Chief of the Task Force.

1230. Not long after our skipper came back to his ship, we weighed anchor and left Hashirajima berth. The *Akigumo* went forward to the Kure Naval Base on the calm surface of Hiroshima Bay as I continued suppressing the joy with which I was filled.

1330. At length we moored the *Akigumo* to the appointed B Berth in Kure Harbor. Our crew now enjoyed mail call as the first letters in weeks arrived at our ship.

After securing our mooring, *Hangen Joriku* (half of the crew on shore leave) was announced.

This evening all the officers of my ship attended a farewell party at the Green (a famous restaurant in Kure) in honor of Commander Arimoto, our skipper who already had received orders of transfer.

I volunteered as duty officer so I stayed aboard the ship and had a sound sleep the first night of my return home.

8. LOOKING BACK ON OUR LONG VOYAGE

At present we have a deep friendship with the U.S.A., and the waves in the Pacific Ocean are very calm and quiet. When I recall the old times of 33 years ago, when we had really strained relations with the U.S.A., superior to the tempestuous ocean, my heart is filled with a deep emotion.

It was duly in the afternoon of 16 November 1941 that we left the Kure Naval Base after the hasty completion of our preparations for war. I did not know then when we would wage war against the U.S.A. and in what battle I would join.

After 40 days of navigation I returned safely to dear Kure Base and could barely finish composing my diary of the Battle. I can tell from my diary, which was written in pencil and the record rather incomplete, how eagerly I wished to write a record at that time. I can easily recall when reading my plain diary today how the angry waves in the Pacific upset us.

When I recall those old times 33 years ago, I believe that we could not have safely reached the final destination near Hawaii with all the ships of our Great Fleet until we had endured the contest of over one month against Mighty Nature like this. And also I believe we could not have had such amazing results at Pearl Harbor without having had a foundation of hardship beyond description for all the crew of our fleet.

It is only common sense that a warship is a boat that runs on the sea and a sailor should serve on board a warship, but I cannot help being much impressed by myself from the fact that such a small ship as *Akigumo* could achieve her long journey of about 8,600 M after her departure from Hitokappu Bay, against the raging swells from which we had a 47° roll to one side on the way out and a terrible pitching from angry waves like mountains on our return.

My diary has the following postscript at the end of it: ''In spite of a long voyage of about one month, I did not feel very tired, rather I felt a little fat.''* From this postscript I can imagine that my view of the big mission and the victory of the big battle could prevent fatigue in body and mind on a month-long voyage even in stormy weather.

The important matters of most concern in the long voyage of the great fleet might be summarized by the following two questions, I think.

The first question is how the fleet could make a cruise so secretly, even though the Pacific Ocean is very large? How could such a large force consisting of over 20 vessels escape enemy patrol nets? How did the fleet make such a cruise without meeting with third power ships? How could they get to their destination safely 220 M north of Pearl Harbor?

These were the greatest problems we faced against the enemy and which we must consider, and I believe that we paid the greatest attention to them. I could easily imagine that not only would we not reach our destination, but a great sea battle might occur on the way to Hawaii, if we were caught by the patrol screen from Midway in the south, or Kiska and Dutch Harbor in the north. Even if the fleet could get to the destination, we expected a strong counterattack by the enemy without fail. Even if we met third power ships, it should give enough warning to U.S. forces to have them take a defensive position.

As I have already stated, we fortunately slipped through all the patrol cordons by the help of God, and I see now that my fears had been an unnecessary anxiety. I really couldn't find any other better expression for our good fortune than the words of ''the Grace of Heaven and the Help of God.''

Of course, naturally, we did not dispatch any wireless indications, remaining under radio silence at all times.

The second question is the internal problem of the Fleet which we must consider seriously. How can a big fleet safely reach its destination together without struggle? For this purpose, not to speak of paying great attention to maintaining the main engines and keeping the crew in good condition, I must say the greatest problem was how to supply enough oil to the ships for their long trip of 8,600 NM, especially for such small ships as the *Akigumo*. This oil supply problem was a most serious matter of concern to everyone.

---

* We believe Chigusa meant ''flat'' rather than ''fat.'' Certainly one can appreciate that anyone who had come through such an operation might feel a little let down at reaching home port —Eds.

It would have been possible to some extent for a large ship to take enough oil almost to supply herself, and also she does not suffer as much distress as a small ship which is at the mercy of the waves like a leaf of a tree. However, big ships cannot make a cruise without escort by destroyers, because it is very dangerous if enemy submarines are about. The reason new destroyers only were selected to join in this battle came from these considerations.

So oil for the destroyers had to be supplied by some means. I was sincerely pleased that all ships could return home after the achievement of their missions because the oil re-supply operation was handled so smoothly. My diary tells me very clearly that often the *Akigumo* had oil supply operations to fill her tanks, whenever she had an opportunity day or night, sometimes by the "alongside" method and at other times by the "astern" method.

Now I would like to answer the following questions from my American friends:

A. Why did the Imperial Navy not occupy the Hawaiian Islands with a landing force?

The first attack that our air force made was a real surprise attack. Although we had a victory in the Hawaiian Battle, as you may understand by my diary, our fleet cruised every day under very serious conditions. Until "X" Day I had spent an uneasy day every day, and I was afraid I could not get to the destination without damage. We had prayed only for our first success in the attack on Pearl Harbor by our air force, and it was a great problem even to get to our destination. So I can tell you that it was considered a great risk to follow up with a landing force at that time.

From the beginning, our Navy only wished for the first success, which was the attack on Pearl Harbor, and did not plan for a second success to occupy the Island at that time. I believe that our Imperial Navy only hoped for the success of the attack on Pearl Harbor, and the reason was that while the Pacific Fleet of the U.S. Navy had been suffering from big damage at the first stage, our Navy wanted to develop other operations without interference in Southeast Asia.

B. Why did the Japanese Air Force not attack Pearl Harbor again after the first success?

As you know, our first attack on Pearl Harbor resulted in heavy damage to the U.S. Navy in Hawaii, receiving rather small damage in return, because it was a surprise attack. But if we had made a second attack, we must expect rather heavy damage because this would not be a surprise attack and we might expect heavy opposition from the U.S. Navy.

Also, the aircraft carriers of the U.S. Navy were not damaged at all by the first attack of our air force, so they would be near Hawaii with their complete powers intact.

I suppose that Vice Admiral Nagumo decided to keep his force's strength for the next operation in view of the heavy damage at Pearl Harbor.

9. THE OIL SUPPLY TO DESTROYER *AKIGUMO*

The oil supply operation to the *Akigumo* was held 19 times during her whole voyage from departure from Saeki Bay on 18 November to her return to Kure Base

on 24 December. The total quantity of oil supplied was about 700 tons. Full tanks
for the *Akigumo* required 600 tons of oil as I had mentioned before. To my memory,
the capacity of each tanker was about 10,000 tons.

In 18 or 19 times, the oil supply was while under way on the ocean, and only
one time was by anchoring at a supply point at Hitokappu Bay. From my experience, refueling by the "alongside" method was easier than by the "astern" method.
Consequently, 14 services were by the "alongside" method and only 4 times by the
"astern" method. Of course, working in the daytime was easier than at night, but
we did it even at night in an unavoidable case. In any case, it was most difficult to
do on rough seas.

Although the oil supply was influenced by the condition of the sea, training for
oil supply operations [was] not neglected. It was true that the more often we had
training, the smoother the operation was. I remembered that we did the oil supply
operation even on pretty rough seas in which we had strong winds of 15 meters (30
kts) and the ship rolled to 15° to one side under fairly large swells. As for 15 m (30
kts) wind, it usually caused pretty high white waves to cover all of the surface. A
roll of 15° was also pretty strong so that it required some effort to remain standing.

Under the motto of "Always keep your tanks filled with oil," we had oil
supplied once a day as our standard, so even at night we did it, if possible. When
we had oil supplied every day, we received about 30 T each time. However, when
Akigumo first received oil from *Kyokuto Maru* on 9 December after the attack on
Pearl Harbor, it required 250 T. The reason came from high oil consumption owing
to our high-speed operation during two days before and after "X" Day. I feel that
the successful operation of our oil supply plan was a key to the success of our attack.
The following data explains our oil supply in detail:

(1) The oil consumption of the *Akigumo*:

SECTION CRUISED

From	To	Oil Consumption
Kure Base	Saeki Bay	17T
Saeki Bay	Hitokappu Bay	150T
Hitokappu Bay	Hiroshima Bay	1,079T
Total		1,246T

(2) The amount of oil supplied to the *Akigumo*:

Name of Tanker	Saeki Bay to/from Hitokappu Bay	Hitokappu Bay	Hitokappu Bay to/from Hiroshima Bay	Total
Toho Maru		48 T (1)	238 T (7)	286 T (8)
Nippon Maru	139.5 T (6)		49 T (2)	188.5 T (8)

Name of Tanker	Saeki Bay To/From Hitokappu Bay	Hitokappu Bay	Hitokappu Bay To/From Hiroshima Bay	Total
Kokuyo Maru			20 T (1)	20 T (1)
Kyokuto Maru			245 T (1)	245 T (1)
Shinkoku Maru			160 T (1)	160 T (1)
TOTAL	139.5 T (6)	48 T (1)	512 T (12)	699.5 T (19)

Note: Number in brackets is the number of times oil was supplied.

(3) Number of times oil was supplied to the *Akigumo:*

Day or Night	Method of Supply		Total
	Astern	Alongside	
Daytime	4	11	15
Nighttime	0	3	3
Total	4	14	18

Note: The above are records of ocean supply; besides these, we had one anchoring supply during daylight at Hitokappu Bay. If this is added to the above records, the number of daytime becomes 16 and the total will then be 19 times.

Now I must give an additional explanation of the damage to my ship, the *Akigumo*. As I stated, the *Akigumo* did not receive damage from enemy action because we did not have a counterattack by enemy forces in the Hawaiian Battle. However, to my astonishment, I found damage to our weapons and cracks in the hull that were caused by the stormy weather we experienced on the Pacific Ocean, and the *Akigumo* had to repair these at the ship repair facility in Kure. The terrible pitching on our return had apparently caused the hull damage.

Although the *Akigumo* was really a very new destroyer, completed just two months before the outbreak of war, she did not have enough time for practical training. It was really too short a time to master the weapons. As for the guns which I controlled, all operators made determined efforts in their training day and night, hoping to put their guns to good use by all means. But I was secretly glad that I could attend the battle only indirectly and wipe out my anxiety.

As luck would have it, the battle was over without any necessity for us to shoot even one shell. However, owing to the unexpected storm on our return way, we got into a tight corner that gave our weapons a rough time. Even though our weapons were very new, they could not stand up against such severe stormy weather, and we were obliged to have them repaired.

It is indeed terrible to have to battle against nature.

10. HOW WE MAINTAINED MORALE AND PHYSICAL STRENGTH

As Executive Officer of the *Akigumo* and in a sense "mother" of the ship, I had always wished that all our crew, that is, my children, could engage in this battle in good health. In plain language that is, I took care of them in various ways, so they would not suffer from illness and not be wounded or swept away by the waves. As the *Akigumo* was a destroyer, we were especially fortunate to have a Naval surgeon on board. (A doctor usually was not on board each destroyer.) So I could feel a bit easy relying on the doctor if I had a patient on my ship.

We were used to feeling extra pressure during alert steaming to watch against the enemy, but when we couldn't even see the enemy airplanes, we were apt to have simple navigation problems. It is no wonder that morale suffered when mentally tired out as such weary steaming continued for a week, only watching to glare at the horizon. It was natural that we did so, because a sailor is only human. Moreover, if it involves navigation under stormy weather, it will be still more enervating.

(1) The methods used to maintain morale for which I worked hard were as follows:

(A) **THE STRICT ENFORCEMENT OF SINGING WAR SONGS:** We strictly enforced singing of war songs every day by all the crew gathered together on the open deck, so far as circumstances could permit. As for the songs, our Navy made it a habit to simply sing 4 or 5 commonplace songs at one time, but I made every effort to let them sing popular songs which I especially selected for the young sailors, who raised their voices from the bottom of their hearts for over a half hour. We could not have the effect we expected, if the sailors did it with bad grace. We couldn't achieve the purpose of our singing until all the crew would positively attend it with great pleasure.

(B) **THE ENFORCEMENT OF EDUCATION THROUGH THE BULLETIN BOARD:** It is very difficult to issue a ship's newspaper every day on a destroyer, being such a small ship and having no space for this as does a large ship. But we felt it was easy to give the same information, or as much of it as we could, utilizing a bulletin board. It was necessary as an incentive for the crew, drawing their eyes and minds toward a bulletin board on which we notified them of the fresh news in as many instances as we could.

Besides the above, we remembered to let the crew know about big news as soon as possible by broadcasting it throughout the ship at the first opportunity.

(C) **THE BULLETIN SHOWING THE SHIP'S MOVEMENT ON A SAILING CHART:** By dotting the location of the *Akigumo* on a sailing chart every day, I could let the crew know their location in the Pacific Ocean. And at a glance the sailors could recall their efforts of the past days of the cruise, and could estimate how soon they would reach their destination. This surely gave them help and encouragement.

(D) **BY SEIZING AN OPPORTUNITY TO GIVE ENOUGH TIME (NEARLY ONE THIRD OF A DAY) FOR THEIR RECREATION:** It was a regulation to permit the crew amusement and music only on Sunday and on festivals when we are aboard ship in normal times. But it was necessary to consider their need for recreation, permitting it, if possible, every day even in wartime when we are on such a long, weary voyage. And we usually beamed the radio news and entertainment from Japan throughout the ship on such occasions.

(E) **THE STRICT ENFORCEMENT OF GYMNASTICS:** It was very difficult to force gymnastics on the crew at the same time, utilizing the narrow deck of a destroyer, particularly when operating in stormy weather. But I did my best to give them such diversions under all possible conditions. I also added games they liked as much as I could, so as to give the sailors a happy familiarity with gymnastics. (Some sailors reacted passively to gymnastics when we had only formal exercise.)

(F) **METHODS FOR BUTTRESSING MORALE BY FOOD:** Giving enjoyment to sailors infuses life into them and cuts mental fatigue. On the sea, the life of every serious day can't be enjoyable without good meals. It was very important to have a good menu for the sailors, so as to give enjoyment to their meals.

Although it was no easy task to plan good menus in such bad situations as limited food budgets and limited storage capacity for food, I did my best to urge our cooks to do so. The many sweet and special foods prepared for our midnight supper of which I wrote in my diary were no exception to this consideration. When I served *Ohagi* with two apples to all the crew for their lunch on the day before "X" Day, I could distinctly see the sailors' determination to do their best with real pleasure.

When we lived on the sea during a long voyage, watching for our enemy, we used to become demoralized without knowing it. Stormy weather also gives a stimulus to it. How to help the sailors keep their original pep is a problem before meeting any enemy, and we seriously considered it. If a sailor is dead tired before meeting his enemy, he cannot fully utilize his fighting strength.

The next matter we considered was how to maintain a sailor's physical strength, that is, the method used to preserve his physical strength. A human being should be like an animal, and live naturally on shore. Seafaring living is unnatural, and it is to be expected that the longer we continue our seafaring lives, the more we interfere with our health. We must consider how we can keep our potential, that is, our physical strength. At least we must keep strong by all means until we meet our enemy.

(2) The method by which we kept up physical strength. My diary illustrated the following methods:

(A) **THE SUPPLY OF VITAMIN SUPPLEMENTS:** Before departure from our Naval Base, we had a proper quantity of vitamins placed aboard the ship, and gave a dose of it to each member of the crew every day, under the direction of our doctor.

(B) **TO ASSURE ADEQUATE SLEEP FOR EACH SAILOR:** By regulation, it was not permitted to stay up for private reasons between lights out and the hour of rising. That is, we have attention to our sailor's sleep, so as to avoid late nights without business and at the same time to give *Toban Tsuridoko* (additional sleep for night duty). A sailor who had night duty, usually for two hours, could sleep until breakfast so far as circumstances permitted.

(C) **STRICT ENFORCEMENT OF GYMNASTICS, RUNNING AND GAMES:** If possible, we did gymnastics twice a day, in the morning and in the afternoon, and occasionally we added running and games.

(D) **STRICT ENFORCEMENT OF ADEQUATE VENTILATION:** We enforced adequate ventilation every day. Inside a destroyer, it is cramped, and the portholes and hatches must always be closed for damage control readiness when operating against the enemy, so the air inside the ship became impure and we used to experience a nasty smell peculiar to a ship. It was absolutely necessary to enforce proper ventilation.

(E) **ADEQUATELY OPENING AND CLOSING THE PORTHOLES:** We could not open portholes during alert steaming, and it was impossible to open the portholes when under stormy weather. But if the air inside a ship becomes impure, it is not only bad for health, but it also aggravates seasickness for young sailors.

If the movement of the enemy and the conditions of the sea were not serious, we did our best to take in fresh air quickly by opening portholes and hatches for even a short time, if possible. During Naval operations in which enemy contact was uncertain, we very carefully opened ports all at one time by order and under control, rather than doing it haphazardly.

(F) **THE STUDY OF ADEQUATE MEALS FOR SEASICK SAILORS:** It was difficult to take a normal meal at a table, when the ship was rolling and pitching in stormy weather. My diary clearly states that we had meals of hard biscuits and rice balls for several days.

The problem which we had to consider seriously was how to serve a suitable meal to seasick sailors. Extreme rolling of a ship was not always happy even for an old sailor who had never been seasick, and especially among young men there were many poor sailors. Some of them wouldn't eat meals of a normal menu. Even though someone has said that seasickness is out of the question in front of the enemy, our physical strength will decrease, if we don't take meals. A sailor is apt to eat food which is good for seasickness or a very light meal even if he feels a little bad.

In addition to physical strength, another problem to which we had to pay attention was sanitation. And I enforced the following:

(A) **ENFORCEMENT OF WASHING HANDS WITH DISINFECTED WATER BEFORE MEALS:** We always heard the announcement of the order, *"Shokutakuban teo Arae!"* (Duty sailors for a meal, please wash your hands!) just before each meal in our ex-Navy. The true meaning of this order is "Please prepare for a crew's meal," but it is worthy of note that "After washing hands please prepare the meals." Normally all the crew made it a habit and practice to wash their hands before meals without fail.

(B) **EDUCATE OUR COOKS WITH A SENSE OF SANITATION:** We had to pay attention to sanitation on the assumption that cooks and kitchens must attain perfection in sanitation.

(C) **THE ENFORCEMENT OF INSPECTION OF MEALS BY THE EXECUTIVE OFFICER:** It was a rule for the Executive Officer to inspect sailors' meals. We called it *Tenken Shoku* (the Inspection Meal). The purpose of this was not only to check the quality and taste, but also to inspect the sanitation.

(D) **USING A BELLYBAND FOR A SAILOR:** I think all sailors used to always wear a bellyband, and it was useful in preventing colds caught during sleep.

Some readers might think that the above are matters of course, and crude methods, but it was not easy to practice these rules in the uncomfortable life aboard a narrow ship. Everything for our crew fortunately went off without a hitch, and there were no stragglers. So all the crew of the *Akigumo* vigorously joined this battle together, and they could carry out their duties completely.

11. OUR DREAM OF THE ORDER OF THE GOLDEN KITE

On a certain evening when we were looking forward to our sally at Hitokappu Bay, before the attack on Pearl Harbor, it was rumored in our wardroom as follows: "This time the Order of the Golden Kite (*Kinshi Kunsho*) will surely be awarded to us. But we will go down with our ship, so our family must receive it. If we should return home alive, of course we will receive it directly ourselves."

Not only the officers but all the crew must have dreamed of the *Kinshi Kunsho*. I can now easily recollect our discussion of the above, even if it was half in jest. To a Japanese military man, nothing was superior to the honor of receiving the Order of the Golden Kite. Of course it was not easy to get it, and it was natural that we could not be eligible for it without distinguished military service. From this rumor you can now easily understand that before the Battle we were very conscious of the Hawaiian Battle, how great and important it would be, and all the crew felt their great responsibility.

At last we had our great success in Battle and we had the honor of receiving a Letter of Appreciation from Admiral Yamamoto, Commander-in-Chief of the Imperial Great Fleet as follows:

"The Letter of Appreciation"

To Task Force

At the beginning of the War the operation by the Task Force that made a surprise attack by their air force on the U.S. Naval Station in Hawaii, and destroyed the major part of the U.S. Naval capital force of the Pacific Fleet and the air force there greatly contributes to future operations.

I recognize these as distinguished military services.

Hereupon I award this Letter of Appreciation to the Task Force.

15 May 1942

Isoroku Yamamoto
Commander-in-Chief, Great Fleet

On looking back to the attack on Pearl Harbor, the meaning of the battle was so great and our defeat of the U.S. Navy was a great success. And it had an important effect upon other battles at the first stage of the war. However, the final results of the Great War in which the Japanese Navy was defeated brought all to naught, whatever big battles we engaged in and whatever success we had on the battlefield. Consequently, we were disqualified for the award.

The above argument surrounding the Order of the Golden Kite has become a funny story now, as an old, fantastic tale, and only the Letter of Appreciation now in my hands makes it a source of reminiscences.

12. THANKING GOD FOR HIS GRACE AND HELP

To be sure, the *Akigumo* was the newest destroyer, but I cannot help wondering if she was too young to participate in the battle so unprepared at that time. However, such thoughts didn't occur to me at that time, and I had done nothing but my best.

In spite of the above conditions, the fact that I could return home safely was rather a miracle, and I was filled with a feeling of gratitude to the grace of Heaven and the help of God. I believe that we could secure the grace and help of God like this as the fruits of the toil of all our crew who put things together under the command of Commander Arimoto, our splendid skipper, to carry out our duties.

Special mention must be made of the achievement of the important mission of the *Akigumo,* with my great pleasure.

Now I quietly recall the old days 33 years ago. After so long a time I am still deeply impressed with the performance of my skipper, Commander Arimoto, and all the crew of the *Akigumo*.

This diary is nothing but a story in which I marshaled only the old facts of all the days in which I earnestly conquered the Pacific Ocean for my life on board the *Akigumo* 33 years ago. But if I was able to answer some of the questions of readers of this diary in which I reported a part of the Task Force's operation in the Hawaiian battle, my joy will be more than complete. At present 33 years after the battle my modest diary comes to life again, and it must feel deep satisfaction for its old description.

13. POSTSCRIPT

The surprise attack on Pearl Harbor was made by the especially selected Imperial Fleet. (And I was engaged in the battle at that time.) Looking back upon the battle, I cannot help being struck with admiration at how fearlessly the plan was put into operation. It was a transocean operation of the largest scale, not only in the last war, but in all history. And it was worth noting that the operation succeeded.

But I surely believe such an operation will not occur again. Only a large-Navy country can attempt such an ocean crossing operation as the Hawaiian Battle, but I must say that if it tries, there will be no chance to succeed in a surprise attack, judging from the present defensive attitude equipped by advanced new weapons. The attack on Pearl Harbor, ventured by the Imperial Navy, will remain a record of the one and greatest surprise operation across oceans in our history.

However, with the progress of the world, a surprise operation by a fleet across the ocean is old-fashioned, and at present, a surprise operation of a new type is very easily carried out. Namely, it will be done by the ICBM which only requires one to push a button. The strong power of this ICBM, which can easily fly several thousand miles, is far superior to the power of our attack on Pearl Harbor. Of course, we can say that this is the best weapon for a surprise attack. This is a weapon unnecessary to fight against Nature, although the *Akigumo* was obliged to endure it for over one month. And it is also unnecessary to get the help of God. In the present situation it is sufficient just to push a button without hard work and we can easily venture to do so.

With the great progress and development of science, the world has become quite changed and I can again feel fear for the future. However, I would like finally to emphasize that we must make our world cheerful, so as not to need surprise weapons. This is nothing but a commitment to make our world truly peaceful. All the countries in the world should better understand each other and also must help each other more, shouldn't they? And all people must do their best to realize their ideal that the world become one.

In conclusion, I wish that we may keep this record of the attack on Pearl Harbor only in our history and we will never again plan a surprise operation. I believe that if my prayer has been answered, the transocean operation to attack Pearl Harbor will go down in history without fail, and the attack on Pearl Harbor will lead to a worthwhile life once again, I am sure.

1. Organization Chart of the Task Force for the Attack on Pearl Harbor

	CLASSIFICATION		COMMANDER	FORCES (SHIPS)	MISSION
TASK FORCE	Air Attack		Commander-in-Chief No. 1 Air Fleet	No. 1 Air Fleet (except No. 4 Air squadron and destroyers) No. 1 Air Squadron (*Akagi* and *Kaga*) No. 2 Air Squadron (*Soryu* and *Hiryu*) No. 5 Air Squadron (*Zuikaku* & *Shokaku*)	Exterminate aircraft carriers and the capital force.
	Guard Force		Commander, No. 1 Torpedo Squadron	Flagship, No. 1 Torpedo Squadron (Cruiser *Abukuma*) No. 17 Destroyer Division (*Tanikaze, Urakaze, Hamakaze, Isokaze*) No. 18 Destroyer Division (*Shiranuhi, Kasumi Kagero*, and *Arare*) *Akigumo*	Guard the fleet on the course. Support air force. Guard airplanes. Escort supply group.
	Support Force		Commander, No. 3 Battleship Squadron	No. 3 Battleship Squadron (Except No. 2 platoon) (*Hiei* and *Kirishima*) No. 8 Cruiser Squadron (*Tone* and *Chikuma*)	Support air force.
	Patrol Force		Commander, No. 2 Submarine Division	No. 2 Submarine Division (Type A class [*IGO*] No. 19, No. 21 and No. 23)	Watch before and behind the fleet. Guard airplanes.
	Destroy Force to Midway		Commander, No. 7 Destroyer Division	No. 7 Destroyer Division (except No. 2 platoon) (*Ushio* and *Sazanami*) *Shiriya*	Destroy airplanes and main facilities in Midway.
	Supply Force	No. 1 Supply Division	Captain of *Kyokuto Maru*	*Kenyo Maru, Kyokuto Maru, Kokuyo Maru, Shinkoku Maru*	Oil supply
		No. 2 Supply Division	Supervision, *Toho-Maru*	*Toho-Maru, Toei Maru*, and *Nippon Maru*	
Advance Troops			Commander-in-Chief of No. 6 Fleet	No. 6 Fleet (Submarine) (except 3 submarines)	Watch enemy fleet. Assault enemy fleet. Secret scout of berth.

2. The Table of Organization for Each Aircraft Carrier

	ATTACK PLANE MARK 97-NO. 3	BOMBER, MARK 99	FIGHTER, "ZERO-SEN"	TOTAL
Akagi	27	18	18	63
Kaga	27	27	21	75
Shokaku	27	27	18	72
Zuikaku	27	27	18	72
Soryu	27	18	18	63
Hiryu	27	18	18	63
Total	162	135	111	408

NOTE: Capacities of each plane:

• Attack plane
  Mark 97—No. 3   "Kanko"

  At 3,000m in height
  Economical speed — 130 kts x 8 hours
  Maximum speed   — 140 kts

• Bomber:
  Mark 99   "Kanbaku"

  At 3,000m in height
  Economical speed — 150 kts x 7 hours
  Maximum speed   — 170 kts.

• Fighter:
  "Zero-Sen"   "Kansen"

  At 3,000m in height
  Economical speed — 180 kts x 8 hours
  Maximum speed   — 380 kts

Introduction to the writer of this book

This book, "Conquer the Pacific Ocean," was written by RADM Sadao Chigusa, Japanese Maritime Self-Defense Force (Ret.).

1. WRITER'S CAREER: He was born in Hiroshima Prefecture in 1908.

Entered the Japanese Naval Academy at Etajima, Hiroshima Prefecture, in 1927, after completing a five-year course at the Hiroshima First Middle School. He graduated from the Japanese Naval Academy in 1930.

2. HIS EXPERIENCE IN THE IMPERIAL NAVY: He made a training cruise to the Mediterranean Sea area aboard the *Yagumo,* Training Squadron, when he was a midshipman in 1931. He was commissioned an Ensign in 1932. When he had the rank of Lieutenant (junior grade) he visited Europe again aboard the *Iwate,* Training Squadron, in 1934.

His duties were mostly at sea on board six destroyers (*Yugiri, Matsukaze,*

Suzukaze, Hayashio, Yudachi, and *Akigumo*), three cruisers (*Mogami, Jintsu,* and *Yubari*) and the aircraft carrier *Zuiho.*

He was engaged in the "Chinese Incident" twice, once aboard the *Jintsu* in 1932 and later aboard the *Suzukaze* in 1937.

He was assigned the duty to equip the destroyer *Akigumo* at Uraga Dockyard, Yokosuka, in the middle of July in 1941. When the *Akigumo* was completed and delivered to the Imperial Navy on 27 September 1941, he was assigned as the Chief Ordnance Officer of the *Akigumo.*

He was promoted to Lieutenant Commander on 15 October 1941. He was engaged in the Hawaiian Battle (attack on Pearl Harbor), Bismarck Island Battle (attack on Kabient and Rabaul) and Indian Ocean Battle (attack on Ceylon Island) on board the *Akigumo,* which belonged to the Task Force. He also joined Midway Battle and First Solomon Sea Battle (first landing operation on Guadalcanal) on board the cruiser *Jintsu.*

He served in the Imperial Navy until World War II ended in 1945, at which time he was the Ordnance Staff Officer at Marizuru Naval Station with the rank of Commander.

Demobilization activity occupied him for about two years in Hiroshima after his Navy service.

3. HIS EXPERIENCE IN THE NEW JAPANESE NAVY: Called back into service when the Japanese Maritime Self-Defense Force (so-called new Navy) started in 1952.

Studied in the Management Training Program, U.S. Army Forces Far East in Yokohama and became a Captain in 1953.

Commander of Escort Division in 1955.

Subsequent study at the National War College in Tokyo in 1956.

Appointed Commandant of Cadets, Defense Academy, 1957, in command of cadets for all three armed services departments.

Directly following service as Cadet Commandant, studied at the Amphibious Warfare Course at Coronado, California, U.S.A.

Next duty was in command of the Osaka Naval Base for four years, reaching the rank of Rear Admiral in 1961.

In 1962, served on the staff of the War College in Tokyo, and was retired on 31 December 1962.

4. AFTER HIS RETIREMENT FROM THE NEW NAVY: He has worked with several American companies to add a plank to the pretty bridge over the Pacific Ocean between Japan and the U.S.A. He lives in Zushi City, near Yokosuka.

5. HIS FAMILY HISTORY: Married to Fumiko Yokotake in 1936, and they have four children, all married.*

A. Kimiko (girl): Born in 1938, has two children. Graduated from Kaseigakuin Junior College in Tokyo.

B. Masao (boy): Born in 1940, has three children. Graduated from Tokyo University, M.S. in Architecture.

---

* We believe the final page of this diary is missing, hence only two of his four children are listed—Eds.

CHAPTER 14

War Diary of the 5th Carrier Division, 1–31 December 1941

T HE 5TH Carrier Division, consisting of the carriers *Shokaku* and *Zuikaku,* under the command of Rear Adm. Chuichi Hara, participated in the attack on Pearl Harbor. While no translator is indicated, we believe this to be the work of Masataka Chihaya, who translated the diaries of the 1st Destroyer Squadron and the 3rd Battleship Division for Dr. Prange.

All times cited are Japanese time.

It has been our custom to make minor grammatical adjustments to bring the translations more in line with normal English usage. However, the messages herein are so historically important that, except for correcting an occasional obvious typographical error or spelling, we have reproduced these messages exactly as originally translated.

SUBJECT: Translation of 5th Cardiv War Diary of December 1941 (*Daigo Koku Sentai Senji Nisshi*)

COVER

5th Cardiv Confidential No. 29-4
From 1 Dec 1941 to 31 Dec 1941
   5th Cardiv War Diary (Operations and general matters)

5th Cardiv headquarters

TEXT
5TH CARDIV HEADQUARTERS WAR DIARY (1 DEC 41–31 DEC 41)

  I. Progress

    1. General situation

      a. In accordance with the strength allocation for the 1st Period of the 1st Stage Operations for the Great East Asia War, this division (minus *Akigumo* and *Oboro*) was organized into the Air Strike Force of the Task Force, and left Hitokappu Bay on 26 November. Generally maintaining 12 to 14 knots (9 knots while refueling), the force sailed to the north sea off Hawaii Island, the anticipated combat area.

b. Arriving at a point about 650 miles north of P.H. at 0200, 7 December, the force headed south with the increased speed of 20 knots, reaching a point 230 miles north of P.H. by 0130, 8 December. From this point the first wave was launched, and the second wave followed it at 0245. In cooperation with the 1st and 2nd Cardivs' attacks upon enemy ships in P.H., the division's air force attacked enemy air bases on Oahu Island, destroying most of the enemy air forces and hangers. Thus enemy fighter interception and counterattack upon our force was crushed. By 0750 all planes except one dive bomber of the *Shokaku* had been received. The force then withdrew generally to the northwest. (Ref. Detailed Action Report No. 1)

c. Reaching a point 750 miles bearing 345 from P.H. by 1200, 9 Dec., the force then headed west at 12 knots generally skirting 700 miles out of Midway Island. On the morning of the 10th, the Force was slated by Task Force Signal Order No. 27 to make an air attack upon Midway, but owing to adverse weather it was delayed until the next fine day.

d. Task Force Signal Order No. 30 on the 15th called for suspension of the air attack on Midway and, instead, for an air attack on Wake cooperating with the Fourth Fleet. But this plan was changed again when Task Force Signal Order No. 34 was issued on the following day, the 16th, whereby the mission of the air attack upon Wake was assigned to the 8th Crudiv, 2nd Cardiv, the *Tanikaze* and *Urakaze*, and the rest was ordered to go straight back to the western part of the Inland Sea.

e. Based upon information obtained after the air raid upon Hawaii on the 8th, it was judged that enemy submarines were ambushing the sea north of Marcus Island, the Southern Islands line centering Chichijima, off Tokyo Bay, the Kii and Bungo Channels to intercept the returning Task Force. Since the 15th this division had maintained daytime anti-sub patrol ahead of the Force and the afternoon patrol to the rear of the Force using a total of 28 planes a day. At 0935, 0950 and 1229 on the 17th, a *Shokaku* anti-sub patrol plane discovered two enemy subs (one quite sure and another not sure) and bombed them, claiming one of them surely sunk and another probably. (Ref. Detailed Action Report No. 2)

f. At night of the same day, the Task Force took a luring course to the south and passed the sea south of Iwojima with a speed of 16 to 20 knots. On the morning of the 21st, the Force joined the 21st and 27th Des. Divs. and the 2nd Tanker Train at a point about 350 miles southwest of Chichijima. After having the Guard Force refueled from the 2nd Tanker Train while sailing toward Bungo Channel, the Tanker Train left us. Arriving at the entrance of the mine-swept channel of Bungo Channel at 0930 on the 23rd, the Force entered the Inland Sea under the help of the Kure Naval Station. At 1833 the Force temporarily anchored at Hiroshima Bay. Leaving there at 1345 of the following day, the 24th, the Force entered Kure at 1600 of that day.

g. In accordance with Task Force Signal Order No. 38, approximately half of the carrier-borne fighters, dive bombers and bombers took off from the ships at 1000 on the 22nd, the fighters going straight to Oita, elements of the dive bombers and bombers to Kanoya after patrolling ahead of the Force (they too went to Oita after patrolling ahead of the Force on the following day, the 23rd), the rest of them straight to Oita. After entering Hiroshima Bay on the 23rd, base personnel and materials of the *Shokaku* and *Zuikaku* were sent to Oita by the *Hatsushimo* and *Yugure* respectively to establish base there.

h. After the 24th, the carriers engaged in preparing for the next operation at Kure, while the air forces prepared at Oita base.

2. Assignment and organization

   a. Principal assignment

      1) Until 1200 of 26 Dec., the force engaged in the surprise attack upon enemy ships and air forces in the Hawaii area, in accordance with the strength allocation for the 1st Period of the 1st Stage Operations.

      2) From 1200 of the 26th on, the force engaged in the Rabaul area invasion operation by the Southern Sea Force in accordance with the strength allocation for the 2nd Period of the 1st Stage Operations.

   b. Fleet organization

      1) Until 1200 of the 26th, the Air Strike Force of the Task Force in accordance with the strength allocation for the 1st Period of the 1st Stage Operations.

      2) From 1200 of the 26th on, the 1st Air Strike Force of the Task Force in accordance with the strength allocation for the 2nd Period of the 1st Stage Operations.

   c. Organization

Flagship *Zuikaku*

2nd ship *Shokaku*

II. Status of personnel

   1. Headquarters

Division commander:	Rear Adm. Chuichi Hara
Division engineering officer:	Engineer Capt. Kikuo Muta
Senior staff officer:	Cmdr. Kyozo Ohashi
Air staff officer:	Lt. Cmdr. Takashi Mieno
Communications officer:	Lt. Cmdr. Tonosuke Otani
Engineering officer:	Lt. Cmdr. Tsuyoshi Yoshida
Code officer:	Chief Warrant Officer Nobuo Kinoshita
Petty officers and sailors attached to the headquarters:	Total 22

2. Number of personnel under the command

Officers:	94
Warrant officers:	123
Petty officers:	696
Sailors:	2,242
Others:	9
Total:	3,164

III. Messages and reports (Ref. Detail Action Report as to these exchanged during the air raid upon Hawaii on the 8th)

From Chief of 1st Bureau, N.G.S., 2100 30 Nov., to Task Force and Advance Force, received at 0930 1 Dec. (Telegram)
"General Staff Telegram No. 973
(Report from Honolulu consul general dated 28 Nov.)"

From CO of Task Force, 0730 1 Dec., to Task Force, received at 0730. (Signal)
"Task Force Signal Order No. 9
This force is already in the anticipated scouting area from Kiska and Midway Islands. Tonight we will pass the 180 degree line and near the enemy zone. More strict air alert and strict look-out against enemy ships suspected to track us will be maintained. Particular attention will be paid not to reveal any light at night and to limit blinker signal as much as possible."

From Chief of 1st Bureau, N.G.S., 2000 1 Dec., to Task Force, received at 0600 2 Dec. (Telegram)
"General Staff Telegram No. 985
(Report from Honolulu consul general dated 26 Nov.)"

From C-in-C of Combined Fleet, 1500 2 Dec., to All Combined Fleets, received at 200 2 Dec. (Telegram)
"Combined Fleet Telegram Operational Order No. 10
The 'X' day is set forth as 8 December. Date of issuance of this order: 1830 of 2 December."

From Chief of 1st Bureau, N.G.S., 2200 2 Dec., to Task Force, received at 0400 3 Dec. (Telegram)
"General Staff Telegram No. 994
(Report from Honolulu consul general dated 28 November.)"

From C-in-C of Combined Fleet, 0910 3 Dec., to all Fleets, received at 1130 4 Dec. (Telegram)
"Combined Fleet Telegram Operational Order No. 11
The ship belonging to Panama, Norway, Denmark and Greece will be treated in accordance with the treatment of the enemy ship."

From CO of 5 Cardiv, 1020 3 Dec., to 5 Cardiv, received at 1020 3 Dec. (Signal)
"From 0300 of 4th on, be ready for the immediate use of 15 knots and also for 20 knots with 20 minutes notice."

From CO of Task Force, 1250 3 Dec., to Task Force, received at 1250 3 Dec. (Signal)
"Task Force Signal Order No. 16 (Excerpt)

The air alert from 4th December on will be carried out as before in accordance with the method 'C' of the 2nd preparation. The alert time will be, barring a separate order, from 15 minutes before the sunrise to 15 minutes after the sunset.''

From Chief of 1st Bureau, N.G.S., 2300 3 Dec., to Task Force and Advance Force, received at 0345 4 Dec. (Telegram)
"General Staff Telegram No. 9
(Report from Honolulu consul general dated 2 December.)

From CO of Task Force 0455 4 Dec., to Task Force, received at 0455 4 Dec. (Signal)
"Task Force Signal Order No. 17

    1. It has already been ordered to go to war on 8 December, but so critical becomes the situation on Far East that one can hardly predict war would not spark out by that time. So far no new information on Hawaii area received and also no indications of our Task Force being detected. But since the enemy intention is by its nature far beyond prediction, strict attention will be directed to immediately meet any unexpected encounter with an enemy.

    2. It is intended that this force will operate as scheduled even if war broke out before 8 December.

    3. Principal naval vessels stationed at Hawaii on 28 Nov. are: 8 BBs, 2 CVs, 11 or 12 CAs and 5 CLs.''

From Chief of 1st Bureau, N.G.S., 1900 4 Dec., to Task Force, received at 2045 on 4 Dec. (Telegram)
"General Staff Telegram No. 18
(Report on the weather broadcast as of 0130 of 4th in Hawaii district)''

From Chief of 1st Bureau, N.G.S., 2030 4 Dec., to Task Force, received at 0500 5 Dec. (Telegram)
"General Staff Telegram No. 24

    1. Report from Honolulu consul general dated 2nd Dec.

    2. Enemy warships and planes activities observed through the enemy radio activation observation.

    3. Report from Honolulu consul general dated 4th Dec.''

From CO of Task Force, 0610 5 Dec., to Task Force, received at 0610 5 Dec. (Signal)
"Task Force Signal Order No. 18

    1. When any of enemy or the Third Power's warship or merchant ship is sighted, her communication equipment will be destroyed if and when necessary to protect secrecy of our intention, and, in case of emergency, she will be sunk.

    2. The ship belonging to Panama, Denmark, Greece will be treated in accordance with the treatment of the enemy ship.''

From Chief of 1st Bureau, N.G.S., 2300 5 Dec., to Task Force, received at 0240 6 Dec. (Telegram)
"General Staff Telegram No. 38
(According to the enemy radio activities observation the planes in Midway district were approximately ten flying boats.)''

From Chief of 1st Bureau, N.G.S., 2130 5 Dec., to Task Force, received at 0310 6 Dec. (Telegram)

"General Staff Telegram No. 33
(Weather broadcast as of 1500 of 5th in Hawaii district)"

From Chief of 1st Bureau, N.G.S., 2200 6 Dec., to Task Force, received at 1200 7 Dec. (Telegram)
"General Staff Telegram No. 42
Information from Honolulu consul general:

1. On 5th the Oklahoma and Nevada arrived in (they have been out of the harbor for eight days), and the Lexington and five heavy cruisers left the harbor.
2. The ships in the harbor as of 1800 of 5th are: 8 BBs, 3 CLs and 16 DDs. 4 Honolulu type cruisers and four DDs are in docks."

From Chief of 1st Bureau, N.G.S., 2100 6 Dec., to Task Force, received at 0300 7 Dec. (Telegram)
"General Staff Telegram No. 51

(1. Report on enemy plane activities west of Hawaii Islands on 6 Dec.
2. Weather broadcast as of 0100 6th Dec. at Oahu Island.)"

From C-in-C of Combined Fleet, 0000 7 Dec., to Combined Fleet, received at 0115 7 Dec. (Telegram)
"Combined Fleet Telegram No. 775
On 3 December I was received in audience by His Majesty and was given an Imperial rescript which will be sent separately. Respectfully I relate it to you. In the audience I replied as follows:
I am deeply appreciated to be honored [with] the Imperial rescript prior to Japan's going to war. I have the honor to tell the Majesty that every man of the Combined Fleet will, with the Imperial order in his mind, do his utmost to accomplish the aim of waging war at any cost and respond your Majesty's trust upon him."

Combined Fleet Telegram No. 775 Separate telegram
Upon the declaration of Japan's going to war, I trust you to command the Combined Fleet. The responsibility trusted upon the Combined Fleet is indeed very important, as the rise and fall of the Empire only depends upon it. You are trusted to demonstrate the strength of the long-trained fleet throughout the world by destroying the enemy force."

From C-in-C of Combined Fleet, 0200 7 Dec., to Combined Fleet, received at 0630 7 Dec. (Telegram)
"Combined Fleet Telegram Operational Order No. 13
The rise and fall of the Empire depends upon this war. Every man will do his utmost to accomplish the mission."

From CO of 5 Cardiv, 1149 7 Dec., to 5 Cardiv, received at 1149 7 Dec (Signal)
"From 0100 of 8th on, be ready for the immediate use of 30 knots and also for the top speed with 20 minutes notice."

From CO of 20 Subdiv, 1500 7 Dec., to COs of advance and Task Forces, received at 1606 7 Dec. (Telegram)
"The enemy fleet is not in the Lahaina anchorage."

From CO of Task Force, 1046 7 Dec., to Task Force, received at 1046 7 Dec. (Signal)

"1. Summing-up of information reaches a conclusion that the estimated enemy strength in Hawaii area are: 8 BBs, 2 CVs, approximately 10 CAs and 6 CLs: more than half of them are in P.H. and the rest most probably under training south of Maui Island. They do not seem to stay in Lahaina.

2. Barring a particular change developing in the subsequent situation, the ship attacking will be concentrated to P.H.

3. So far no indications observed of the enemy being particularly alerted, but do not relax attention at all.''

From Chief of 1st Bureau, N.G.S., 1700 7 Dec., to Task Force, received at 2130 7 Dec. (Telegram)
''General Staff Telegram No. 61 (Excerpt of Honolulu consul general's report)

1. On 7th, no barrage balloon used in Honolulu district, and battleships were not protected by torpedo-defense nets.

2. No air patrols carried out in Hawaii Islands area.

3. The Lexington and Enterprise have been out of the harbor.''

From Chief of 1st Bureau, N.G.S., 1800 7 Dec., to Task Force, received at 2240 7 Dec. (Telegram)
''General Staff Telegram No. 65 (Excerpt of Honolulu consul general's report)

1. Excerpt of Honolulu consul general's report
   a. In the evening of 5th (local time), the Utah and a seaplane tender entered the harbor. The ships in the harbor on 6th are: 9 BBs, 3 CLs, 3 seaplane tenders and 17 DDs, in addition to 4 light cruisers and 2 DDs in the dock. All of heavy cruisers and carriers were out of the harbor. No unusual indications observed on the fleet so far.
   b. Honolulu is quiet with no black-out.

2. The Navy General Staff is firmly convinced of the success of the operation.''

From C-in-C of Combined Fleet, 0700 8 Dec., to Combined Fleet, received at 0759 8 Dec. (Telegram)
''Combined Fleet Telegram 791
The U.S. Asiatic Fleet ordered to go to war with Japan.''

From Chief of Staff of Combined Fleet, 0710 8 Dec., to Task Force received at 0800 8 Dec. (Telegram)
''Combined Fleet Telegram 792
The U.S. Fleet in P.H. was ordered to sortie from the harbor.''

From Chief of Staff of Combined Fleet, 0730 8 Dec., to Task Force, received at 1650 8 Dec. (Telegram)
''Combined Fleet Telegram 794 (Excerpt)
There are likely eight enemy ships 50 miles west of Oahu Island.''

From CO of Task Force, 1245 8 Dec., to Task Force, received at 1245 8 Dec. (Signal)
''From the sunrise of 9th the following air patrols will be carried out: bearing 0 to 120, Akagi bearing 180 to 240, Kaga bearing 240 to 0, 5 Cardiv. The distance to be covered, generally 300 miles but those patrol lines to be directed toward the rear of the force may be shortened as required. Make the level bomber and dive bomber ready for the torpedoing and dive bombing and wait for orders.''

From Navy Minister, 1920 8 Dec., to all Navy, received at 0820 9 Dec. (Telegram)
''Navy Ministry Telegram No. 946
Message to all men of the Navy

Facing the unprecedented crisis of the Empire, the Imperial rescript declaring war was issued. And, both the War and Navy Ministers were summoned in audience of His Majesty today to be given another Imperial rescript addressed to the Imperial Army and Navy.

We are deeply appreciated to be given such a warm Imperial rescript. Everyone will have the Imperial rescript into his mind and assist the Emperor's great deed, by close cooperation of the Army and Navy and also by demonstrating the results of longtime hard training thus achieving the aim of the operation."

From CO of Task Force, 1930 8 Dec., to Task Force, received at 1930 8 Dec. (Signal)
"Till the sunrise of tomorrow the fighters will be kept in the 1st Degree Preparation."

From CO of Task Force, 0200 9 Dec., to Task Force, received at 0200 9 Dec. (Signal)
"The fighter cover of tomorrow will be made as follows:

1. The first duty planes will be launched at 0250 and the fourth duty planes will be received at 1250. The duty hour will be two hours each.
2. Following the take-off of the next duty planes the landing of the duty finished planes will be made."

From CO of Task Force, 0450 9 Dec., to Task Force, received at 0450 9 Dec. (Signal)
"Congratulation for the sake of our country that the brilliant result was achieved through the good fighting of your men. But there remains still a long way to go. I trust you to tighten string of your helmet after the victory and do further efforts to accomplish the final aim."

From CO of Shokaku to CO of 5 Cardiv, received at 1206 9 Dec. (Signal)
"A number of the available planes for the tomorrow's operations: 16 fighters, 25 dive bombers and 25 level bombers. (Remark: those of Zuikaku: 17 fighters, 26 dive bombers and 26 level bombers."

From CO of Task Force, 1100 9 Dec., to Task Force, received at 1100 9 Dec. (Signal)
"As a result of the air scout no enemy sighted within 300 miles circle. Be ready for the immediate use of 26 knots."

From Chief of 1st Bureau, N.G.S., 1100 9 Dec., to Task Force received at 1300 9 Dec. (Telegram)
"General Staff Telegram No. 104
Flying boats, estimated three to six, in the Midway reported they would arrive the Pearl Harbor at 1330 today."

From CO of Task Force, 1220 9 Dec., to Task Force, received at 1220 9 Dec. (Signal)
"In view of the fact that the enemy detected the direction of us yesterday, the enemy is supposed to detect our movement from our sending telegrams today. Particular alert will be requested therefore."

From CO of 5 Cardiv, 1600 9 Dec., to 5 Cardiv, received at 1600 9 Dec. (Signal)
"Be ready for the immediate use of 20 knots and also for 24 knots with 30 minutes notice."

From C-in-C of Combined Fleet, 1640 9 Dec., to CO of Task Force, received at 2150 9 Dec. (Telegram)
"Combined Fleet Telegram Operational Order No. 14
As far as the situation permits, the Task Force will launch an airraid upon the Midway Island on its return trip and destroy it completely so as to make the further use of it impossible."

From C-in-C of Combined Fleet, 1740 9 Dec., to Task & Advance Forces, received at 0600 10 Dec. (Telegram)
"Combined Fleet Telegram Operational Order No. 15
The Task Force commander is relieved of commanding the Advance Force."

From CO of Task Force, 0553 10 Dec., to Task Force, received at 0553 10 Dec. (Signal)
"Task Force Signal Order No. 27
This force will join with the Tanker Train for refueling and after that will attack Midway to destroy it in accordance with the Combined Fleet Telegram Operational Order No. 14. Details will be ordered by separate orders."

From CO of Task Force, 0615 11 Dec., to Task Force, received at 0615 11 Dec. (Signal)
"On 10th C-in-C of the Combined Fleet was given the following Imperial rescript:
Upon the outbreak of the war the Combined Fleet, under the good planning and with the brave action, demonstrated its great deed by destroying the enemy fleet and air forces in Hawaii area. I was rejoiced very much. I expect your men to do further efforts to accomplish the final aim."

From Chief of 1st Bureau, N.G.S., 2330 11 Dec., to Combined Fleet, 1st Air Fleet and 4 Fleet, received at 0315 13 Dec. (Telegram)
"General Staff Telegram No. 152
Radio activities observation information (excerpt)

1. Several flying boats seem to be at Midway. They flew for considerable hours on 8th and 11th.
2. In the vicinity of Wake Island two radio directions belonging to flying boats, carriers, watch or supply ships were detected."

From CO of Task Force, 0400 12 Dec., to Task Force, received at 0400 12 Dec. (Signal)
"Summing up each division's brief action report, the least estimate of the battle result achieved in the Hawaii airraid and our losses sustained are:

1. Sunk: 4 BBs (one of which exploded with explosion of her magazine, and the rest broken out of their hulls or capsized), 1 or 2 heavy or light cruiser, and one tanker.
      Severely damaged or sunk: 2 BBs, 2 CLs and 2 DDs
      Damaged: 2 BBs (such damage as one torpedo hit or two 888 kg. bombs hit) and 4 CLs
2. 16 hangers and 222 parking planes set on fire. 14 planes shot down. Summarizing the aboves, 450 planes set on fire. In addition to this, many planes were strafed though they were not set on fire.
3. Losses: 9 fighters, 15 dive bombers and 5 level bombers. (This includes those that made forced-landing after the attack.)

From C-in-C of Combined Fleet, 2300 12 Dec., to Combined Fleet, received at 0900 13 Dec. (Telegram)
"Combined Fleet Telegram No. 810

1. On 10th C-in-C of the Combined Fleet was given the Imperial rescript which will be sent by the separate telegram.
2. I replied to His Majesty to the following effect: It is my greatest honor and appreciation to have been given such a warm Imperial rescript. We also have the firm determination not to settle upon the lees and do our best to satisfy your Majesty."

From CO of Task Force, 0820 13 Dec., to Task Force. (Signal)

"As to the Combined Fleet Telegram Operational Order No. 14, the following recommendations will be soon made, and a decision will be given accordingly.

In either case, the force will first proceed to a point "L" where a refueling will be made.

1. First plan:
   From "L" point the force will speed down to south, and, in cooperation with the Fourth Fleet, invade Wake. Then, Midway, Johnston and Palmyra will be occupied, enemy land based air forces destroyed, paving the way for an invasion of Hawaii.
2. Second plan:
   The force will return straight to the homeland and preparations for the next operations will be speedily made there."

From C-in-C of Combined Fleet, 2250 13 Dec., to Combined Fleet. (Telegram)
"Combined Fleet Telegram Operational Order No. 18
The following countries will be treated in accordance with the enemy countries: Panama, Denmark, Greece, Cuba, Haiti, Honduras, Guatemala, Salvador, Nicaragua, Costa Rica and Dominica."*

From CO of Task Force, 0720 14 Dec., Task Force. (Signal)

1. The anti-sub alert will be tightened.
2. Preparations will be made on each carrier so as to have all dive bombers ready for anti-sub attacks. The degree of readiness will be ordered separately."

From C-in-C of Combined Fleet, 0800 14 Dec., to Combined Fleet received at 1330 14 Dec. (Telegram)
"Combined Fleet Telegram No. 823

1. On 12 December C-in-C of the Combined Fleet was given another Imperial rescript which will be sent to you by separate telegram.
2. I replied to His Majesty as follows: We are again deeply impressed by having been given another warm rescript."

From CO of Task Force, 0808 14 Dec., to Task Force. (Signal)

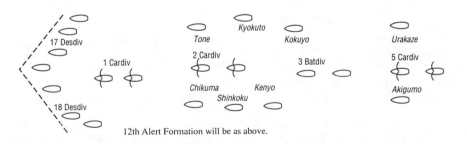

12th Alert Formation will be as above.

From C-in-C of Combined Fleet, 0910 14th Dec., to Combined Fleet, received at 1640 14 Dec. (Telegram)
"Combined Fleet Telegram No. 824
The Imperial rescript given to C-in-C of Combined Fleet:
The air force of the Combined Fleet demonstrated its great strength throughout the world

* Dominican Republic—Eds.

by annihilating the main strength of the British Asiatic Fleet at South China Sea. I deeply appreciate their deed.''

From C-in-C of Combined Fleet, 0200 15 Dec., to Task Force, received at the same day. (Telegram)
"Combined Fleet Telegram Operational Order No. 19

1. Since the outbreak of the war, the 24th Air Flotilla had repeated air attacks upon Wake Island inflicting considerable damage upon enemy installations and air force. On 11 December, however, the invasion force lost two destroyers owing to several remaining fighters and suspended the invasion for a while, and is now preparing another offensive at Roi, the Marshall Islands.
2. The Task Force will support the invasion operation of the South Seas Force by destroying enemy forces on Wake Island with an appropriate air force.''

From CO of Task Force, 0805 15 Dec., to Task Force. (Signal)
"Task Force Signal Order No. 32

1. This force will attack Wake Island after having refueling and conference at Truk where is reached on 22nd.
2. The 1st Supply Train accompanied by the Kasumi will go down to Truk intensifying the anti-sub alert, after departing the formation at the sunrise of 16th.

From CO of Task Force, 0807 15 Dec., to Task Force. (Signal)
"Task Force Signal Order No. 30

1. The Wake Island invasion operation has stalemated because of the resistance of the remaining enemy fighters.
2. As soon as refueling ends, the Task Force will speed down to south to destroy enemy force on Wake Island thus supporting the invasion operation by the South Seas Forces.
3. The attack on Midway Island instructed by the Combined Fleet Telegram Operational Order No. 14 is cancelled.

From CO of 24th Air Flotilla, 1330 15 Dec., to CO of Task Force, received at 0010 16 Dec. (Telegram)
"24 Air Flotilla Telegram No. 196
(Situation of Wake Island)

From Chief of Staff of Combined Fleet, 1620 15 Dec., to Cs-in-C of Combined Fleets, received at 0400 16 Dec. (Telegram)
"Combined Fleet Telegram No. 844 (Combined Fleet's informations on enemy subs No. 1 Extracted.)
Enemy subs sighted by the noon of 15th are as follows:

1. On 11th, about two subs in the vicinity of the entrance of the Tokyo Bay. On 10th, about two within 100 miles of the Hahajima.
2. From 13th on, one or two subs in the vicinities of the entrance of Bungo Strait.''

From Chief of 1st Bureau, N.G.S., 2200 15 Dec., to Task Force, received at 0200 16 Dec. (Telegram)
"General Staff Telegram No. 199
Information on enemy subs southeast of Japan Proper (Excerpt)

1. One sighted by a plane on 13th northeast of Marcus Island.

2. According to the enemy radio activities observation, at night of 14th one sub each observed in bearing of 49, 64, 65 and 66 from Chichijima. (It is estimated they are within 400 miles circles from the island.)
3. Some are operating off the Tokyo Bay and Bungo Channel.

\# From CO of Task Force, 1530 15 Dec., to Task Force, received at 1750 16 Dec. (Telegram)
"Task Force Telegram No. 854
Place the radio transmitter under the second degree control."

\# From CO of Task Force, about 1600 of 16 Dec., to Task Force, received at 1715 16 Dec. (Signal)
"Task Force Signal Order No. 34

1. The 8th Cruiser Division commander will command the 2d Carrier Division, 8th Cruiser Division and two destroyers of the Guard Force, and after cooperating the Wake invasion operation with its air force will return back to the west of the Inland Sea as soon as possible.
2. Until a separate order given, the 8th Cruiser Division commander will command the 1st Supply Train.
3. The remaining forces will return back to the west of the Inland Sea via north of Ogasawara Islands.
4. The Task Force Signal Orders No. 30 and No. 32 are cancelled."

\# From CO of Task Force, 1622 16 Dec., to Task Force. (Signal)
"The Wake attack force will depart the formation as its commander decides. Hope good luck."

\# From Chief of Staff of Combined Fleet, 1020 17 Dec., to Cs-in-C of Combined Fleet, received at 1035 17 Dec. (Telegram)
"Combined Fleet Telegram No. 861
Combined Fleet informations on enemy subs No. 2

1. According to the enemy radio activities observation, there appeared, from 2330 of 15th to 0200 of 16th, ten subs in an area from bearing 50 to bearing 68 from Chichijima, one sub bearing 18 from Truk and one sub each from bearing 87, 107, 121 from Ushiomisaki.
2. On 14th one enemy sub was sighted in the western part of the Inland Sea, but no further informations obtained in spite of a search of it."

\# From CO of Task Force 1045 17 Dec., to 5 Cardiv. (Signal)
"This afternoon, the 5th Cardiv will search enemy submarines suspected following our force, its detail being at disposal of the division commander."

\# From CO of 5 Cardiv, 1100 17 Dec. (Signal)
"From 1400 on, be ready for the immediate use of 24 knots."

\# From CO of Shokaku, 1107 17 Dec., to CO of 5 Cardiv. (Signal)
"One sub surely sunk."

\# From Chief of Staff of Yokosuka Naval Station, 1200 17 Dec., to Chief of Staff of Combined Fleet, received at 1530 17 Dec. (Telegram)
"Yokosuka Naval Station Telegram No. 185

On 13th a submerged sub sighted near Tsurugizaki, but subsequent every day search didn't see it any more. At 0730 of 17th an enemy sub sighted east of Hachijojima and was attacked by planes. In view of the result of the enemy radio direction detecting, enemy subs seem gradually concentrating toward north to northeast of Chichijima.''

\# From CO of No. 53 Base (probably Marcus Island), 1300 17 Dec., to CO of Yokosuka Air Group, received at 0500 18 Dec. (Telegram)
"No. 53 Base Telegram No. 27 (Excerpt)
At 0530 three subs sighted 60 miles bearing 80 from Marcus Island heading north.''

\# From CO of Task Force, 1335 17 Dec., to Task Force. (Signal)
"Changing the schedule, this force will go down south after the sunset of today, and will head for the western part of the Inland Sea via south of the South Iwojima. Particular attention will be paid against enemy subs today.''

\# From CO of Task Force, 1400 17 Dec., to C-in-C of Combined Fleet. (Telegram)
"Task Force Telegram No. 845
Task Force Brief Action Report No. 1 (Excerpt)

1. Ships:
   4 BBs, sunk, 2 BBs severely damaged and 2 others considerably damaged.
   2 CAs or CLs sunk and 4 others considerably damaged.
   2 CLs and 2 DDs severely damaged. 1 tanker sunk.

2. Airplanes and hangars
   16 hangars set on fire and 2 others destroyed. 450 planes destroyed.

\# From CO of 5 Cardiv, 1440 17 Dec., to 5 Cardiv. (Signal)
"Be ready for the immediate use of 20 knots and also for 24 knots with 20 minutes notice.''

\# From Chief of Special Intelligence (Enemy radio activities observation), N.G.S. to Combined Fleet, received at 0420 18 Dec. (Telegram)
"General Staff Telegram No. 213
Radio information (excerpt)
Nine enemy subs are operating in Chichijima district.''

\# From CO of Task Force, 1610 17 Dec., to Task Force. (Signal)

1. As probability is great that enemy subs would be met tonight, the alert will be tightened.
2. Today two enemy subs sighted and sunk.

\# From CO of Task Force, 1630 17 Dec., to C-in-C of Combined Fleet (Telegram)
"Task Force Brief Action Report No. 2
At 0935 of 17th an enemy sub was sunk by bombing at a point 680 miles bearing 31 from Marcus Island. At 1229 of the day another sub heading north was also attacked 20 miles bearing 300 from the first sighted sub, presumably sunk but not sure. In view of enemy subs this force will change the schedule and return back to the homeland via south of Ogasawara Islands arriving there on 23rd.''

\# From CO of Shokaku, 1230 19th Dec., to CO of 5 Cardiv. (Signal)
"Kogi Maru* sighted 55 miles bearing 240 from Akagi at 1230. Its course is east.''

* Possibly *Koei Maru*—Eds.

From Chief of Staff of Combined Fleet, 1630 19 Dec., to Chiefs of Staff of all Fleets, received at 0038 20 Dec. (Telegram)
"Combined Fleet Telegram No. 876
Combined Fleet information on enemy subs. Estimate on enemy subs as of 19 Dec. (Excerpt)

1. One to four enemy subs each off Tokyo Bay, Bungo and Kii Straits.
2. Three or four subs along the Nampo Island chain."

From CO of Task Force, 1630 20 Dec. (Signal)
"Task Force Telegram and Signal Order No. 2
(Matters concerning the limit of the public release of this operation.)

From C-in-C of 5 Fleet, 0900 18 Dec., to CO of 7 Base Force (at Ogasawara), received at 1230 18 Dec. (Telegram)
"5 Fleet Telegram No. 424 (excerpt)
A full cooperation will be given to guard the Task Force."

From CO of Task Force, 1520 18 Dec., to Task Force. (Signal)
"Enemy subs sighted near Marcus Island yesterday are heading north so that it is quite probable this force would meet them. Strict alert will be kept."

From CO of 7 Base Force, 1220 18 Dec., to 1st Air and 5 Fleets, received at 1550 18 Dec. (Telegram)
"7 Base Force will carry out the following patrol for the return of the Task Force (excerpt)

1. On 19th and 20th, Chichijima Air Group will scout a fan area, a distance of advance being 150 miles, from bearing 90 to 180 from the island.
2. From 0800 of 19th, 4 minesweepers, 2 sub-chasers and 2 patrols will sweep the area from a point 24 N, 145 E toward the direction of 139."

From C-in-C of Yokosuka Naval Station, 1330 18 Dec., to CO of 53 Base and others, received at 1800 18 Dec. (Telegram)
"Yokosuka Naval Station Telegram No. 197
Yokosuka Naval Station Force will carry out the following patrol for the return of Task Force. (excerpt)

1. The 53 Base (Marcus Island) will scout on 18th an area (detail omitted) and on 19th a fan area, a distance of advance being 550 miles from bearing 300 to 320 from Marcus Island.
2. The Yokosuka and Kisarazu Air Groups will carry out scouts (details omitted)."

From CO of Task Force, 1030 19 Dec. (Signal)
"Task Force Signal Order No. 36

1. This force will join with 21st and 27th (minus 1 DD) Desdivs, Arare and 2nd Tanker Train at 0900 of 21st at a point 22–20 N, 138–30 E, and reach near Okinoshima at 1300 of 23rd. After passing through the second mine-cleared channel, the formation will be discontinued.
2. After the formation is discontinued (in case of the carrier division, after unloading necessary materials for bases), each unit will go to Kure where repairs and replenishments will be made. The 1st Cardiv (minus the desdiv) will temporarily anchor off Gunchu at night of 23rd.
3. The distribution of bases is set forth as follows:
1st Cardiv: Iwakuni
2nd Cardiv: Usa

5th Cardiv: Oita
3 BB Div, 8 CA Div and 1 Des Sqd: Kure''

From CO of Task Force, 1130 19 Dec. (Signal)
"Task Force Signal Order No. 37
After 1000 of 20th, all seaplanes of 3 BB Div and 1st Des Sqd will carry out the anti-sub patrol on the scheduled course of the Task Force and its vicinity. Details will be at disposal of 3 BB Div commander. The air officer of the Hiei will command this force. After that, the force will go to Chichijima by sunset, and on 21st will search enemy subs in the Nampo Islands. It will return back Kure via Yokosuka by 24th.''

From CO of Task Force, 1340 20 Dec. (Signal)
"Task Force Signal Order No. 38
The carrier borne air force will carry out the anti-sub operation as follows:

1. 22nd:
   a. At 1000 hours, each carrier will launch approximately half of her fighters, dive bombers and level bombers. Fighters, in groups those of each carrier each, will go to Kanoya. Dive bombers and level bombers will go to Kanoya, too, after carrying out the following patrols. (Details omitted.)
   b. The 5 Cardiv will carry out an advance patrol ahead of the force and an anti-sub patrol.
2. 23rd:
   a. At 0630, all remaining fighters and bombers will be launched to carry out patrol missions toward the direction of 335. After that mission, they will proceed to previously arranged bases. Depending upon the situation, however, they may fly over to Iwakuni via Kanoya and Saeki.
   b. The detachment commander dispatched to Kanoya base will offer the anti-sub patrol over the main force and the supply force from 0900 to sunset and will send all planes to the prearranged base by 24th.''

From Chief of Staff of Combined Fleet, 2230 20 Dec., to Chief of Staff of 1st Air Fleet, received at 0240 31 Dec. (Telegram)
"Combined Fleet Telegram No. 889
On 19 Dec, enemy sub sighted and attacked in the western part of the Inland Sea but not certain whether they were sunk. Efforts are now being made to search them. The Inland Sea is, therefore, considered not absolutely safe from enemy subs as off seas. Much care is requested to be made . . .''

From CO of Task Force, 1445 21 Dec., to Task Force. (Signal)
"Task Force Signal Order No. 40
Since enemy subs are suspected to have penetrated into the Inland Sea, this force arriving Okinoshima at about 1000 23rd will continue the alert formation until Hiroshima Bay where the formation will be discontinued.''

From CO of 5 Cardiv, 0703 22 Dec., to 5 Cardiv. (Signal)
"The movement of the planes designated to take off today will be as follows:

1. Fighters will go to Oita Air Base.
2. After carrying out the designated patrol mission, element of bombers may go to Oita Base as the skipper of carriers decides.''

From CO of Task Force, 0850 22 Dec., to Task Force. (Signal)

"Task Force Signal Order No. 43

1. (Omitted)
2. Upon request of the 5 Cardiv commander, the Guard Force commander will share two destroyers for transportation of personnel and materials necessary for that division's base training after the arrival to Hiroshima Bay.''

From CO of 5 Cardiv, 1033 22 Dec., to 5 Cardiv. (Signal)
"This division's third base training will be carried out as follows:

1. Period: From 24th Dec. to a specific day to be designated by a separate order.
2. Base to be used: Oita Base
   Planes to be sent: All of the carrier borne planes.
3. Base commander: Zuikaku's air officer.
4. Communication and other: (omit)''

From CO of Task Force, 1045 22 Dec., to Task Force. (Signal)
"The Tanker Train will discontinue the formation and go to Kure with its best speed.''

From CO of 5 Cardiv, 1250 22 Dec., to Task Force. (Signal)
"Zuikaku's 8 fighters, 15 dive bombers and 15 level bombers and Shokaku's 9 fighters, 14 dive bombers and 13 level bombers took off.''

From CO of 1st Dessqd, 1631 22 Dec., to Task Force. (Signal)
"The destroyers requested by the Task Force Signal Order No. 43 to cooperate with the 5 Cardiv are designated as Akigumo and Isokaze.''

From Kure Defense Sqd commander, 1650 22 Dec., to Chief of Staff of 1st Air Fleet, received 0200 23 Dec. (Telegram)
"Kure Defense Sqd Telegram No. 105

1. Since 17th four destroyers have been used at successive nights to sweep enemy subs in an area from Okinoshima and Fukashima line to about 40 miles to north from that line with no events.
2. At night of 22nd, eight destroyers are sweeping a 40 miles belt starting from the Okinoshima light toward bearing 150 down to 32 degrees latitude.
3. On 22nd the east channel was swept with no events.''

From CO of 5 Cardiv, 0720 23 Dec., to Task Force. (Signal)
"Zuikaku's 10 fighters, 9 dive bombers and 10 level bombers and Shokaku's 8 fighters 12 dive bombers and 12 level bombers took off. They will go to Oita after carrying out the designated patrols.''

From CO of 1st Dessqd, 0817 23 Dec. (Signal)
"The destroyers requested by Task Force Signal Order No. 43 to cooperate with 5 Cardiv will be changed as Hatsushimo and Yugure.''

From CO of 1st Air Fleet, 1830 23 Dec., to C-in-C of Combined Fleet, Chief of N.G.S. and Navy Minister. (Telegram)
"1st Air Fleet Telegram No. 871
The Task Force (minus 8 Crudiv and 2 Cardiv) arrived at Hashirajima.''

From C-in-C of Combined Fleet, 1845 23 Dec., to Task Force. (Signal)
"Congratulation for your success. I am grateful for your painstaking efforts.''

From CO of Task Force, 0738 24 Dec., to Task Force. (Signal)

1. After a message is given today each division will go to Kure as the division commander decides.
2. (Omit)
   (Note) C-in-C of Combined Fleet gave this message to the men and officers of the Task Force at 1030 of 24th.

\# From C-in-C of Combined Fleet, 1030 26 Dec., to all commanders of Combined Fleet, received at 1220 26 Dec. (Telegram)
"Combined Fleet Telegram Order No. 30
The strength allocation for second stage of the 1st period operations will be taken: effective from 1200 hours."

I. Battle Lessons

1. Pitchings and rollings of the Zuikaku class carriers are much more than those of the Akagi and Soryu class. A remedy step should be taken.
2. The Zuikaku types' radius of action proved sufficient for that kind of operation. At the time they left Hitokappu Bay on 26 Nov. they had approximately 5,500 tons fuel. On 29th Nov. approximately 350 tons was refueled from a tanker, and on the 24th when she got back to Kure she still had approximately 1,700 tons of fuel.

The division's position as of noon of each day:

1 Dec:	42–32.5, 178–31	16 Dec:	35–25, 164–55
2 Dec:	42–6.5, 175–0	17 Dec:	34–11, 160–24.5
3 Dec:	41–31.5, 169–5	18 Dec:	29–29, 156–40
4 Dec:	40–0, 163–50	19 Dec:	25–46, 151–3.5
5 Dec:	36–45, 160–46	20 Dec:	22–17, 145–25
6 Dec:	34–26, 152–30	21 Dec:	22–50, 138–1.5
7 Dec:	30–17, 156–55.5	22 Dec:	27–19, 133–45.5
8 Dec:	26–11, 158–01	23 Dec:	8.9 miles bearing 110 from
9 Dec:	33–29, 161–31.5		Mizunoko light
10 Dec:	39–39.5, 164.53	24 Dec:	Hiroshima Bay
11 Dec:	39–24, 169–47	25 Dec:	Kure
12 Dec:	39–42.8, 174–21.5	26 Dec:	Kure
13 Dec:	39.23, 179–38	27 Dec:	Kure
14 Dec:	28–18.5, 175–22	28 Dec:	Kure
15 Dec:	36–57, 169–20	29 Dec:	Kure
		30 Dec:	Kure
		31 Dec:	Kure

CHAPTER 15

War Diary of the
1st Destroyer Squadron,
1–31 December 1941

T HE 1ST Destroyer Squadron consisted of nine destroyers—*Akigumo, Arare, Hamakaze, Isokaze, Kagero, Kasumi, Shiranuhi, Tanikaze,* and *Urakaze*—under the command of Rear Adm. Sentaro Omori in his flagship, the light cruiser *Abukuma.*

Many of the messages recorded herein were also recorded in the diary of the 5th Carrier Division; however, a number were not. As in the case of the 5th Carrier Division, we are reproducing all the messages exactly as in the original translation by Masataka Chihaya, except we corrected misspellings and typographical errors.

All times are Tokyo time.

According to a note in Prange's handwriting, this diary is complete.

Dai Ichi Suirai Sentai Senji Niishi
(War Diary of the 1st Des. Sqd.)
Ji Showa Juroku Nen Junigatsu Ichi Nichi Itaru
Showa Juroku Nen Junigatsu Sanjuichi Nichi
(From 1 Dec. 1941 to 31 Dec. 1941)
Dai Ichi Suirai Sentai Shireibu
(1st Des. Sqd. HQ)

1. Proceeding

   (1). General situation and enemy situation:
   The same as described in Combined Fleet Operational Order No. 1 and Task Force Operational Order No. 1.

   (2). Assignment and Organization:

   (a). Organization
   Assignment: Guard Force of Task Force
   Commander: 1st Des. Sqd. Commander
   Forces: *Abukuma,* 17th Des. Div., 18th Des. Div., and *Akigumo.*

   (b). Mission:
   As the Guard Force of the Task Force, this force engaged in guard, look-out for air, and escort of the supply groups.

   (c). Position:

6 Dec.	The *Arare* and the 2nd Supply Group composed of *Toho Maru, Toei Maru* and *Nippon Maru* separated from the main group heading for Kure.
7 Dec.	The *Kasumi* and the 1st Supply Group composed of *Kyokuto Maru, Shinkoku Maru, Kenyo Maru,* and *Kokuyo Maru* separated from the main group.
8 Dec.	Two series of airraids were made upon Pearl Harbor and military installations and air bases.
9 Dec.	The *Kasumi* and the 1st Supply Group composed of *Kyokuto Maru, Shinkoku Maru, Kenyo Maru* and *Kokuyo Maru* joined the main force.
16 Dec.	The *Tanikaze* and the *Urakaze* separated from the main group to cooperate with the Wake invasion operation.
17 Dec.	*Kagero, Hamakaze* and *Isokaze* made attacks on two enemy submarines with depth charges. Result unknown.
21 Dec.	The *Arare* and the 2nd Supply Group composed of *Toho Maru, Toei Maru* and *Nippon Maru* joined the main force. The 27th and 31st Des. Divisions (minus *Hatsuharu*) joined the main force and were placed under my command.
22 Dec.	The *Arare* and the 2nd Supply Group separated from main force.
23 Dec.	The Guard Force (minus *Kasumi, Tanikaze* and *Urakaze*) arrived at Hashirajima anchorage. The 27th and 21st Des. Divisions (minus *Hatsuharu*) were released from my command.
24 Dec.	The Guard Force (minus *Kasumi, Tanikaze* and *Urakaze*) arrived at Kure.
25 Dec.	The *Kasumi* arrived at Kure.
26 Dec.	The command organization for the Second Phase of the First Stage Operation was issued.
29 Dec.	The *Tanikaze* and the *Urakaze* arrived at Kure.

2. Status of Personnel:

(1). Headquarters:

(a). Ranks, names of officers:

Commanding officer:	Rear Adm. Omori, Sentaro
Squadron engineer officer:	Engineer Capt. Tanaze, Yasuri
Staff officer, senior:	Cmdr. Arichika, Rokuji
" ", gunnery:	Lt. Cmdr. Mikami, Sakuji
" ", communications:	Lt. Iwasa, Kyosuke
" ", engineering:	Lt. Cmdr. Yoshikawa, Tsutomu
Attached:	Sub-Lt. Warrant rank Matsumura, Jisuke
Attached:	Chief Warrant Motoda, Isaburo

(b). Petty officers and sailors: 27 men.

(2). Total number of personnel under the command:

Abukuma	456
17th Des. Div.	964
18th Des. Div.	948
Akigumo	234

3. Messages:

From CO of Task Force, 1 Dec. [to Task Force], received at 0753 1 Dec. (Signal or telegram signal)*
"Task Force Signal Order No. 9.
This force is already in the anticipated scouting area from Kiska and Midway Is. Also tonight we will pass the 180 degree line and near the enemy zone. More strict air watch-out is required and strict watch-out for suspected enemy vessels tracking this Force. Particular attention will be paid not to reveal any light at night and to limit blinker signals as possible."

From CO of Guard Force, 0900 1 Dec., to Guard Force and Supply Group, received 1 Dec. (Signal)
"Guard Force Signal Order No. 10

1. Blinker signals will not be used at night except in case of emergency.
2. Strict look-out will be kept with increased fighting spirit."

From C-in-C of Combined Fleet, to 1st Combined Signal Unit, received at 0450 2 Dec. (Telegram)
"Combined Fleet Operational Order No. 8.
It is requested at this moment to make every effort to seek a training base of the American Fleet in Midway area and an information of the British vessels in the Indian Ocean area. For this purpose, if necessary, you might issue an instruction to the enemy radio interception group under command of 81st Signal Unit."

From CO of Task Force, 2 Dec., to Task Force, received at 0500 2 Dec. (Signal)
"I-23 submarine seems to drop out the formation and to be following up the force from the rear. Take care of lookout."

From CO of Guard Force, 0535 2 Dec., to Guard Force and Supply Group, received 2 Dec. (Signal)
"Guard Force Signal Order No. 11
In order to make immediate response of gunfire while being refueled, each ship will make preparation for emergency break-off of refueling and also standing by for guns."

From CO of Task Force, 2 Dec., to Task Force, received 0540 2 Dec. (Signal)
"Task Force Signal Order No. 11
Revisions in the Task Force secret operational order No. 1:

1. The course through point 'N' either of First or Second course, both passing through points 'H' and 'O,' will be cancelled out and it will pass through the point 'L' (35 degree north and 160 degree east).

* This was by signal —Eds.

2. The staging point of the Supply Group, point 'N,' will be shifted to point 'L' (35 degree north and 160 degree east).''

\# From CO of Task Force, 2 Dec., to Task Force, received 0722 2 Dec. (Signal)
"Task Force Signal Order No. 12.
While the Airraid Force heads south with high speed from 'D' point, the submarine division will guard the rear of the main force following it with appropriate distance. After the main force reverses its course take the ordered position.''

\# From CO of Task Force, 2 Dec., to 18th Des. Division, received 0855 2 Dec. (Signal)
"Bring up I-23 which is seen in the direction of 170 degrees.''

\# From CO of Task Force, 2 Dec., to Task Force, received 1145 2 Dec. (Signal)
"Task Force Signal Order No. 13.
The commanding officer of the Guard Force will indefinitely let two destroyers take positions at 15 kilometers (5 kilometers at night) in the direction of 135 degrees on both sides of the Third Battleship Division to guard the rear of the force.''

\# From CO of Guard Force, 1250 2 Dec., to Kasumi and Arare, received 2 Dec. (Signal)
"Kasumi and Arare will go out of the formation at 1215 and will act as ordered by Task Force Signal Order No. 13. Stress will be made in before-dawn and after-dusk guards. Refueling will be made at appropriate time from Kyokuto Maru and Kokuyo Maru.''

\# From CO of Task Force, 3 Dec., to Task Force, received 0455 2 Dec. (Signal)
"Task Force Signal Order No. 14.
The 'X' day was fixed 8 Dec.''

\# From CO of Guard Force, 1032 3 Dec., to Task Force, received 3 Dec. (Signal)
"In event of* 5th Carrier Division will separate from the force to make air raid upon Midway in accordance with the Task Force Operational Order No. 1. Urakaze and Akigumo will accompany them.''

\# From C-in-C of Combined Fleet, 0910 3 Dec., to All Fleets, received 1350 3 Dec. (Telegram)
"Combined Fleet Operational Order No. 11
Ships of Panama, Norway, Denmark and Greek will be treated in accordance with the treatment of enemy ships.''

\# From CO of Task Force, 4 Dec., to Task Force, received 0424 4 Dec. (Signal)
"Task Force Signal Order No. 16.

1. The air guard after 4 December will be successively carried out according to the method 'C' of the Second preparation. The alert time will be, without separate orders, from fifteen minutes before the sunrise to fifteen minutes after the sunset.
2. Arms-equipments of torpedo planes and dive-bombers will be by degrees shifted to the arms-equipment of the day of the airraid. In event of a surprise encounter with the enemy after that, the first attack will be carried out with prepared equipment.''

\# From CO of Task Force, 4 Dec., to Task Force, received 0530 4 Dec. (Signal)
"Task Force Signal Order No. 17.

---

* Evidently an omission here, but the sense of the message is clear —Eds.

1. To start the war on 8 December was already ordered, but so critical became the situation on Far East that one can hardly predict the war would not spark out by that time. So far no new information on Hawaii area has been received and also no indication of our Task Force being detected. The enemy's intention is naturally far beyond predicted. Strict attention will be therefore directed to prepare for unexpected encounters.
2. It is planned that this force will operate as planned even if the war starts before 8 December.
3. Principal naval vessels stationed at Hawaii on 28 Nov. are: eight battleships, two carriers, eleven or twelve heavy cruisers and five light cruisers.''

From CO of Task Force, 5 Dec., to Task Force, received 0640 5 Dec. (Signal)
"Task Force Signal Order No. 18.

1. When any of enemy's or Third Power's naval vessels and merchant ships is sighted, her transport equipment will be cut off if necessary for protecting our intention, and, in case of emergency, she will be sunk.
2. Ships of Panama, Denmark, Greece will be treated with accordance to the treatment of the enemy ships.''

From CO of Task Force, 5 Dec., to Task Force, received 0815 5 Dec. (Signal)
"Task Force Signal Order No. 19.

1. The point 'F' in the paragraph of the 1st Supply Group, Task Force Top Secret Operational Order No. 1, will be shifted to the point of 34 degrees north and 162 degrees west. The rendezvous time to the main force at the point 'F' will be changed to 0900 of 9 December. By 0800 of the same day the 1st Supply Group will be the point 'F.'
2. After finishing fueling at the point 'F' the 1st Supply Group together with Kasumi might separate from the main force. In this case, the force will return back the west of Inland Sea via the point about a hundred miles north of 'G' and 'H,' with the details being at disposal of the commanding officer.
3. In case of the rendezvous with the 1st Supply Group could not be made, it is planned that destroyers in guard missions be refueled from carriers and Abukuma and Tanikaze from the Third Battleship Division.
4. The 2nd Supply Group with Arare will proceed to the point 'L' via the point about a hundred miles north of 'G' and 'S' after departing from the main force and wait subsequent orders.
5. The main force will head to the point 'L' maneuvering 800 miles outside of Midway Is. after through the point of 'F'.''

From CO of Guard Force to Guard Force, received 5 Dec. (Signal)
"By 6 Dec. each ship will carry out the following training and preparation:

1. Battle training and firing test of each machine-gun (four rounds per each gun).
2. Assuring of arms, equipment and engines so as to make preparation for full employment of the fighting strength and full maintaining of it.
3. Completion of battle preparations, particularly for the defense against bridge-strafing attacks.
4. Stripping off some preparations for cold weather which could cause some trouble for full employment of the fighting strength.''

From CO of Task Force, 6 Dec., to Task Force, received at 0425 6 December (Signal)

"Task Force Signal Order No. 21

1. Kasumi and Arare will, at appropriate time, eliminate their names and signs from their chimnies.
2. The Supply Groups will make every effort to avoid foreign ships even after 8 December."

From CO of Task Force, 6 Dec., to Task Force, received at 0735 6 Dec. (Signal)
"Task Force Signal Order No. 22

1. The Kasumi will take the position of 15 kilometers (5 kilometers at night) rear of the Third Battleship Division and with the sunrise of 7 Dec. the position will be shifted.
2. The positions of Abukuma and the Third Battleship Division in the 1st Alert Formation on 7 Dec. will be shifted to positions of five kilometers rear of the 8th Cruiser Division and the Abukuma respectively.
3. After refueling to the 2nd Carrier Division, the Kyokuto Maru and the Kokuyo Maru will take their positions of 'T-6' and 'T-8' respectively."

From Chief of Staff, Combined Fleet at 1400 5 Dec., to Chief of Staff, 1st Air Fleet, received at 0630 6 Dec. (Telegram)
"Combined Fleet Telegram No. 705.
By 1200 of 5 December little difference has been observed in the communication condition of Hawaii area since the General Staff telegram No. 842 reported it. Still no indication of Hawaii being more alerted. Additionally the Saratoga was judged in the Hawaii area."

From C-in-C of Combined Fleet at 0950 5 Dec., to flagships of Combined Fleet, received at 0510 6 Dec. (Telegram)
"Combined Fleet Telegram No. 703.
Around 1500 of 4 December, one submarine sailing under water was sighted 50 miles north-east and another 50 miles north-west of Papua Is. Again at about 1000 two submarines were sighted 240 miles west of the island. Enemy submarines seem to be deployed on the front."

From C-in-C of Combined Fleet on 0000 7 Dec., to Combined Fleet, received on 0100 7 Dec. (Telegram)
"Combined Fleet Telegram No. 775
On 3 December I was received in audience by His Majesty and received an Imperial rescript which will be sent separately. Respectfully I relate it to you. In the audience I replied as follows:
I am deeply appreciated to be honoured the Imperial rescript prior to the beginning of the war. I have the honour to tell the Majesty that every man of the Combined Fleet will, with the Imperial order in his mind, do his utmost to accomplish the aim of waging the war at any cost and respond to your Majesty's trust upon them."

"Imperial rescript (Combined Fleet Telegram No. 779)
With the declaration of the war, I trust upon you to command the Combined Fleet. The responsibility trusted upon the Combined Fleet is indeed very important, as the rise and fall of the Empire depends upon it. You are trusted to demonstrate the strength of the long trained fleet throughout the world, by destroying the enemy forces."

From the C-in-C of Combined Fleet on 0200 7 Dec., to Combined Fleet, received on 0620 7 Dec. (Telegram)
"Combined Fleet Operational Order No. 13

The rise and fall of the Empire depends upon this war. Every man will do his utmost to accomplish his mission.''

From skipper of I-72 on 1255 7 Dec., to Advance Force and Task Force, received on 1433 7 Dec. (Telegram)
"The enemy is not in the Lahaina anchorage. 1255"

From Chief, First Bureau, General Staff on 1800 7 Dec., to Task Force, received on 2120 7 Dec. (Telegram)
"General Staff Telegram No. 65
The Navy Section, General Staff, is firmly convinced the success.
1. 'A' information:
    a. In the evening of 5th (local time), the Utah and a seaplane tender got in the harbor. Ships in the harbor on 6th are: nine battleships, three light cruisers, three seaplane tenders and seventeen destroyers, in addition to four light cruisers and two destroyers in the dock.
    b. All of heavy cruisers and carriers were out of the harbor.
    c. No unusual condition was observed on the fleet.
2. Six flying boats and twelve land planes spotted on the Wake Island on 4th reconnaissance were also confirmed on the enemy communication activities. It is sure that the 22nd commander was there.
3. Two flying boats on the Midway Is. left there at 0600 on 7 Dec. for the Johnston Is.
4. Telephone contacts made with Japanese and civilian in the Oahu Is. from 1330 to 1400 of today reported Oahu Is. was very calm and no black out.
5. Two amphibious planes reported by the General Staff Telegram No. 61 were found out to be planes of the Saratoga in the west coast. No indication of small type planes' activities in the Hawaii area.''

From Attack wing on 0300 8 Dec. (Telegram)
"The enemy fleet is in the Pearl Harbor. Make 'attack preparation formation.' "

From Attack wing on 0319 8 Dec. (Telegram)
"All forces will make the dashing."

From Attack wing on 0321 8 Dec. (Telegram)
"Surprise attack succeeds."

From C-in-C of Combined Fleet on 0700 8 Dec., to Combined Fleet on 0830 8 Dec. (Telegram)
"Combined Fleet Telegram 791
The United States declared the war against us.''*

From Chief of Staff, Combined Fleet on 0710 8 Dec., to Task Force, received at 0805 8 Dec. (Telegram)
"Combined Fleet Telegram 792
The American fleet in the Pearl Harbor was ordered to get out the harbor. 0634.''

From Chief, First Bureau, General Staff on 0800 8 Dec., to Task Force, received on 0915 8 Dec. (Telegram)

---

* The United States did not declare war formally until Monday 8 December. This is the same telegram that, in the 5th CarDiv Diary, appears as "The U.S. Asiatic Fleet ordered to go to war with Japan "— Eds.

"General Staff Telegram No. 81
Enemy patrol planes of Hawaii are reporting eight warships at 21–10 north, 160–16 east heading 90 degrees, 0600. They were estimated to be enemy scouting force."

From C-in-C of Combined Fleet on 0730 8 Dec., to Task Force, received on 0845 8 Dec. (Telegram)
"Combined Fleet Telegram No. 794
The enemy communication interception indicated there were likely eight warships at the point of 'Tsu-tsu-hi,00.' "

From Chief, First Bureau, General Staff, on 0800 8 Dec., to Chief of Staff, 1st Air Fleet, received at 1000 8 Dec.
"General Staff Telegram No. 79
Likely either of the American fleet commander or the Fourteenth Naval District Commander issued the following urgent message to the whole fleet (?): 'All ships will get out of the Pearl Harbor to form a task force.' Inform the 8th Task Force which will take command of destroyers group, combat force."

From Chief of First Bureau, General Staff on 0700, to Task Force, received on 1000 8 Dec. (Telegram)
"General Staff Operational Telegram No. 80
The enemy is pointing out our task force in the direction of 178 degrees from 'AIB' (Translator's note: Japanese code name of someplace in United States.)"

From CO of Advance Force on 0950 8 Dec., to Task Force, received on 1220 8 Dec. (Telegram)
"From the flag ship of the Pacific Fleet to ships under command. Ships believed to be enemy carriers are pointed in the direction of true north."

From C-in-C, 1st Air Fleet on 0200 ? 8 Dec., to C-in-C, Combined Fleet, received on 1910 8 Dec. (Telegram)*
"1st Air Fleet Telegram No. 483
I will return back via 1st route. But, point 'L' is shifted to the point of 35–00 north, 160–00 east."

From Navy Minister on 1840 8 Dec., to all Navy, received on 1955 8 Dec. (Telegram)
"Navy Ministry Telegram No. 163
At 1140 today the Imperial Rescript declaring the war against the United States and Great Britain was issued."

From CO of Task Force at 0800 8 Dec., to C-in-C, Combined Fleet and Chief, General Staff, received at 2200 8 Dec.
"Task Force Telegram No. 844
Two battleships sunk, four severely damaged and about four cruisers severely damaged were certain. Many enemy planes destroyed. Our losses were about thirty planes."

From CO of Task Force on 8 Dec., to Task Force at 1100 8 Dec. (Signal)
"Task Force Signal Order No. 25

---

* Something is wrong here, as indicated by the translator's question mark. If Nagumo dispatched this telegram at 0200, it would mean a delay of 17 hours in its receipt. And it is incredible that Nagumo would have broken radio silence a mere 10 minutes after his first wave set course for Hawaii. It is more likely that the initial damage report (TF Tel. No. 844) was the first such action —Eds.

1. This force will head north, making strict precautions for oncoming enemy forces tonight. Tomorrow morning we will seek enemy forces nearby to destroy them.
2. Tonight the seventh Alert formation will be continued. The distance of 'A' and 'B' will be shifted to four kilometers and that of 'D, C, and F' to six kilometers.''

From CO of Guard Force at 1240 8 Dec., to Guard Force, 8 Dec. (Signal)
Guard Force Signal Order No. 14
''From 1330 on, the twenty-six knots moment alert and the full speed fifteen minutes alert will be made.''

From CO of Task Force on 8 Dec., to Task Force, received at 2350 8 Dec. (Signal)
Task Force Signal Order No. 26

1. ''Till the new order is issued, the seventh Alert formation will be kept on. But, the distance of 'A and B' will be shifted to four kilometers and that of 'D, C and F' to six kilometers at night.''*
2. Abukuma and Tanikaze will make their ways ahead to the point 'F,' from where, after refueling, will lead the Supply Group to join the main force. The main force is to make the way of twenty-six knots to 230 degrees till the rendezvous.
3. Refueling to other destroyers will be begun in the night of 9th.''

From Navy Minister at 1920 8 Dec., to all Navy, received at 0845 9 Dec. (Telegram)
''Navy Ministry Telegram No. 946.
Message to all men of the Navy.
Facing the unprecedented crisis of the Empire, the Imperial Rescript declaring the war was issued. Both Army and Navy Ministers were summoned in audience of His Majesty to be given another Imperial rescript addressed to the Imperial Army and Navy. We are deeply appreciated to be given such a warm Imperial rescript. Everyone will take up the Imperial rescript into his mind and assist the Emperor's great deed, by close cooperation of both army and navy and also by demonstrating the results of longtime hard training, thus achieving the aim of the operation.''

From Chief, First Bureau, General Staff at 1100 9 Dec., to Task Force, received at 1150 9 Dec. (Telegram)
''General Staff Telegram No. 104
Flying boats estimated three to six in the Midway reported they would arrive the Pearl Harbor at 1330 today.''

From Navy Minister at 0940 9 Dec., to CO of Task Force & Combined Fleet, received at 1410 9 Dec. (Telegram)
''Navy Ministry Telegram No. 102.
Accept my congratulation for the wonderful deed the Task Force and the Advance Force achieved, under the close and splendid planning, in daring the determined attacks upon far Hawaii Islands and destroying the enemy fleet and air forces there.''

From C-in-C of Combined Fleet at 1640 9 Dec., to C-in-C of 1st Air Fleet, received at 2155 9 Dec. (Telegram)

---

* On 6 December the Second Supply Group composed of Toho Maru, Toei Maru and Nippon Maru under the escort of Arare departed from the main force heading for Kure. On the following day, 7 December, the First Supply Group of Kyokuto Maru, Shinkoku Maru, Kenyo Maru and Kokuyo Maru departed from the main force escorted by Kasumi. On 9 December the main force joined with the First Supply Group —Trans.

"Combined Fleet Operational Order No. 14
The Task Force will, as long as the situation permits, repeat air raids upon the Midway Island on her return trip, to destroy it completely so as to make the use of it impossible."

From Navy Minister at 2000 8 Dec., to all C-in-Cs of fleets, received at 1000 9 Dec. (Telegram)
"Navy Ministry Telegram No. 945
I was received in the audience of His Majesty today together with the War Minister and was honoured the following Imperial rescript: 'Since the outbreak of the Sino-Japanese Incident, my army and navy forces have fought bravely for more than four years and half to punish the rebellious enemy people, but the situation has not yet been settled. With the realization that it was deeply rooted in the antagonism of the United States and Great Britain involved, I have made the Government to settle the situation through the peaceful means. The United States and Great Britain, however, not only have failed to show their sincereness seeking the peace, but have intended to force the Empire give the way, by increasing their political and military threats upon us. I decided therefore after all to declare the war against both the United States and Great Britain to maintain the Empire's existence and self-defense, and to secure the ever-lasting peace of the East Asia. Trusting upon your men's loyalty and bravery, I expect to accomplish the aim of waging the war and also to maintain the glory of the Empire.'
Receiving the Imperial rescript, I replied together with the War Minister to the Emperor to the effect: that it is my greatest honour to have been given such a warm Imperial rescript in the unpreceding crisis of the Empire, and that we have the honour of promising His Majesty to response the Majesty's trust upon us, by making our utmost under the close cooperation."

From C-in-C of Combined Fleet at 1940 8 Dec., to Task Force & Advance Force, received at 0610 10 Dec. (Telegram)
"Combined Fleet Operational Order No. 15.
The Commanding officer of the Task Force is released of commanding the Advance Force."

From Chief, First Bureau, General Staff at 1130 11 Dec., to Task Force & Advance Force, received at 1545 11 Dec.
"General Staff Telegram No. 494
The enemy radio activities intelligence indicated that at 0518 of 11th December the Chief of Ship-maintenance Bureau sent a telegram to Chief of the Pearl Dock Yard, at the same time informing it to the commanding officer of the fighter group of the Enterprise and the Chief of the Puget Sound Dock Yard. Together with the information at hand it is judged that at 1330 of 10th December a carrier, accompanied by two heavy cruisers, which is supposed to be the Enterprise is heading to Puget Sound for repairing, at the point of 'Tsu-Chi-Ya-46.' It seems likely that patrolling planes are offering patrol service ahead of the carrier."

From C-in-C of Combined Fleet at 1300 11 Dec., to Combined Fleet, received at 0835 13 Dec. (Telegram)
"Combined Fleet Telegram No. 810

1. On 10 Dec. Commander-in-Chief of the Combined Fleet received the Imperial rescript which will be sent by the separate telegram.
2. I replied to His Majesty to the effect: that it is my great honour and appreciation to have been given such a warm Imperial rescript, and we have the firm determination to do our best to satisfy your Majesty, without settling upon the lees."

"Combined Fleet Telegram No. 812

That the Combined Fleet demonstrated the great deed upon the outbreak of the war, by severely destroying the enemy fleet and air forces stationed at Hawaii under the excellent planning and with brave action, rejoiced me very much. I expect your men to do further efforts to accomplish the final aim.''

\# From Chief of Staff, Combined Fleet at 1300 11 Dec., to Chief of Staff, 1st Air Fleet, received on 13 Dec. (Telegram)*
"Combined Fleet Telegram No. 809

1. The following steps are planned to be taken chiefly for the anti-submarine operation of the Task Force, heading for the west of the Inland Sea:
    a. The 21st and 27th Des Divisions will sweep enemy submarines out of the Bungo Strait and, by noon of 19 December, will be at the position of 150 miles north of Chichijima. From there they will be placed under the operational command of the Task Force till the arrival in the west of the Inland Sea.
    b. The Nihoro group of the Kisarazu Air Corps and the Minamitorishima group of the Yokosuka Air Corps will move in the Chichijima Island around 18th and 19th December respectively to cooperate with patrolling the sea area around the Ogasawara Gunto (the Bonin Archipelago).
    c. The headquarters will make arrangement to the Yokosuka and Kure Naval Bases if necessary.
2. Toward the evening of 10 December four enemy submarines were confirmed at the south of the Hahajima.''

\# From C-in-C of Combined Fleet at 0800 14 Dec., to Combined Fleet, received at 1400 14 Dec. (Telegram)
"Combined Fleet Telegram No. 823.

1. On 12 December Commander-in-Chief of the Combined Fleet was again given another Imperial rescript which will be sent to you by a separate telegram.
2. I replied to His Majesty to the effect: that we are again deeply impressed by having been given another warm rescript.''

\# From C-in-C of Combined Fleet at 2250 13 Dec., to Combined Fleet, received at 0730 14 Dec. (Telegram)
"Combined Fleet Operational Order No. 18
The following countries will be treated in accordance with the enemy countries: Panama, Norway, Denmark, Greece, Cuba, Haiti, Honduras, Guatemala, Salvador, Nicaragua, Costa Rica, and Dominica.''†

\# From CO of Task Force on 15 Dec., to Task Force, received at 0800 15 Dec. (Signal)
"Task Force Signal Order No. 30

1. The invasion operation of the Wake Island stalemated because of the resistance of the remaining enemy fighters.
2. As soon as refueling finishes, the Task Force will head south to destroy enemy forces on the Wake Island, thus supporting the invasion operation of the island of the South Seas Force.
3. The attack on the Midway Island ordered by the Combined Fleet Order No. 14 is cancelled.''

---

* Again, we believe an error in date or time is involved, for there seems to be no reason for a two-day delay in reception —Eds.
† Dominican Republic—Eds.

From C-in-C of Combined Fleet at 0300 15 Dec., to Task Force received at 0610 15 Dec. (Telegram)
"Combined Fleet Operational Order No. 19

1. Since the outbreak of the war, the 24th Air Sqd. repeated airraids upon the Wake Island, inflicting considerable damages upon enemy installations and air force. On 11 December the invasion force lost two destroyers owing to several remaining fighters and suspended the operation for a while, and is preparing another offensive at the Marshall Islands.
2. The Task Force will assist the invasion operation of the South Seas Force, by destroying enemy forces on the Wake Island with appropriate force."

From CO of 7th Sub. Sqd. at 1300 15 Dec., to Task Force, received at 0820 15 Dec. (Telegram)
"7th Sub. Sqd. Telegram No. 402
One or two submarines of this force have been within the radius of 30 miles from the Wake Island for watching mission."

From CO of Task Force at 1800 15 Dec., to 2nd Supply Group, received at 1830 15 Dec. (Telegram)
"Task Force Telegram No. 847.
Make haste to Truk."

From CO of Guard Force at 1539 15 Dec., to Task Force on 15 Dec. (Signal)
"Tanikaze and Urakaze were designated destroyers to be employed in the Wake invasion operation."

From CO of Task Force on 15 Dec., to Task Force, received at 1925 15 Dec. (Signal)
"Task Force Signal Order No. 32

1. This force will attack the Wake Island, after refueling and conferences at Truk, arriving there on 22th.
2. The Supply Groups accompanied by the Kasumi will make haste to Truk, intensified the anti-submarine guard, after getting out of the formation at sunrise of 16th.
3. Refueling of 16th will be cancelled."

From Chief of Staff, Combined Fleet at 1700 15 Dec., to Chief of Staff, Yokosuka Naval Base, received at 2040 15 Dec. (Telegram)
"Combined Fleet Telegram No. 845
As the return of the Task Force delays, it is asked that the dates of removing the Kisarazu and Yokosuka Air Corps will be postponed four days respectively."

From CO of Task Force on 16 Dec., to Task Force, received at 1550 16 Dec. (Signal)
"Task Force Signal Order No. 34

1. The commanding officer of the 8th Sqd. will command the 2nd Air Sqd. and the 8th Sqd. together with two destroyers of the Guard Force, and cooperating the Wake invasion operation with the air force, will return back the west of the Inland Sea as possible.
2. The commanding officer of the 8th Sqd. will control the First Supply Group till another order changes this.
3. The remaining force will return back the west of the Inland Sea through the north Ogasawara Channel.
4. Task Force Signal Orders No. 30 and No. 32 will be cancelled."

From C-in-C of 1st Air Fleet at 1500 16 Dec., to 2nd Supply Group, received at 1620 16 Dec. (Telegram)
"Head for Kure instead of heading for Truk."

From C-in-C of 1st Air Fleet at 1530 16 Dec., to 1st Supply Group and Kasumi, received at 1850 16 Dec. (Telegram)
"1st Air Fleet Telegram No. 850
1st Supply Group will suspend to go to Truk and move under the command of the Commanding officer of the 8th Sqd. Continue the present mission till another instruction is received."

From CO of Task Force at 1530 16 Dec., to C-in-C of the Fourth Fleet, received at 2000 16 Dec. (Telegram)
"Task Force Telegram No. 849
The Task Force cannot afford full cooperation because of fuel problem. The 2nd Air Sqd., 8th Sqd. and two destroyers will separate from the main force and make airraid upon the Wake Island around 20th. As those forces cannot stay the area for a long time, it must be understood that the force will retire the area after making almost single air raid on enemy air force and installation."

From CO of 8th Sqd. at 2020 16 Dec., to First Supply Group and Kasumi, received at 2100 16 Dec. (Telegram)
"8th Sqd. Telegram No. 1.
The First Supply Group and Kasumi will join us at the point of 60 miles in the direction of 180 degrees from the point 'K' at 0600 of 18th December."

From CO of Task Force at 1630 17 Dec., to Second Supply Group and Arare, received at 1810 17 Dec. (Telegram)
"Task Force Telegram No. 857.
The Second Supply Group and Arare will join us at 22–20 north and 138–30 east at 0900 of 21st Dec., making round two hundred miles south and east of the Chichijima under intensified guard against submarines."

From C-in-C of 1st Air Fleet at 1600 17 Dec., to C-in-C of Combined Fleet, received at 1910 17 Dec. (Telegram)
"1st Air Fleet Telegram No. 858
It is requested that 21st and 27th Des. Divisions will join us at the point of 22–20 north and 138–30 east at 0900 of 21st December."

From C-in-C of Combined Fleet at 0020 17 Dec., to C-in-C of 1st Air Fleet, received at 0400 17 Dec. (Telegram)
"Combined Fleet Telegram No. 854
The 27th and 31st (minus one destroyer) Destroyer Divisions will go to Tokuyama for refueling after 0800 of 17th under the command of the commanding officer of the 27th Des. Div., and, after sweeping enemy submarines north of the Chichijima, will join the Task Force at the point of 170 miles true north of the Chichijima at 0600 of 20 December. With the rendezvous with the Task Force, they will be placed under the operational control of the Task Force."

From C-in-C of Combined Fleet at 0040 18 Dec., to CO of 21st Des. Div., received at 0535 18 Dec. (Telegram)
"Combined Fleet Telegram No. 866

The 27th and 21st (minus one destroyer) Des. Divisions will, after a proper anti-submarine operation, move as requested by the 1st Air Fleet Telegram No. 858.''

\# From CO of Task Force at 1400 17 Dec., to C-in-C of Combined Fleet, received at 0930 18 Dec. (Telegram)
"Task Force Telegram No. 845
Task Force Outline Battle Report No. 1

1. Firmly convincing the good luck and God's help with the glory of the Imperial Throne upon us, the Task Force proceeded two hundred miles north of the Pearl Harbor at dawn of 8 December. Despite of much difficulties caused by big rolling listing to ten degrees at max. because of long swells then prevailing total of 361 planes of fighters, dive-bombers, torpedo planes and seaplanes successively took off the ships, starting from 0100 hours. Penetrating through the prevailing close clouds and fierce fire barrages, those planes carried out the airraid upon Hawaii as same was scheduled from 0330 to 1500. At 0900 the Force received air forces and all of the Force withdrew generally in the direction of NNW as planned.
   No encounter of the enemy air forces except several flying boats attempting to trace of us.

2. Results (those considered reliable based upon summarized studies by means of photographs.)
   (a) Sunk:
       Four battleships: one of the California type exploded bomb-hitting on her magazines, each of the Maryland and the Arizona broken out of her hull with torpedoes and bombs, one unidentified exploded with torpedoes. Either of two heavy cruisers or light cruisers: Four torpedoes and five 250 kilograms bombs hit. One oil tanker: Five 250 kilograms bombs hit.
   (b) Severely damaged (those considered impossible or very difficult to be repaired)
       Two battleships: one of the California type inflicted four torpedoes and four 250 kilograms bombs and one of the Maryland type inflicted three 800 kilograms bombs and several of 250 kilograms bombs with big fire. Two light cruisers and two destroyers. Each inflicted more than one 250 kilograms bomb.
   (c) Considerably damaged (considered possible to be repaired):
       Two battleships: one of the Nevada type inflicted two 800 kilograms bombs and set fire, and another Nevada type inflicted one torpedo. Four second class cruisers: totalling seven 250 kilograms direct hits.
   (d) Aircraft and installations on land: Fourteen planes shot down, sixteen hangars set on fire and two destroyed. More than 222 planes being out of the hangars set on fire by strafing and bombing. Summarizing the aboves, 450 planes were estimated set fire. In addition of this figure many planes were destroyed by strafing and bombing, though they were not set on fire.
       In addition of this, it is certain that the unprecedentedly brave surprise attack made by the special attack force of the Advance Force could inflict a severe blow upon the enemy.* It is believed therefore that, within one and half hours since the outbreak of the war, the main body of the enemy Pacific Fleet Combat Group and the enemy army and navy air forces in the Hawaii area were all but annihilated.

3. Our losses:
   Nine fighters, fifteen dive-bombers and five torpedo planes were lost chiefly because of the enemy defense fire barrage.

---

* Nagumo referred to the midget submarines, which inflicted no damage —Eds.

4. Lessons:
   (a) The 800 kilogram bombs type 5 and the ''91'' type torpedoes proved their predominant effectiveness that either of five to eight direct bombs hits or approximately same number of torpedoes could inflict the fatal blow upon any of the existing battleships on sea.
   (b) Any reduction of the effectiveness (TN)* was not observed in this attack in spite of the fierce enemy defense barrages. Out of 49 800 kilograms bombs type 5, more than eleven could make direct hits. More than 35 torpedoes out of 40 could make run and hit against the targets despite of the shallow waters.
   (c) Results of duel fighting in the air indicated that abilities of enemy large type planes were a little inferior than previously published.''

From Chief, First Bureau, General Staff at 1000 18 Dec., to Chief of Staff, Fourth Fleet, received at 1330 18 Dec.
''General Staff Telegram No. 227
Since dispatching the telegrams in the air from the Task Force is considered to offer much disadvantages, in view of that many enemy submarines are gathering around the vicinity of the task force, your appropriate steps are requested to be taken.''

From Chief of Staff, Combined Fleet at 1140 18 Dec., to Chief of Staff, Task Force, received at 1330 18 Dec.
''Combined Fleet Telegram No. 869

   1. In view of informations regarding the appearance of the enemy submarines, this headquarters considers your south rounding down course under indirect covers adequate.
   2. The enemy ability of detecting our forces through radio activities could not be neglected. It seemed that the submarine discovered on 17th attempted to encounter Japanese forces, detecting them. Your close attentions are requested therefore. Information regarding enemy submarines will be sent to you as much as possible.
   3. Total of seven destroyers of the 21st and 27th Des. Divisions left Tokuyama at 0830 of 18th heading for the rendezvous point requested by your telegram No. 858.''

From CO of 53rd Air Base at 1530 18 Dec., to CO of Yokosuka Air Corps, received at 2050 18 Dec. (Telegram)
''53rd Air Base Telegram No. 30
The following air patrols for guarding the Task Force were carried out today. No enemy was sighted.
   Four patrol line in the directions of 30 15 0, 345 degrees from the Minamitorishima (Marcus Island) with the advance of 450 miles each.''

From C-in-C of Fourth Fleet at 1530 18 Dec., to CO of 5th Sqd., received at 2110 18 Dec. (Telegram)
''Fourth Fleet Telegram No. 656
South Seas Force Operational Order No. 25
The commanding officer of the Saipan Defense Force will intensify the anti-submarine operation in its jurisdiction area with the 23rd Des. Div. and others till the Task Force passes through the south of the Ogasawara Islands.''

---

* It was the common assumption among the military experts that the effectiveness of the force somewhat reduced in the face of the enemy —Trans.

\# From CO of Task Force on 19 Dec., to Task Force, received at 1135 19 Dec. (Signal)
"Task Force Signal Order No. 37

After 1000 hours of the next 20th, all seaplanes of the 3rd Sqd. and the 1st Des. Sqd. will carry out the anti-submarine operation on the scheduled course of the Task Force and its vicinity. Details will be at disposal of the 3rd Battleship Sqd. Commander. The air officer of the Hiei will command this force.

After this mission this seaplane force will go to Chichijima and commanding enemy submarines in the Nanpo Archipelago area on 21st, will return back Kure via Yokosuka by 24th."

\# From Chief, First Bureau, General Staff at 1210 19 Dec., to Chief of Staff, 1st Air Fleet, received at 1330 19 Dec.
"General Staff Telegram No. 240

The enemy radio activities interception indicated that four submarines which had been detected in the direction of ENE from the Ogasawara Archipelago were still detected in the direction of 54–62 degrees from Chichijima, with little change in their radio activities. It seemed likely that the Task Force had not been tracked by them."

\# From Chief of Staff, 4th Fleet at 1640 19 Dec., to Chief of Staff, 1st Air Fleet, received at 1750 19 Dec. (Telegram)
"4th Fleet Telegram No. 672

The 5th Naval Base is patrolling the area between the Iwojima and the Mougue Island (northern end island of the Mariana chain of the islands) with three special submarine chasers and one patrol boat."*

---

* On 21 December the Second Supply Group (*Toho Maru, Toei Maru,* and *Nippon Maru*) accompanied by *Arare* joined the main force and the 27th and 21st (minus *Hatsuharu*) Des. Divisions also joined the main force.

On the following day, 22 December, the Second Supply Group together with *Arare* separated from the main force.

On 23 December the Guard Force (minus *Arare, Tanikaze,* and *Urakaze*) arrived in the Hashirajima anchorage in the Inland Sea —Trans.

CHAPTER 16

War Diary of the 3rd Battleship Division, 4–25 December 1941

THE 3RD Battleship Division consisted of *Hiei* and *Kirishima*, under the command of Vice Adm. Gunichi Mikawa, and was a part of the Support Force of the Pearl Harbor Task Force.

This translation is by Masataka Chihaya. His translation bears the notation, "Part of the original of this J. document was missing." The reader will note that this diary begins on 4 December rather than 1 December. Also, Mr. Chihaya omitted the messages sent and received during this period. No doubt this is because these are covered thoroughly in the diaries of the 5th Carrier Division and the 1st Destroyer Squadron.

All times are in Tokyo time.

War Diary of the 3rd Battleship Division
(*Dai San Sentai Senji Niishi*)
December 1941
(The preceding part omitted)

On 4th and after 11th: Third alert
On 5th, 6th and 10th: Second alert (Third alert at night)
On 7th, 8th and 9th: First alert (Second alert at night)

At 0530 of the 4th, changed course to 145 degrees and at 0435 of the 6th the 2nd Supply Group separated. At 0200 of the 7th, arrived at point "D" and at last turned in the attacking course.

Since intelligence indicated that the existence of the enemy main force in Pearl Harbor was certain, the departure point of the first attack wave was shifted to the point 230 miles north of Pearl Harbor. At 0346 the 1st Supply Group separated. On or after 0600 this force was alerted for immediate readiness for 24 knots and at the same time fifteen minutes' readiness for top speed.

It had been almost cloudy by the 7th, the day before the attack. A southerly wind of 13 to 18 meters per second speed prevailed, sometimes with maximum speed of 23 meters per second. Despite this bad weather, the task force could carry out ocean refueling as scheduled. This success was believed to be chiefly attributable to the complete utilization of the results of sincere training and preparation, improvement of equipment, and the sincere efforts of crews, in addition to good luck blessed by God.

On the 7th the Imperial Rescript addressed to the Commander-in-Chief of the Combined Fleet was related. It said:

> With the declaration of war, I trust you to command the Combined Fleet. The responsibility entrusted to the Combined Fleet is indeed very important, as the rise and fall of the Empire depends upon it. You are entrusted to demonstrate the strength of the long-trained fleet throughout the world by destroying the enemy forces.

Deeply appreciating the warm Imperial Rescript, all officers and men firmly determined to fulfill the responsibility entrusted to them by the Emperor, by destroying the U.S. Pacific Fleet with utmost efforts.

Received message from the Commander-in-Chief of the Combined Fleet which said: "The rise and fall of the Empire depends upon this battle. Further efforts of every man is requested."

Employing the transocean tactics which the enemy had long planned, on the contrary, we will forestall them the next morning by launching a disastrous blow upon them. The morale of all men is very high, receiving the messages from the Commander-in-Chief of the Combined Fleet and the commanding officer of the task force. We don't care anything for either life or death, but to destroy the U.S. Pacific Fleet.

This signal flag of "Z" reminds us of the signal flag of "Z" which was hoisted in the sea battle of the Japan Sea thirty-eight years ago. Nothing more contents us, as fighting men, than to look at the same signal hoisted when we are about to meet the enemy's Pacific Fleet on the Pacific Ocean. There is none who does not make up his mind to accomplish a great deed comparable to that accomplished by his ancestors, thereby making the Empire everlasting.

On the 8th, half cleared up and partly with thick clouds. The wind came from E to ENE with the velocity of 12 to 15 meters per second. Good visibility suitable for flight. Pretty rough sea. On or after 0030 the 3rd Battleship Division was alerted for immediate readiness for top speed.

At 0100 aircraft of the 8th Cruiser Division started. At 0148 the first attack wave started, and at 0200 two reconnaissance planes, one from each ship, left. At 0220 took position of the Seventh Alert Formation. At 0252 the second attack wave left.

At 0300 the reconnaissance reports of the 8th Cruiser Division's planes proved it certain that the enemy fleet was in Pearl Harbor. With the message sent from the *Akagi*'s plane at 0322 saying "surprise attack succeeded" as the first message, reports of bombing and torpedoing the enemy airfields and fleets successively were received.

The attack of the first and second attack waves which lasted about one and one-half hours annihilated the enemy Pacific Fleet and achieved brilliant success. Damages inflicted upon the enemy were as follows:

Sunk:	Four battleships, two heavy or light cruisers and one oil tanker.
Severely damaged:	Two battleships, two light cruisers and two destroyers.

Damaged: Two battleships and four light cruisers.

Estimated: 450 planes destroyed.

Sixteen hangars set afire and two destroyed.

Nine fighters, fifteen dive bombers and five torpedo planes lost.

With the report of the Hawaii operation reaching the Emperor, the following Imperial Rescript was given:

"That the Combined Fleet demonstrated its great deed upon the outbreak of the war, by severely destroying the enemy fleet and air forces stationed at Hawaii, under excellent planning and with brave action, rejoiced me very much. I expect your men to make further efforts to accomplish the final aim."

The warm Imperial Rescript was given to the result which could only be done with the help of good luck, by the illustrious virtue of His Majesty. There was none who did not appreciate it. All men determined to accomplish the final aim, keeping in their minds the following answer of the Commander-in-Chief of the Combined Fleet to the Emperor:

"It is my great honor and appreciation to have been given such a warm Imperial Rescript, and we are firmly determined to do our best to satisfy your Majesty, without settling upon the lees."

On or after 0800 of the 8th, this force was alerted for immediate readiness for 26 knots and at the same time fifteen minutes' readiness for full speed. On or after 1045 it was shifted to immediate readiness for 26 knots.

At 0540 the first attack wave returned and at 0633 the 3rd Battleship Division's planes were lifted on board. At 0645 the second attack wave returned.

After receiving the returning planes, the task force retired generally in the direction of 330 degrees at 20 to 26 knots. Received no encounter with enemy planes or vessels.

On or after 1349 of the 9th, this force was alerted for immediate readiness for 20 knots and at the same time thirty minutes' readiness for 24 knots. At 0012 of the 10th, changed course to 345 degrees and joined the 1st Supply Group at 0300. At 1244 took position of the Second Alert Formation.

At 0535 of the 11th, changed course to 265 degrees. Since the afternoon of that day the weather became bad and the wind increased with the maximum speed reaching twenty-five meters per second.

At 0435 of the 16th, changed course to 330 degrees and at 0530 the 1st Supply Group, accompanied by the *Kasumi,* separated. At 1635 the 8th Cruiser Division, the 2nd Carrier Division and the *Tanikaze* and *Urakaze* separated from the main body to head for attacking Wake Island. At 1730 changed course to 255 degrees. A southwesterly wind prevailed with the maximum speed reaching 25 meters per second.

At 0945 of the 17th and also at 1225 anti-submarine patrol planes discovered enemy submarines at the positions of 34–00 N, 160–10 E and 34–11 N, 159–39 E. They were certainly sunk by bombing and depth charges. At 1700 turned course to 200 degrees.

At 0912 of the 18th, turned course to 235 degrees. Seaplanes catapulted from the 3rd Battleship Division and the *Abukuma* at 1100 of the 20th made searching flights over the scheduled course of the task force returning to Chichijima. At 1210 changed course to 270 degrees.

At 0200 of the 21st, the 2nd Supply Group, together with *Arare* and the 21st and 27th Destroyer Divisions, joined the force. At 0610 took the position of the Four-teenth Alert Formation and changed course to 335 degrees at 1035 of that day. Since 0942 of the 23rd, anti-mine preparation was made and at 1025 entered the cleared channel of Bungo Strait. Passing through the cleared channel at 1340 and then through Iyonada and Tsurishima channels, arrived at Hashirajima anchorage at 1825 of that day.

At 1100 of the 24th, received the messages of the Chief of the General Staff and the Commander-in-Chief of the Combined Fleet. Left the anchorage at 1330 head-ing for Kure and arrived there at 1600 of that day.

At Kure efforts were chiefly made for maintaining ships, weapons and engines, and for replenishment and recreation in preparation for future operations.

Status of the enemy:

Pre-war intelligence indicated it was certain that the U.S. Pacific Fleet was training with Pearl Harbor as its main base, but it also pointed out that part of them were always out for training base. Later information disclosed that Lahaina anchor-age, which had been supposed to be a training base, was not used. The task force was very anxious therefore to get detailed information as to the whereabouts of the training groups of the U.S. Pacific Fleet which were supposed to be training only in the area south of the Hawaiian Islands.

An information received on the 2nd said:

"Two battleships, *Oklahoma* and *Nevada;* one carrier, *Enterprise;* two heavy cruisers and twelve destroyers left the harbor while five battleships, three heavy cruisers, three light cruisers and twelve destroyers entered the harbor."

Another information received on the 3rd indicated:

"Six battleships, seven heavy cruisers (of which two were not certain), four light cruisers, eighteen destroyers, four submarines, the *Lexington,* twenty-six other vessels were in Pearl Harbor on the afternoon of the 29th."

An information on the 4th further pointed out that the U.S. ships usually left the harbor on Tuesday returning on Friday, or left the harbor on Friday, returning on Saturday of the following week, and also that in each case they used to stay in the harbor about a week. These informations led to the conclusion that the U.S. vessels anchoring in the harbor on the 5th (Friday) might leave the harbor, thereby making their locations unknown to us. Everyone prays to God to have the U.S. Fleet now in the harbor stay a little longer.

Every effort was made to get information through specifically arranged com-munications and radio intelligence, but it was not until the 7th, the day before the attack, that a long-awaited information was finally received. It said, "On the 5th the *Oklahoma* and *Nevada* entered the harbor and the *Lexington* with five heavy cruisers left the harbor."

This led to the following conclusion: eight battleships, seven light cruisers and sixteen destroyers were in Pearl Harbor at 1800 of the 5th. It now became certain that the bulk of the U.S. Pacific Fleet was in Pearl Harbor, moreover with no room for doubt that they would stay in the harbor at the time of the attack. Everybody was convinced of providential help.

The estimate of the enemy situation made by the Commander of the Task Force:

1. The summary of the enemy situation is as follows:
   Eight battleships, two carriers, about ten heavy cruisers and about six light cruisers are in the Hawaii area, more than half of which are in Pearl Harbor and the remainder are most likely in the vicinity south of Maui Island for training. It is not likely that they are in Lahaina anchorage.

2. Air attacks upon enemy vessels will be concentrated on Pearl Harbor as long as no particular change is observed tonight.

3. So far the enemy does not seem to be alerted particularly, but it is requested to maintain strict alert.

After sunset of the 7th, a message sent from *I–72* submarine confirmed that the enemy was not in Lahaina anchorage. Ultimately the reconnaissance flight of the 8th Cruiser Division's seaplanes assured that the main body of the enemy was in Pearl Harbor.

1. Factors which affected the operation

   (a) Despite the bad weather throughout the operation, the refueling, about which we had been most concerned, was smoothly carried out except for a very few days and the astronomical observation could be made successfully at the necessary times, thus assuring that positions by it were possible.

   (b) All of the enemy battleships stayed in Pearl Harbor at the time of the attack, as quite usual as before.

   (c) The fact that the politico-military evolution of Japan was smoothly carried out, coupled with the fact that our secrecy security measures were adequately taken up, contributed to the success of the surprise attack on Pearl Harbor. Dispatching Ambassador Kurusu to America and also dispatching the *Asama Maru* could camouflage Japan's real intention. The absolute radio silence of the task force did not leak anything. The precise broadcasts from the Tokyo Signal Corps contributed to swift communication of important telegrams and easy receiving of enemy messages, thus again contributing to obtaining enemy intelligence information.

2. Status of personnel

   (1) Headquarters

      (a) Ranks, names of members

Commanding officer	Vice Adm. Mikawa, Gunichi
Engineering officer	Engineering Capt. Okumura, Yoshio
Staff officer (Senior)	Commander Arita, Yuzo

Staff (Gunnery)	Commander Takaya, Kiyoshi
" (Communication)	Lt. Comdr. Mori, Torao
" (Engineering)	Engineering Lt. Comdr. Takeuchi, Yoshitaro
Code Officer	Senior Petty Officer Sato, Sakae

(b) Petty officers and others

Sailors	18
Paymasters	7
Others	1

(2) Total number of men under the command

Officers	222
Warrant officers	160
Petty officers	1,333
Sailors	3,662
Others	23
Total	5,400

3. Messages and reports (Omitted)*

5. General proceeding of the operation

DEC. 1ST

Position: 42–32.5N, 179–30W.†

Cloudy, wind SSE of 12 meters, 13C (temperature).

Visibility of 15 kilometers.

In the daytime, First Alert Formation while at night Third Alert Formation. Heading for the operational area with Third Degree Patrol. Course 91, speed 12 knots. Since 1300 hours 14 knots.

Division gunnery training.

DEC. 2ND

Position: 42–11.5N, 175–02W.

Cloudy, SSE wind of 12 meters, 13C, vis. 20 km.

At 0345 speed 16 knots, at 0404 9 knots and at 1600 12 knots.

At 0400 began refueling, which was finished at 1100.

Amounts of oil refueled: *Hiei,* 354 tons; *Kirishima,* 469 tons.

DEC. 3RD

Position: 41–39N, 169–10W.

Cloudy, SSW wind of 17 meters, 13C, vis. 10 km.

---

* No paragraph 4 is included in the translation. It is not known whether this was one of the items missing from the original, whether the translator omitted it as of no interest, or whether 5 was simply a typographical error —Eds.

† In the Japanese Navy the position as of noon of the day was usually mentioned —Trans.

At 0400 9 knots, at 0600 12 knots and 1155 9 knots.

DEC. 4TH

Position: 40–09N, 163–08W.

Cloudy, SSW wind of 18 meters, 14.2C, vis. 8 km.

At 0530 course, 145 degrees.

From today on, the wind increased in speed with maximum speed of 23 meters. In the afternoon it decreased, and at 1500 hours it became 11 meters.

DEC. 5TH

Position: 36–40N, 160–39W.

Cloudy, E wind of 8 meters, 13C, vis. 12 km.

At 0502 speed 9 knots, at 0719 14 knots, at 0840 9 knots and at 1230 5 knots.

Second Alert (Third Alert at night).

Division gunnery training.

DEC. 6TH

Position: 34–26.8N, 158–33.3W.

Cloudy, SSW wind of 18 meters, vis. 10 km.

At 0344 speed 9 knots.

At 0435 2nd Supply Group separated.

1910 course 156 degrees.

DEC. 7TH

Position: 29–12N, 156–55W.

Cloudy, NE to NW wind of 10 meters, vis. 10 km.

At 0200 hours reached point "D" from which it is the attacking course. Since intelligence pointed to the existence of the enemy main force in Pearl Harbor certain, point of "F" was shifted to the point 230 miles north of Pearl Harbor. At 0340 the 1st Supply Group separated. At 0700 made way on course of 180 degrees with speed of 20 knots. Took the position of the Sixth Alert Formation. From this day on, the First Alert (the Second Alert at night).

DEC. 8TH

Position: 26–17.5N, 157–11.8W.

Clear, ENE wind of 19 meters, 22C, vis. 35 km.

At 0100 reached point "F." Seaplanes of the 8th Cruiser Division started.

At 0148 the first attack wave started.

At 0200 seaplanes of the 3rd Battleship Division started.

At 0220 the Seventh Alert Formation.

At 0252 the second attack wave left.

At 0540 the first attack wave returned.

At 0633 seaplanes of the 3rd Battleship Division were picked up.

At 0645 the second attack wave returned. After receiving the second attack planes on board, the Force generally kept its course at 330 degrees with 20 to 26 knots.

DEC. 9TH

Position: 33–28.5N, 161–31.7W.

Cloudy, SW to S wind of 7 meters, 18.5C, vis. 30 km.

At 0210 carrier-borne planes left on a reconnaissance mission. They returned at 0830.

Division gunnery training.

DEC. 10TH

Position: 37–40N, 164–35W.

Clear, S to SW wind of 8 meters, 15C, vis. 30 km.

At 0012 course 345 degrees.

At 0015 speed 20 knots. At 0300 joined the 1st Supply Group.

At 1244 the Second Alert Formation. Since 1405, 12 knots.

DEC. 11TH

Position: 39–32N, 169–46W.

Part clear, W to WSW wind of 10 meters, 13C, vis. 20 km.

At 0409 speed 14 knots.

At 0535 course 265 degrees.

At 0945 speed 12 knots.

Maximum wind speed of this day, 25 meters.

From this day on, the Third Alert Patrol.

DEC. 12TH

Position: 39–46N, 174.15W.

Cloudy, NW wind of 13 meters, 12C, vis. 25 km.

DEC. 13TH

Position: 39–21N, 179–41W.

Cloudy with fog, SW wind of 17 meters, 17C, vis. 12 km.

At 1030 speed 9 knots and at 1225 course 255 degrees.

At 1533 12 knots.

DEC. 14TH

Position: 38–20.5N, 175–24E.

Partly clear, NW to N wind of 10 meters, 13C., vis. 35 km.

At 1020 speed 14 knots.

At 1052 the Twelfth Alert Formation.

At 1145 speed 12 knots.

At 1300 speed 14 knots.

DEC. 15TH

Position: 37–3N, 169–07E.

Cloudy, SSW wind of 14 meters, 17C, vis. 30 km.

At 0635 speed 12 knots.

At 1000 speed 9 knots.

Great swells.

DEC. 16TH

Position: 35–23N, 164–54E.

Cloudy, SSW wind of 20 meters, 20C, vis. 18 km.

At 0435 course 230 degrees.

At 0530 the 1st Supply Group with *Kasumi* separated.

At 1027 12 knots, and at 1335 9 knots.

At 1635 the 8th Cruiser Division, the 2nd Carrier Division and the *Tanikaze* and *Urakaze* separated from the Force heading for Wake Island.

At 1730 course 255 degrees.

At 1936 speed 12 knots.

Today wind prevailed, reaching the maximum speed of 25 meters.

DEC. 17TH

Position: 34–15N, 160–09E.

Partly clear, a wind of 5 meters, 18C, vis. 30 km.

At 0500 14 knots, and at 0620 12 knots.

At 0900 14 knots and at 0953 16 knots.

At 1707 course 200 degrees.

At 0940 attacked with bombs and depth charges an enemy submarine sighted at 34–00N, 160–10E. Certainly sank it.

At 1225 again sighted an enemy submarine at 34–11N, 159–39E and attacked it.

DEC. 18TH

Position: 29–28.5N, 156–39E.

Clear, west wind of 14 meters, 23C, vis. 35 km.

At 0912 course 235.

DEC. 19TH

Position: 25–48.5N, 151–05.3E.

Partly cloudy, NNE wind of 12 meters, 23C, vis. 30 km.

At 1506 speed 9 knots and at 0647 speed 16 knots.

At 1230 met two navy land-based bombers and at 1438 met the minelayer *Koogi Maru.**

DEC. 20TH

Position: 22–15N, 145–25E.

Partly cloudy, NE to ENE wind of 10 meters, 25C, vis. 25 km.

At 1057 speed 20 knots, and at 1210 course 270.

At 1304 speed 14 knots, at 1447 speed 18 knots and at 1804 speed 20 knots.

Two seaplanes of the Division, one from each ship, and a seaplane of the *Abukuma* made a reconnaissance flight over the scheduled course of the task force, returned to Chichijima.

DEC. 21ST

Position: 22–49N, 138–01.5E.

Partly cloudy, ESE wind of 10 meters, 25C, vis. 25 km.

At 0735 speed 18 knots.

At 0800 the 2nd Supply Group together with the *Arare* and the 21st and 27th Des. Divisions joined the force.

At 1035 course 335 degrees.

DEC. 22ND

Position: 27–19N, 135–43.5E.

Cloudy, W wind of 12 meters, 23C, vis. 25 km.

At 1031 speed 16 knots.

DEC. 23RD

Position: 31–32N, 132–08.8E.

Clear, N wind of 7 meters, 16C, vis. 25 km.

At 0500 speed 20 knots, at 0903 course 350 degrees.

---

* Possibly *Koei Maru*—Eds.

At 1003 speed 16 knots and entered the cleared channel of Bungo Strait at 1025.

At 1141 speed 18 knots.

At 1340 passed through the cleared channel. Speed 20 knots.

At 1530 the Guard Force left the Formation.

At 1822 arrived in Hashirajima anchorage.

DEC. 24TH

Position: Hashirajima anchorage.

Partly cloudy, SW wind of 7 meters, 14C, vis. 25 km.

At 1330 left the anchorage for Kure.

Arrived in Kure at 1600.

At 1100 received messages of the Chief of the General Staff and the Commander-in-Chief of the Combined Fleet on board the *Akagi*.

AFTER DEC. 25TH TO THE END OF THIS MONTH:

Position: Kure.

CHAPTER 17

Submarine Operations, Extracts, December 1941–April 1942

T HIS IS another of the many studies prepared in the Military History Section, Headquarters, USAFFE, in Tokyo during the Occupation. As mentioned in the foreword to this volume, this study, like other such monographs, was prepared from memory and fragments of other documents. For details, see this study's foreword and preface. The principal compiler of this monograph was Capt. Tatsuwaka Shibuya, a submarine expert who was assigned to the staff of the 1st Air Fleet on 9 November 1941. Prange knew Shibuya well and interviewed him a number of times.

Of particular interest is the account of the submarines' part in the Pearl Harbor attack. As an example of the high regard in which the Japanese Navy held the submarines of that operation versus the taking for granted of the airmen is found on p. 18. The compilers could seriously believe that "the confusion in Pearl Harbor" was caused by the six midget subs, not the attacking aircraft, and that these subs, rather than the air raid, occasioned the American message "giving general warning."

A notable feature of Japanese submarine operations was the failure to exploit fully the submarine's capability against Allied commercial shipping, in sharp contrast with Germany's U-boat warfare in the Atlantic.

[COVER SHEET]

Japanese Monograph No. 102

SUBMARINE OPERATIONS

December 1941–April 1942

Prepared by
Military History Section
Headquarters, Army Forces Far East

Distributed by
Office of the Chief of Military History

Department of the Army

[1953]

FOREWORD

This monograph was compiled by Capt. Tatsuwaka Shibuya, former staff officer of the Combined Fleet. Due to the lack of official documents this record was compiled partially from the recollections and personal papers of Captain Shibuya and Comdr. Yasuo Fujimori, former staff officer (operations) Imperial General Headquarters, and partially from fragmentary battle reports of the Submarine Force. Additional material was obtained by interrogation of former Japanese officers of the Submarine Force.

Additional monographs covering the operations of Japanese submarines during World War II are as follows:

TITLE	PERIOD	MONO. NO.
Submarine Operations in the Second Phase Operations, Part I	Apr 42–Aug 42	110
Submarine Operations in the Second Phase Operations, Part II	Aug 42–Mar 13	111
Submarine Operations in the Third Phase Operations, Part I	Mar 43–Nov 43	163
Submarine Operations in the Third Phase Operations, Part II	Nov 43–Mar 44	171
Submarine Operations in the Third Phase Operations, Part III	Mar 44–Aug 45	184
Imperial Japanese Navy in World War II	Nov 41–Aug 45	116

14 January 1952

[*Page V:*]

PREFACE

Through Instructions No. 126 to the Japanese Government, 12 October 1945, subject: Institution for War Records Investigation, steps were initiated to exploit military historical records and official reports of the Japanese War Ministry and Japanese General Staff. Upon dissolution of the War Ministry and the Japanese General Staff, and the transfer of their former functions to the Demobilization Bureau, research and compilation continued and developed into a series of historical monographs.

The paucity of original orders, plans and unit journals, which are normally essential in the preparations of this type of record, most of which were lost or destroyed during field operations or bombing raids, rendered the task of compilation most difficult; particularly distressing has been the complete lack of official strength reports, normal in AG or G3 records. However, while many of the important orders, plans and estimates have been reconstructed from memory and therefore are not textually identical with the originals, they are believed to be generally accurate and reliable.

Under the supervision of the Demobilization Bureau, the basic material contained in this monograph was compiled and written in Japanese by former officers, on duty in command and staff units within major units during the period of operations. Translation was effected through the facilities of Allied Translators and

[*Page vi:*]

Interpreters Service, G2, General Headquarters, Far East Command.

This Japanese Operational Monograph was rewritten in English by the Japanese Research Division, Military History Section, General Headquarters, Far East Command and is based on the translation of the Japanese original. Editorial corrections were limited to those necessary for coherence and accuracy.

[*Page vii:*]

TABLE OF CONTENTS

[*Page 1:*]

SUBMARINE OPERATIONS, NOVEMBER 1941–APRIL 1942

In November 1941, the submarines of the Japanese Navy suitable for use as first line strength consisted of 30 submarines of the newest type and 18 submarines of older types of almost equal efficiency. The second line strength consisted of 12 very old submarines which could only be used in the coastal waters of Japan or for training (see appendix I). In addition to these 60 submarines the Japanese Navy had under construction at the time 18 submarines to be completed by the end of 1942 and 11 to be completed by the end of 1943. Approval had been granted for the construction of an additional 38 submarines after the end of 1942 (Chart 1).

OPERATIONAL POLICY FOR SUBMARINE WARFARE

The fundamental operational policy for submarine warfare was formulated by the Japanese Navy in November 1941, at the time when it became necessary to prepare for the war with the States, Britain and the Netherlands. This policy called for the early annihilation of the enemy fleet by the coordinated efforts of submarine units, the surface fleet and the air force.

The United States Fleet in the eastern Pacific was the principal target of submarine operations and the United States, British and Netherlands Fleets in the Far East were classified as secondary targets. Disruption of enemy commerce on the key sea routes by submarine warfare was to be conducted against the United States, Britain and the Netherlands. These operations were to be conducted

[*Page 2:*]

Chart No. 1
Approved Submarine Construction
(November 1941)

	UNDER CONSTRUCTION TO BE COMPLETED BY THE END OF 1942	
Type I–15	I–27, I–28, I–29, I–30, I–31, I–32, I–33, I–34, I–35, and I–36	10
Type I–176	I–176, I–177 and I–178	3
Type RO-100	RO–100, RO–101, RO–102 and RO–103	4
Type I–9	I–11	1
	Total	18
	UNDER CONSTRUCTION TO BE COMPLETED BY THE END OF 1943	
Type I–15	I–37, I–38 and I–39	3
Type I–176	I–179, I–180, I–181 and I–182	4
Type RO-100	RO–104 and RO–105	2
Type RO–35	RO–35 and RO–37	2
	Total	11

APPROVED FOR CONSTRUCTION
TO BE STARTED BY THE END OF 1941

Type I–18	6
Type I–52	3
Type I–54	3
Type I–9	1
Type I–176	3
Type RO–100	10
Type RO–35	12
Total	38
Grand Total	67

[*Page 3:*]

only in such a manner as not to interfer [*sic*] with the objectives of the main operation which would vary in accordance with the progress of the Fleet Operation.

The distribution of submarines Japan had at the outbreak of the war and the assignment of duties thereof naturally had to be decided in accordance with the mission to be performed and the ability of particular submarines to perform the task. The organization of fleets was also decided with the same purpose in mind.

The 1st, 2nd and 3rd Submarine Squadrons which had the greatest operational ability and consisted chiefly of the newest type submarines made up the 6th Fleet (Chart 2). The 6th Fleet was organized under a single commander with the aim of destroying the United States Fleets in the eastern Pacific. The 4th and 5th Submarine Squadrons, which were next to the first line strength but included old type vessels and those somewhat inferior in operational ability, were attached to the Combined Fleet. The principal mission of those squadrons was the destruction of surface strength in the Southern area and support of the invasion operations in the Philippines, British Malaya and the American Fleet after the outbreak of war, it was intended that two submarine squadrons, along with the 6th Fleet, were to engage in interception operations by shifting quickly to operations in the western Pacific.

The 6th Submarine Squadron, which was nearly equal in efficiency to the first line strength and consisted of submarines with mine-laying facilities, was attached to the 3rd Fleet and was assigned

[*Page 4:*]

Chart No. 2
Assignment of Submarine Units
(Beginning of the War)
COMBINED FLEET

4TH SUBMARINE SQUADRON	5TH SUBMARINE SQUADRON
Kinu (Lt Cruiser-Flagship)	*Yura* (Lt. Cruiser-Flagship)
18th Submarine Division	28th Submarine Division

I–53, I–54, I–55
19th Submarine Division
I–55, I–57, I–58
21st Submarine Division
RO–33, RO–34

Nagoya Maru (Tender)

I–59, I–60
29th Submarine Division
I–62, I–64
30th Submarine Division
I–65, I–66
Rio de Janeiro Maru
(Tender)

SIXTH FLEET (SUBMARINE FLEET)
(FLAGSHIP-LT. CRUISER *KATARI*)

1ST SUBMARINE SQUADRON
I–0 (Flagship)
1st Submarine Division
I–15, I–16, I–17
2nd Submarine Division
I–18, I–19, I–20
3rd Submarine Division
I–21, I–22, I–23
4th Submarine Division
I–24, I–25, I–26
Yasukuri Maru (Tender)

3RD SUBMARINE SQUADRON
I–8 (Flagship)
11th Submarine Division
I–74, I–75
12th Submarine Division
I–68, I–69, I–70
20th Submarine Division
I-71, I-72, I-73
Taigai (Tender)

2ND SUBMARINE SQUADRON
I–7 (Flagship) I–10
7th Submarine Division
I–1, I–2, I–3
8th Submarine Division
I–4, I–5, I–6
Santos Maru (Tender)

THIRD FLEET
6th Submarine Squadron
Chogai (Lt
Cruiser-Flagship)
9th Submarine Division
I–123, I–124
13th Submarine Division
I–121, I–122

FOURTH FLEET
7th Submarine Squadron
Jingai (Lt
Cruiser-Flagship)
26th Submarine Division
RO–61, RO–62, RO–63
27th Submarine Division
RO–65, RO–66, RO–67
33rd Submarine Division
RO–63, RO–64, RO–68

KURE NAVY DISTRICT FORCE
I–52, RO–31 (Training only)
6th Submarine Division
RO–57, RO–58, RO–59

[Page 5:]

chiefly as support for the invasion of the Philippines, Dutch East Indies and British Malaya. The remaining submarines capable of front line operations were selected from the submarines of second line strength and were organized as the 7th Submarine Squadron. This squadron was attached to the 4th Fleet, with the assignment as a defense force to operate chiefly in the inner south sea and Japanese waters. Those vessels of second line strength which were unsuitable for operations in the open sea were attached to the Kure Navy District Force as a component of the Homeland defense force and were assigned to the training of submarine crews.

[*Page 6:*]

SUBMARINE OPERATIONAL PLANS

The Commander in Chief of the Combined Fleet, assuming that war with the United States, Great Britain and Netherlands would break out while Japan was still at war with China, issued on 5 November 1941 the following fundamental operational policy:

a. In the eastern Pacific, the American fleet would be destroyed and her supply route and line of operation to the Orient severed.

b. In the Western Pacific, the campaign in Malaya shall be conducted to sever the British line of operation and supply to the Orient as well as the Burma Route.

c. The enemy forces in the Orient shall be destroyed, their strategic bases captured, and important areas endowed with natural resources shall be occupied.

d. Strategically important points shall be captured, expanded in area and strengthened in defensive forces in order to prepare for a prolonged war.

e. Enemy invading forces shall be intercepted and annihilated.

f. Successful operations shall be exploited to crush the enemys' [*sic*] will to fight.

Based on this operational policy, the operational plans of the Combined Fleet in the first stage of the war were prepared. The Submarine Force (6th Fleet), the Carrier Striking Force, the

[*Page 7:*]

South Seas Force, the Northern Force and the Main Force were to engage the United States Fleet. The Carrier Striking Force was to commence hostilities with a surprise attack on the enemy fleet in the Hawaiian Islands. The Submarine Force was to advance secretly to the Hawaiian area prior to the opening of hostilities and support the Carrier Striking Force by observing and attacking the enemy fleet stationed in that area. A unit of the Submarine Force was also to attack the enemy fleet berthed in Pearl Harbor with midget submarines. These midgets, manned by a crew of two men, had a 46 ton displacement submerged. They were 23.9 meters in length and 1.85 meters in breadth and depth each. After release from the deck of the mother submarine, they were propelled by batteries and motor power at a speed of 19 knots and were capable of running for 50 minutes underwater. They were armed with two 45 cm torpedoes.*

[*Page 8:*]

The South Sea Force, while carrying out the campaign against the enemys' strategic points in the South Sea, was to be prepared to engage the enemy fleet around Australia, while the Northern Force was to be prepared for possible Soviet Intervention. The Main Force was to stand by in the western area of the Inland Sea, and take action when occasion demanded, in order to support the entire operation.

The Southern Force was to destroy and sweep away the enemy fleet in the Philippines, British Malaya and the Dutch East Indies and, in cooperation with the army, gradually take over these areas.

In the event the United States Fleet assumed the offensive and appeared in the Western Pacific, the Southern Detachment Fleet and the 3rd Fleet were to temporarily assume operational duties in the Southern area, while the bulk of the Combined Fleet was to intercept and engage the invading United States Fleet.

[*Page 9:*]

PLANS FOR THE HAWAIIAN OPERATION

The Pearl Harbor attack was to be a surprise attack, initiated by an air attack, which would be sudden and complete. The submarine attack was necessary to obtain subsequent cumulative effects. The first priority was given to an air attack by the Carrier Striking Force. The principal aim of the Submarine Force therefore, was to render the result of air-attack more effective. Its principal operational duties were the secret preliminary reconnaissance of Lahaina Anchorage and of strategical points in the Aleutians and the South Pacific areas the tracking down and destruction of the enemy fleet which might run out of Pearl Harbor escaping the air attack and the interception of any counter-attack against the Carrier Striking Force by the enemy fleet. Participation of the Submarine Force in the attack [called] for an attack by midget submarines against the enemy fleet in the harbor and the rescue of crews of aircraft of the Carrier Striking Force which might be forced down.

In the event the attack by the Carrier Striking Force on Pearl Harbor succeeded, the Submarine Force was to maintain submarine patrol and reconnaissance of Pearl

---

* In 1934 two midget submarines were built by Capt. Kishimoto Kaneji at Kure Navy Yard for experimentation. It was intended that they be used as auxiliary weapons carried on board fast surface vessels. The two experimental models without conning towers had the shape of a torpedo. As the result of further experiments a small conning tower was fitted to each of them. They were called "A-targets" for confidential purposes.

Again in 1936, another two were built and were launched successfully from the *Chitose* (seaplane tender) in 1937. Mass production of this type was started in Kure under strict secrecy. In the summer of 1941 the seaplane tender *Chiyoda* was converted to a midget submarine carrier capable of carrying 12 midgets in her hanger and of launching them through a hinged door at her stern. Necessary training was started of personnel to operate the midgets. At the end of October 1941, the commander in chief of the Combined Fleet decided to use midgets in the Pearl Harbor Operation —Eds.

Harbor for a long period of time after the Carrier Striking Force had withdrawn to home bases. The disruption of enemy surface traffic between [*the*] West Coast of North America and Hawaii and submarine attacks on enemy air bases lying between Hawaii and Samoa Islands were to be carried out.

In compliance with the above operational duties, the com-

[*Page 10:*]

mander of the Submarine Force formulated the Task Organization of his forces for the opening of hostilities. For command of the over-all operation the commander of the 6th Fleet, Vice Admiral Shimizu Mitsoyoshi, was to be aboard the flagship *Katori* stationed in the Kwajalein atoll. The commander of the 1st Submarine Squadron, Rear Admiral Sato Tsutomu, was to command the 1st Submarine Group consisting of the I–9, I–15, I–17, and I–25. The mission of this Group was to patrol the sea northeast of Oahu, tracking down and annihilating any escaping vessels and in readiness for intercepting any counter-attacks against the Carrier Striking Force. Assigned the same mission was the 2nd Submarine Group under the command of Rear Admiral Yamazaki Shigeteru, commander of the 2nd Submarine Squadron. The 2nd Submarine Group, composed of the I–1, I–2, I–3, I–4, I–5, I–6 and I–7 was to patrol the area between Oahu and Molokai. The commander of the 3rd Submarine Squadron, Rear Admiral Miwa Shigeyoshi, was to command the 3rd Submarine Group composed of the I–8, I–68, I–69, I–70, I–71, I–72, I–73, I–74 and I–75. This group was to patrol the area south of Oahu and in addition to the mission assigned the 1st and 2nd Groups, the 3rd Group was to make prior reconnaissance of the Lahaina Anchorage and during the attack was to rescue the crews of downed aircraft from the Carrier Striking Force. Also the Submarine I–74 was to be in the vicinity of Niihau on the day of the attack. The Special Attack Unit, composed of the I–16, I–18, I–20, I–22 and

[*Page 11:*]

I–24 under the command of Capt. Sasaki Hankyu, commander of the 3rd Submarine Division, was to attack the enemy fleet in the harbor with midget submarines. The submarines I–10 and I–26 under their respective commanders was [*sic*] to scout the Aleutian and South Pacific area. The Submarine force was to be supplied by the supply ships *Ondo, Toa Maru, Aratama Maru* and No. 2 *Tenyo Maru,* which would be in the vicinity of Kwajalein or off the Homeland.

Besides the above forces, attached to the Carrier Striking force from the 6th Fleet to perform patrol duties were the submarines I–19, I–21 and I–23. In addition to acting as the Patrol Unit in front of the Carrier Striking Force, this unit was to rescue the crews of downed aircraft and be prepared to resist counterattack.

Immediately after the air raid the Carrier Task Force commander was to assume command of the Submarine Force for a three-day period, for it was anticipated that the two forces would be operating in the same area.

The Patrol Unit attached to the Carrier Task Force naturally was to be under the direct control of the Task Force commander when the latter advanced or withdrew after the airraid. However, in the event the unit was found unnecessary in checking counter-attacks of the enemy fleet, it was scheduled to return to the command of the Submarine Force as early as possible.

After the attack had been completed and submarines had returned to the control of the 6th Fleet the plan called for the

[*Page 12:*]

1st and 2nd Submarine Squadrons to remain in the area for patrol and observation and to attack enemy vessels. The 3rd Submarine Squadron was to destroy surface traffic between the United States and Hawaii.

In advancing to Hawaiian waters, secrecy was of the utmost importance. The Submarine Force was to proceed on the surface by night and under water by day within a radius of 600 nautical miles of the Aleutians, Midway, Johnston and Palmyra Islands. Taking into consideration the secrecy of advance, the time of starting the war, the speed of each submarine, and the time of completing preparations for war, the time to commence action and the routes were selected. The 1st and 2nd Submarine Groups were to depart Yokosuka around 20 Nov 41, pass between the Aleutians and Midway north of Oahu and be within 300 miles of Oahu around 3 December 41. The 3rd Submarine Group was to depart Saeki around the middle of Nov 41 and Kwajalein around 25 Nov 41, proceed eastward from Kwajalein, passing south of Johnston and north of Howland and Palmyra, reaching their station south of Oahu around 2 Dec 41. The Special Attack Unit was to depart Kure around 20 Nov 41, pass south of Midway and north of Johnston arriving off Oahu around 2 Dec 41.

Although the secrecy of movement of the Special Attack Unit with midget submarines aboard was threatened thereby, the unit had to take the shortest route by passing between Midway and Johnston Islands because it was impossible to move forward the departure date of the mother submarines due to the delay in the preparation

[*Page 13:*]

of the midgets.

On the assumption that the Carrier Striking Task Force would carry out the airraid on 8 December, it was planned that all submarines of the Submarine Force, except the reconnaissance unit for strategic points, were to arrive within 300 nautical miles of Oahu on 3 December and thereafter gradually tighten their dispositions arriving at close position for observation by the day before the attack.

The I–72 and I–73 were in charge of the secret pre-attack reconnaissance of Lahaina Anchorage and it was decided that both submarines should report their observation results by the 7th at the latest. In the event any enemy fleet was found in the Lahaina Anchorage, disposition of submarine groups with Oahu as its nucleus was expected to be changed so that its center would be transferred to Lahaina. Furthermore, it was decided that in this case the submarines of the Submarine Force should penetrate into the anchorage from three mouths, Pailele, Kalehi and Auau Channels, after the airraid of the Carrier Striking Task Force and carry out attacks on the fleet.

The mother submarines for the midget submarines were to be within 100 nautical miles of Pearl Harbor after sunset on 6 December, and there, all preparations for launching the midget submarines were to be completed. The mother submarines were to approach within 10 nautical miles of the mouth of the harbor secretly and launch the midget submarine after locating the harbor entrance.

[*Page 14:*]

The attack was to be delivered between the first and the second waves of air attacks by the Carrier Striking Task Force, but the scheduled attack could be postponed until after sundown of the same day if circumstances required it. Each midget submarine, after launching attacks on the enemy fleet, was to sail counterclockwise around Ford Island, get out the harbor and proceed to the rendezvous. The mother submarines were to surface some seven nautical miles west of Lanai Island on the night of the attack to pick up midget submarine crews. However, if the rescue was not possible on the first night, another attempt was to be made on the following night.

It was decided that the I–10 would execute the reconnaissance of Fuji, Samoa and Tutuila and the I–26 of the Aleutian Islands by 5 December. Furthermore, it was decided that, if they found a powerful enemy force, the submarines would keep the force under observation. If there was no such force, the submarines were to advance to a point halfway between Hawaii and the West Coast of North America by the time of the outbreak of war.

It was pre-arranged that, in the event war was not to be commenced because of a favorable turn in the diplomatic situation while the Submarine Force was underway, it would turn back home without further orders.

[*Page 15:*]

THE HAWAIIAN OPERATIONS

About the middle of November 1941, the 3rd Submarine Group, initiating the move on Hawaii, left Saeki for Kwajalein and the others followed almost as pre-arranged. The I–10, on strategic reconnaissance, set out from Yokosuka toward Fiji* and Samoa on 16 November, and the I–26 toward Kiska and Adak on 19 November. The submarine of the Patrol Unit of the Striking Force left Yokosuka on 20 November for Hitokappu Bay, there jointed [*sic*] the Carrier Striking Force and set out toward Hawaii on the 25th.

The Commander in Chief of the 6th Fleet who commanded the Submarine Force went on board the flagship *Katori* and arrived at Kwajalein on 5 December by way of Truk. The Commanders of the 1st, 2nd and 3rd Submarine Squadrons who respectively commanded the 1st, 2nd and 3rd Submarine Groups proceeded to Hawaii on board the flagsubmarine, I–9, I–7, and I–8, respectively.

The 1st, 2nd and 3rd Submarine Groups and Special Attack Unit bound for

[*Page 16:*]

---

* After reporting no enemy in Suva Bay, Fiji Islands, I–10's patrol plane was lost, whether to British gunfire or accident is not known. I–10 searched for it fruitlessly for three days —Eds.

Hawaii steered east as scheduled and from about 3 December gradually closed in on Hawaii. On the day before the attack, they completed the planned disposition (Chart 3). The strategic reconnaissance unit sighted no enemy vessels or planes either at Kiska, Adak, Dutch Harbor or Suva except for an Astoria type cruiser which was witnessed by the I–10 off Pago Pago Harbor on 4 December. The I–20 and I–26 were half way between the Hawaiian Islands and the American Mainland on the eve of the war. The Patrol Unit which had accomplished the Striking Force separated from the main force on 7 December and proceeded ahead at full speed. By the time of the attack on the following day, it had moved forward between the Striking Force and Oahu and completed its deployment.

[*Page 17:*]

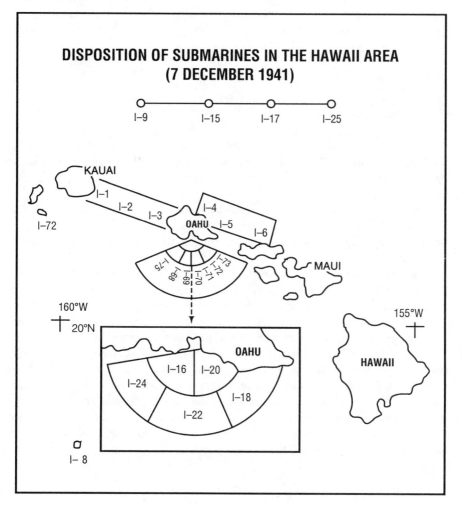

DISPOSITION OF SUBMARINES IN THE HAWAII AREA
(7 DECEMBER 1941)

Chart No. 3
Organization of the Special Attack Unit
Captain Sasaki, Hanku, Commander

	MASTER OF THE SUBMARINE	COMMANDER OF THE MIDGET SUBMARINE	CREW OF THE MIDGET SUBMARINE
I–22	Commander Agata, Kiyo	Lt. Iwasa, Naoji	Petty Officer 1c Sasaki, Naoji*
I–16	Commander Yamada, Kaoru	Lt. (j.g.) Yokoyama, Shoji	Petty Officer 2 c Wada, Sadamu**
I–18	Commander Otani, Kiyonori	Lt. (j.g.)*** Furuno, Shigarani	Petty Officer 1 c Yokoyama, Shigenori
I–20	Commander Yasuda, Takashi	Ensign Hiroo, Akira	Petty Officer 2c Katayama, Yoshio
I–24	Commander Hanabasa, Hiroshi	Ensign Sakamaki, Kazuo	Petty Officer 2c Inagaki, Kiyoshi

* Elsewhere Naokichi
** Elsewhere Yokoyama, Masaharu, and Uyeda, Tei.
*** Elsewhere Shigemi

Thus each submarine took up a position to watch over Pearl Harbor. Prior to this the I–71, I–72 and I–73 carried out secret reconnaissance missions around Lahaina Anchorage and reported to the Striking Force that no major unit of the United States Fleet was stationed there.

Security of secrecy was the supreme watchword among the submarines of the Submarine Force in the Hawaii Area and this was carried out so well that it is believed today that there was no chance of being discovered by the enemy till the day of the attack.

The Special Attack Unit approached the mouth of Pearl Harbor about 2300 on 7 December, and from there dispatched their midget submarines. The operation could be carried on without any interference, due to the lack of enemy surveillance. It was presumed that the midget submarines penetrated deep into Pearl Harbor and, after sunset, attacked unguarded ships anchored in the Harbor.

Each submarine which had dispatched its midget submarine kept on watching enemy forces around the mouth of the Bay until sunset of the day of the attack and returning to the rendezvous points after sunset, they carried on a search all through the night, but could not find a single one of their midget submarines. On the night of the 9th the search was again carried out, but it too was unsuccessful, therefore, the commander of the attack unit, deviating from the schedule, kept up the search again on the following day but it

[Page 18:]

too was in vain.

Reliable information on the effectiveness of the midget submarine attack could not be obtained. It was believed that they caused a certain amount of damage to the enemy fleet considering the confusion in Pearl Harbor as witnessed by one or two submarines. A radio message of success from one of the midget submarines and an intercepted plain message dispatched from the United States forces giving general warning supports this belief.

When the air attack of the Carrier Striking Force commenced on 0330, 8 December, the Submarine Force Commander, preparing for the possible sortie of the enemy fleet from Pearl Harbor, ordered all submarines except the Special Attack Unit to exercise strict surveillance.

The next day, it was found that the enemy had taken strict precautionary measures in southern Oahu and it was confirmed that antisubmarine nets were laid between Diamond Head and Barbers Point. The Commander of the Submarine Force therefore ordered the 3rd Submarine Group, which had been stationed south of Oahu, to move further south.

After completing the air attack on Hawaii, the Carrier Striking Force withdrew northward of Hawaii and on 9 December 1941, the Carrier Striking Force Commanding Officer released the three submarines, which had been accompanying his force as the Patrol Unit, and directed them to return to the command of the Submarine Force.

CHAPTER 18

Japanese Study of the Pearl Harbor Operation

T HIS IS one of many such studies prepared by the Japanese following major engagements. The name of the author is not given, and obviously the text is the product of the memories of many who had been involved in the project. It is interesting to note that Comdr. Mitsuo Fuchida, who led the air attack on Pearl Harbor, was assigned to Yokosuka in late 1942 to work on similar studies of the battles of the Indian Ocean, Coral Sea, and Midway. The translator is likewise unknown, and obviously the translation was made during the Occupation of Japan. We have made no attempt to check and/or correct any of the figures cited herein, preferring to let this study stand on its own.

This document is reliable and valuable as it pertains to plans, preparations, and actions of which the Japanese had direct knowledge. Their claimed results, however, are far off base and serve merely as an indication that damage estimates made under wartime conditions are seldom if ever accurate. For instance, as late as the summer of 1942 when this study was made, the Japanese obviously did not know that *Pennsylvania* had been in drydock. And they mistakenly credited themselves with two oil tankers sunk. They greatly overestimated U.S. air strength on Oahu. As an example, they credited Ford Island with 100 flying boats, whereas only 35 were there on 7 December.

It is noteworthy that the Japanese gave credit first of all to ''providential help, far beyond human help.'' Their American opponents would be more inclined to call it luck, but undoubtedly it was a factor.

In view of the ''radio silence'' controversy, we call attention to the fact that fuses were removed and keys sealed, so that ''the strictest radio silence was perfectly carried out.''

Page 8 of this study is missing.

[COVER SHEET]

August 1942 (estimate)

DAI TOA SENSO SENKUN (KOKU) (HAWAII KAISEN NO BU) DAI ICHI HEN

Lessons [air operation] of the Sea Battle off Hawaii, Vol. I.)

Compiled by
Yokosuka Naval Air Corps
Air Branch Committee, Battle-lessons
Investigating Committee

Note: On the back of the cover the Chief of Document Section, Second Demobilization Bureau endorsed this document as follows:

23 March 1948

It is confirmed that this document containing two pages of index, sixty pages of text and one map with no cover is one of the original copies of the documents, compiled by the Yokosuka Naval Air Corps and the Air Branch Committee, Battle-lessons Investigation Committee in August 1942 (date estimated), based upon recollection of those who were concerned with the operation.

[*Page 2:*]

INDEX

INTRODUCTION

LESSONS

INTRODUCTION

The Sea Battle off Hawaii, based upon a splendid operational concept, carefully and adequately executed at the outbreak of the war, was the naval operation in which the Japanese fleet succeeded in making a surprise attack upon the American fleet in Pearl Harbor, delivering the fatal blows upon enemy battleships and land-based air forces. Its importance in the field of strategy was very great; no other operations could have more influence upon subsequent operations.

From the tactical point of view, however, it was exclusively one of struggles for key positions. It could not be adopted, therefore, as a guiding operation for all sea operations as it was. Anyhow, it was the precious record of battle in which our naval air forces, after long, hard efforts and with firm determination to die for the country, knocked down the old enemy with a single blow. Not only was it a good example of our launching a surprise attack upon the outbreak of war, one of the Japanese traditional tactics, but it was the unique one which determined the outcome of the long-discussed problem—"battleships or aircraft"—thus stimulated a revolutionary change in naval tactics.

[*Page 3:*]

LESSONS
1.
Tactics

Since the outcome of initial operations has great influence upon the whole war situation as well as upon the morale of the forces, and they also have rich opportunities for successful surprise attacks, they should be carefully prepared and splendidly conducted so that the enemy main forces might be knocked out by a fierce and valiant forestalling attack before they could complete their preparations.

This Sea Battle was a typical instance of launching a surprise attack at the outset of war which has been one of our navy's traditional tactics. In this operation, the political and strategical evolution was so well conducted that, taking the good opportunity which arose, our navy succeeded in launching a surprise attack, and achieved a great result.

It is to be regretted that, since the enemy carriers had been out of the harbor at the time of our striking, with no information as to their whereabouts available, we missed a good chance of destroying them. Nevertheless, the great achievement of sinking four battleships and destroying four others, together with approximately 500 planes wiped out, contributed to raise the morale of the people as well as of the whole forces. Also it very much facilitated the subsequent overall operational conduct of the war.

a. The success of the surprise operation was attributed to the following factors:

1. It was favored by providential help.

Such facts described as follows should be regarded as providential help, far beyond human help:
The voyage to the attack area, which had been expected to be a very rough one, was actually so comparatively calm that not only scheduled

[Page 4:]

refueling but maintaining equipment and personnel, in particular flying crews, in good condition, was possible. Continuous cloudy weather with poor visibility also helped the Task Force to conceal its movement, with the result that no single plane or ship had been met on the way.

Despite the thick cloud over Oahu Island on the day of the attack, there was a clearance over Pearl Harbor that made bombing possible.

The main elements of the enemy fleet were in the harbor on the scheduled striking day.

2. The political and military evolution was well conducted.

It seemed that the United States mistakenly believed that Japan could be brought to her knees by bluffing, underestimating Japan's strength, its attitude being quite the same as that of Russia in the Russo-Japanese War. Additionally, our sincere efforts for a settlement of the negotiations between the United States and Japan seemed to strengthen her conviction that Japan would not fight. Therefore we could deploy the forces very secretly. The switch-over from diplomacy to strategy was perfectly carried out.

3. We could surprise the enemy.

The Hawaii air attack was a great operation which was carried out, passing the Rubicon. The enemy never even dreamed of such a splendid operational concept. We surprised the enemy completely.

4. Concealment of the plan.

The fact that the plan of this operation had been kept perfectly secret throughout the operation also contributed to the surprise of the enemy. The following steps were taken for this purpose:

Studying of this operation was limited as much as possible. Combined Fleet operational orders covering the Task Force's Hawaii air

[Page 5:]

attack were only distributed among the Task Force.

Only after the arrival at Hitokappu Bay were the Task Force's operational orders distributed among the Task Force.

Selection of the advance course was good. There were three advance courses considered, one being the northerly course, another being the central course passing along the Hawaiian Islands, and the last being the southerly course via the Marshalls. The northerly one had advantages of keeping out of the enemy land-based air forces' patrol range as well as the merchant marine course, but it was much affected by meteorological conditions, causing many difficulties in refueling and also in navigation. To this the central and southerly courses were quite contrary in both respects. Whether a surprise attack could be launched or not, together with the feasibility of refueling, were two great factors in determining the success of the operation. Finally the northern course was adopted, on the ground that refueling could be improved by training.

STRICTEST RADIO SILENCE. In order to keep strict radio silence, thorough steps such as taking off fuses in the circuit, holding and sealing the keys were taken. During the operation, the strictest radio silence was perfectly carried out.

RECONNAISSANCE IMMEDIATELY PRIOR TO THE ATTACK. The operation exclusively depended upon whether the surprise attack could be made or not. Since desired information on the enemy had been generally obtained, reconnaissance operations prior to the attack were abandoned, except the reconnaissance flight just preceding the attack, which was to reach the target thirty or forty minutes before the arrival of the attacking forces.

[*Page 6:*]

In order to mask the situation, improved sight-seeings in Tokyo by sailors of the Yokosuka Naval Barrack were made on 5 and 7 December 1941.

During the Task Force's stay at Hitokappu Bay, the Ominato Minor Naval Station kept strict guard near the anchorage and took steps to suppress sea traffic and dispatching of mail and telegrams. Dispatching mail from the Task Force was also suppressed. Those ships which had stationed there for refueling were released to return only after 8 December.

The Main Force and the 12th Combined Air Corps exchanged false communications so as to pretend that the Task Force was still under training in the Kyushu area.

In order to camouflage the fact that the situation was getting serious, the *Tatsuta Maru* was ordered to head for America in the early part of December. She put about upon receipt of word of the outbreak of war on 8 December.

5. Supremacy of mental power.

Every man participating in this operation recognized its importance and took it as an honor to participate in the epoch-making attack. Inspired by the honor, they were inflamed with loyalty to their country. The morale of the whole fleet was at the highest point.

That bombers repeatedly tried to attack again and again through intense anti-aircraft gunfire until they were sure of their attacks, and the fliers had agreed not to request returning directions to the carriers even if they lost their returning way lest their dispatches would offer clues to the enemy of their carriers—those firm determinations not to care for their own lives were considered as contributing very much to the success.

[*Page 7:*]

6. Concentration of powerful forces.

It was a very proper step that carriers of the 1st Air Fleet were concentrated in the operation. Had half of them been saved for other missions, the effective attack would not have been achieved and it was certain that it would have suffered damage by enemy encounters.

7. Crack units with thorough preparations.

[*Page 8 missing; page 9:*]

8. Personnel

(a). Training

The 1st Air Fleet concentrated its carriers in one group instead of dispersing them, aiming to concentrate all air forces under one commander and to annihilate an enemy with its powerful single blow.

This principle made it necessary to familiarize flying commanders and crews with the same operational concept and also to improve the fighting power of the group of carriers as well as that of individual carriers. The air forces of the 1st and 2nd Carrier Divisions made their group training as follows:

Kagoshima Base	Torpedo-attacking planes of 1st Carrier Division and leading bombers of the 1st Air Fleet
Tomitaka Base	Dive bombers of 1st Carrier Division
Izumi Base	Torpedo-attacking planes of 2nd Carrier Division
Kasanohara Base	Dive bombers of 2nd Carrier Division
Saeki Base	Fighters of 1st and 2nd Carrier Division

(All training was under the control of the Fleet.)

Since the 5th Carrier Division was organized later, its training was carried out independently as follows:

Usa Base	Torpedo-attacking planes
Chita Base	Dive bombers
Omura Base	First stage training of fighters
Oita Base	Second stage training of fighters

(Fighters trained at first at Omura and later moved to Oita for training in carrier-borne operations.)

[*Page 10:*]

Group training was emphasized as much as possible for air forces except leading bombers. In the latter part of October four trainings of fighter groups against dive-bomber and torpedo-attacking plane groups were held. In the early part of November, three trainings with all carrier-borne air forces except fighter groups were made from carriers in accordance with the Hawaii air attack plan.

The air forces therefore made big progress in group operations so that they felt no fear in carrying out the operational plan.

(b). Bombing

Bombing drills against the moving *Settsu* (target ship) had been almost continuously carried out since August. Leading level bombers concentrated in Kagoshima Base used to make a single-plane bombing against *Settsu* twice a day. Dive bombers started from their bases to dive bomb almost twice a day. In a drill held on 24 October the following records were obtained:

Level bombing   Probabilities of striking targets   50% (Max. 75)
                       Probabilities of hitting targets   10% (Max. 17)

Dive bombing   Probabilities of hitting targets   40% (Max. 55)

(Weather: calm, wind velocity 15–20 meters per second, unsteady air conditions, target's speed 16–18 knots, free evasive action)

Bombing drills against stationary targets had been carried out as often as possible. Since 26 November* a drill against *Settsu* was made once and about two weeks' training was made upon the target, the same size as a *California*-type battleship, which had been made on the beach of Osaki. As far as bombing against stationary targets were concerned, the men came to have a firm confidence of destroying many ships with a single blow.

(c). Torpedo attacking

Since the targets seemed likely to be in shallow waters, particular emphasis was placed in training of torpedo-attacking in

---

Should be October. On 26 November the task force sortied from Hitokappu Bay—Eds.

[*Page 11:*]

shallow waters to find out adequate data for that sort of attack. Experimental torpedo attacks were made against stationary targets in Kagoshima Bay, using self-recording torpedoes. Finally towards the last stage of training, the following two methods were decided upon:

Method A: Launching altitude: 20 meters
              Launching speed: 140 knots
              Angle of elevation: 0 degrees

Method B: Launching altitude: 10 meters
              Launching speed: 100 knots
              Angle of elevation: up 4.5 degrees

Fliers were so earnest that they used to make their torpedo-attacking approach before landings, even in transportation missions. They made big progress so that they had firm confidence in the operation. Also, practices were made against the fleet about ten times.

(d). Air duel fighting

Emphasis was placed on group fighting. Even fliers of poor ability could engage in air duel fighting of three against six. Studies were also made for encountering tactics of dive bombers and torpedo-attacking groups. In the latter part of October, four trainings were made for fighters against dive bombers and torpedo-attacking planes operations.

(e). Landing-on-carriers practice

Owing to comparatively large-scale reshuffling before the operation, there had been many fliers who were not familiar with landing-on-carriers practice. Moreover, efforts had to be made to have carriers available for that practice, for during that period carriers were engaged in one-by-one repairing.

Most of the training time for young fliers was therefore used in landing-on-carriers practice which was the fundamental technique

[*Page 12:*]

for all carrier-borne operations. Landing-on-carriers practice during dusk, moonlight and dark night was assigned to skilled fliers, so that half of the fliers became able to make landings-on-carriers during dark night.

(f). Night practice

Night practice was made as often as possible. Consequently half of the torpedo-attacking planes of the 1st and 2nd Carrier Divisions could make night torpedo attacks in the face of searchlight flashes, with approximately 70–80% hitting probabilities.

2. Warships

(a). Unloading of unnecessary materials
All unnecessary materials which would be dead weight and inflammable were unloaded. They were:

All boats except two large boats and two cutters, weapons for practice purposes, documents, fuel for boats, gangways, tents, cars, chests, etc.

(b). Steps taken for lengthening radius of action
In order to lengthen radius of action, fuel was overloaded as follows:

AKAGI:

300 tons of drummed oil, 250 tons in trimming tanks, 900 tons in reserve oil tanks, totaling 1450 tons

2ND CARRIER DIVISION:

100 tons of drummed oil, 400 tons of canned oil, 200 tons in trimming tanks, totaling 700 tons

8TH CRUISER DIVISION:

100 tons of drummed oil, 480 tons in trimming tanks and water-proof compartments, totaling 580 tons

CL *Abukuma* and destroyers could not be overloaded with fuel for fear of their strength of hulls and also their stability.

[*Page 13:*]

With the operation depending upon whether refueling could be made, each ship about three times practiced refueling from the tankers *Kenyo Maru* and *Kyokuto Maru* in the period from the middle of November.

Accordingly, the following methods were to be used: battleships and carriers will be followed by tankers, and cruisers and destroyers will take a side method in calm water and in other cases they will take a method of following the tankers.

On the way to Hitokappu Bay in the latter part of November, the 2nd Carrier Division, 8th Cruiser Division and the Guard Force refueled to such an extent that each ship practiced ten times.

The tankers assigned to the fleet were: *Kyokuto Maru, Kenyo Maru, Shinkoku Maru, Toho Maru, Nippon Maru, Toei Maru,* and *Kokuyo Maru.*

In view of the aforementioned refueling practice the following equipment was installed on tankers:

Leading ways in the bow and stern for the hose

Derricks and buffers for side-refueling

Spare hoses, and slings and slips

In addition, the *Hichiro Maru,* an ammunition ship, the *Hoko Maru,* a food-stuff ship, and the *Dai Ni Kyoei Maru,* a gasoline tanker, were assigned to the fleet.

3. Weapons

Preparations for weapons were generally completed as planned. It was so late, however, that Type 5 800 kg. bombs and Type 99 250 kg. bombs were discovered not to fit the torpedo-attacking planes and the dive bombers respectively, and that the adjustments could not be finished by the date of the fleet's sortie from Saeki Bay. They were finally completed at Hitokappu Bay by the fleet's own repairing teams.

Also, adjusting work to prevent fighters from self-vibration man-

[*Page 14:*]

aged to be finished just before the fleet sortied from Saeki Bay. Torpedo-adjusting workers aboard carriers were also busy with adjusting new torpedoes equipped with stabilizers for shallow waters and also with strengthening the air chamber of other torpedoes. They could manage to finish their adjustments by the early part of November with the help of the Yokosuka Air Corps.

4. Gathering of information

Necessary information was smoothly obtained through General Headquarters. In particular, the miniature models of Oahu Island and Pearl Harbor, the recent information on Hawaii from a staff officer of the General Staff which was received at Hitokappu Bay and the data from the Consul General in Honolulu (A Information)—all these were quite effective in facilitating the operation.

The special information section was organized in the fleet and it intercepted enemy communications and broadcasts.

c. The use of carrier groups

It was a very proper step to have planned to exploit the striking power of carriers to the fullest extent by concentrating carriers in one group, under the circumstance that there was a good possibility of a successful surprise attack and also of neutralizing enemy encounters by a single blow. However, such a use of carrier groups cannot be applied in all cases.

d. Reduction of effectiveness in battles

In view of several past sea battles in which our navy engaged, it was widely conceded that the effectiveness of battling technique would make for a comparative reduction in actual battles. The effectiveness of our air forces participating in the operation proved that there was no reduction in effectiveness compared with those of peacetime. They were:

[*Page 15:*]

LEVEL BOMBING:

Squadrons participating: 7 (five planes each)

Squadrons whose bombs covered the targets: 6; its percentage: 86%

Hits: 13 bombs; its percentage: 37%

(These figures were concluded only from those which were accurate.)

DIVE BOMBING:

Number of bombs dropped: 65

Hits: 38 bombs; its percentage: 59%

TORPEDO-ATTACKING:

Number of torpedoes charged: 40

Number of torpedoes which ran: 39

Number of torpedoes which hit: 36

Its percentage: 90%

The reasons why such effectiveness could be obtained:

1. Valiant fighting spirit and a strong sense of responsibility.
   There were a lot of good examples. Level bombers which were handicapped by cloudy weather, bad air conditions and colossal smoke caused by the attacks tried to bomb again and again in the face of intense defense gunfire until they were sure of making hits. Also torpedo-attacking planes fired at very close range and, realizing just prior to charging torpedoes that they were aiming at the wrong targets, made bold turnings to the right targets amid fierce gunfire.

2. Firm confidence after hard training under conditions similar to war.
   Practicing bombing against the *Settsu*, level bombing made such great progress that they abandoned the customary concept of bombing with a nine-plane formation and adopted a five-plane formation in bombing against sta-

tionary targets, thus increasing the number of attacks. Torpedo-attacking also was practiced in shallow waters, about 12 meters deep, in narrow Kagoshima Bay, finally reaching confidence in the shallow-water torpedo attack.

[*Page 16:*]

The aforementioned factors were the most important ones which contributed to preventing effectiveness from being reduced in the operation, but the following ones were also to be considered:

1. Our navy succeeded in making the surprise attack and met little opposition.

2. There were crowded targets in the harbor and they were stationary.

3. The torpedo-attacking group, dive-bomber group and fighter group played their roles to the fullest extent, having firm confidence in each other and displaying their combined strength.

2.

Air Duel Fighting

(Strafing strips inclusive)

1. Machine gun

   (a). 7.7 mm. machine guns are not powerful and of little value. Not less than 13 mm. machine guns are necessary for future planes.

      (1). Strafing by 7.7 mm. machine guns proved unexpectedly powerless; even five or six strikes could not set planes on fire.

      (2). There were two planes which received enemy 7.7 mm. bullets on their cylinders, but no damage was inflicted upon them.

   (b). 20 mm. machine gun ammunition for the Zero fighter must be increased. 20 mm. machine gun ammunition proved very powerful, to the extent that two strikes generally could set fire to planes on the ground. However, sixty rounds per gun proved very insufficient to make powerful strikes. At least about two times the present rounds are necessary.

2. Receiving fighters

   (a). How to receive fighters.
      In the operational plan some elements (approximately one or two flying squadrons) of the 1st and 2nd waves had been designated

[*Page 17:*]

to guide fighter groups to the carriers when they returned. As it turned out, however, only some small elements of fighters could join the designated units; the remainder joined with nearby bomber groups.

This proved that small groups of bombers designated to guide fighters would not be effective for that sort of purpose owing to their own exhaustion of strength, time delays due to engagements and some errors in contacting rendezvous. It is considered better to have all bombers designated to guide fighters when they return.

(b). Rendezvous points with fighters.

Three rendezvous points were chosen, the principal one being fixed on the point twenty miles in the direction of 340° off Cape Kaena. In such a surprise operation like the Hawaii operation, encountered by no enemy fighters, a rendezvous point with fighters like this proved very proper as it could be checked accurately by apparent objectives on the island in sight. However, keeping in mind a case of an unsuccessful surprise attack meeting enemy encounters while rendezvousing, rendezvous points well apart from the land should be selected. In such a case, preparations would be taken to drop smoke bombs on the sea to mark the spot and to facilitate rendezvousing.

(c). Rendezvousing altitude.

In this operation the altitude of fighters for rendezvous was fixed at 1,500 meters while that of bombers at 1,000 meters. In general cases, however, the altitude for contacting rendezvous is better less than 500 meters and beneath clouds in cloudy weather.

(d). Communication.

It was an effective method of receiving fighters that, keeping in mind cases of fighters failing to make contact with bombers, bombers were scheduled to broadcast radio signals toward which fighters could be guided by the "radio-direction-detecting-instrument." Should radiophones able

[*Page 18:*]

to contact fighters directly be equipped in bombers designated to receive fighters and be used together with the radio-direction-detecting-instrument, they seem to give much help in rendezvousing. It must be kept in mind, however, that comparatively much practice is necessary for successful results.

(e). Fighter-receiving lines by use of planes.

In case of enough strength being available, though they were not in the operation, preparing the fighter-receiving line with planes on their returning way or marking the fighter-receiving line with dropped smoke bombs was considered an effective means of receiving straggling fighters.

Also elements of surface forces should be designated to lay smoke screens if necessary.

(f). A need to increase the navigating ability of fighters.

Although fighters could not join with the designated bombers as planned, almost all fighters could make their way back to the carriers, joining with the nearby bomber groups. However, in case of meeting fierce enemy encounters or decisive battles at sea they might likely fail to join with even nearby bombers and have to return back to the carriers by themselves. In such cases, it would be impossible for them to do so, with such poor navigating abilities as at present. Urgent measures such as equipping with navigating instruments and increasing the abilities of radio should be taken for increasing the navigating abilities of fighters.

(3). Ground strafing

(g). Ground strafings are better executed to destroy parked planes from the leeward as long as permitted.

At Wheeler and Barbers Point air fields, ground strafings were made from the beginning without any control, so that flames and

[Page 19:]

smoke arose elsewhere preventing continued attacks on undamaged planes.

When many planes attempted to make simultaneous strafing attacks from other directions through poor visibility, there was much danger of colliding with each other. Therefore, a plan should be made to control strafing attacks in such cases.

(b). During the first wave striking, fighters met comparatively little opposition from the ground defense gunfire, but they met opposition in the second wave, striking with comparative damage.

In general cases, fierce enemy defense gunfire must be expected in ground strafing, as in the second wave strike. Therefore, in order to limit expected damage and also to increase effectiveness of the attacks, it is better to reconnoiter the ground before strafing to find out enemy defense gunfire positions, and to neutralize them with elements of the forces while strafing.

(c). It is quite necessary to retain elements of the forces as guards in the air even if there is no enemy interceptor in the air, while ground strafing.

Fighters which, after strafing Bellows Field, were about to strike Kaneohe airfield, circling at an altitude of 2,000 meters, were surprised by nine enemy interceptors. This is attributed to lack of attention to the air. In any case, close attention to the air is unavoidable.

(d). Strafing is apt to be loosely conducted when too many objectives are presented, as in the operation. Shower firing without any definite targets proved, in general cases, of little effect, even if many objectives come in crowds. A precise firing, aiming at one target, should be conducted in one strike of strafing.

[Page 20:]

3.

Attacking

1. Effectiveness of weapons

(a). Although the limit of effectiveness of 800 kg. bombs (No. 5) and 91-type torpedoes against the present battleship class could not be checked, owing to insufficient confirmation of results, the enemy's holding up of information concerned and also to overconcentrations or gaps in the attacks, the Hawaii operation proved their magnificent effectiveness. Either of several hits or 800 kg. bombs (No. 5) released from the over designated altitude or several torpedoes would be able to give a fatal blow to present-type battleships.

Presuming that the enemy undoubtedly would take steps to strengthen armor and improve underwater compartments, efforts should be made immediately, without being contented with the success of this operation, to study more effective weapons.

(b). It was proved that a single hit of 800 kg. bombs (No. 5) could sink a present-type battleship instantly when it hit on certain points. Every one of their hits also proved that it caused fire beneath the armored deck.

(c). A single hit of 91-type torpedoes did not seem to inflict serious damage to a battleship, but more than three torpedoes were considered enough to give a fatal blow to her.

(d). 250 kg. bombs dropped from dive bombers were not sufficient to give a fatal blow even to a cruiser, much less a battleship. 250 kg. and 500 kg. bombs (No. 4) should be completed immediately to increase penetrating effectiveness.

(e). 98-type 250 kg. bombs for land operations with attached instant fuses could destroy and set fire to a lot of parked planes on aprons.

[Page 21:]

(f). 97-type 60 kg. bombs for land operations and 99-type 60 kg. bombs proved effective to set fire to inflammable objectives on the ground.

2. Distribution of targets

Information on enemy situations and reconnaissance reports are fundamental issues for planning target distribution of an air raid upon an anchored fleet. In particular, careful consideration should be given to planning target distribution for an air attack upon irregularly dispersed objectives in narrow waters.

(a). The 1st Air Fleet divided targets in accordance with areas, and keeping in mind some errors involved in the beforehand research, the second and third plans for target distribution were made.

(b). Such priorities as giving the most easy-to-attack targets to torpedo-attacking planes, and also as making their charges precede any other attacks, were given to torpedo-attacks which were to be placed under restraint. This contributed to the great success of nearly destroying the American fleet.

(c). Further studies in detail of the damage from the attack, however, indicated that there were overconcentrations of attacks and also some gaps which had not been damaged. This was considered attributable to the following factors:

(1). Some errors in identifying ships in the aircraft reconnaissance report.

(2). Visibility was very much hampered by colossal smoke caused by burning flying boats on Ford Island which dive bombers of the first wave struck preceding torpedo attacks, contrary to the original plan.

(3). Aside from those ships instantly sunk, attacks were overlapped as damages inflicted could not be realized immediately.

[*Page 22:*]

(4). As torpedo-attacking planes attacked with long-distance intervals for fear of water spouts expected to be caused by torpedo hits, they failed to observe attacks by the preceding planes, thus causing overlaps in the attacks.

(5). Attacks were more restricted than expected. The torpedo-attacking had to be conducted from one side, as most of the enemy ships moored along the coast.

(6). It is human nature to seek an easy-to-attack objective. These factors should be kept in mind in subsequent operational plans.

From now, it seems that level bombers and torpedo-attacking planes overlapped their attacks, concentrating on the same objectives. However, there was no alternative in the pre-war planning stage, because the effectiveness of 800 kg. bombs (No. 5) and 91-type torpedoes was not yet ascertained and also because the effectiveness reduction in battlefields had to be kept in mind—though they had firm confidence in level bombing and torpedo-attacking in shallow waters. In view of the battle lessons of this sea battle, it is considered better to assign level bombers different targets from those for torpedo-attacking planes, in case of the attacking strength being limited.

3. Sequence of attacks

In attacking an enemy fleet at anchor in a defended harbor, a common sequence of attack is to assign the torpedo-attacking planes and the level bombers—the main striking forces—to the enemy fleet, after neutralizing the air with fighters and also silencing enemy defense gun positions with dive bombers. But, in such a surprise operation with much possibility for success, such as the Hawaii operation, it was considered a proper step to make the torpedo-attacking planes—though

[*Page 23:*]

the main striking force, but the ones most vulnerable to enemy defense gunfire—attack at first with fighters in order to facilitate their attack, as planned by the 1st Air Fleet.

4. Dive bombing

(a). The bomb-releasing altitude for dive bombing for 400 meters which was adopted by the 1st Air Fleet proved proper. This was considered one of the principal causes of the good results, marking 59% hit percentage.

(b). Dive bombers of the second wave circled over targets before attacking to confirm results of the first wave. This step was considered proper in this operation, although it would be impossible in case of being intercepted by enemy interceptors or attempting to make a surprise attack on fleets at sea. If the situation permits, however, it is to be adopted.

(c). Dive bombers interval—The course of the attack proved that, when bombs with delay fuses of 0.2 second were used from an altitude of 400 meters, there was no fear of bomb detonation to bombers. Therefore, the proper dive bomber interval is considered to be 400 to 500 meters, in order to increase bombing effectiveness and also to facilitate the regrouping of dive bombers after bombing.

(d). Withdrawal after bombing—Dive bombers had better withdraw immediately at high speed after bombing, sometimes with zigzag movements within twenty degrees changes of course.

(e). Regrouping after bombing—As regrouping after mixed fights is usually very difficult, it is necessary that dive bombers should join immediately nearby

[*Page 24:*]

planes after bombing, thus keeping their self-defense abilities, should be further stressed.

5. Torpedo-attacking against ships at anchor

Matters taken into consideration in planning torpedo-attacking against ships at anchor were obstacles in the air (balloon barrages, etc.), torpedo-defense nets, and a method of torpedo-attacking in shallow waters. The latter was finally solved after hard efforts of concerned departments just until the outset of the war, but the problem of torpedo-defense nets could not be solved after all. It was only our luck that torpedo-defense nets were not prepared by the enemy. As such a lucky chance is inconceivable in the future, efforts should be made to find out possible methods of cutting down enemy torpedo-defense nets as well as of making torpedoes skip over the nets.

6. Attacking enemy air bases

The result of the attack taught that air attacks on enemy air bases, if necessary, would be divided into attacks on hangars and those on parked planes, and suitable bombs and fuses for those purposes should be used.

7. Torpedo-attacking

(a). The firing interval of torpedo-attacking should be shortened as much as possible. Water spouts caused by torpedo hits fired by the preceding plane can be avoided when torpedoes are fired from points more than 500 meters from the targets. Actually, intervals between planes were 1,500 to 1,800 meters and too far.

(b). When torpedoes are fired too near the targets, firing movements would become very difficult and much damage would have to be expected.

[*Page 25:*]

(c). Regrouping after torpedo-attacking—As torpedo-attacking planes are apt to be dispersed after attacking, stress should be laid on their joining nearby planes immediately after attacking, thus maintaining their self-defense abilities.

8. Special training of bomb-sight men

Level bombers demonstrated their excellent abilities in the operation in spite of cloudy weather and bad air conditions. This is exclusively attributed to hard training. The Imperial Navy had established a so-called special training of bomb-sight men in order to give a special training to those who were to guide the leading bombers and the 1st Air Fleet had trained them for the past year. This was also thought to have given a great hint as to future air training.

However, it must be reminded in conducting training that most bomb-sight men of the leading bombers were below the warrant officer rank, and had not yet received operational training. They themselves also confessed that they had been at a loss how to select targets in each strike.

Further efforts should be made for this training. At the same time, studies must be made so as to let the command plane directly control the leading bombers, fully utilizing the inter-unit telephone.

4.

Reconnaissance

1. The training of the estimate-navigation method should be stressed, and at the same time navigation instruments should be improved.

Throughout the operation there were several cases of accidents caused by navigational errors as well as the case that on 9 December many scout planes failed to return to the carriers. The case on 9 December sufficed to show lack of estimate-navigation ability, though most of

[*Page 26:*]

these fliers were spare crews and, in addition, the carriers took different movements from the schedule.

Returning to carriers has become easy in these days by means of radio-direction-finding, but radio restriction on carriers should, of course, be expected. Even if radio-direction-findings are available, they are valuable only for returning. The estimate-navigation method is absolutely necessary for keeping accurate navigation on the designated course. Together with a radical increase of the plane's radius of action, its ability therefore might have great influence in the future, not only on the problem of returning but on composing scouting areas. The estimate-navigation method should be further stressed and trained.

Additionally, the present navigation instruments has been little improved for a long time; their capacities seem awfully inadequate for the expected radius of action of planes in the very near future. However hard training by means of the present instruments might be made, satisfactory results could not be achieved. Their improvement seems to be most urgent.

2. A need to minimize the size of the aero-camera.

The present portable aero-camera is too heavy and large; it is not suitable for damage-photographing and forcible reconnaissance photographing as it was in the operation. For those purposes, such a long-focused camera like that is not necessary. A small-size camera easy to handle was badly needed.

3. Identification of ships is very important; it should receive hard training.

The *Chikuma*'s plane mistook light cruisers for battleships in its report. This was considered to have caused some over-concentration of attacks.

[Page 27:]

As conduct of reconnaissance has great influence upon the outcome of operations, its importance should be stressed to concerned fliers and hard training for it should be made. In particular, reconnaissance of many ships irregularly anchored in a complicated area as in this operation is of the utmost difficulty; preparatory studies and preparations are indispensable.

4. In view of the importance of reconnaissance, proper fliers should be assigned to the reconnaissance mission.

In reference to the abovementioned matter, the most able flier should be assigned to the very important and difficult reconnaissance mission. In particular, in such an important reconnaissance mission that the outcome of a major operation depends upon it, consideration should be given to assigning able reconnaissance officers.

5.

Communications

1. Utilization of enemy messages

Efforts should be made as much as possible to utilize enemy messages. It is quite necessary to have a permanent enemy-message-interception group in task forces.

(a). In this operation the enemy did not pay much attention to preventing its own radio communications from being intercepted and in defending messages being decoded. Therefore, the Task Force's enemy-message-interception group, composed of a Paymaster Sub-Lieutenant (Chief), a commissioned Warrant Officer and approximately ten men, easily intercepted enemy messages and obtained very valuable information for the conduct of the operation.

Those enemy messages utilized by the group are:

[Page 28:]

(1). Messages indicating incoming and outgoing planes in the Hawaii area (plain code)

(2). Aircraft communications practice in the Hawaii area

(3). News and weather broadcasts by radio (plain words)

(4). Plain messages exchanged during the air raid upon the Island indicating the confused situation, and some intentions and movements.

(b). Dive bombers and fighters utilized the Honolulu radio broadcast by means of the "Kulucy" (not sure of its spelling) type radio-direction-detecting instrument and facilitated their flights to there.

2. Protection of communications

(a). Protecting communications from being intercepted

The American shore communication stations seem to be effective in utilizing our radio activities. Stringent control of radio activities is necessary therefore in near waters of powerful enemy stations.

In case of messages being radioed out of necessity, attention should be paid, expecting that the enemy would never fail to utilize them.

In this operation the strictest radio activities control had been maintained in the Task Force. As soon as planes which had finished attacking began to contact the carriers, the enemy detected radio-directions and gave them to nearby American Fleets.

Reference:

(1). The Task Force had an experience on its returning way from the Hawaii Operation that enemy submarines assembled in its vicinity as soon as messages were transmitted.

[*Page 29:*]

(2). Soon after the 2nd Submarine Squadron's submarine engaged in a watching mission near Oahu Island dispatched a message at night, enemy patrol boats approached her. She also received an enemy daytime air attack at the expected time after transmitting a message.

(b). Protection of messages

Since plain messages present good information to the enemy able to judge our situation, it should be further stressed never to use plain messages except in very unavoidable cases.

When the Task Force attacked Pearl Harbor, the enemy was so upset that they used mostly plain messages to such an extent that we could imagine the whole situation as it was.

3. Preparation of communications

(a). Adjustments and maintenance of communication instruments

The Task Force used radio instruments for the first time on the day of the attack, since they had been fixed at the base approximately twenty days before, and proved they worked well. As paper flaps had been inserted between key points of some transmitters on board the *Akagi* to keep the strictest radio silence, control circuit tests were made on the day before the attack, with the result that most of them were found out of working order owing to some remaining paper flaps and gathering rust. Only the early discovery saved mishaps.

(b). Preparation of instruments

Sufficient spares of crystal pieces of aero-radio should be prepared.

Smooth operational communications would be impossible at the present level of aero-communication without help of crystal pieces.

[*Page 30:*]

Sufficient crystal pieces should be prepared beforehand, taking operational plans and communication plans into consideration.

In the operation, the *Akagi* had difficulties in supplementing necessary crystal pieces for interceptors, leading bombers as well as spare waves. 30% allowance for the full number would be better kept.

4. Aero-communication waves

In order to assure swift and precise communications even in the face of intense mix-ups and strong interference by the enemy, one or two spare waves should be reserved for the important "A" wave, though such waves least interfered with by others are very hard to get in wartime. At the same time, intense studies should have been made to discover the most suitable waves for the whole action area.

The investigation since several days before the attack revealed that the "A" short wave for air operations of the 1st Air Fleet had intense mix-ups with the station with the code name of "JAH." Fortunately, the station was Koyama Transmitting Station in Japan using that wave toward America, so on the day of the attack upon Hawaii the mix-up with that wave was weakened. It is considered necessary to make careful preparatory investigations beforehand to get such necessary information as that for planning.

6.

Maintenance

1. In view of heavy losses by enemy bullets, the following points should be taken into consideration in preparations:

(a). The following items should be reserved over their full numbers:
Fighters: Front glass, tanks in wings and tanks in fuselage.
Dive bombers: Front glass, tanks in wings, tail wheel and tail wheel support

[*Page 31:*]

Torpedo-attacking planes: Front glass and wheels

(b). The following items should be reserved as fixed-number items:
Fighters: Landing gears controlling lever and spinners
Each plane: Functioning oil tanks

2. High capacity gasoline filtering equipment should be installed.
Ship gasoline tanks have some chances of water and dust getting in. It takes a lot of time for refueling gasoline by means of filtering skin with low capacity.

[*Page 32:*]

APPENDIX

I.

Outline of the plan

1. Organization

Task Force commanded by CinC, 1st Air Fleet

AIR ATTACK FORCE COMMANDED BY SAME

Strength: 1st Air Fleet (less 4th Carrier Division and its Destroyer Division)
Mission: Annihilation of enemy carriers and battleships

GUARD FORCE COMMANDED BY CO, 1ST DESTROYER SQUADRON

Strength: Flagship of 1st Destroyer Squadron, 17th and 18th Destroyer Divisions and DD *Akigumo*
Mission: Guarding the course, supporting the Air Attack Force and alert for the air (additionally, escorting the Supply Train)

SUPPORTING FORCE COMMANDED BY CO, 3RD BATTLESHIP DIVISION

Strength: 3rd Battleship Division (less its second half) and 8th Cruiser Division
Mission: Supporting the Air Attack Force

PATROL FORCE COMMANDED BY CO, 2ND SUBMARINE DIVISION

Strength: *I-91, I-21* and *I-23*
Mission: Patroling ahead and rear of the Force and alert for the air

MIDWAY BOMBARDING FORCE COMMANDED BY CO, 7TH DESTROYER DIVISION

Strength: 7th Destroyer Division (less its second half)
Mission: Destroying aircraft and major installations on Midway Island

SUPPLY TRAIN COMMANDED BY SKIPPER OF *KYOKUTO MARU*

First Supply Train commanded by skipper of *Kyokuto Maru*
Strength: *Kenyo Maru, Kyokuto Maru, Kokuyo Maru* and *Shinkoku Maru*
Second Supply Train commanded by skipper of *Toho Maru*
Strength: *Toho Maru, Toei Maru* and *Nippon Maru*

ADVANCE SUBMARINE FORCE COMMANDED BY CINC, SIXTH FLEET*

Strength: Sixth Fleet (less three submarines)
Mission: Watching and attacking enemy fleet, and secret reconnaissance of enemy anchorages

---

* Advance Submarine Force was also under the control of the CinC of the 1st Air Fleet for the operation —Eds.

[*Page 33:*]

2. Air forces organization

  (a). Reconnaissance force

    Preceding reconnaissance: Two "Zero type" seaplanes of 8th Cruiser Division

    Reconnaissance and guarding: Four "95 type" seaplanes of 3rd Battleship and 8th Cruiser Divisions

  (b). Attack Forces

Commander in general: Comdr. Fuchida, a wing commander of *Akagi*

The First Wave under the direct command of Cmdr. Fuchida

  First Group commanded by Cmdr. Fuchida

    First Attack Unit commanded by Cmdr. Fuchida

      15 "97 type" Torpedo-attacking planes

      Targets: Warships

    Second Attack Unit commanded by Lt. Cmdr. Hashiguchi

      14 (15)* "97 type" Torpedo-attacking planes

      Targets: Warships

    Third Attack Unit commanded by Lt. Abe

      10 "97 type" Torpedo-attacking planes

      Targets: Warships

    Fourth Attack Unit commanded by Lt. Cmdr. Kusumi

      10 "97 type" Torpedo-attacking planes

      Targets: Warships

  Special group under the command of Lt. Cmdr. Murata

    Special First Attack Unit commanded by Lt. Cmdr. Murata

      12 "97 type" Torpedo-attacking planes

      Targets: Warships

    Special Second Attack Unit commanded by Lt. Kitajima

      12 "97 type" Torpedo-attacking planes

      Targets: Warships

    Special Third Attack Unit commanded by Lt. Nagai

      8 "97 type" Torpedo-attacking planes

      Targets: Warships

    Special Fourth Attack Unit commanded by Lt. Matsumura

      8 "97 type" Torpedo-attacking planes

      Targets: Warships

  Second Group commanded by Lt. Cmdr. Takahashi

    Sixteenth Attack Unit commanded by Lt. Sakamoto

      25 (27) "99 type" dive bombers

      Targets: Wheeler air field

    Fifteenth Attack Unit commanded by Lt. Cmdr. Takahashi

      26 (27) "99 type" dive bombers

      Targets: Ford and Hickam air fields (9 planes to Ford and the remainder to Hickam)

---

* Figures enclosed in parentheses indicate planned planes to participate in the engagement —Eds.

[*Page 34:*]

Third Group under the command of Lt. Cmdr. Itaya
    First Air-control Unit commanded by Lt. Cmdr. Itaya
        9 "Zero type" fighters
        Targets: Hickam and Barbers Point
    Second Air-control Unit commanded by Lt. Shiga
        9 "Zero type" fighters
        Targets: Same as those of First Air-control Unit
    Third Air-control Unit commanded by Lt. Suganami
        8 (9) "Zero type" fighters
        Targets: Wheeler and Barbers Point
    Fourth Air-control Unit commanded by Lt. Okajima
        6 "Zero type" fighters
        Targets: Barbers Point
    Fifth Air-control Unit commanded by Lt. Kaneko
        5 (6) "Zero type" fighters
        Targets: Kaneohe
    Sixth Air-control Unit commanded by Lt. Sato
        6 "Zero type" fighters
        Targets: Kaneohe

The Second Wave under command of Lt. Cmdr. Shimazaki
    First Group under the direct command of Lt. Cmdr. Shimazaki
    Sixth Attack Unit commanded by Lt. Cmdr. Shimazaki
        27 "97 type" Torpedo-attacking planes
        Targets: Hickam
    Fifth Attack Unit commanded by Lt. Ichihara
        27 "97 type" Torpedo-attacking planes
        Targets: Ford and Kaneohe (18 planes to Kaneohe, and the re-
            mainder to Ford)
Second Group under the command of Lt. Cmdr. Egusa
    Eleventh Attack Unit commander by Lt. Chihaya
        18 "99 type" dive bombers
        Targets: Warships
    Twelfth Attack Unit commanded by Lt. Makino
        26 (27) "99 type" dive bombers
        Targets: Warships
    Thirteenth Attack Unit commanded by Lt. Cmdr. Egusa
        17 (18) "99 type" dive bombers
        Targets: Warships
    Fourteenth Attack Unit commanded by Lt. Kobayashi
        17 (18) "99 type" dive bombers
        Targets: Warships
Third Group commanded by Lt. Shindo
    First Air-control Unit commanded by Lt. Shindo

9 "Zero type" fighters
Targets: Hickam
Second Air-control Unit commanded by Lt. Nikaido
9 "Zero type" fighters
Targets: Ford and Wheeler
Third Air-control Unit commanded by Lt. Iida
9 "Zero type" fighters
Targets: Kaneohe and Bellows
Fourth Air-control Unit commanded by Lt. Nono
8 (9) "Zero type" fighters
Targets: Same as above

[*Page 35:*]

II.

Outline proceeding

1. Outline proceedings of the Task Force and the Advance Submarine Force

After secretly completing the operational preparation in parallel with the diplomatic negotiations becoming tense, the Advance Submarine Force left the homeland in the middle of November to take a position of watching the enemy fleet. The Task Force assembled in Hitokappu Bay by 22 November and sortied from there at 0600 on 26 November. The Force continued its advance on strict alert for submarines and aircraft, refueling as scheduled.

On 6 December the 2nd Supply Train departed after refueling the 2nd Carrier Division and the Guard Force. On the next day, the 1st Supply Train also left the Force after the final refueling to the Guard Force. By 8 December the Force reached the point about 200 miles north of Oahu Island.

All men aboard realized that "the rise and fall of the Empire depended upon this battle" and determined in their minds to "do their utmost efforts." At 0130 the first wave rose in the air and at 0245 the second wave followed it. They succeeded in annihilating enemy warships and aircraft, and returned to the carriers from 0545 until 0830. The Force then withdrew to the north.

By this blow the main force of the American Pacific Fleet and most of the enemy air forces in the area were destroyed, but no other information on the enemy was available. Under this circumstance, the Task Force commander determined to withdraw, giving up another air attack. His decision was based upon the following judgments:

A. Almost an expected result had been achieved by the first air strike; further major damages therefore could not be expected by another strike.

[*Page 36:*]

B. Even in the first strike enemy defense gunfire showed its rapid response, making the later attacks forcible ones. Fierce encounters would have to be expected in the second and more strikes, so disproportional losses on our side for the expected results would have to be risked.

C. According to intercepted enemy messages, it was almost certain that at least about 50 enemy large-type planes still remained and moreover the whereabouts of enemy carriers, heavy cruisers and submarines were unknown.

It was considered also disadvantageous to stay long within the range of the enemy land-based air force, because the Force hardly covered more than 250 miles of reconnaissance area and also could not rely upon reconnaissance of the Advance Submarine Force alone.

On the 9th the Force joined with the 1st Supply Train and refueled the Guard Force. Then it continued on its way, keeping 700–800 miles outside of the enemy air bases. At 1630 of the 10th, the Support Force for the Wake Operation, composed of the 8th Cruiser Division, 2nd Carrier Divison and DDs *Tanikaze* and *Urakaze*, left the Force.

On the 17th, *Shokaku*'s submarine-scouting planes discovered enemy submarines at 0935 and 1129 hours and sank them. In view of the information obtained indicating enemy submarines gathering in the area of the Bonin Islands, the course of the Force was changed to go around south of the Volcano Islands, arriving in the western Inland Sea on the 23rd. (See the action map.)

2. Outline of the air attack proceedings

(a). The First Attack wave

43 fighters, 51 bombers and 89 torpedo-attacking planes under the command of Cmdr. Fuchida, a wing commander of the *Akagi*,

[*Page 37:*]

left the carriers at 0130 and, making formation at 0140, made their way at the altitude of 3,000 meters.

At 0300 the enemy situation reports of the 8th Cruiser Division's planes were received. At 0319 the order ''all forces will charge'' was given and at 0323 ''successful surprise attack'' was reported. In the face of fierce defense gunfire, each force attacked the enemy at 30 to 60 minutes in accordance with the plan. From 0545 until 0830 all planes returned to the carriers except three fighters, one dive bomber and five torpedo-attacking planes.

(b). The Second Attack Wave

35 fighters, 78 dive bombers and 54 torpedo-attacking planes* under the command of Lt. Cmdr. Shimazaki, a wing commander of the *Zuikaku*, left the carriers at 0245, arriving off Kahuku Point at 0424. Then they attacked as planned for 30 to 60 minutes amid intense gunfire. They returned from 0700 to 0830, with six fighters and 14 dive bombers missing.

(c). The preceding reconnaissance planes left their ships at 0100 and the guard planes at 0200. They made reconnaissance flights as scheduled, and all returned to their ships from 0700 until 0800.

---

* Actually high-level bombers. There was no torpedo attack in the second wave —Eds.

3. Alerts for enemy ships and planes

    (a). Since departure from Hitokappu Bay on 26 November, strict alerts had been kept until 7 December with Alert Positions No. 1–No. 3. Three to six planes for aircraft and six planes for submarines had been alerted on deck with readiness of five to 30 minutes' notice. From sunrise to 30 minutes after sunset on 8 December, Anti-air Alert Position No. 1-B was maintained, with three to six fighters of each carrier in the air and another three to six fighters on deck with readiness of one to five minutes' notice.

[*Page 38:*]

    (b). Two to four seaplanes had been reserved to be used against submarines immediately if necessary.

    (c). From sunrise to 30 minutes before sunset of the 9th, the Anti-air Alert Position No. 1-C was taken up, with three fighters of each carrier in the air, and another three to six fighters on deck with readiness of one to five minutes' notice.

        The anti-submarine guard mission was assigned to the 5th Carrier Division. Four planes were in the air on duty. From sunrise time, the following search was carried out to guard the Force from enemy surface ships:

(1) 2nd Carrier Division:	From 0° to 120° in direction
Akagi	From 120° to 180°
Kaga	From 180° to 240°
5th Carrier Division:	From 240° to 360°

        (2) Advance: Generally 300 miles, but in case of rear searching it may be reduced as warranted.

    (d). From the 10th on, the Anti-air Alert Position No. 2-c had been kept. The anti-submarine guard was also assigned to the 5th Carrier Division, and two planes guarded the scheduled course while another four took the position of close watch over the Force.

    (e). On the 20th, all seaplanes of the 3rd Battleship Division and 1st Destroyer Squadron advanced to Chichijima Air Corps in the Bonin Islands, after mopping up enemy submarines south of the Bonin Islands. On the next day, they further advanced to the Yokosuka Air Corps, mopping up enemy submarines west of the Islands.

    (f). On the 23rd, from a point about 200 miles from land, approximately half of all serviceable planes advanced to the Kanoya Air Corps, mopping up areas ahead of the Force.

    (g). On the 23rd, the remaining force advanced to the Kanoya, Saeki and Iwakuni Air Corps, also mopping up areas ahead of the Force.

[*Page 39:*]

The force which had advanced to the base on the preceding day also made anti-submarine flights to the Force.

4. From 1831 to 1857 on the 8th, the 7th Destroyer Division (less *Akebono*) made a surprise bombardment upon Midway Island.

5. At 1935 on the 17th, a *Shokaku* submarine-scouting plane attacked a submerging enemy submarine at about 34-0 N, 160-45 E, and sank it.

At 1229 on the same day, *Shokaku*'s plane also discovered a periscope and attacked it at about 34-13 N, 100-08 E.

III.

Results

1. Results of attack

(a). Against ships

(1) Level bombing (altitude 3,200 meters)*

Akagi:	First Squadron	(E)	5 bombs released of which 2 hit
	Second Squadron	(D)	5 bombs released of which one hit
		(C)	on (C) and another on (D)
	Third Squadron	(C & D)	5 bombs released. Due to smoke, damages inflicted unknown, but some hits conceivable.
Kaga:	First Squadron	(C & D)	5 bombs released, of which one hit on (C) and another on (D)
	Second Squadron	(B)	5 bombs released, of which two hit on (B) and another on a transport (a)
	Third Squadron	(D)	4 bombs released, of which one or two hits estimated, although smoke prevented from observing results.
Soryu:	First Squadron	(C & D)	5 bombs released, of which one hit on (C) and another on (D)
	Second Squadron	(A)	5 bombs released, of which no hits observed.
Hiryu:	First Squadron	(B)	5 bombs released, of which two hits on (B)
	Second Squadron	(G)	5 bombs released, of which results unknown owing to smoke.

---

* Letters in parentheses indicate target ships —Eds.

[*Page 40:*]

In total, 49 bombs released from the bombers and more than 13 hits recorded. With regard to target ships, see page 39 [of original; see pp. 40–41 this version].

(2) Dive bombings

Akagi:	21st Sqdn.	(RU)	3 bombs dropped, results unknown.
	22nd Sqdn.	(HE)	3 bombs dropped, results unknown.
	23rd Sqdn.		(estimated to have attacked battle-ships) Results unknown.
	25th Sqdn.	(NU)	3 bombs dropped, one of which hit.
	26th Sqdn.	(E)	3 bombs dropped, results unknown.
	27th Sqdn.	(E)	3 bombs dropped, estimated five hits. (Note: These figures contradict each other)
	Total:		Fifteen bombs and perhaps three more dropped, of which one hit.
Kaga:	21st Sqdn.	(A′)	3 bombs dropped
	22nd Sqdn.	(A′)	"
	23rd Sqdn.	(A′)	"
	24th Sqdn.	(A′)	"
	25th Sqdn.	(A′)	"
	26th Sqdn.	(E & D)	3 bombs dropped, two on (E) and one on (D) hit.
	Total:		27 bombs dropped, of which 8 hits with 13 probable hits.
Soryu:	21st Sqdn.	(Ro & Ho)	3 bombs dropped, of which one hit on (Ro) and two on (Ho).
	22nd Sqdn.	(NI & destroyer)	3 bombs dropped, two hits on (NI).
	23rd Sqdn.	(G & Ri)	3 bombs dropped, one hit on (G) and two on (Ri).
	24th Sqdn.	(H, Ho & Ni)	3 bombs dropped, and each hit on the target.
	25th Sqdn.	(G)	2 bombs dropped, and two hits on the target.
	26th Sqdn.	(*Omaha,* I & D)	3 bombs dropped, one hit on (I).
	Total:		17 bombs dropped, of which 14 hit.
Hiryu:	21st Sqdn.	(Chi)	2 bombs dropped, and two hits on the target.
	22nd Sqdn.	(E & Ni)	3 bombs dropped, and two hits on (E) and another on (Ni).
	23rd Sqdn.	(Ni)	2 bombs dropped, and two hits on the target.
	24th Sqdn.	(Ha & G)	3 bombs dropped, and two hits on (Ha) and another on (G).

[*Page 41:*]

	25th Sqdn.	(Ha & G)	3 bombs dropped, one hit on each target.

26th Sqdn.	(E)	3 bombs dropped, and all hit on the target.
Total:		16 bombs dropped, of which 15 hits were marked.
Grand Total:		65 (+3) dropped, of which 38 were hits and more than 13 hits were probable.

(3) Torpedo-attacks.

Akagi	First Sqdn.	3 torpedos charged, of which two hits on (D) and another on (F).
	Second Sqdn.	3 charged, of which two hit on (F).
	Third Sqdn.	3 charged, of which two hit on (G) and another on (D).
	Fourth Sqdn.	3 charged, of which three hit on (F).
Kaga:	First Sqdn.	3 charged, of which three hit on (D).
	Second Sqdn.	3 charged, of which two hit on (F).
	Third Sqdn.	3 charged, of which each torpedo hit on (A, D & F).
	Fourth Sqdn.	3 charged, of which one hit on (F).
Soryu:	First Sqdn.	2 charged, and each one hit on (Ni & G).
	Second Sqdn.	2 charged; all hit on (O).
	Third Sqdn.	2 charged; all hit on (O).
	Fourth Sqdn.	2 charged; all hit on (O).
Hiryu:	First Sqdn.	2 charged; all hit on (D).
	Second Sqdn.	2 charged; all hit on (Ni).
	Third Sqdn.	2 charged; all hit on (F).
	Forth Sqdn.	2 charged; all hit on (Ni).
	Grand Total:	40 torpedoes charged, of which 38 torpedoes made hits.

(4) Results.

Target Name:	(A)	Maybe *Oklahoma* or *Nevada*	One torpedo hit and eight 250 bomb hits and 13 350 bombs (not sure)	Damaged
"	"	(B)	Maybe *Arizona* or *Pennsylvania*	Four 800 bomb hits	Severely damaged. Big fire
"	"	(C)	Maybe *California* or *Tennessee*	Three 800 bomb hits	Sunk

[Page 42:]

| Target Name: | (D) | Maybe *West Virginia, Colorado* or *Maryland* | Nine torpedo and three 800 bomb hits and one 250 bomb hit | Perhaps sunk |

"	"	(E)	same	Two 800 bomb hits and twelve 250 bomb hits	Severely damaged Big fire
"	"	(F)	Maybe *Arizona* or *Pennsylvania*	Twelve torpedo hits	Sunk
"	"	(G)	Maybe *West Virginia, Colorado* or *Maryland*	Three torpedo and five 250 bomb hits	Damaged
"	"	(H)	Maybe *Nevada* or *Oklahoma*	One 250 bomb hit and one more probable	Slightly damaged
"	"	(O)	*Utah*-type ship	Six torpedo hits	Sunk
"	"	(Ni)	*Brooklyn*-type light cruiser	Five torpedo and six 250 bomb hits	Perhaps sunk
"	"	(Ru)	Tanker	Three 250 bomb hits	Sunk
"	"	(Ha)	Tanker	One 800 bomb hit	Sunk

(b). Attacks on air bases

Damages inflicted upon enemy air forces were as follows:

Ford: Estimated strength: approx. 100 flying boats
First Wave: *Shokaku*'s dive bombers destroyed 23 planes.
Second Wave: *Kaga*'s dive bombers destroyed one plane and
Shokaku's dive bombers another one.
In addition, one hangar was set on fire. It was therefore
believed that about ten planes in the hangar were also destroyed.

Hickam: Estimated strength: 40 4-engine planes, 100 twin-engine
planes and several assault planes
First Wave: *Akagi*'s fighters and *Kaga*'s destroyed eight and
seven planes respectively. *Shokaku*'s dive bombers
also destroyed another seven.
Second Wave: *Akagi*'s fighters destroyed two planes. *Zuikaku*'s
level bombers scored 13 planes destroyed.
Besides, 12 hangars were destroyed, with approximately 120
planes in the hangars also destroyed.

Wheeler: Estimated strength: Approx. 200 fighters, 10 assault planes
and several night fighters
First Wave: *Soryu*'s fighters destroyed 17 planes, *Zuikaku*'s
dive bombers another 60 planes.
Second Wave: *Kaga*'s dive bombers scored one plane destroyed.
Besides, six hangars with approx. 90 planes inside were
set on fire.

[*Page 43:*]

Barbers Point: Estimated strength: About 80 carrier-borne planes.
First Wave: Fighters of *Akagi, Kaga, Soryu* and *Hiryu* destroyed
11, 15, 12 and 22 planes respectively.

Second Wave: Dive bombers of *Kaga* scored two more destroyed.
Hiryu's dive bombers destroyed several more.

Kaneohe: Estimated strength: Approximately 50 flying boats.
First Wave: *Zuikaku*'s fighters destroyed 32 planes and 4 more
probable.
Second Wave: Fighters of *Soryu* and *Hiryu* scored 6 and 2 planes
destroyed respectively.
In addition, one hangar with approx. 10 planes inside
was set on fire.

Bellows: Estimated strength: 35 2-seated double-wing planes were
spotted by reconnaissance.
First Wave: *Shokaku*'s fighters scored 3 planes.
Second Wave: *Hiryu*'s fighters destroyed 3 planes.

Shot down: First Wave:

Akagi:	One transport, one training plane and one B-17
Kaga:	One training plane
Soryu:	Four planes and one more probable
Hiryu:	None
Zuikaku:	One plane by dive bombers

Second Wave:

Akagi:	One plane by dive bombers
Kaga:	Two planes by dive bombers
Soryu:	Two fighters
Hiryu:	Two fighters by fighters and one flying boat by dive bombers

Total: 265 (5) planes were completely destroyed or shot down.

---

1. The above-mentioned figures include only planes set on fire or those shot down; those seriously damaged exclusive.
2. Eight planes which *Zuikaku*'s level bombers destroyed at Hickam were included in the number. They were regarded as completely damaged, as set on fire.
3. Besides the above-mentioned figures, *Kaga*'s dive bombers set fire to two more planes, but they were not included, as the airfields where those two planes were set on fire were unknown.
4. The figures in parentheses indicate those which were not certain.

[*Page 44:*]

2. Damages received

(a). Attacks against ships

	LEVEL BOMBING	DIVE BOMBING	TORPEDO- ATTACKING	TOTAL
Participating strength	49	78	40	168
Shot down	0	14	3	17

Missing	0	0	2	2
Forced landing	0	0	1	1
Damages only to be repaired in naval yards	0	0	0	0
Damages able to be repaired in the fleet	5	54	8	67

(b). Attacks on air bases

	LEVEL BOMBING	DIVE BOMBING	TOTAL
Participating strength	54	51	105
Shot down	0	1	1
Missing	0	0	0
Damages to be repaired in naval yards	1	0	1
Damages able to be repaired in the fleet	13	17	30

(c). Attacks on air bases

Participating	79
Shot down	3
Missing	6
Damages able to be repaired in the fleet	24

PART IV

Aftermath

CHAPTER 19

An Intimate Look at the Japanese Navy

Masataka Chihaya

T HIS EXTRAORDINARY work deserves a section to itself. Seldom if ever
has an officer of any Navy written a more devastating critique of his
service's strategy and tactics. It cannot be entirely charged up to the
20/20 vision of hindsight, for on at least one occasion the author spoke out
publicly against a major policy and was as publicly slapped down for his
pains. This study is undated but was obviously written in the mid-1940s,
when the sting of defeat was still sharp and when no one could have predicted
Japan's amazing resurgence.

Just as he pulls no punches in assessing the Imperial Japanese Navy's
shortcomings, he is amazingly generous in his praise of the U.S. Navy—its
planning, execution, utilization of men and materiel, and the courage, daring,
and dedication of the individual officers and men.

This study is not just a "period piece," of interest only to historians and
World War II buffs. Its principles are timeless and deathless and would repay
study not only by naval officers seriously concerned with learning by the
mistakes of the past, but by anyone interested in the psychology of large
organizations and the pitfalls that await the unrealistic, the overambitious, and
the overconfident.

TABLE OF CONTENTS

FOREWORD
THE "ONE BIG BATTLE" IDEA OF THE JAPANESE NAVY

The Japanese navy had studied the United States for a good many years, knew the United States thoroughly, at least should have known. If so, why did this Navy wage war on her and get itself wiped out? This is a great question.

This question has been asked of us by quite a few of the American naval officers who came over with the Occupation Forces. This is a question entertained not only by American naval officers, but by a good many of us, too. The Japanese people are really mystified, because they know that the Japanese navy had always kept itself aloft of politics, domestic and international, devoting itself unswervingly and exclusively to the business of the navy. No thought had been more foreign to it than to think and make itself an instrument of Imperialist policy.

Half a year has already passed since the armistice was signed on the *Missouri*, 2 September 1945. The signing was a historic scene. Since then, almost a year has just flown. No sign of the beginning of a revival from the exhaustion of war is yet in evidence. Debris all over the country greets our eyes. Then chaos and confusion. Not even assurance for tomorrow's food. We are far ahead of food! Not one single thing but reminds us vividly of defeat, defeat and defeat.

"If this war had not occurred?" "Why did such a war break out?" Such a question constantly haunts us: "Didn't you foresee all this?" a good many American officers have asked me.

I have served the Navy for over 18 years. In all this time, I have been put through many difficult kinds of experiences. By far the greater part of my time has been spent on the seas, or the foremost front line, on the fleet. During the war, important offices were assigned to me—positions at the center as a member of the staff,

[*Page 2:*]

brilliant jobs for an officer of my grade. But after brilliancy, the darkness is so much the darker! I now feel full of shame. I have survived the war and am a spectator of the defeated motherland. I feel rueful, painfully rueful, to think that as a member of the defunct Imperial Navy I am not quite free from the responsibility for this utter, bottomless defeat, a defeat that has beaten itself hollow.

Why has such a complete defeat been inflicted on the Japanese navy? This question is not so puzzling to me as it may appear to many. I feel I can account for it in my own modest way. Although modest, I am convinced that I am right. To throw light on this point is the purpose of the booklet.

This booklet abounds in exposures, but exposure is not my object. I mean it for confession, for expiation for the great guilt in which I feel I have a share, however modest. I am just stating truths, not half truths but whole truths. I hold myself wholly responsible for every statement contained herein.

In Chapter I, I have started my discussion from the character of the education which Japanese naval officers were put through; then, from the angle of that education, I have tried to analyze the war psychology of the Japanese naval officers, and from the analysis so attained I have come to the conclusion which I have mentioned at the very start of this booklet: The Japanese naval authorities had confounded the war with the battle; confusion of thoughts had misled them to identify a particular scene of a battle with the whole phase of the war. Shame! I have noticed this after I have been put out of the navy. Wisdom has come too late!

Of course, this is my own view. Many will differ. I am sure, however, that to this view of mine there will be supporters galore.

[*Page 3:*]

In Chapter II, I have stated how this confusion of thought worked itself out in practice, in war operations. In doing this, I have cited the American side of the corresponding factors, as I have thought such a treatment will add to the clarity of my explanation.

The events I have cited belong mostly to the period before the battles around the Marianas in June of 1944. After that, no more balance, or semblance of it, existed between the American and the Japanese navies. For America, it had become just a chase, a hunt, a scavenger operation. There were no more battles worthy of the name, worthy of the description for my purpose. I have left out the instances the citing of which I have considered useless.

[*Page 4:*]

CHAPTER I

The Judgment of the Japanese Navy on the War with the United States

Ever since the Russo-Japanese War (1904–05), in spite of everything competition continued to grow between the Japanese and the American navies. The American navy has always been the imaginary enemy of the Japanese. Up until 1931, when Japan started a policy of expansion in Manchuria, however, Japan did little more than endeavor to keep something like a balance against the American navy— balance in figures, desk theories, more of speculation, play of fancy, than a practical issue of burning urgency. This was the character of our study of the American navy, largely academic. This also we have realized only as late as now.

A sudden change came with our planning a positive expansion policy in Manchuria, in 1931. Concretely and objectively, the Japanese policy came into head-on collision with the American policy. Japan grabbed Manchuria, extended her claws to China proper. Friction produced heat, and in the heated atmosphere many incidents happened, the Panay Incident amongst the rest. The explosion then looked already imminent, but did not actually occur. Both sides kept the brake pressed tight, especially the American side. But even as late as this, the inevitability of the Japanese-American war, if matters were left to develop freely, did not come home to the Japanese navy. Their idea of the Japanese-American naval war remained vague and indefinite. Hence the naval authorities did not yet begin to lay a concrete plan of war, a scheme of expansion adequate to answer the requirements of the pressing situation.

When, however, Nazi Germany started their *blitzkrieg* against Poland in September 1941 and set World War II ablaze, its repercussion on this side of the world deepened the crisis. Japan's attitude became increas

[*Page 5:*]

ingly violent. The friction with the U.S., which stood for equal opportunity, no war, the Nine Power Treaty, and all that, began to produce sparks. When Ambassador Grew in his address at the American Club welcome party emphasized the necessity of rectifying American-Japanese relations on a sound, peaceful basis and used the word "MUST," we came to feel that war was inevitable. It was really from about this period that our navy set about studying the war in all earnest. This would look unbelievable, nevertheless it is quite true. Our exercises and training suddenly became very serious, violent, exhaustive, even murderous.

Combustible materials that lurked here in Japan began to catch fire from the Nazi conflagrations in Europe. Smoldering continued for some time. All this while, what specific efforts were made to avert the crisis? A study of this subject will be interesting, but to my deep regret sufficient first-hand information is not available, so I have to leave it out.

SOME STUDIES ABOUT THE
AMERICAN-JAPANESE WAR

A few minutes' walk from the Meguro station of the government railway, on the left-hand side of Meguro street, going towards the city center, there is a black, four-storied building of the ex-Naval College standing prominently in the midst of a measureless stretch of debris. It is a solid, squat structure in which as recently as a year or so ago, young officers, commanders and lieutenants were educated for a space of two years in various branches of sciences related to sea warfare. They were taught what they had to do, and how, if we were to beat the American navy. Strategy and tactics, war histories of American and Japan, even economics and laws were included in the school curriculum. The role this college played was big, as big as the role played by similar institutions

[*Page 6:*]

in other countries. Staff membership of the Navy Department, general staff and the fleet was composed mainly, if not to the similar extent in the army, of the graduates from this college.

An inquiry into the method and substance of education imparted in this institution will therefore throw a sidelight on the studies of the American-Japanese war as they were undertaken by the Japanese navy. Such an inquiry at the same time will afford an explanation of the mental processes that led the Japanese navy to make up their mind to fight this fatal war.

I am one of the last graduates from this college. After the graduation of my class, which took place during the war, the college was closed forever. Here is an episode that will give a glimpse of the atmosphere in the institution. This is rather digression, but the story will be interesting enough to justify a little diversion. Just before graduation, our opinions were invited on the education given in the college.

It was then in the beginning of 1944. The Gilberts and Marshalls had already fallen into American hands. Melancholy prevailed around Rabaul. I gave my opinions as follows:

> I do not think the college will be reopened in the course of this war. If by good luck it should be opened again, it would be necessary to thoroughly revise the curriculum and the methods of teaching. The current system is utterly out of focus, lacks coherence between each line of studies, leads nowhere after all. The phenomenon named war must be scientifically analyzed. Speaking of the instance of the present war, it should have been studied at a very early date if Japan could at all undertake and manage such a war. What would be the particular features of such a war?—if such features were clearly envisioned. Then what counter-measures should and could have been adopted in order to cope with them. These would form the major premises, and within the framework of these major premises, a coherent, well-dovetailed plan of education should have been formulated. The study of a subject such as the movement of the fleet should be treated as no more

[*Page 7:*]

than a sub-section of this fundamental system. The present unfavorable drift of the war cannot but be the consequence of the very imperfect traditional system which lacks unity of purpose and evenness of attention. A thorough reconsideration is very badly needed . . .

I replied to some such effect. A few days later the professor in charge of my class called all the classmates into the hall and served an animadversion.

"We have requested you," he started, "to express your views on the educational policy of the college." Then he mentioned me by name and continued, "Lieutenant Commander Chihaya has slandered the present war policy and the policies of his seniors. Such behavior is very much to be regretted . . ."

Such an attitude was very unsatisfactory to me. They hated criticism. But from this isolated fact, one will be able to guess the atmosphere of self-complacency that filled the institution. Apparently they felt everything was perfect humanly. I will later dwell upon further details.

THE STRATEGY AND THE TACTICS OF THE JAPANESE NAVY

Strategy and tactics are alike means to win a war. The difference in the last analysis is one of scale. On the small scale, it is called tactics; great tactics is strategy. This is the way I understand it. The Oriental school of strategy and tactics made very much of the maneuvering of fighting forces. The Japanese navy was also devoted to this idea. Its idea of strategy and tactics was based on this tradition and modified under the influence of the late Admirals Masayuki Akiyama and Tetsutaro Sato, who distinguished themselves as strategists during the Russo-Japanese war. The central ideas were "forestalling and concentration." They had studied these points, and the results were fruitless. In such a study they took into consideration the precedents

[*Page 8:*]

in the war histories of America and Great Britain. The merits of such endeavors, serious and arduous, are amply discernible in the stages of developments that had led up to the outbreak.

The attack on Pearl Harbor is an example of this spirit of forestalling and concentration. The units that took part in this attack composed the greatest of the task forces ever displayed in the history of sea warfare before that date. The *Akagi, Kaga, Soryu, Hiryu, Shokaku* and *Zuikaku*, all carriers, composed the main body. They succeeded in getting the jump on the American navy and managed it beautifully in the beginning. Then step by step the luster wore off, grew dimmer and dimmer and at last the whole outfit just melted away into nothingness. The process was tortuous and elaborate. I will dwell on it later. Here let it suffice to mention that the thought patterns, specific ideas, that governed the actions of the Japanese navy all through this period are worth serious study and attention, containing much that will interest strategists of the future. But unfortunately the true value of such lessons then escaped the attention of the Japanese naval authorities. They were short and narrow-sighted, just like a horse in harness. The American navy's vigilance saw through everything. They have got at the secrets of our weakness.

The Japanese navy attributed great value to the night attack, the last trump card for a navy of inferior power. The result scored by this tactic was not small. Dashing into the ranks of the enemy fleet and giving daredevil attacks on what comes to hand under the protection of darkness and firing secret long-range torpedoes etc. were some of the most prominent features of the methods adopted by our navy. Torpedoes driven by oxygen must still remain in the memory of experts of foreign navies. The reports about these weapons must have pretty much gotten on their nerves.

[*Page 9:*]

Our oxygen torpedo was at least 10 knots speedier than the speediest torpedo then known in the world. Its range was almost twice as great as the announced figures. When we mentioned this torpedo in the navy documents, we always discounted 10 knots on the speed and one-half on the range, but nobody even seemed to doubt the veracity of such reports. After making such a large allowance, the published figures still looked quite decent.

The recognition by the navy of the importance of the air forces, if not sufficient in itself, was much superior to the army, and was at least commendable. Even before the war, the cry was heard for a strong air force, for converting into carriers the *Musashi* and *Yamato,* then the biggest battleships under construction. Indeed the advocates of this conversion were many among the farsighted men. The study of aviation and serial tactics was pretty advanced, correct and accurate except as regards the requisite quantity and the capacity of production. That must be admitted, when we remember the results scored by our task forces already mentioned, by the so-called "Zero Fighters," and the efficiency of torpedo planes proved in the shallow water of Pearl Harbor. The Zero Fighter lost its value as the war progressed, and at last came to nothing. But they had their very heydays. In the course of 1940 they flew from Hankow far away to distant Chengtu and delivered crushing blows. Nothing wonderful now after the F6F, P-38, P-51, and P-47, but in those days the feat was nothing short of amazing. They were then wonderful machines.

The navy's land-based "96" bomber which flew up from Saishu Island southwest off Korea and Formosa, crossed the China Sea and attacked the Shanghai and Hankow districts were also first-class planes in those days. Planes which succeeded in firing torpedoes into the shallow waters (12–13ms) of Pearl Harbor and accurately hit the marks were the

[*Page 10:*]

"97" torpedo planes. Good airplanes were they indeed, of which the Japanese navy could well be proud in the light of those days.

This was the result of a serious, almost fanatical study. It was the case of an honest effort justly rewarded.

Admiral Togo's fleet revolution by 16 points at the time of the Battle of the Japan Sea, and Vice Admiral Kamimura's arbitrary modification of Admiral Togo's order to turn around the fleet unit by unit into a wholesale revolution of the entire fleet on the same occasion, have since become the subject of unqualified admiration, and there has grown a tendency to consider these tactics as the unique cause of the victory in that engagement. This was very unfortunate!

As a result of this misconception, the strategy and tactics taught in the Naval College has become a maneuver on a chessboard, the Japanese and the American navies pitted fleet against fleet and fighting out the whole war in one decisive stroke—one imaginary once-for-all decisive battle which was always made to develop in favor of the Japanese side. They fooled themselves in a study of a picture warped by prejudice. A student criticized it: "How will the American navy come out into the seas near Japan and stake a decisive battle under conditions obviously unfavorable to them? Such an idea is self-complacent, self-satisfying, a dream of a fool's paradise . . ." This hits the nail on the head.

One big decisive battle was always imagined, they had no other picture. As to how such a decisive battle would take place, what if the battle turned out to be indecisive, or a defeat? Honestly, such questions were never seriously studied.

An instance will be given here of the error that did actually result from such missions in the study of naval warfare. The submarine flotilla used in the attack on Pearl Harbor had not been intended to

[*Page 11:*]

be sacrificed in one fell blow like that. On that occasion our special submarine flotilla gave the attack in concert with the air forces, and all the crews except sub-lieutenant [Kazuo] Sakamaki perished with their craft. However, to speak the honest truth, that had not been the program. Those special submarines had been designed for further uses on the high sea in the "decisive battle" of the navy's imagination. These craft were of high speed and short cruising radius. They were the least fit for such an operation as the attack on Pearl Harbor which would require long periods of secret activities. Directly after the announcement of the attack on Pearl Harbor, a vice admiral who designed that craft said to me in tears, "Alas, I would never have designed such craft if they were to be used in such a manner. This is murder of the crews. What a pity! It were much better I had never designed such a weapon!" His voice still remains in my ears.

Again, ever since the battle around the Solomons, we continued to be painfully harassed by the daredevil activities of the American torpedo corps. This painful experience makes us question why our navy, which had attached so much importance to the night attack, was not equipped with torpedo craft. At the time when the problems of the torpedo craft were hotly discussed in England and Italy, our navy also studied the subject, but is said to have come to the conclusion that such a type is of no use where waves are high, as in the seas near Japan, and given up the idea. That reason is very simple indeed, but quite misguided.

Recalling the experiences all went through, we find many more factors that are open to criticisms. The overestimate of the power of the techniques due to an imperfect study of the subject is one of

[*Page 12:*]

them. Vice Adm. Tetsutaro Sato, a strategist of the Japanese navy, put down the formula: Force $= \frac{1}{2} MV^2$ (M: Quantity of force) (V: Power of technique), which means: Inferiority in quantity can be made up only by superiority in efficiency.

Such a conclusion is only abstractedly correct. It is a travesty of the law of energy. A grave inaccuracy vitiates the conclusion, in that a 100 percent super efficiency all by itself will make possible a victory against a force quantitatively superior. But how can we make an accurate comparative estimate of the respective fighting forces? Practically, this is an impossible proposition—just a formula, nothing more, of no practical value, nothing we can rely on. I recall a classmate of mine, an expert mathematician, who did not accept this formula unconditionally, questioned its accuracy, studied it carefully and said to me, "Force $= M\sqrt{V}$ is more correct." I cannot help feeling he was more accurate than the expert vice admiral.

Let me cite another instance. While I was in the Naval College, we tried a deck maneuver, fancying a situation in the middle of 1944. I was favored with the honor of being appointed "The Commander-in-Chief of the United States Navy." In this capacity, I planned an attack on the Japanese main islands with the task forces. The Japanese came out and attacked us with their long-awaited *Ginga-Tai* (The Milky Way Corps), consisting of about 50 planes, which was not yet in existence at this time. The final verdict delivered was quite unfavorable to me. My "American Fleet" was declared annihilated. I absolutely refused to acquiesce in such an erroneous judgment. I protested firmly. "The real fighting power of the Japanese forces is several times superior to that of the American forces" was the explanation.

Such stupidity was overpowering. In those days, the efficiency of

[*Page 13:*]

one Zero Fighter was estimated equal to about 10 Hellcats treasured by the American navy. They dreamed such a dream and were happy. As I have mentioned, our strategy and tactics emphasized "Forestalling and concentration" as precious mottoes. At the same time we believed in "Offense" as the best "Defense." But did they pay much attention to defense? It would not seem they did. The omission was conspicuous, notorious. The punishment came soon—telling, convincing, painful. This error found expression in the lack of understanding of, indifference and inattention to the problems of the maritime traffic protection, aerial defense, and the protection of warships and transports. These omissions have each one of them proved fatal to the life of the navy afterward. On the protection of maritime traffic and aerial defense I will dwell later. Here I will discuss only problems related to the protection of the warships and transports.

Since the *Queen Mary* and the *Indefatigable* of the British navy were sunk without much ado during World War I, all the naval powers have shown renewed interest in the study of this problem of the protection of the surface craft. Of the rest, the American navy's interest in this problem looked the keenest. Since the commencement of this war, considering the great liability of capital ships and carriers to conflagration, all the navies of the world have introduced a great reform. The counter-measures adopted by the American navy have been thorough and exhaustive, which has been proven in the absolute impregnability of the *Franklin* and the *Bunker Hill* in the battle of Okinawa.

Against such an attitude on the part of other navies, let us ask what our navy has done for its part. Look at the results. The *Yamato* and *Musashi*, the greatest capital ships of the world, displacing 60,000 tons and equipped with 18 inch guns, built under strict secrecy even from the Japanese naval personnel, were both sunk, one in the Battle

[*Page 14:*]

of Okinawa (April 1945) and the other in the Sibuyan Sea (October 1944), both by the American task forces. More surprising was the fiasco experienced at Midway in the course of 1942. The *Akagi, Kaga, Soryu,* and *Hiryu,* which indeed consti- tuted the hope of Japan, became just so many masses of fire before the attacks of the American forces. Very soon they disappeared from the surface of the water. The *Shinano,* which was originally intended to be the sister ship of the *Yamato* and the *Musashi,* but was later converted into a carrier, was sunk in the area south of Japan Proper toward the end of November 1944. The *Unryu,* laid on the keel soon after the Midway disaster, was sunk in the China Sea in the course of December 1944. All of these were victims of American submarines.

Our famous Zero Fighter was a perfectly defenseless plane. This feature is said to have amazed the American experts. Also we had a defenseless bomber which our pilots nicknamed "*ichishiki* lighter," it caught fire so easily. It was the nightmare of our pilots.

The above are some of the salient features of the Japanese navy's strategy and tactics. Now let me shift my eyes to other departments of the navy's functions.

THE WAR SERVICES OF THE JAPANESE NAVY

The term "war services" is made to include searches, scouting, patrolling, protection of sea transportation and other related services. To such a conception of the war services there may be objections on various grounds, but for our present purpose, this is enough.

The war services in themselves are dry, unostentatious works. But their impor- tance is supreme. Endurance, steadiness, and regularity characterize them. Without those qualities, no result can be accomplished. It was decreed, unfortunately, that the Japanese racial quality was not suitable for them. The Japanese like swashbuck- ling jobs

[*Page 15:*]

in which there is much "showing and thrill." The strategy and tactics based on the idea of a "decisive battle" is characteristically Japanese. The war services that called for steady, untiring, regular, quiet effort naturally had little interest for them. Few have studied how to develop efficiency with enough zeal. Those farsighted few who cried out to call attention to the importance of the war services just cried in the wilderness. Thus the war services were shamefully neglected and produced a con- sequence that proved irretrievable when the great moment came.

To start with the replenishment of supplies. Of the supplies, the most important was fuel. Japan does not produce her own fuel. Just before the outbreak of the war, about 6 million tons of oil was kept stored, which would last the navy for two years, the navy alone; the requirements of the army and for civil purposes exclusive. The army and the civil interests were not so sensitive as the navy in this respect. At the time of the outbreak of the war, the storage in their hands was rather poor.

The navy having been the largest fuel consumer, its voice carried the greatest influence, and it would be expected it had thought of the fuel requirements of the entire nation. But actually it did not. It minded its own business only, and when the war came and the army, the civil departments, industries and the general public began to run out of fuel, especially of liquid fuel, the navy was forced to accommodate those requirements out of its own stock.

If it was capable of such an oversight in such an important department of national requirements, one can well size up its caliber of attention in other respects.

The Japanese navy was planned exclusively on the "One Decisive Action" theory, and this idea led to a great oversight also in its

[*Page 16:*]

attention to the problem of cruising radius. Of the many warcraft that took part in the attack on Pearl Harbor, how many felt sure of their fuel supply? Could they compare against the American task forces that easily cruised about, comparatively carefree in this respect, one month, two months, attacking here, there, everywhere. What a vast difference, a difference "as between heaven and earth," as our idiom puts it! Shortly after the outbreak, there were fortunate occasions for the Japanese navy to engage in pursuit engagements. But always the poor cruising radius came in its way. Did not some of the commanders once in a while use this drawback as an excuse to cut short the pursuit?

A serious shortage was also revealed in ammunition supply. When the war broke out, all the craft departed from the various bases after loading more or less prescribed quantities of ammunition. After their departure the magazines at Yokosuka, Kure and Sasebo completely ran out of 25 mm machine-gun bullets. How often were we harassed during the whole course of the war by the want of ammunition! After the middle period of the war, the average quantity of ammunition for the anti-aircraft was (believe it or not) only 100 rounds (about 19 minutes and finis!), for the machine guns only 1,000 rounds (also about ten minutes), and no chance for replenishment. What wonder is there that our anti-aircraft and machine guns were completely overpowered by American air attacks?

What most seriously troubled the Japanese navy during the war was the difficulty in recruiting the crew. In the middle part of the war, the shortage of officers was keenly felt. The difficulty of the situation was beyond description. Since about the autumn of 1944, or the Philippine campaigns, we tried the attack by the so-called "Special

[*Page 17:*]

Attack Corps." Meantime, criticism began to make itself heard to the effect that the "Special Attack Corps" contained few graduates from the Naval School. This was true, but what we could not make public was the painful circumstance that most of the graduates from the Naval School young enough to join the "Special Attack Corps" had long since been dead. Of one class from one-half to two-thirds had been killed. Such a high death percentage was unprecedented. It became almost impossible even to supply the leaders for the "Special Attack Corps." Once in the course of 1944, I happened to be stationed in one of the South Sea islands where there were about 12,000 naval men, amongst whom the graduates from the Naval School counted only 15, of whom again those ranking below lieutenant were only two. One may well guess how rapidly we were running out of men. Had such a fear never occurred to the Personnel Bureau of the Navy Department before it was too late?

Again the status regarding the submarines and anti-submarine measures was even more exasperating. At the London conference of 1931, the equal ratio was agreed upon between Great Britain, the United States, and Japan. The submarine was Japan's main dependence, so great importance was attached to it. But here also the fatal "One Decisive Battle Theory" prevailed and influenced the whole scheme. Submarines were to be active in "the Decisive Engagement between Fleets," all plans were laid on this idea. Great Britain's hard experiences at the hands of German submarines during World War I were remembered, but not heeded. A mere memory!

Submarines' roles and activities in the war that was to come had not been envisioned clearly enough. Consequently the features of the future American-Japanese war were not studied thoroughly in relation to their activities. The thoughts were confined to the maneuvers on the

[*Page 18:*]

chessboard, no farther, no wider. When the real war came, what merits could be credited to the submarines farther than the sinking of the *Yorktown* in the area near Midway in 1942 and the *Wasp* in the Coral Sea and some other exploits not worth special notice? On the other hand, they committed ridiculous stupidities such as the long vigils they kept around the small bits of an island like Johnston, from time to time carrying out bombardments to break the tedium and seek diversions. Sending of scattered, almost aimless, shells into the State of Oregon is another piece of bright flashes that will fascinate a fool only. In the periods before the war, submarine exercises were confined to its roles in fleet engagements. We heard almost nothing about its function as a devastator of sea trade. On the contrary, was not the foundation of our strategy completely upset by the activities of American submarines?

Further, our anti-submarine tactics were shiftless beyond description. No efforts had been made in the study of counter-submarine measures except those visualized in fleet engagements, and even in this limited field they had not succeeded in hitting upon one single method that was sure and reliable. Not only that, they had consulted the American motion pictures and drawn the most self-complacent of conclusions, believe me! to the effect that Americans are people used to easy, luxurious habits, lacking the quality to endure the hard life in submarines, so we need have not much fear of them. This was our unique dependence in fighting the American underwater fighting forces. If we were not defeated, it would have been a miracle indeed! "Why invite the nightmare and let it disturb our comfort? Let us put a lid on distasteful subjects and forget about them." This was the idea.

Suppose one asked our naval authorities what they had thought of the British efforts against the German submarines during World War I, or the Joint British-American arduous study of the measures to cope

[Page 19:]

with the submarine dangers that became increasingly serious since the outbreak of World War II, or if they thought the fleet hastily improvised of trawlers and catcher-boats sufficient to combat American submarines? To such queries did they have any real answers full of convictions? I am sure they had none at all.

In 1930 Commander Frost, the treasure of the American navy, remarked about the submarine something to the effect that they were weapons fit for use by Americans, because Americans are possessed of all the requisite qualities for handling them—alacrity, decision, initiative, etc.—so if submarines easy to operate and capable of developing efficiency were given them, they would be sure to beat any other races in the successful operation of this type of vessel. He was right, right beyond all dispute. Did such a remark claim the attention even of a few seconds of our naval authorities? Did they regard and lightly pass over the experiences of John Paul Jones, this incarnation of American indomitableness and inflexibility, of the *Essex* during the British-American war, or of the *Alabama* in the American Civil War, the astounding exploits accomplished by them in the attack on marine traffic? Did they treat them as mere episodes to amuse their idle hours? The omissions were grave, almost criminal.

PREPARATIONS BY THE JAPANESE NAVY

General [Erich] Ludendorff spoke of "Total War." Kindred expressions came on the lips of the Japanese people about 1937 when the China Incident broke out. Total War, Defense state, Super-defense State etc. flooded the community. The Institute for the study of total war was created. In this movement the army led, the navy just followed in a mood rather apathetic.

[Page 20:]

The navy's idea of national defense was narrow. This narrowness came from the peculiar traditional conception of tactics. Under the influence of such a conception, they did not take much interest in the problem of total war. In fact, the circumstances of World War I, at least as far as the navy was concerned, were not of the nature to stimulate and develop the total war idea. In other words, they set before themselves the big chessboard called the Pacific Ocean, on which they put the chessmen and played maneuvers. They did nothing beyond that. The army's effort to develop the total war idea fell rather flat on the navy. Half asleep, they entered World War II. The defective ideas on preparedness and productive capacity, the serious lack of recognition in every respect, became threateningly conspicuous as the war went on. The errors looked irretrievable and found expressions in the dwarfish airplane production and lame marine transportation.

Airplane production capacity for 1941 was about 2,500 for the navy and the army respectively. Production of aluminum for the same year was 56,000 tons, which is a figure quite amazing—amazingly modest. The oil shortage was 8,000,000 tons. This was Japan's preparedness when she entered the modern war on her own hook. After the fall of Attu, Frank Knox, secretary of the U.S. Navy, is reported to have said, "Japan was either unable to understand modern war or not qualified to take part in it." This was about the correct sizing up of Japan's position at the time.

With regard to marine transportation capacity, they had never undertaken the study of this all-important subject. The navy at least had never studied it. I have never heard it had been undertaken anywhere. In the light of Britain's and America's bitter experience in marine transportation during World War I, from time to time there had been some

[*Page 21:*]

who dwelt on the gravity of this problem in the event of a war, but that went only so far and no farther. It was only a general and abstract dissertation. It is doubtful if anyone had imagined a particular war and computed the tonnage such a particular war would have required.

Then what about the navy's guidance of maritime transportation? Before the war there were built the superior "K" class freighters, built first by the Kawasaki Dockyard and then by other builders. This type of freighter was the first of its kind in the annals of the world's shipping. The navy gave subsidies so as to facilitate their conversion into seaplane tenders. I am interested to know what else the navy has done in its relation to shipping.

Now from another angle, what about the naval forces to be spared for the protection of sea traffic? Was our navy perfectly satisfied with the trawlers? If that is the case, they have learned nothing from the experience of other Powers in World Wars I and II. They have no excuse for such an oversight. Or if they entered the war, well knowing the inadequacy of such protection, their guilt and responsibility are appalling, unforgivable.

THE COOPERATION BETWEEN THE ARMY AND NAVY

At no time in the history of war was the importance of close cooperation between the army and navy so keenly felt as in the Pacific warfare during World War II. It was indispensable, imperative, urgent. The United States, which attained perfection in such cooperation, has triumphed. Japan, which has utterly failed in effecting it, has been beaten hollow. There is indeed no name for the utter mess the disunity between the army and navy brought about. Now let me ask what kind of studies had been undertaken about such cooperation between the two

[*Page 22:*]

arms of the defense forces before the war. Just some very limited, localized attempts. There was the exchange of college teachers between the army and navy to study such cooperation. Also some maneuvers were practiced by joint forces of college students, but even this only insofar as regarding landing operations. Just an academic item to fill up the curriculum! A joint study of the broader aspect of the problem in anticipation of a particular war had never been undertaken.

Instead of cooperation, the army had studied how to protect its position against the navy, and vice versa. Their mutual studies in this direction were extensive and thorough. The spirit of rivalry just got the better of both of them. Little else was left in their minds. To expect from such misguided parties a study, however cursory, of cooperation in the event of war with the United States was out of the question. The case of landing operations excepted, the cooperation between the army and navy on a broad strategical line in the event of war with the United States had never become an object of serious study before the war.

When the war started, instead of cooperation, opposition and antagonism characterized every feature of relations between the army and navy. The enmity was especially marked in the defense of Japan Proper. The navy stood for absolute resistance based on purely academic arguments, leaving concrete practical details entirely out of regard, while the army, showing very lukewarm interest (in the navy's estimate) in the Pacific war, advocated concentration of efforts around the Marshalls and Marianas. The latter's main aim was the reinforcement of the supply route. Heated discussions ensued. To an observer in a detached position, the army's contention looked right, but true to the traditions, without enough justifying reasons the navy did not yield to the army's views. The two were just like ice and fire, no chance of a compromise.

[*Page 23:*]

As regards air defense, the navy was far in advance of the army, in both thought and practice. Conscious of this superiority, the navy demanded priority. The army, just for face's sake, insisted on equality. The two bickered and fell out at every chance. This nonconformity weakened Japan's defense system just like a cancer. This circumstance is public property. The country suffered. In working out the details of operations and war services, collisions and irritations were multitudinous, piling up mountain high. I will cite some other examples. Since autumn 1943 the army planned a submarine transportation system. They remembered the bitter experiences undergone by surface craft in the conveyance of supplies to the Solomons and New Guinea since autumn of 1942. For the construction of these submarine transports, they had to engage shipbuilders that had had almost no experience of submarine building, as the builders that had taken orders for submarines building for the navy were all engaged, not available. Reckless enough! The whole plan ended in a complete fiasco. It could not be otherwise in the nature of things.

As regards serial warfare, the navy and the army were just like enemies. They hated each other, almost fought. Exchange of secrets and experiences, the common use of airplanes and other instruments, could not even be thought of.

The disagreement, lack of understanding and cooperations between the army and the navy are among the most important causes that led to our swift defeat. A fat book could be written on this subject, were the materials available.

THE JUDGMENT ON THE ESSENTIAL FEATURES
OF THIS WAR

What sort of features did our navy visualize and anticipate as to the development of the war? To confess the shameful truth, the picture

[*Page 24:*]

they had drawn on their mental canvas was nothing but a decisive battle between the two massed fleets. I have already touched this point when I dwelt on the education in the Naval College. I will add here another instance. The navy's basic strategy of the war was built around the idea of one decisive battle between the massed fleets under the walls of the unsinkable fortresses (islands) of the Mariana group. Laudable efforts were made on the study of such a strategy. But the fundamental solution of this problem really depended on the treatment of the Marshall Islands which constitutes the advance post of the Mariana group.

When we adopted a decisive fleet battle strategy based around the Mariana group, the American navy was sure to proceed and attack in the direction of the Marshalls in the first place. Taking such a strategy on the part of the American navy for granted, the first problem we were to solve was whether the Marshalls were to be given up or not. Two birds could not be struck with one stone. One had to be given up. A quick decision had to be taken; however, no decision was taken. To this all-important problem they never paid attention worthy of the name. The preparations for their pet ''Decisive Battle'' around the Marianas ought then to have been fairly good. For them, obsessed with this idea, we would naturally expect this, but that was not the case. They were the slave of One-Big-Battle idea, but the preparations they made for it did not go much beyond the ''Blueprint Stage.'' Ideas were poor, leadership sorrowfully ineffectual in every respect.

And when the war actually broke out, they were suddenly and rudely awakened to every defect, felt as if they were taken by surprise and cried aloud in distress. Shame! They got just what their inattention deserved. Even to such important items as the supply provision, reinforcement of the Marianas fortifications etc., which the Decisive Battle

[*Page 25:*]

should necessarily have involved, they were criminally inattentive. Such a deplorable state of affairs was undeniably due to the failure to anticipate along broader lines the feature of the naval war that would be fought. It had never occurred to our naval authorities to make a thorough study from this angle. They had committed a serious crime of omission and got a punishment which they rightly deserved. And then, when the B29, the radar, the atomic bomb came to greet them, they just stood aghast, stunned with surprise, lost in thought with folded arms, their hands hastening for the sword with which to kill themselves in despair. Pity! The causes responsible for such omissions are galore, of which the Japanese war records is certainly among the most important.

In the Sino-Japanese war of 1894, in the Russo-Japanese war of 1904, favorable circumstances blessed them with victories, but a close study will reveal the fact that in these two wars the Japanese navy was not put to such severe tests as the American navy had been in its war with Britain in the past century. Our victories took very much of the nature of good luck, while American victories in their past wars on the sea were wrung with desperate efforts from the hands of hard fate. They fought a grim fight and triumphed. Ours were won certainly with stiff fighting, even then there were plenty of elements of luck. Moreover, it would be clear to a detached observer that the importance of the naval victories in the above two wars look rather exaggerated. For the final victory in the war as a whole, a large credit must be given to other circumstances that had little to do with the naval battles. For the final surrender of the Imperial Chinese government, the annihilation of the Chinese fleet in Wai-hai-ei was one of the important causes, but not all the causes. It would be more appropriate to say that the Imperial Chinese government surrendered to its own debility. It became

[*Page 26:*]

suddenly aware of its own hopeless impotence and sued for peace. Likewise did it fare in the Russo-Japanese war. The decisive victory of the Battle of the Japan Sea was one of the potent factors for the early return of peace, but the direct and most important factors were the anxiety of the Romanoffs for the safety of the throne amidst the many threatening symptoms of a nearing revolution and the powerful hand of Mr. Theodore Roosevelt, who used his good offices between the warring nations. The Japanese navy had certainly attached too much importance to factors of lesser merit. Dazzled by the brilliant victories, they concluded erroneously that victory was brought about solely by the single stroke of a decisive engagement. A blind belief that spelled disaster!

The navy's appraisal of merits was quite out of focus. In the education at the Naval College, the great figure of Admiral Heihachiro Togo was always the center of homage. The students were taught to believe Japan won the sea fight chiefly because of Togo's supreme leadership throughout. On the other hand, the figure of Admiral Gombei Yamamoto was entirely overlooked. In spite of his insuperable merit, the latter had been left somewhat out in the cold by the navy. He was not even created a fleet admiral. Such an atmosphere pervaded the entire navy. Togo's calligraphy was especially coveted. His busts were in evidence everywhere. There are almost no calligraphies of Admiral Yamamoto to be seen anywhere—he rarely wrote as a calligrapher. This circumstance of apparently little significance speaks a great deal. Admiral Yamamoto was the man who created the navy that crushed the sea forces of Imperial Russia. He deserves merit No. 1; at least he should rank equal with Admiral Togo.

[*Page 27:*]

OUR IDEAS ABOUT AMERICA AND GREAT BRITAIN

"Those who know the enemy as well as ourselves never suffer defeat," says Sun, the great Chinese strategist. The navy, which abides by his teachings, had always studied the American navy with deep interest. The army had paid little attention to America.

The histories of the American and European wars formed one of the curricula of the Naval College. A good amount of time is allotted to this course. Compared with that, the study of modern America by the Japanese army may be called almost "indifferent." In the army's purview there was no other Power except Russia.

Rashly and headlong, they went exclusively at Russia, Russia only! They forgot everything else.

Here is an episode to show how very cool the army's interest was in the study of modern America. When in the course of 1943 the initial activities in North Africa of the M4 (Sherman) tank, the pride of the American army, were reported, I put a question to a professor of the Military College who used to come to the Naval College to teach tank warfare, asking what measure the army had in mind to cope with this new weapon. He replied he did not know what the M4 tank was. The great authority in the Japanese army on tank fighting did not know the M4! You can guess the rest.

On the contrary, the Japanese navy had always studied the American and the British navies. By studying and emulating their examples, it had attained a considerable development. In the study of strategy, we knew pretty well our enemies' potentials. The examples frequently cited of Admirals Farragut's and Dewey's heroic behaviors in dashing across the mine fields used to cause the blood of our young officers to boil with the spirit of emulation. The blocking of Port Arthur during the Russo-Japanese war of 1904–05 took its cue in a large measure from the

[*Page 28:*]

American example at Santiago during the Spanish-American war. Commander Akiyama, who was a member of the naval staff at the time of the Russo-Japanese war, had studied the American naval tactics in the Spanish-American war when he stayed in Washington as an attaché in 1898. The blocking of Santiago gave him an especially deep impression. A few years later, he blocked the Russian fleet in Port Arthur.

Pearl Harbor was the grave where it was the dear ambition of all young naval officers to be buried. In the attack on it, nine had met the fate they had so dearly wished. Who knows their challenge was really the example set on 27 February 1865 by Lieutenant Jackson when he dashed on the small *David* into Charleston Harbor? But here also can be traced a hint of the naval tactics in the narrow sense which formed the tradition of our navy.

In the study of the two navies of both Britain and America alike, they have limited their attention to naval tactics in the narrow, limited sense. For instance, the measures adopted by the American navy at the time of World War I, such as the speedy expansion of naval armament through quick building and training, did not leave a lasting impression on our naval mind. How these factors constituted great elements in America's naval strategy, how they influenced the progress of events all through the war, points like these did not particularly interest our navy! They were just surprised and that was the end of it. Likewise it fared in the study of the British navy. They took interest in the battles of Jutland, of Dogger Bank, the landing operations at Dardanelles, in the blocking of Zeebrugge etc., while such problems as the devastation wrought on the Allies' sea traffic by German submarines, the counter-measures adopted against it, the influence of German warfare on

[*Page 29:*]

Britain's political and economic conditions, on the circumstances which did not allow Britain to take positive measures against the menace, but forced her to remain satisfied with counter-measures of just negative character, indeed such problems of far-reaching consequence never did arouse much interest in the minds of our navy men. I do not know how to account for such an omission. Moreover, they studied almost nothing about the American army and the British army!

After the outbreak of war, the harassment they underwent at the hands of the air arm of the American army was indeed immeasurable. Before the war started, how much time and effort had they devoted to the study of the American air forces, how much fighting potential had the Japanese navy attached to this branch of America's fighting power? It looks like it did not worry about such questions.

A GENERAL JUDGMENT

When Ambassadors Nomura and Kurusu were conducting negotiations at Washington in the late season of 1941, the key to the serious question whether or not we should go to war with America was in some sense held by our navy. In the event of such a war, the chief role was of course the navy's, not the army's. If the navy had firmly objected to the opening of the war, certainly the army could have done nothing, however violent, rash, and reckless was the attitude of its radical elements. Whatever leadership was under the army's control at the time, could they come to any decision, with the navy showing a resolute opposition? No!

At this crucial moment, what did our navy do? They left the decision of this grave problem to the decision of Premier Konoye. What lack of the sense of responsibility when the very existence of the empire hung in the balance! It is reported that the navy took such an attitude because they knew Premier Konoye had been opposed to the war. Why did they not show their opposition positively, in no ambiguous language? "Out of

[*Page 30:*]

regard for the army's feelings," it is further reported. If this report is true, our navy had only the army on its mind. It forgot the empire!

When at last they adopted the momentous decision, they had Admiral Shimada, as the Navy Minister of the Tojo Cabinet, assume all responsibility for it. Admiral Shimada is a character of the so-called "Oriental Hero Type," just rough-hewn, lacking precision of thought and a clear-cut sense of responsibility in the western sense of the word. To have selected such a misfit as a minister to represent the navy was in itself a fatal blunder, for which the leader of the navy back of him should answer.

How did the leaders of the navy facing this stupendous crisis conceive the American-Japanese war on which the curtain was just lifting? It is impossible to know how, but we may guess almost correctly from the angle of the education they had gone through. I have been put through the same system of education, so I can easily put myself in their position and imagine the picture of the American-Japanese war in their mind. I will try to guess their minds by their surroundings.

Of course, there are individual differences in the reaction to the influence of the surroundings, but such influence can be sometimes too powerful for such individual differences to make themselves felt, individuality all engulfed and absorbed and annihilated. Exactly this was the case. The current was sweeping, overpowering. Individuals were just overwhelmed, obliterated. This is my conclusion, from the surroundings and traditions I have already described. I am convinced my conclusion is correct. The navy just drifted into the war by inertia.

Our navy has committed a great omission in sizing up America's war potentiality. The leaders of the navy had imagined "One Big Battle," further than which they could not think. In them the American-Japanese

[*Page 31:*]

war was the American-Japanese *battle,* whence I have derived the title of this booklet. I say this because if we had considered our positions from a cool, detached viewpoint, it should have been quite clear that there was not one chance against a hundred that we could win a war against America. There was not one iota of hope. In the initial stages we might have secured a couple of victories, but after that how could we have forced such a huge, resourceful country as America to sue for peace? It was impossible. The impossibility was manifest to the man in the street. But according to the judgment based on the navy's pet "One Big Battle" idea, the year 1941 was the most propitious year to enter upon the war with America. In the imagination of our navy leaders there was an "American-Japanese Great Naval Maneuver," to be carried out according to the schedule and finished in a week with themselves ultimately coming out triumphant.

Our navy scanned the battlefield of Europe where the German Nazis were making a stiff fight. On the Pacific chessboard which they pictured to themselves, the Japanese navy could hold a superior position. After the occupation of Hawaii, the Japanese naval task force would have been the most powerful fighting power afloat. The "Zeke" was also the airplane that would have set defiance to any airplane that so far had appeared on earth. The storage of heavy oil ran nearly 6 million tons. Furthermore, as far as fuel was concerned, as the supply was already definitely cut off as a result of economic severance declared by the United States, a day's delay spelled a day's disadvantage.

As one Jingo put it, "Missing this opportunity, Japan is headed for sure ruin. This is the one supreme moment. Now or never! Japan is at the crossroads! We must make a supreme decision!"

Boiled down, this cast of thought amounts to this: "Missing this

[*Page 32:*]

chance, there will never come another chance for an American-Japanese Great Naval Maneuver on the Pacific!"

Underneath there lurked the idea: "Unless we stood up now, should we not lose our face to the army, to which we are several years in advance in fighting preparedness? If we let slip this opportunity, our position would become untenable against 'America'? No! Against the Army'?" I cannot but suspect that such was the navy men's mentality, when we boil it down to its essence. Whether they were conscious of this or not, that is another problem.

Until late in the autumn of 1941, the Nazis' offensives were successful everywhere. They rolled up the whole of Europe before their sweeping onslaught. A chance came when they directed their attack on the Soviet Union. They began to wilt before the Russian dogged tenacity, were checked, began to retreat. Their war aim was entirely baffled. Thus the European situation began to indicate a serious aspect. Came the turning point.

Judging from the angle of the European situation, Japan's offensive started in the winter of 1941 was not a wise move. Those who started it saw only the draughtsmen on the chessboard, not those waiting outside (available resources), much less the thoughts taking shape in the brains of the American opponent.

Apart from this, did the all-important question of how to wind up the war ultimately ever occur to their half-infatuated mind? Perhaps it did. Perhaps vague uneasiness threw a shadow on their minds. Did they try to forget such an uneasiness by chanting Chinese epic poems of classic antiquity with a hoarse voice? Chinese classics furnish plenty of heroic passages of little practical use but aptly fit for those trying to seek shelter from the bogey of their own threatening nightmares. Those gripped

[*Page 33:*]

in the clutches of a nightmare shout to scare away the hideous shadow of a demon. Did some of the great leaders of our navy not emulate such examples?

"Let us seek life in death itself!"

"Before a supreme decision, even a demon shrinks."

"Here lies a serpent athwart my path. I have drawn my invincible blade to cut it in twain. Down comes the stroke. The snake just stirred. But lo! It was the tip of the beard of a huge dragon!" The hero sang himself hoarse. The discovery made his knees give way!

Would-be heroes in an oriental fable keep such passages ready in their memory so they may repeat them aloud when checkmated, to hide their own confusion. The mental cast of an opium fiend! I am sure our leaders of the navy tried to "seek life in death," to stake the whole issue on the chance of "One Big Battle." They set forth to stake the 2,600 years in one suicidal stroke. What an adventure, what a stupid idea, a silliness that surpasses one's imagination!

CHAPTER II

The war that was started on such a miscalculation has developed into the war that we have discovered. It has been a severe, dangerous, intense, breathtaking, cruel and by and by a losing, hopeless, and finally an annihilating war, and the annihilated party was the party that started it. To our adversary it was far from being such a war; even the remarkable success accomplished at Pearl Harbor, undoubtedly the greatest success through the entire period of the war, did mercilessly expose the weakness of the Japanese navy. For the systematic progress of this comment on the naval war, a discussion here of the Pearl Harbor attack would be very helpful. So I will do it.

[*Page 34:*]

LESSONS OF THE BATTLE OF HAWAII

On 26 November 1941 our fleet started from Hitokappu Bay of the Kurile Island group. It sailed due east across the Pacific. The waves were high. At dawn of 8 December, from the north of the Hawaii islands flew 360-odd planes up into still-dark skies and dashed a surprise attack on the American Pacific Fleet anchored there and the air forces. The result was brilliant. We succeeded in destroying the greater part of the American airplanes and most of the larger units of the American navy that happened to be there. On our part the loss was negligible indeed. We lost only 29 aircraft and one submarine engaged in scouting at the mouth of the harbor. As a battle it was an unrivalled success; however, the value was questionable from the war standpoint, as a way to start a war against Great America.

The attack was to be started after the declaration of war. But due to some impediment in communications, it has actually turned out to be an attack without notice, just a sneak attack and was branded as such. The navy had become a violator of international law. This single circumstance was fatal to Japan's honor on the one hand, while it aroused the martial spirit of the entire American people, adding infinitely to their fighting power. In the impact on the American mind, "Remember the Maine" must have paled into nothingness as compared with "Remember Pearl Harbor." At the moment when the leaders of the navy devised such a tactic, did it occur to any single one of them for one single moment how such a mode of attack would work on the American mind?

Then did they utilize the result of the first attack for the subsequent operations of the war? In the first place, why did they not follow it up with a close second? And a third? Was a landing possible?

[*Page 35:*]

At the time of the outbreak I was serving as a staff member in charge of the construction of the so-called "Hope of Japan," the battleship *Musashi* at Nagasaki of later atomic bomb fame. When I heard over the radio of the attack on Pearl Harbor, my whole nerve just tingled. I remember indulging in a discussion on the abovementioned two points with some of my friends. One conclusion was that they should have followed the advantage without letting the enemy catch its breath. As it actually was, this did not take place. Admiral Nagumo, who then commanded the task force, gathered the units and withdrew from the battle areas without trying a second coup. Why such a course of tactics? The reasons may be guessed as follows:

1. First was the problem of fuel. Of the units taking part in the attack, those that could operate on their own fuel supply were only the carriers *Kaga*, *Shokaku* and *Zuikaku*, the battleships *Hiei* and *Kirishima*, the cruisers *Tone* and *Chikuma*. As regards the light cruisers such as the *Abukuma* and the destroyers, it had been planned to give them up in midocean in case fuel could not be replenished at sea. This difficulty besetting the fuel supply was certainly one of the important causes that prevented the navy from carrying out the second attack on Hawaii.

2. The lost airplanes were only 29, but the damaged ones that called for repair

were pretty many. We did not have ready sufficient numbers with which to deliver the second attack. In other words, our navy had thought of just one attack.

3. "We have given a crushing blow. We have made a record which is enough. The adventure of the second attack is not worth the risk, is not necessary." This is the philosophy. They thought and argued in altogether Japanese fashion, the mentality of our champion wrestler in

[Page 36:]

the national *Sumo* game, triumphantly retiring amid handslaps and acclamation from the ring. Just like a wrestler in such a position, our navy felt their business was through. They were playing a game, just sporting. A chase, a pursuit—such ideas were entirely alien to their minds. This will furnish the answer to the question why they did not undertake a landing. They had not even dreamed of it.

In reaping the full harvest of a victory the navy's thought lacked thoroughness and perfection in such a way. Much less did it occur to them to derive useful lessons from such experiences for future improvement. They never did mercilessly, critically, thoroughly pass this great experience under severe examination and appraise the results. On the contrary, it may even be said this spectacular victory even poisoned the navy's mind and put it on the track of their final undoing. The victory was so great that the elation expelled victory irrevocably.

Two days later, on 10 December off Malay, the navy's air forces attacked the *Prince of Wales,* the British dreadnought flying the flag of Admiral Phillips, and the *Repulse,* with the remarkable success of sinking both of them almost instantly. This phenomenal success has demonstrated the enormous values of the air forces and the task forces. It meant a revolution in naval warfare. But has our navy continued their effort in this direction farther on? Alas, no! They made some endeavors to increase the production of airplanes, but not of carriers. The serious effort to increase the carriers started after the loss of the *Akagi, Kaga, Soryu* and *Hiryu* in the attack on Midway. Only after this terrific disaster did they set about building carriers with bloodshot eyes.

As I have mentioned already, at the time of the Pearl Harbor attack I was in Nagasaki serving as a staff member attending to the construction

[Page 37:]

of the battleship *Musashi.* Alongside, the *Izumo Maru,* the would-be Japan's No. 1 passenger steamer, was being converted into a carrier named *Junyo.* The naval staff and all the personnel of the dockyard engaged in the building of this latter had to make room, so to speak, for those engaged in the construction of the battleship *Musashi.* The latter looked so much more important, carried in the consciousness they were attending to a job of minor importance so much more prestige. The demonstration beyond dispute of the tremendous value of the carriers in those two memorable engagements did not destroy this complex. The navy's mind was so slow to change, the slave of inertia!

Further, they had made no very serious study in the operation of the task forces. In other words, they admitted nothing but the anthem of the "Irresistible Imperial navy" that began to be chanted in a general sort of way all over Japan since 1940.

They became simply puffed up, self-conceited, vain, a damned fool. The great superiority of the different types of aircraft that took part in the attack on Pearl Harbor could be admitted. There were perhaps no matches for them in the entire world about this time. But the excessive confidence in their abilities soon changed into making light of others and the evaporation of the spirit of emulation.

Against this, what did the American navy learn? At the time we could know nothing except the relieving of Admiral Kimmel of his post and the opening of the Investigation Committee to pry into the cause of the Pearl Harbor disaster. But the subsequent activities of the American sea forces all over the Pacific area are quite eloquent of what lessons the American navy learned from this experience. One year after the signing of the armistice, reading the announcement by the Pearl

[*Page 38:*]

Harbor Investigation Committee of the result of their investigations we felt deeply struck by the excellently scientific attitude with which the American government has treated this problem. Our complete defeat was in the due course of matter. Now that we can account for our defeat, we have behaved just to concede the victory to the Americans. If our navy had been in America's place, would they have taken the attitude the Americans did take? By all means, No!

We scored a victory of which we could well be proud, but subsequently we committed a blunder that more than offset the brilliance of the early victory. America, [which] had suffered a terrible calamity at first, secured from it a moral benefit that far outweighed the material damages. I will discuss the series of blunders committed by our navy subsequently on the battlefield of the Pacific.

THE JAPANESE NAVY'S CLEVERNESS IN HANDICRAFT WORK

In the broad, comprehensive survey of the American-Japanese war, our navy had committed a stupendous error that has ultimately cost the national existence, but within the framework of this narrow "One Big Battle" conception, it has made an accomplishment worth unstinted commendation. But this accomplishment was available only during the short initial period. After this period was over, the fundamental, greater errors in the survey of the general situation begat one error after another until the attainment in the field of small handicrafts was rendered useless.

In the attack on the two British battleships off Malay two days after Pearl Harbor, about eighty navy planes took part. They displayed a feat that almost revolutionized aerial warfare. Later our *Musashi* and *Yamato* underwent a similar experience at the hands of the American task forces. The German *Tirpitz* met the same fate, at the hands of

[*Page 39:*]

British heavy bombers.

In the initial stage of the war, the Zero fighters did develop great efficiency. They went far south from the tip of Formosa, holding control of the skies of Manila, and in two short months brought pressure to bear on the Dutch East Indies. Even allowing for the lack of preparedness on the part of the Allies, this was a great accomplishment. Later investigations have revealed the damages suffered by our air forces figured considerably less than what had been anticipated by the authorities. They were agreeably surprised. The rates of our damages were one-tenth of those on the part of the Allies, which fact gave rise to the view that on the Japanese navy's Pacific chessboard the strength of the Zero Fighters was ten times as powerful as the American air forces.

When in 1942 the United States navy, as the first step of turning from defense to offense, landed its crack First Marine Corps under [Vice Adm.] R. L. Ghormley, just like the proverbial bolt out of the blue, in the corners of Tulagi and Guadalcanal Islands, our cruiser squadron was at anchor under Vice Admiral Mikawa in Rabaul. Composed of the A-class cruiser *Chokai* and the B-class cruisers *Kinugasa, Kako, Aoba, Furutaka,* two more light cruisers, and one destroyer—altogether eight in number—with a show of fighting spirit sweeping everything before it, the squadron heaved anchor on the night of 8 August, sped south to Guadalcanal like a hurricane and rushed on the American fleet under Rear Admiral Crutchley consisting of the *Vincennes, Quincy, Astoria, Chicago*—and the Australian cruiser *Canberra*.

The battle of Savo Island took place. "Cutting down whatever came within reach," as we say it, displaying our navy's superb dexterity in the night attack, beat the American fleet wherever we met, sinking all the enemy war vessels except the *Chicago,* then cruising around west to east off the southern tip of Savo Island, fought through in the most

[*Page 40:*]

brilliant manner. The quickness of decision and action, the dashing spirit, displayed on this occasion was really a trick of light, a legerdemain. That was verily a great power that made all this possible. "The Tokyo Express," so called by the Allies in those days, started from this venture and continued until about the middle of 1943. All in all, it was a brave show. Nevertheless, experts wondered why on this occasion Vice Admiral Mikawa did not double back, follow up the advantage of such a brilliant victory and make a clean sweep of the Lunga anchorage. About this I will write later.

Since the landing of the American troops on Guadalcanal, the sea areas around the Solomon group became the focus of the American-Japanese naval warfare. Here the sea forces of the contending parties were concentrated. The Japanese navy had not yet completely recovered from the great disaster suffered at Midway. It was building the Third Fleet to take the place of the carrier squadron that was shattered and annihilated around Midway. It was, however, decided to send what had been already completed of this Third Fleet to the Solomons area. The great opportunity was fast ripening. Frank Knox, secretary of the Navy, sensed the development and predicted the nearness of a decisive engagement in the Solomons area. Our navy on its part also took warning, felt determination becoming ever more steel-like.

On the night of 25 October 1942, the main force of the Third Fleet was sailing in solemn silence southeastward in the area northwest of the Solomons, without noticing at the time that it was heading toward the trap set by the American navy. They were not aware of the American night contact planes that were constantly escorting them. Theirs might have been the fate of a rushlight before the wind. If they had continued steering in that way, by the dawn of 28 October they must have become the

[Page 41:]

target of a concentrated American attack, and the situation should have attained a completely different development, but it was not so decreed. An American airplane, perhaps by mistake, dropped bombs, very fortunately for us. We now feel like interpreting this step as an error, as then our fleet that had been fated for destruction would get full credit for snatching the laurel of victory from the hands of the American navy on which fortune had been smiling.

The bomb attracted the notice of Admiral Nagumo, who was the commander-in-chief at the time of the Pearl Harbor attack and now of the Third Fleet. He ordered the whole fleet to turn around. He had judged the American fleet to be near. He gave the second order to the entire fleet to make ready for an attack in the morning. This was a Parthian-like counterattack which turned out to be quite successful. We sank the *Hornet,* the regular carrier from which flew the air forces under Doolittle that raided Tokyo on 18 April 1942. We inflicted further pretty substantial damages on the American fleet. On our part, we suffered damages to the *Shokaku* and the *Ryujo,* both carriers, from bombs, but we succeeded in putting out the fire before it did much harm. It was an engagement very dangerous, to say the least. Tactically this was a defeat for us. We escaped a disaster merely by a sleight-of-hand that we had practiced a good many years. But such luck coming from a long-practiced trick of course could not long continue. This was about the last success. Like infantile paralysis, our limbs gradually became numbed and shrank.

There was just one other successful piece of hand tricks. This was about a fortnight after the battle of Santa Cruz in the course of the Guadalcanal fights. It is known among us as the Third Solomon Battle. It happened this way:

[Page 42:]

About the same time as the sea battle around Santa Cruz, we were giving the third general attack on the Guadalcanal airfield with a division of land forces, which ended in failure before the terrific gunfire of the American Marine Corps. A reinforcement was sent. In consequence of such operation by our army, our navy planned a positive measure of attack on the same island, which invited a counterattack from the American navy. An engagement resulted.

On 12 November 1942, a squadron consisting of the battleships *Hiei* and *Kirishima,* one light cruiser and 14 destroyers undertook the attack on Henderson airfield. Our purpose was the frustration of the Guadalcanal air bases. Through a squall and utter darkness we steered. Before midnight we reached a point south of Savo Island, whence we trained our guns on Henderson airfield. They were loaded with special shells for airfield bombardment. Elevated high up, gunners were waiting for the order to fire, when the American fleet appeared on this side of the airfield, rather close to the mouth of the Lunga River. Directly a change of aim was ordered. The *Hiei*'s searchlights began to throw lights.

A free-for-all fight without any precedent in the record of sea battles developed.

The American fleet commanded by Vice Admiral Callaghan consisted of the *Atlanta*, the *San Francisco*, the *Portland*, the *Helena*, the *Juneau* (all cruisers) and 8 destroyers. They had been waylaying the Japanese fleet. The ships fought at close quarters, almost falling aboard of each other. It was chaos, confusion. Some destroyers crossed the enemy lines. We missed the antiquated rams very badly. We lost the *Hiei* and two destroyers. She was hit in the steering room, into which the sea leaked. In the afternoon it hung around by Savo Island. Toward the evening it was sunk by air attacks.

[*Page 43:*]

The damage on America's part was also serious. According to her official announcement, the American navy lost 2 cruisers and 4 destroyers, suffered some more damages. Nevertheless, they succeeded in preventing the Japanese from bombarding the airfields. Looked at [it] from our angle, we not only failed to attain the primary object we had gone out for, we had just managed to escape disaster by a sort of sleight-of-hand, an outmoded operation which still at this late date could display some effect. Two days later, there took place a battleship engagement again in the area adjacent to Guadalcanal on which occasion our favorite sleight-of-hand ceased to tell any more.

During July 1943 there was fought a series of engagements between the two navies' light craft around Jula Bay and Colombangara Island on the occasions when the American forces came to attack in the direction of New Georgia. In these battles our training and favorite game surrendered completely before American science and new weapons. We lost a large number of light craft. These areas came to be called "The Graveyard of Japanese destroyers."

After the battle of Santa Cruz, the American and the Japanese naval forces did not meet for two years. When we met again in June of 1944 when America came to take the Marianas, what a change! The American navy and the Japanese were then as alike as cheese and chalk. Our fleet under Vice Admiral Ozawa's command consisted of the double-armored carrier *Taiho, Shokaku, Zuikaku* (alike regular carriers) and six auxiliary carriers. The fleet looked majestic but was sadly poor in real fighting power. Since 1942 we had fought hard and continuously in the directions of the Solomons, Marianas, Marshalls, under a pressure that never relented. America had given us no breathing space. After Pearl Harbor the recovery of American sea power was astoundingly rapid. Amer-

[*Page 44:*]

ica's stupendous industrial efficiency left us far, far in the rear. Through their experience of the Gilberts, Marshalls, Solomons, New Guinea, the American navy had become an institution invincible in defense, irresistible in offense. The difference between the two contending navies became world-wide. We had to fight a dwarf's battle against a giant.

About this time we undertook a plan of attack very similar to what Americans call a "Shuttle Attack." We had not meant to copy the American prototype. The "Shuttle" was to travel back and forth between the Japanese carrier squadron gathered to the east of the Philippines and our bases around Guam Island. The sharp-eyed Americans quickly saw through our scheme. When our airplanes flew up from the carriers about 500 miles west of the Marianas, the American aircraft had anticipated them, gone ahead and waited in the skies over Guam, where ours were to land scant of fuel and munitions, after a long flight, in the course of which they delivered the planned attack on the targets on their route. Theirs were fresh, full of vigor. Ours were used up, tired out. One after another they fell victims to the American fighters. In one single day, the Japanese carrier forces just vanished.

In those days, on the Marianas bases were kept spread the newly-organized First Aerial Force, the treasure of the navy, under the command of Vice Admiral Kakuta, the most intrepid of the Japanese navy's soldiers. This squad was the crackest of the cracks in the navy's command. Each type that composed it was given a name emblematic of its character. The fighters included such names as "Tiger," "Panther," and the like, the attack corps consisted of "Hawks," "Dragons," and so forth. "Pheasant" was found among the scouting planes. This was really the hope of the navy. Up until the beginning of 1944 they kept

[*Page 45:*]

an independent position of their own, not coming under the command of the commander-in-chief of the Combined Fleet. They belonged directly to the navy's General Headquarters. They had kept on training day after day waiting for the "Day."

When the Marshalls fell, and the fall of the Marianas looked imminent, they went out on the Pacific arena as the defender of the foremost front. This was about the same time as the first sally of the American forces in the attack on the Marianas, 23 February 1944. The navy's expectation from this particular aerial corps had been great indeed!

In May 1944, they met in conference in Manila to discuss the operations of the next period. I took part in it. I put the following question to the operations Chief of the First Air Fleet staff.

"Captain, we will depend on you."

"Do! We will show you what we can."

"Will it be the double?" said I to him, who is very fond of cards.

"Yes, yes!" he answered back excitedly. "Yes, yes! It is going to be the double, re, re, re, re-double."

The result, however, was "down, down, all down!" It was an annihilation.

The "Tokyo Express," which demonstrated some results in the Solomon area in the course of 1942, gradually paled before the fast-improving scouting operation on the part of the American navy. The radar in particular was an anathema to it. In 1944 in Leyte the two battleships *Yamashiro* and *Fuso,* the *Mogami* (cruiser), and 3 destroyers disappeared altogether, except only one destroyer, in an instant. Of this squadron almost nothing was traced except TB boats.

It was as if they fell victim to some magic. We began to lose con-

[*Page 46:*]

fidence in ourselves, a positive self-contempt. The last thing welcome to a soldier came to possess him—"Fear!" After the Battle of Leyte, there even appeared a convoy commander who showed hesitation and reluctance, a phenomenon that had never been witnessed in our navy.

In July 1945, the *Haguro,* a cruiser that survived the Leyte disaster, undertook transportation in force from Andaman Island, met four British destroyers in Malacca Strait at night and was sunk.   It was a battle which to the Japanese side only was an unexpected encounter. To the enemy it was a planned engagement. Pitiful is the status of a fighter who has lost all confidence in himself!

IF THEY GAVE US A MONTH MORE TO PREPARE!

What were the main causes that have robbed the Japanese navy, once so full of spirit, so sure of itself, now made it so passive, nervous, even tremulous? The American war-engine that progressed from day to day, the scale of production that we could not even dream of, against this the slowness in the training of crews, slowness, smallness, narrowness in everything on our part—well, there were factors galore. But of all of these by far the most important was the tremendous speed of the American operations.

Not once or twice but many a time, we were chagrined to see the speedy actions by the enemy completely frustrating at the last minute the final great fruit of our labors, ceaseless and arduous, extending over a period of weeks and months, involving plenty of bloodshed and material sacrifices. On such occasion the bitterness of disappointment just drove us crazy. It was not difficult for us to foresee approximately the directions, the dates or the character of the enemy's next moves and operations, but our surveys and speculations lacked accuracy and precision. Always there was some slip. They always came when we did not expect them.

[*Page 47:*]

The ideas of the Japanese strategists became exclusively defensive only when Rabaul was forced into inaction between the pressure from the East, from the direction of the Solomons (early in 1944) by way of New Georgia (1943), an operation that developed from the defensive-offensive actions started in the summer of 1942 at a corner of the Solomons, and the aerial flanking movement directed from the west by way of Lae and Salamoa in New Guinea. If they had had a broader strategic understanding of the position, they should have turned "exclusively defensive" already by the time of the fall of Guadalcanal. All this while they were wavering between offense and defense.

Indeed, since we transferred the navy's air forces from around Rabaul to the Truk area and the army's air forces to the middle region of New Guinea in order to cope with the American attacks against the Gilberts in November 1943 and the Marshalls in January 1944, our strategy came to assume a purely defensive character, just resisting and defending without any definite end. It became the so-called "Defensive delaying (dragging) strategy." American forces advanced as they pleased, sweeping everything before them. Our forces in New Guinea retreated west and west as long as the land features allowed such continuous retreat without depending on modern means of locomotion. It was a tragic retreat made imperative by the misery of defeats. To the Pacific isles supplies were entirely cut off. Indescribable hardships and famine gripped our fighting forces in the vise-like clutches of the American forces. Still they maintained their spirits. They continued to fight and resist, but all such endeavors were just empty, fruitless struggles before the terrible speed of the American onrush, a speed that defied all our imagination and calculation.

There was one expression that was constantly on the lips of our

[*Page 48:*]

men: "If the American gave us a respite of just one month!" A pathetic remark that will stay long in our memory. Americans came always one month too early, ahead of our plan! Let's see.

On 7 August 1942 a detachment of the American navy commanded by [Vice Adm.] A. A. Vandegrift landed on the Lunga airfield in the northwestern part of Guadalcanal without meeting much resistance. This airfield had been built by the navy's civil engineering squad after two months of indescribable struggles with epidemics and all imaginable hardships. We had practically built this airfield for the American Marines to take and use. The following day, 9 August, we were to celebrate its completion. Such is the irony of fate. We just prepared the ground for our ensuing desperate fight in the jungle that was kept up for six long months against Americans, epidemics and famine, that ended in a complete defeat.

In the case of Biak Island also where the American forces landed on 27 May 1944, our navy's memorial day, if they had come only a month later, they should have found more than one division of our land forces and a good number of heavy guns on the cliffs of Bosnik on the southern coast of the island.

In the battles between the task forces that had not met for a pretty long time, indeed in these engagements that at last culminated in the fall of Saipan and Guam into America's hands, our naval planes could have given more effective attacks and accomplished greater results if America had come a month later. Invariably it was always "one month too early."

In the battles during April 1945 that finally resulted in the fall of Okinawa it fared likewise. If there had been a delay of one month on America's part, a reinforcement of one regiment would have been sent

[*Page 49:*]

for the defense of Katena airfield that dominated the northern and central parts of Okinawa. Also the Kikusui Flying Forces stationed in Kyushu, which was in fact, Japan's last unit of air forces, could have accomplished a fair showing, if America's arrival came a little later. We were always "one month behind." Just as in a rugby game, we were always chased, hunted, pestered, driven about here and there and up against the wall, all the time without the shortest breathing space. Finally we fell tired, exhausted, unconscious! They finally sent us an atomic bomb instead of a referee with a whistle, just to close the lid. There was no ceremony of the victor and the vanquished shaking hands in cordial fellowship after the match was over, but the disgrace of a surrender without conditions was just forced on us.

A FOOL JUST REPEATS

Apropos of American rugby, a friend of mine who had been educated in America said to me once, "In American rugby it is thought the most stupid thing to repeat one and the same trick over again and get beaten. The Japanese navy should carefully remember this and not play 'a fool that remembers just one thing'!" This features more or less, or rather very strongly, the strategy and tactics of the Japanese navy. "With our scant resources we had no alternative," it may be answered. But this does not dispose of the matter.

As I will explain later, the Battle of Midway was a disaster that was irrevocable, a blunder that could not be unmade.

Our navy always repeated the same blunder more or less. In the Battle of Midway, the greatest of blunders committed during the whole course of the war, a blunder that was irrevocable, that could not be unmade! The "Tokyo Express" of unexpected fame in the battles of the Solomons: the old-fashioned amphibious operations that properly belonged

[*Page 50:*]

to the medieval ages, which finally collapsed before the Allies' improved counter-attacks in the landing operation at Rabi (in the southern tip of New Guinea): In all these cases the failure came always as a result of repeating the same old method. The fruit was always a disaster. Maybe such a propensity is in the race. The navy stuck to traditions to the last man, to the end of time, and perished with the tradition!

DEFECTIVE SCOUTING

Defective scouting has always vitiated the drawing and enforcement of the tactical plan.

Before the advent of the aircraft, unlike in land warfare, sea forces were usually kept in the dark as to the condition of the enemy, its positions and its size, its strength. The undue importance attached to the "offense" side of our navy's tactics had inclined it to make light of scouting. In maneuvers, the enemy's conditions could be guessed. They had always had a pitched, decisive battle in view. When the enemy's conditions became unknowable, the referee gave the necessary information as if by God's command so that the maneuver might be continued. Such evil practices left bad influences on the navy's mind. They came to expect, in spite of themselves, the likewise in real war. Just before the outbreak some warnings about our poor scouting were given; however, it was too late. They roused almost no interest.

There were a few cases of successful scouting. Scouting, just before our attack on Pearl Harbor, those practiced in the direction of Fiji and Samoa, and also around the islands of the Marshalls, the Solomons and the Admiralty before the battle of the Marianas during June 1944, in these cases scouting was fairly well conducted. They invariably exercised very favorable influence on the warfare that followed. The cases of disasters invited as a result of insufficient scouting were numerous. Let me cite some instances.

[Page 51:]

The fiasco at Midway is one instance. We could not size up the enemy's strength. On 26 October 1942 in the battle of Santa Cruz again, we met a disaster, had indeed a hairbreadth escape. The cause was the lack of scouting in the direction of the Ellice and the New Hebrides groups. They knew the importance of doing it, but somehow omitted it. The omission soon invited the punishment.

On 7 August 1942, when the American forces came landing at the Solomons and Tulagi, about ten each of flying boats and seaplanes had been far out towards Tulagi. In spite of the mission assigned them of scouting the southeastern side of the Solomons, they could not effect their missions. Moreover they were all devoured on the surface by hunting dogs, American vessels, before they even flapped their wings to fly.

In February 1944, after the fall of the Gilberts and the Marshalls, we spared what we could not well spare and assigned a part of the very scanty air forces to the defense of the Solomons and Truk. Such precaution notwithstanding, a part of the American task forces came in a surprise attack on these islands on 27 February. It was America's answer to ours at Pearl Harbor, as they much publicized it. Our defense forces could not make an effective counter-attack. The damages were appalling: 320 airplanes, 2 cruisers, 4 destroyers, 26 transports. Large enough damages! An ample compensation for Pearl Harbor!

Then on 10 September when the Americans came attacking at the Visayas section of the Philippines, the major part of our First Air Forces, composing the main units of the Philippine defenses, was burnt on the ground. We had looked forward to a decisive duel when the enemy came. When the enemy did come, we were just taken unawares.

A month later, in the great sea battle of Leyte, perhaps the last of its kind in history, the Japanese navy played the role of a blind

[Page 52:]

lion rushing in a dark night. They had known almost nothing of the formidable obstacles lying ahead.

When in 1945 the war theater shifted to the sea near Japan, we had no means of knowing the approximate features of the American forces, even the symptoms of their approaches. Their bombardments of Kamaishi, Hidachi, even of the Bohahu peninsula lying right in front of Yokohama Naval Station were to us a surprise attack. We had anticipated nothing beforehand.

RUNNING AND CHASING FIGHT

To go back, on 8 August 1942 at the Battle of Savo Island, our 8th Fleet under Vice Admiral Mikawa's command passed through the anchorage of Guadalcanal with lightning speed and delivered a crushing blow which rendered the American fleet almost powerless, but it did not continue the chase. This omission makes no common sense, indeed is unaccountable. Why did he not immediately press upon the American transports which then had lost all the convoy protection and had to spend a few hours before the night was over roaming on the dark seas, trembling at the nightmare of the Japanese fleet? If Vice Admiral Mikawa had taken the decision, turned his fleet and opened a fresh attack, a few pages of the history of the Pacific war might have had to be rewritten. Now everybody, Japanese and American, who is at home with the progress of events involved in that engagement, is mystified by his omission to do that. Everybody who reads the history of the Pacific war, when he comes to this section, will shake his head and feel curious about his motive. Perhaps he did not like the risk.

Had not Vice Admiral Mikawa been aware of the great result accomplished by his fleet? Or did he just not care to? He and his men had gone out with a determination to conquer or perish. They did not perish but conquered with an almost harmless victory, suffering no wounds worthy

[*Page 53:*]

of the name. Exultingly they steered northward off the eastern coast of Savo Island. They were feeling a sense of relief after great actions and catching their breath in a relaxed atmosphere.

The captain of the *Chokai,* flagship of Mikawa's fleet, was standing speechless, grim on the bridge.

"Let us turn around and attack, Admiral!" he called to the Vice Admiral. The latter was standing on the right corner of the bridge. He made no reply. No replies came from any one of the dark figures standing around him. The fleet continued to steer northward. At the admiral's mentality on this occasion we can only guess. The following are two reasons advanced for his mysterious attitude:

1. The Japanese fleet had used up all of the first-time attack's torpedoes. The fleet formation was in a deranged status. The preparation for a fresh attack required several hours.

2. The fresh attack might be successful, but lingering around in the battle area meant the risk of meeting counterattacks after dawn by fresh American task forces suspected to be nearby. The Admiral meant to avoid this risk.

Before the Admiral started on this expedition he hoisted a signal: "We now start to attack the enemy that is coming." By this "enemy" did he mean the American warships only? If so, he finished his mission by having annihilated most of the American warships. Or did he mean by "enemy" the whole American fighting forces? If so, why did he spare the fleet of transports under convoy?

Whatever his reasons for this omission, they are feeble. He should have continued chasing the enemy's transport fleet and finished it, as his captain suggested. This decision had to be taken in a few minutes. That these few minutes of supreme importance were idly wasted meant a

[*Page 54:*]

disaster for the future of the navy, the future of this war. Truth to tell, there was no particular convincing reason. It just so developed. Predestination! We study consolation after the event.

To go back to February 1942. About this period, the war progressed in our favor. Our forces on land and sea were irresistible, swept everything before them. They took Singapore, Timor, Celebes. Now the opportunity was ripe for the invasion of Java, which had been marked as the object of the first period warfare. In Java, there was a fleet under the command of Vice Admiral [C. E. L.] Helfrich of the Dutch navy, composed of about six cruisers. They lay in wait; an encounter with the Japanese navy had been expected.

When the Japanese fleet pressed near Java convoying the landing troops, they came unexpectedly to an encounter with the Allied fleet under Dutch [Rear] Admiral [K. W. F. M.] Doorman's command. That was the first engagement fought in broad daylight on the Pacific. The Japanese fleet was under the command of Vice Admiral Takagi, who later died in Saipan, and consisted of the cruisers *Haguro* and *Nachi*, two light cruisers and 14 destroyers, which were under the protection of absolutely superior air forces. The Allied fleet was composed of the Dutch cruisers *DeRuyter*, *Java*, Australian cruisers *Exeter*, *Perth*, an American cruiser *Houston* and 9 other destroyers.

The battle was an exchange of shells at a great distance. The Allied fleet frequently changed course in an effort to avoid hits. Vice Admiral Takagi, being possessed of spotting planes catapulted from his ships, knew quite well the shells did not hit. For reasons that could not be accounted for, he never approached nearer than 20,000 meters. During two hours, the Japanese navy just wasted 20 c.s. shells. During the latter half of the duel, the Japanese made a general charge.

[*Page 55:*]

By means of long-distance oxygen torpedoes, we succeeded in sinking two destroyers. The Allied fleet fell into confusion and serious danger. At this crucial moment, the Japanese fleet stopped fire and steered around northward, letting the Allied fleet escape.

The reasons given for this stop-fire order were the recognition of something like the explosion of mines, the coming in sight of the Soerabaya lighthouse which meant that our fleet was already within the mine area and the menace of the enemy's submarines. Whatever the reasons, we missed big game. Light craft are for fighting at close quarters. Why instead of coming into close quarters did they just exchange shells at a long distance and waste them?

There is another instance of a similar kind. Toward the end of March 1943, Vice Admiral [Boshiro] Hosogaya, commander-in-chief of the 5th Fleet, cruised toward the North Pacific convoying the troop ships that went to Attu. Our fleet consisted of the two first-class cruisers *Nachi* and *Maya*, two light cruisers and four destroyers. When they were sailing through the area south of Kommandorski Island, they met the American fleet commanded by Rear Adm. C. H. McMorris, consisting of the *Salt Lake City*, the *Richmond* and four destroyers. The encounter developed into what we named the Battle of Kommandorski Island.

Quite by accident, we succeeded in deploying the fleet on the eastern side of the American fleet, which meant cutting off their route for a retreat. Our forces were overwhelming. In spite of that, we did not press close on the American fleet. We engaged only in a long-distance running gunfire duel. Toward the end of the fighting, our fleet stopped chasing in order to avoid the torpedoes from the

American destroyers which came charging on us to protect a cruiser that looked disabled by

[*Page 56:*]

our hits. It is to be admitted, however, that our commander's staff were not aware of this circumstance on the enemy's side. It was noticed only by a scouting plane whose message to this effect somehow failed to reach our command. This instance of Kommandorski Island was a real tragedy, just a half-way measure, failure to fight it out and accomplish the enemy's annihilation. There were indeed few instance of a thorough fighting, fighting to the finish, in the record of the Japanese navy.

The only instance in which the Japanese navy fought throughout to the finish was the Battle of Tsushima, 27–28 May 1905, when Admiral Togo continued the chase till the enemy's fleet was either sunk or had surrendered. He did this because he had learned to realize the importance of chasing the enemy to the bitter end and as the result of his one-and-a-half year's personal experience of constant fighting. Two battles in particular, one on 10 August 1904 in the Yellow Sea, when the Russian fleet made a sally from Port Arthur, and the other four days later on 14 August 1904, in the sea of Japan off Urusan, Korea, when Kamimura's fleet engaged the Russian Vladivostok fleet.

On the former occasion, Togo caught the Russian fleet just when it was steaming out of Port Arthur in an attempt to escape and seek shelter in Vladivostok. They had not had much fighting spirit. The fight began from a little after noon and continued for over five hours. The zeal and spirit to fight at close range was wanting, so not much substantial effect was obtained. Only just out of sheer good luck we hit the *Tsarevitch,* the Russian flagship, causing the death of the Russian commander-in-chief, thus scattering the nerve center of the Russian fleet, and succeeded in forcing the Russian fleet to give up their plan to escape to Vladivostok.

[*Page 57:*]

On the other occasion, on 14 August 1904, in the battle off Urusan, Korea, we sank the *Rurik,* a heavy cruiser, and gave chase to others which did not bring any result. We gave it up after a while and returned to the rescue of the crew of the *Rurik.* On this occasion we gave up the chase reportedly because the magazines were almost empty. A close examination after the fight revealed, however, that although the magazines were empty, there still remained a good amount of shells and powder beside the guns and in the passages of transportation. The story is told of Commander Sato, senior staff officer, later Vice Admiral, gnashing his teeth and stamping the ground when this discovery was made. These two failures had taught Admiral Togo the great value of continuing the chase to the limit. When he met the Baltic fleet off the island of Tsushima on 27–28 May, the following year (1905), he made good the valuable lessons.

Thus the Japanese navy has scant instances of a successful chase. I think fundamentally this is due to racial character. The Japanese are not seekers of perfection, lack the spirit of thoroughness, generally speaking. This is why I said: the Japanese navy just cannot help stopping the chase. It just cannot go to the limit. It reflects the character of the race, is just preordained. Our national game of wrestling is well illustrative of this racial propensity. The wrestling game is governed by a number of very complicated, minute rules, the disregard of just a single one of which spells decision. It is not necessary to utilize the rule-breaker's mistake to one's own advantage. In most cases, a mistake in itself means a decision. At all events, Japanese wrestling is not a game to the finish. A display of just one brilliant feat is all that is desired. Whether there still

[*Page 58:*]

remains a surplus of fighting strength or not, that is absolutely irrelevant. This suits the public taste. They don't feel like seeing it through to the bitter end even in such a simple game. This feature comes to the fore in a fighting game of a far vaster scale.

AMBIGUOUS WAR AIM

What was the object of the warfare as conceived by the Japanese navy? The annihilation of the enemy, making a clean sweep of it? Or passively, just defense to death? It cannot be aught else. Sometimes the objectives of strategy and of tactics are confounded. Such seems an almost idle question as long as the war continues favorably. But a doubt begins to rise when we begin to lose as the case was with us since the early summer of 1942.

The result of the Midway battle was treated as one of the greatest secrecies of the Japanese navy. We were not allowed to know anything about it at the time. We were also quite in the dark as to the nature of the orders previously given to the crews who took part in it. But looking back to the event from now, we cannot help entertaining a deep doubt about the objective our navy then had aimed to attain. The doubt will explain itself in the next section.

SELF-CONCEIT

The Midway battle was the most splendid defeat the Japanese navy had scored in its history up to that date. More splendid were yet to come, though the four regular carriers which constituted at that time the basic strength of the main fighting forces were lost in one stroke. Not only were we compelled to give up the objective which we had aimed to attain by that attack, but this defeat forced us to revise the whole plan of our Pacific warfare. But there was nothing to wonder about it. We had as good as planned for it. If we had escaped that terrible disaster on that occasion, we should have met the same fate somewhere else

[*Page 59:*]

in the Pacific theater, perhaps in the course of 1942. We cannot help feeling this way. That defeat was also something preordained. Why? Because it was visited on the Japanese navy to penalize its absurd self-conceit.

The Midway tactics had been a blunder from beginning to end. Previous to undertaking this unfortunate stroke, the Combined Fleet Staff held a meeting to study the plan of this operation. At this meeting the commander of the imaginary American force marked in red planned a system of tactics that turned out to be very similar to what was later actually pursued by the American forces. But the director of the maneuver commanded the withdrawal of this tactical plan. He said such a chance was impossible. Somehow it was taken for granted that the American task force would never appear in the seas near Midway. The commander of the Red (American) forces is said to have protested with tears in his eyes: "If my plan of tactics does not suit your plan of the maneuver, I do not object to putting such a chance out of reckoning, the chance of the American task forces appearing in the seas near Midway. But in the real plan of warfare I will most earnestly solicit that you will calculate with such a chance and study proper measures to cope with it."

There were also not a few who had expressed grave concern or seriously expostulated with those who promoted this fateful plan. Nevertheless, the conceited operation commanders, who believed in the "Enemyless navy of Nippon," scoffed at such warnings and forced their ideas through. They put into operation a plan that had not taken the American task forces into reckoning and harvested a result that made them almost faint in alarm. They discovered that there *was* an enemy to the Japanese navy! And this enemy was more than a match!

Let me write a little more about this sea fight.

[*Page 60:*]

There is, it seems to me, something fundamentally out of focus in our plan for this Midway battle.

Why did our navy attack Midway? Why in connection with it did they attempt to take the Aleutians? To preclude these islands being used as air bases from which to attack Japan? Such a guess evinces only their ignorance of the topography, since the land features of these islands are not fit as the base for long-range big bombers such as the B29. There are others who assert that the attempt was preparatory to an attack on Hawaii. But how could we hope to take Hawaii at this stage if we could not take it on the first occasion when the circumstances were far more favorable? At this period (Midway) the balance between the two navies was already turning in favor of the United States. The impossibility of taking Midway was obvious.

The last possible reason is "it was necessary as a preparation for the great fleet battle between the two navies," the idea long cherished by the Japanese navy. But neither does this offer a satisfactory explanation. In the first place, of the six regular carriers then possessed by the Japanese navy, the *Shokaku* and the *Zuikaku* were then under repair from the damages suffered in the Battle of the Coral Sea. The *Akagi, Kaga, Soryu,* and *Hiryu* were the four available for the purpose. If this had been meant as preparatory to the long-cherished "Great fleet battle," why did they not wait two more months when the repairs should have been finished and the six carriers all made available?

Secondly, why add such encumbrances as Midway and the Aleutians, if the "decisive fleet battle" was envisaged? The possession of two such islands wouldn't be of any help for this purpose. As it actually was, the movement of our task forces was hindered in no small measure by this attempt to take those islands. For one thing, the

[*Page 61:*]

preparation tended to reveal the secrets of the general plan. It was suspected the Americans had known everything before we were there. Nevertheless, the plan was forced and met the fate it deserved.

No less an error was committed by our task forces. After the Battle of Pearl Harbor, they went out to the Indian Ocean, and caught the British carrier *Hermes*, the cruisers *Dorsetshire* and *Cornwall* and sank them without much effort and swelled with pride. In the Battle of the Coral Sea, the two carriers *Shokaku* and *Zuikaku* scored fair results and aroused a spirit of emulation on the part of the crews of the four other carriers who had not yet had an encounter with the American task forces.*

The crews of these four carriers that later met their doom at Midway were in high spirits. They had felt like a conqueror before making the test of strength, a very encouraging sign indeed, but such an attitude and mentality is fatal in modern warfare for which no cautions can be too deep, no plans too minute and exact. Men full of hope and in high spirits are apt to be reckless. Such was fate. The final doom was there written on the wall. Only there were no eyes to read it. It could not be said of them "Everything was done that was humanly possible."

Before the attack on Midway, the caution employed by our fleet against the American task forces was not enough. One day before the attack, that is, on 5 June, a part of our fleet was discovered by the enemy and attacked. They had not taken any warning from this and approached Midway in a general happy mood. On the morning of 6 June, the

[*Page 62:*]

American air forces appeared like the proverbial bolt out of the blue from a corner of the heavens, one formation close after another. Bombs from the "Dauntless" set each one of our carriers on fire. The peculiar weakness of the Japanese warships, the relatively weak defense armory, especially against fire, soon revealed itself. The four stately carriers became four big fireballs in no time and soon disappeared with 250 airplanes. It was a blow plumb on the nose of swelling pride. The conceit done to dust. It was a defeat almost unprecedented in the history of naval warfare, in scale and intensity. Against this heavy sacrifice the *Yorktown*, a carrier, was our only score. After this battle, the battle between the two navies was completely broken. They became the offensive, we the defensive. Our doom was sealed.

The vicissitude of our navy's fortune during this war is very much akin to the vicissitude of our general fortune through the whole course of events from the outbreak of the Manchurian Incident in September 1931 down to the present downfall. It is a real tragedy, but does it not tell something of the racial propensity, racial fate?

Now let me look at the other side and discuss the rock-like solidity of the American attitude in every phase of their actions.

---

* Note: The *Shokaku* and the *Zuikaku*, being younger than the four other carriers *Akagi*, *Kaga*, (the 1st Air Squadron), *Soryu* and *Hiryu* (2nd Air Squadron), were possessed of newer equipment, but their crews were not as experienced as those of the other four.

The American navy was cautious, all attention all through. Nothing apparently escaped their attention. On 21 February 1942, their task forces appeared to the east of Rabaul and met the attack by our navy twin-engined land-based bombers. From this they immediately took warning, turned around and withdrew beyond our reach, and came back no more.

The movement of their task forces and their amphibian operations ever since the end of 1943 were characterized by elasticity no less than solidity. Their intrepidity increased in proportion to the weakening of our counterattack, but what was wonderful was the feature that their

[*Page 63:*]

intrepidity never became recklessness. Constantly on the alert, they never showed us an unguarded point, never gave us an opportunity to take advantage of. Especially impressive was their fighting ability demonstrated in the battle between the task forces that developed out of the Saipan battle. The behavior of the carrier groups under Vice Admiral [Marc A.] Mitscher's command, in covering the landing, in meeting the Japanese fleet, in chasing it when it retreated, aroused our admiration. Their actions were quick, defiant, unfathomably cautious. They formed and reformed, spread and gathered, horizontally and vertically, as if under the wand of a magician. We looked at each other, shook our heads, smiled smiles of despair and praise. At last we were satisfied we were defeated.

SUBMARINE WARFARE

The Japanese navy committed a good deal of errors in the fields of strategy and tactics which it had spent many years of intense effort to study. Well, then, in the field of those activities which had remained outside the ken of their attention, they just bungled.

Let us look at our submarines.

In this type of vessel there was equality of ratio between America, Britain and Japan. That was the London arrangement. Our navy attributed an immense hope to the future of the submarines. Within the framework of the London Treaty, we did our utmost to improve and perfect this particular branch of the sea forces. At the time of the outbreak of the war, the winter of 1941, we had thirty-odd vessels each on the first and the second lines. But their major portion had been built and equipped for the purpose of the fleet engagement, the dream of our navy. I have already discussed the main aim of our submarine operations. Their

[*Page 64:*]

mission had not included the disturbance of marine traffic except in a very few cases.

When the war broke out, it was not long before the weakness of the flotilla came to reveal itself. As the war went on developing, we had to employ it for a mission we had not even dreamed of before the war.

In the proper fields of the submarine's mission, it had very little to show. It sank the *Yorktown* at Midway, the *Wasp* in the area south of the Solomons in the autumn of 1942. It scouted successfully the condition of the air bases in the direction of Hawaii and the Southern Pacific. These were certainly merits, but not important enough to change the strategical or tactical features of the war. They pale to almost nothing when compared with the accomplishments of the American submarines which in the opinion of our navy before the war were ''not much to think about.'' When in the course of 1944 the long-awaited battles between the task forces around the Marianas were fought, they sank by one stroke our newest double-decked carrier, the *Taiho,* and the *Shokaku,* manned by veterans who had fought at Pearl Harbor, the Coral Sea and Santa Cruz. They decided the fate of the battle almost at the moment it opened.

Then again, in the battle of Leyte, in October 1944, which was for the Japanese navy veritably a gamble for the throne a few days before the battle, in the area north of Palawan Island, American submarines attacked the First Attacking Forces under Vice Admiral [Takeo] Kurita's command, which had steered out of the Bay of Brunei, Borneo, and sank the first-class cruisers *Atago* and *Maya,* and further inflicted serious damage on the *Takao,* forcing it to leave the line. By this telling blow, they succeeded in casting a dark shadow on the prospect of the forthcoming main engagement. Subsequently, while those same forces were passing

[*Page 65:*]

through the Philippine Islands, it underwent a violent attack from the American 38th task forces and lost the great dreadnought *Musashi,* nicknamed the ''Hope of Japan,'' and several others. This made the Japanese sally into the Bay of Leyte a mere matter of good luck. The American task forces owed this phenomenal success to the constant contact their submarines managed to keep with the Japanese fleet.

Then again on 22 November 1944, the *Shinano,* a carrier that was to be the greatest and the most powerful of the world, was sunk on the sea south of Japan Proper, by an American submarine.* The *Unryu,* a regular carrier launched after the Midway battle, and three converted carriers quickly followed the *Shinano* to watery graves, an accomplishment of such amazing nature that the American submariners themselves perhaps had not had the nerve to hope for. The belief that the submarine was the friend of the weak was completely disproved. Like everything else, it helps the strong only.

The result scored by a submarine raider cannot in the nature of things be accurately known unless the other party publishes it also. But even judging from the result reported by the Japanese side alone, not very much was accomplished in this direction. During the first half of 1942 our submarine flotilla accomplished some result on the Indian Ocean and other areas, that was all. But against the immense tonnage of the Allied marine force, this was a mere drop in the bucket.

When the battles of the Solomons were opened in summer 1942, our marine transportation in that theater was completely blocked by the Allies' overwhelmingly superior air forces and American naval power,

---

* Note: The *Shinano* was originally planned as the *Yamato*'s and *Musashi*'s sister ship, but was later converted into a carrier after the opening of the war.

[*Page 66:*]

which circumstance compelled us ultimately to use the submarines for transporting supplies to the front lines. Their mission as the disturber of the enemy's traffic thus ended almost entirely. But even this new mission to transport supplies was never productive of satisfactory results. What supplies we could manage to send thereby was little more than a few drops of water on a red-hot iron. Nevertheless, for various reasons we had to do it. As far as we were concerned, the battles grew daily more violent, bloody, exasperating.

In this process, the damages suffered by our submarines were terrific, 27 vessels altogether were lost. The total loss of submarines during the whole course of the war is 130. The effect was demoralizing on the spirit of the crews. The necessity mentioned above of diverting the use of the submarines to the transportation of supplies was one of the important reasons for its modest showing as traffic raiders. Nevertheless, we cannot overlook the navy's inattention before the war to the submarine as a traffic raider. Such a thought had never seriously engaged their minds. By way of illustration, I will state briefly the pre-war administration of the submarine policy.

In the course of 1942, German submarines developed the peak of their efficiency on the Atlantic. Much hope was pinned on submarine warfare in consequence. In spite of that, the new building program for that fiscal year included only ten middle-sized and two small-sized craft. It was as late as 1943 that we set about seriously building submarines as traffic raiders. Even then our limited resources did not permit us to build very much more than a hundred units. Already by this time Anglo-American counter-submarine measures had been quite developed and almost wholly succeeded in suppressing the German submarines' activities.

[*Page 67:*]

By the time of our surrender in 1945, we had a pretty good number of special-type submarines patterned after but improved on those used in the attack on Pearl Harbor. This class is known as "the *Koryu* type." Further, we had ready a still smaller type known as "The *Kairyu* type," then another capable of developing very great speed under water, and lastly one that basked in the honor of being admired by the Allied navy as the world's greatest submarine craft. It was known as the *I-400* type.

Our navy's policy regarding the submarine had undergone such a vicissitude, which circumstances will attest beyond dispute lacked one definite, consistent idea—just a pell-mell of thoughts. Constant changes necessarily produced delays. "No! not that, not this" repeated ever and anon ultimately resulted in heaps of unfinished submarine hulls in the dockyards all over the country that never tasted water. Just scrap that had gone on heaping. The navy's submarine flotilla might as well have an exhibition of the "Different Types of Submarines"! Their types were so many and various that even a man in the profession like myself cannot remember them. Cruiser-type, Large-type, Transportation-type, "Rogo"-type, midsized "Rogo"-type, small-size "Rogo"-type, "Hago"-type and whatnot. If indeed we had thoroughly studied submarine warfare and been possessed of one consistent, definite idea, we could have developed an efficiency that the American navy and marine traffic might have felt. At least we could have made it too dangerous for the Allied traffic on the Pacific to go on without a powerful convoy.

COUNTER-SUBMARINE WARFARE

Before the war, on our side, we had made light of the American submarines. We had thought we could dispose of them easily. They have disposed of us easily. They have dealt us a death blow.

And what is more, our navy had never realized its own vulnerabil-

[*Page 68:*]

ity to the submarines until it received such a death blow. At least its concern did not become keenly serious until then. True, up until the middle of 1942 the menace from the American submarines was not very serious; we were on the offensive. About this period, the American navy was building submarines and training the crews in a great hurry. From this knowledge we did not take warning. Neither did we much heed the precious lessons afforded by the German submarines. Unless we had contrived some especially efficient counter-measures, not only could we not hope to eliminate its menace, we stood to suffer a blow that was really fatal. This point had never been noticed.

That we had not undergone much damage from American submarines until about the middle of 1943 was not due to our strong defense, but to inactivities on the enemy's part. In the nature of things it was nothing we could take any credit for. We had been sleeping a sleep of safety which it was up to the enemy to disturb at any time, not the kind of positive safety which America and Britain had wrung from the enemy by airplanes, radar, by an overwhelming number of scouting craft. The inattention by our navy to this point proved fatal and decisive in favor of our enemy. We were punished irrevocably: We had refused to open our eyes.

In the latter half of 1943, America's preparations for submarine warfare had become complete. They had started to be active, very active. The mass attack by submarines carried out in close concert with scouting operations that were absolutely superior, a system of attack that had been foreseen in the German submarine warfare on the Atlantic, caused the losses of Japanese trade vessels to mount very speedily and to look endless.

[*Page 69:*]

The slow-witted Japanese navy decided to wake up. In November 1943 they established the Marine Traffic Protection Headquarters, whose mission it was to control the navy's entire convoy operations, while at the same time they set about speeding the building of convoy craft. The size of the forces placed under the command of this new institution was so small that it just aroused sympathy or laughter. Three converted carriers, about thirty convoy craft and one single squad of air forces, that was all. However efficient the organization of this new so-called Protection Headquarters might be, they could do nothing with such modest means. The enemy paid respect to this new institution by increasing our losses of steamers to over 400,000 tons per month. The convoys and the convoyed very often vanished together. Our fighting power decreased very rapidly in consequence, the supplies from the southern regions on which we largely depended having been speedily and considerably reduced. The war prospect became increasingly gloomy. The mother of these disasters was primarily the navy's erroneous conception of strategy. They could not shake off the fetters of traditions, remained a slave of fatal inertia.

I have already stated the lack of attention before the war to the urgency of increasing the efficiency of the convoy system. This is what they did after the outbreak. In 1942 they built just two convoy ships. In 1943, 35 were launched. The program for 1944 contained 112. A fat volume can be written on the vast importance of the convoy institution in war time, how the inadequacy of the system damagingly affected the country's fighting power in these crucial periods. Here I will limit the discussion to the fields of my own observation.

New convoy ships could be used only for main transportation routes. Branch routes could claim only old ships. The convoys were converted

[*Page 70:*]

from trawlers and catcher boats used for arctic fishing. The transport fleets, however, were helpless before the Allied submarine flotilla equipped with radar and all other imaginable new weapons of attack. In daytime our transports managed to cruise under the protection of the air forces. After dark they could seek safety only in ports of refuge, which, however, were far from being absolutely safe. The enemy's scouting often detected and bombed them. Along with the increase of the danger, supplies ebbed in proportion. Frequently a couple of days' route under normal conditions now required more than ten days. In consequence, the fighting power of the front line withered very rapidly.

Lastly, I will describe numerically how thoroughly efficient the Allied submarine warfare was in their attack on our transportation lines. Before the war, the total tonnage of our merchant fleet was almost 6,000,000 tons. At the time of Japan's surrender, we had only about a million tons left. By far the larger percentage of this enormous loss was due to submarine attack. Indeed, Japan's fighting power was nearly annihilated by the submarines and task forces. I will cite one instance of the daring feats displayed by the American submarine forces.

Since the early summer of 1945, the American submarine flotilla came into the Japan Sea through the straights of Tsugaru, Soya and Tsushima across areas where about 10,000 mines (if of old, rather primitive types) had been laid and wrought havoc to Japanese shipping. This was really a very daring feat, the invasion into the sea area which we had always considered as our territorial waters since our phenomenal victory at the battle of Tsushima in 1905. To this day, it is a mystery to us where and how the American submarines managed to slip through the mine-strewn areas. They were aggressive, defiant, fearless to the Nth degree.

[*Page 71:*]

TRANSPORTATION OF WAR SUPPLIES (LOGISTICS)

The Pacific War was a war of transportation. This impression is deep. We lost practically in the war of transportation. Not a few in our navy feel this way, and ruefully. In the old days, the naval bases were fixed in definite locations. Out of them the fleet went to fight, and returned after fighting. It fared differently in the Pacific war. The fighting area was immensely broad. The air forces came in as a new factor. Bases had to be advanced or withdrawn according to the vicissitude of the war. Further, naval warfare partook increasingly of the nature of land warfare. All such changes in the method of war operations consequent to the introduction of new factors could not fail to effect the problem of supply transportation, which had become far more difficult and complicated. Very unfortunately, the Japanese navy had never visualized such a possibility before the war. Naturally they were re-sourceless. Entering the war without full preparations in this respect—paucity of materials was always the stumbling block in their way—they could not cope with the fast-developing situation and at last invited a disaster that was irrevocable. But this was an inevitable fate.

I have discussed already how transportation affects war operations. Let me continue this discussion a little further. At the time of the battles around the Marianas, we had reckoned on Palau as the prospective scene of the main fighting operations. Why did they select Palau instead of the Marianas that had fallen into American hands? This was not an erroneous calculation as to where we should expect the enemy's next attack, but rather due to the impossibility of going farther eastward because of fuel supply considerations. The Japanese navy's cruising radius was not more than 1,000 sea miles at that time. Our task forces were based in those days in Tawi-Tawi, Sulu Archipelago, from whence

[*Page 72:*]

Palau was the limit of the cruising range; we could not go farther east.

Then again in mid-October 1944, the American task forces came to attack Formosa. Our night attack air forces went out to meet them. Our crews fought intrepidly, but this was their first campaign. They lacked experience. They thought erroneously that the pillars of flame that stood up before them were all "enemy ships blown up." They had not reckoned their own airplanes that burst into flames. Inevitably the consequence was that their reports were very much exaggerated, if in good faith. Believing these reports and jumping with joy, they ordered a chase after the American fleet that was still sound and whole. The units that went out on this chase had a hairbreadth escape from annihilation, because the American fleet was not fleeing in a confusion of defeat, but just going back in order to prepare for the succeeding operations. Further, on that occasion, in the operation directing quarters there took place a heated discussion as to whether to send northward the First Attacking Forces then anchoring at Brunei in Borneo. The key to this problem was fuel. At length the attempt was given up. The First Attacking Forces under the command of Vice Admiral Kurita continued to stay there for ten more days, then it left for its grave, Leyte Gulf.

In April 1945 our last fleet, including the mammoth battleship *Yamato,* sailed out from the Inland Sea on its last one-way sally to Okinawa and met the crack American task forces that came to attack Okinawa and met her doom. There was no clever way to make up for the vast difference in fighting power. In the discussion that decided the dispatch of our last resources, the chief item upon which the decision hung was whether we could manage to procure only a few thousand tons of fuel required for the trip of the fleet to Okinawa, that was only 1,000 sea miles. In fuel also as in many respects we were at the end of our tether.

[*Page 73:*]

On such poor resources what effective plan of warfare could we hope to draw? It was a problem that essentially permitted of no real solution. This circumstance gave rise to endless bickerings between the operation directors and procurement quarters. The former was nervous, over-nervous. When an operationist draws a plan, he bases the actions directly on the plan he has drawn. In his mind, manpower and materials are already there. Actually such factors become readily available after at best a few weeks, sometimes a few months. Those in charge of the procurement of such factors often fail to notice in the press of work that the materials, by the time they are ready, have ceased to be of any use. Such a tendency would usually increase as the tide of war is developing unfavorably and transportation becomes harder.

Also, from the purely technical point of view, we must consider the absence of interchangeability of weapons. Between the navy and the army which are simultaneously engaged in the same landing operations, the weapons are often not interchangeable reciprocally. For example, while battles were raging furiously at Iwojima or Okinawa islands, there came a call for more munitions. On such occasions the weapons for the navy and the army had to be sent separately by air. If such is the case for land war engines, one can imagine the difficulties in the case of those for naval operations. What is more surprising is that even within the same navy, such lack of interchangeability of weapons exists insurmountably. Parts of a gun very often are not interchangeable. Splendid weapons, a good many of them, have very often ceased to be available due to the failure to procure parts.

Japan's fighting forces have been forced to do battling under such unfavorable circumstances all along the lines and in every quarter of the extended battlefields, in the Solomons, New Guinea, everywhere.

[*Page 74:*]

On the New Guinea front lines, in the early autumn of 1943, we lost Lae. Then in the short space of six months, we lost Finchhafen, Saidor, Hollandia and Aitave one after another. It was quick work, and our forces were driven into the depths of the dense primordial forests where they struggled constantly with starvation, epidemics and fear of a fight. It was really hell on earth. Of the Japanese army that counted over 140,000 in July 1943, only a little over 10,000 survived in August 1945. It was a drastic reduction, and of this only 3 percent fell in actual fighting. Epidemics and starvation did the rest of the work. The tragedy was appalling.

THE SEA BEE

The Japanese navy also had this institution, which was created after the outbreak. The great activities the air arm of our naval force kept up during the four months from December 1941 to March 1942 made the creation of the Sea Bee imperative. Along with the increasing activities of the naval forces on land, the Sea Bee was speedily increased and reinforced. At the time of our surrender in August 1945, they numbered 200 units comprising far over 100,000 men, without including those who had already melted before the advance of the Allied forces. They should be given credit for what they have accomplished with the primitive instruments with which they were equipped when they were first organized. A trundle, a pick-axe, were all that was at their disposal. From them, equipped with such primitive implements, we could not expect much. Nevertheless, they have accomplished very substantial results. Just by way of an instance, a squad of just half-equipped engineering forces that went to the marshy lands of Mimika in the remote regions facing the Arafoera Sea in New Guinea has completed an airfield

[*Page 75:*]

in the face of all imaginable difficulties, insufficient supply of instruments, even of pick-axes, the dearth of materials of all kinds. This was our airfield on the farthest front line in those areas, constituting a very important air base for scouting the regions in the direction of Hollandia since the spring of 1944.

The Sea Bee is not properly a fighting unit, but their contribution to this war was great. Since the commencement of counterattacks by the Allies, they took active part in fighting with guns in hand. More than half of the Japanese forces stationed in Guadalcanal when the American forces landed there consisted of our Bee forces. In spite of their great merits, our navy refused them the status of a regular soldier. They were treated only as civilians in military service, which meant a great disadvantage for them, inconveniences in various respects. A revision was repeatedly suggested in vain. It was really a shame that will stay long in history as an unpardonable error and omission.

There was another circumstance that seriously handicapped the activities of this Bee force. It was bad organization, and from such a badly-organized institution the navy, which lacked knowledge and experience in civil engineering, often demanded services which from the civil engineering standpoint bordered almost on the absurd. For such a blundering attitude there was no excuse but the great urgency of fighting requirements and complete ignorance of civil engineering technicalities on the part of the authorities.

When in early autumn of 1943 the defense lines of Lae and Salamoa were broken through and the defense of New Guinea began to be discussed, it was ultimately decided to make the last defense by deploying the air forces to the western part of New Guinea. With this end in view, we

[*Page 76:*]

set about extending the airfield in Bavo, situated close to the neck of Vogelkop Peninsula and Sorong in the western extremity of the island, and building a new big one at Saga 60 km. west of Bavo. The civil engineering squad sent to accomplish this task included the three best-equipped units belonging to the navy. They were in truth victims to the dreams of those who planned such an absurd scheme on their desks.

Such a plan was conceivable on the desk only. They had not actually surveyed the land features by exploring the terrain on foot. They just sent airplanes flying over and spying out the land from the midheavens. The result was a sketch quite roughly made, quite inadequate for such an enormously important purpose. The field they selected for the air base was a low marshland. The building work was gone over again and again. The obstacles remained unconquered. Failure looked certain. The authorities on the spot were alarmed, cabled to Tokyo explaining the difficulties and asking for a change of plans, to which the answer was an invariable "Do your best. Overcome the difficulties no matter what the sacrifices are." Tokyo never consented to a change.

Meantime, from the eastern section of New Guinea and Australia, air attacks began to be feared. Men became nervous. For the space of half a year they kept on doing their utmost in an effort to convert the marshland into a solid strip. In May 1944, Biak Island, scarcely 200 miles distant from Saga, fell into American hands. The airfield was still under construction. It was not finished enough even to take light planes. The attempt at last was given up in its entirety. Then we had to carry out a withdrawal under the enemy's air control. Several thousand men's strenuous effort sustained for half a year and several hundred carloads of materials were just wasted. Not one single runway was completed. This is not due to the difference in the building tech-

[*Page 77:*]

nique of the two countries. The failure in the last analysis was to be ascribed to the inferior brains in the leading sections. When we compare this clumsy result with what our enemy accomplished all the way from Guadalcanal through Admiralty Island, Biak Island, Saipan etc. to Okinawa, building huge airfields in good numbers with inconceivable speed, we cease to wonder why we were utterly beaten. Our enemy was our superior in every respect.

THE DISPOSITION OF MANPOWER

The efficiency of material factors is dependent on the manpower which is properly organized. Was the organization of such manpower adequate? Appointments were fair, done exclusively on the score of ability and character, that is, our authorities did their conscientious best to place the right man in the right place. Given warrantable ability, promotion was quick and without unfair limitation. There were admirals, commanders-in-chief who did not go through the Naval College, the gate to honors. The standing in the class in the Naval College as well as in the Naval Cadet School was never decisive. But slavish to traditions and prejudice, the best men without exceptions were grouped in the operational centers, more concretely in the Tokyo Naval General Headquarters, the staff quarter of the Combined Fleet and the Naval Department Bureau of Naval Affairs. Civil administration, communications, scouting, transportation, supply procurement and so forth were held in secondary position. There was almost no interchange of personnel between these departments and the operational department, with the inevitable result that the personnel in each quarter did not know each other, hence the relations between the two departments were not quite smooth and cordial.

Sectionalism grew and intensified, each section was satisfied with itself, refusing to cooperate, forgetting the greater cause, the promo-

[*Page 78:*]

tion of which only could ultimately assure the strength, power and the safety of the whole.

Another very important factor in the appointment of personnel is the fixing of responsibility, the problem of where to place and fix the responsibility for an action conceived and undertaken. Look at what the United States did in this respect. To probe the tragedy of Pearl Harbor, in the summer of 1945 they organized a committee to investigate in a very minute manner where properly the responsibility for that disaster should be made to belong. They did this in an attempt to preclude the repetition of such a misfortune. On the other hand, look at the condition in Japan. Before the war, our navy used to be pretty strict in ascertaining and questioning the responsibility for every piece of action. For instance, in 1933 occurred an event that had been almost without a parallel in the annals of shipbuilding. In rough weather a torpedo (light destroyer) just capsized. This led to the discovery of a great structural defect common to all types of light craft including cruisers. This defect was soon eliminated by a thorough reconstruction. On this occasion the navy organized a committee to investigate the problem of responsibility. The investigation was prosecuted pretty thoroughly, resulting ultimately in the punishment of the responsible parties. The extent and depth of the investigation undertaken on this occasion, however, bear no comparison to the scale and thoroughness of the American investigation of the Pearl Harbor responsibilities.

After the outbreak of the war, an effort in this respect was continued, if on a rather modest scale. When the battleship *Mutsu* blew up and sank in Hiroshima Bay in June 1943, again when the world's largest carrier, the *Shinano,* sank like an anchor when attacked by an American submarine in the area south of Kii promontory, a committee for an investigation was organized. Both these occurrences having been matters

[*Page 79:*]

coming under the jurisdiction of the Supreme Command (as against the administration), no particular disciplinary measures were taken in consequence. The Oriental philosophy of war teaches: "No attempt should be made to interfere with the commander on the front," true to which our commander's responsibility in both cases was not questioned. For the failure to continue the pursuit of the enemy fleet I have already mentioned, and then even for the unprecedented fiasco of Midway, the responsibility was not questioned. This was really the greatest defeat suffered in the history of Japan's naval warfare. The practice of leaving responsibility unquestioned gave rise to untold evils. The voice of criticism was hushed for one thing.

Progress just stopped dead. It killed the spirit of emulation. When an official retires from a position of responsibility, it is customary for him to greet his seniors and comrades in the following way: "I have held the post for so many years, gentlemen, and I attribute it thoroughly to your generous support that so far I have not been guilty of grave errors." This is practically a confession that he has always endeavored to avoid errors and responsibilities and has not used initiative.

Unless driven to the wall, unless placed in the position of a rat cornered by a cat, he will not act. Such a spirit is fatal to a soldier. The fatality was at last proven!

FORECAST OF THE FUTURE

For the reasons and factors mentioned above, the situation developed rapidly in favor of the enemy. But did the brains of the men in high quarters respond to the changes swiftly enough? No, they did not. On the contrary, to confess the honest truth, their brains inclined to harden. There was indeed a symptom of sclerosis in evidence. When they appeared to be in deep meditation, they were really sleeping. When they

[*Page 80:*]

awoke, they just as good as stampeded. They could not cope with the changes that were kaleidoscopic. They stayed handbound. When they started to change, the changes were quick and frequent. For instance, in starting the war they decided upon the sphere which we had to take and keep secure and under control for the successful prosecution of the war. The first sphere our navy had in view was that enclosed by Burma, Andaman, Sumatra, Java, the Sunda chain of islands, West New Guinea, Bismarck Islands, and the Marshalls. This was the original sphere we had undertaken to secure. In the course of the war, we changed this seven times.

The first change took place in January 1942. It came about this way: Operations were started on 8 December 1941 and went on very smoothly and rapidly. The Allies had been unprepared. Our progress looked like a typhoon that rolled up dry leaves. It was fondly called "superhuman swiftness." The progress was much quicker than had been expected. The damages suffered were not of much consequence. The leaders of the operations swelled with pride. They proposed a change of the sphere to be conquered and retained. The sphere first decided upon was extended and made to include Port Moresby, New Caledonia, Fiji and Samoa to the south, and Midway to the east. This change is a witness to a very poor forecast of the future of the war, as proven by subsequent developments.

This new plan met its first disappointment at Midway. It met the second disappointment in the impregnable pass of Stanley. The occupation of Morseby turned into a dream.

They changed the plan for the second time when the Americans began their attack on a corner of the Solomons. But this change was not anything rooted in a far-sighted view of the future of the war. It was of a patchwork sort. It just meant a discontinuance of offensive warfare and a decision to defend by the line of the Solomons and New Guinea.

[*Page 81:*]

In consequence, America and Japan fought around the Solomons with desperation. Our navy put in as many forces as were then available in these battles and consumed them very quickly. Already by this time, due to the increasing difficulty of transportation, the reinforcement of forces around the Solomons, Gilberts and Marshalls became well-nigh impossible. Those who were dazzled by the apparent (on the map) importance of those quarters and refused to see the grim realities of the situation obstinately refused to lend ears to the warnings to strengthen the defense of the inner Marianas lines. As late as the summer of 1943, the defense works in the direction of the Marianas consisted only of airfields, one each at Saipan and Tinian, absolutely no army forces, a few antiaircraft guns. No more.

Taking some lessons from the experience at Attu gone through in the course of May 1943, they drew a plan to reinforce the defenses of the Mariana and Caroline islands. This is the third change of the plan. On this occasion there was a heated discussion between the army and the navy, the former standing firmly for strengthening the defense of the inner lines, while the latter persisted in fortifying the Solomons. In consequence of such a circumstance, actually very little was accomplished. The decision at length was taken in September, and some more or less result was attained towards the end of the year. This was wasted in indecision.

In November 1943, American forces came attacking the Gilberts. If instead they had come directly to the Marianas, we would have had no preparation to defend them. If indeed the American forces had done that, the history of the Pacific war should have been somewhat briefer. The whole course of history might have been considerably shortened. Already our navy had been very much weakened by the loss of the air forces in

[*Page 82:*]

the course of the long fights around the Solomons, and more particularly in the battle of Bougainville during November of 1943, where we lost a large portion of air forces including carrier air forces. The defense forces were really almost nil in the Marianas. It was only in the course of 1944 that the defense of the Marianas was strengthened.

Believe it or not, it was only after we had fully tasted the efficiency of the American task forces around the Gilberts and Marshalls that the Japanese navy realized for the second time the value of the carrier air forces and admitted the undeniable fact that the real propelling force behind the American task forces was the tremendous power of their air arm. We had been given bitter experiences in the Coral Sea, Midway and Santa Cruz, but they concluded that, however powerful the American air forces might be, we could easily dispose of them by properly utilizing the myriads of unsinkable air bases (islands) scattered all over the sea areas in that direction. By such a conclusion our navy just deceived themselves, discounting the power of the American carrier air forces. The fact had escaped their notice that though one carrier cannot compare against one land base, the offensive power will increase at geometrical progression when the number of carriers goes on increasing, more specifically if the offensive power of one carrier is one, two units may develop a power of two, three may furnish four, four may six, seven or even more. For the acquisition of this knowledge we have been made to pay exorbitant prices at the Gilberts and the Marshalls. When we became wise, it was too late.

Now they came to conclude that Japan's one chance lay in a decisive duel with the American task forces. They hastened to prepare for this venture using the Marianas and Carolines as the bases of the operation.

[Page 83:]

On this plan they decided in May 1944. It was known as Plan *A-Go,* and is the fourth of the seven changes. According to this plan, the land-based units belonging to the First Air Fleet under Vice Admiral Kakuta's command were sent to the Mariana and Caroline bases, while the carrier-based air forces belonging to the First Task Forces under Vice Admiral Ozawa's command were dispatched to the Caroline areas. They aimed at a one-stroke decisive engagement. (The reason why the Mariana areas were not selected as the prospective theater of such engagement has already been stated.) All such literally life-consuming exertions by the First Air Fleet, the First Task Forces or the Mid-Pacific Fleet under Vice Admiral Nagumo's command, and the Japanese civilian residents in those regions, did not prove sufficient to make good the great mistake committed in the beginning of 1942 by Japan's war leaders who became overconfident as a result of the small success which just chance helped them to win. The initial mistake was indeed very serious. Not that alone, their survey of the war future even after 1942 was also wrong, far wide of the mark. They wasted the whole of 1943, doing nothing so far as the defense of the Marianas was concerned. This omission affected the whole course of the war very damagingly. The result was not only the undoing of the Japanese navy, but the crumbling of the last defense of the empire.

The Japanese navy went out to meet the American fleet which came to attack the Marianas in June 1944. Orders were given to the First Air Fleet and the First Task Forces to attack the enemy as had been planned. These units, however, just melted away before the American irresistible 58th Task Forces, which disposed of our forces just like a toy-thing. This marked the end of our navy's initiative for good and ever. We consumed the air forces which had composed the center and backbone of our fighting strength, complete consumption in one stroke,

[Page 84:]

leaving no chance of replenishment in the foreseeable future. The carrier-based air units in particular suffered a damage that was absolutely beyond repair. From this date, the war became one of pursuit for the United States and of retreat for Japan. We had to accept the inevitable.

Now a new plan was again formulated. We had decided to face the American naval forces which were coming on the Philippines with the remnant of the navy's air forces and the surface craft. This new plan was named *Sho-Go,* which meant "Number Victory." This decision was taken in July 1944. It was the fifth of the seven changes.

The forces available according to this "Number Victory" plan were the land-based joint air forces organized by the combination of the First and Second Air Fleets, the First and Second Attacking Forces and the Task Force. The land-based air forces numbered about 600 airplanes, but we could not depend very securely on their real fighting efficiency. The surface craft force consisted of the *Yamato* and the *Musashi* and seven other battleships, fifteen cruisers and about forty destroyers, but they were not well balanced. The carrier squadron had not yet recovered from the serious damages suffered the previous year in the Marianas areas, and so could not take part in the scheme. It was a fleet that did not include the air forces.

There was no contrivance to make up for this deficiency. We had to accept this damaging inferiority by all means, which circumstance compelled us to adopt a special system of attack later known as the "Special Attack Corps." This bloody or bloodless institution speaks for the poverty of our sciences. It was an idea born of an attitude which had made everything of spirit and nothing of material. Superstition begot such a monster, a heart-rending deformity that the genius

[*Page 85:*]

of the Japanese fighting spirit gave birth to for want of any alternative. If we only had had an equal force, if not a superior one, such could well have been dispensed with. Tragic and pathetic as the idea is, our American enemy gave some of them the nickname of "Baka Bomb," an idiot bomb. It was a V-plane manned by a live human being. This is a brave proposition, but when compared with the American "BAT" or the German V weapon, it testifies to the inferiority of the Japanese sciences. Our sense of shame burns when we think of so many promising youths victimized to this institution. But in those days we felt for want of an alternative upon such a measure to seek salvation out of certain defeat and ruin. They tried to seek relief in the popular maxims such as "find life in death," "wait for providence's dispensation after all human measures have been exhausted" and so forth. Now that everything has been irrevocably decided and our excitement subsided, we feel tormented by deep remorse. The Victory Number and the Creation Number did not prove true to their names. The recovery of the general situation became just hopeless.

The decisive battles of the Philippines started in October 1944 and came to the logical conclusion. Luzon fell in January of 1945. Japan's life line of transportation to the South Seas was cut off. The last fight became inevitable in the seas near Japan proper. Okinawa was naturally selected as the first theater of such a fight. The plan was drawn up in the course of March 1945 under this hypothesis. It was the sixth of the seven changes. The plan was known as "The Heaven Number Tactics."

The idea of "The Heaven Number Tactics" was to coordinate the actions on land and sea. It aimed to concentrate air attacks from the bases in Kyushu and Formosa, thereby upsetting and frustrating

[*Page 86:*]

America's offensive against Okinawa and so preparing to pave the way to winding up the war. The attainment of the objective looked easier than in the case of the Philippines, inasmuch as the operations were to be based in Japan Proper. It was to be regretted that our crack 9th Division had been shifted from Okinawa to Formosa to provide for the Philippine warfare the previous year. Besides, it was rather discouraging to miss "the fire" in the spirit of the army air forces when the

Okinawa battle was started. These two factors for pessimism, even if they had not existed, might not have meant much difference to the American operation staged on a scale gigantic beyond all proportions. Only we wished there had been more enthusiasm in the army's airmen.

Much to our grief, Okinawa fell at last. We had to plan preparations for the defense of Japan Proper. We drew up the 7th plan of the seven, the last plan, the conclusion. This plan was named the "Final Plan." For the navy this meant a plan for the air forces only, because by this time our navy had very little left in matters of surface craft. We had only small submarines and the Special Attack motor boats, the so-called *Shin-yo-tei*. It was a sorry remnant of the navy that four years before asserted a tremendous prestige on the western side of the Pacific Ocean. We had no trump card to meet the American assault on our motherland. We felt we lacked even the courage to doubt it. We had no chance to test our "Final Plan" in practice. The atomic bomb forestalled it. We threw up our hands. The fate of the empire was sealed.

The above is a frank description of our plan of operations for the defense of the empire. Our navy's leadership was faulty and defective. A review of its activities up until the end of 1943 reveals

[*Page 87:*]

beyond dispute that it lacked foresight, or more properly what foresight it had was entirely wrong. Moreover, it was very slow in awakening to the errors they had committed. They were not quick enough to change their ideas and attitude. Their errors resulted first in the fall of the Marianas, which meant practically a "Decision" for the entire warfare. After this, the war meant for the American navy successive stages of pursuit until it ended in Japan's acceptance of the Potsdam Declaration.

The errors in the forecast were not confined to the field of war operations only. Similar errors were in evidence everywhere. The state structure of Japan is very complicated, and this complication meant death to efficiency in many other respects. For one thing, it has killed the spirit of cooperation everywhere. More positively, it has been productive of ill will, irritation, the spirit of enmity between the different departments, between the Supreme Command and the administration, the army and the navy, between the bureaus of the same department, between each unit of the same fighting forces. At last it has unmade the old, venerable empire, alas!

THE LACK OF HARMONY AND UNITY

Short-sightedness, deficiency of endurance, reckless impatience that feature the Japanese character as a race, characterized the Japanese activities everywhere during the war.

From such fundamental shortcomings was born the fatal lack of unity in thought and actions. There was no well-unified, coordinated leadership. Actions were sporadic, which meant "planlessness." Between the government and the General Headquarters, the army and the navy, and everywhere there was no unity of thought, no unity of action.

The great defect of the Japanese character is the lack of cooperative spirit. Besides, we are very exclusive. These defective traits

[*Page 88:*]

of the Japanese character have wrought immense damages throughout the whole course of the war. These shortcomings have incapacitated us for team work, for a big enterprise, the success in which should necessarily presuppose a well-concerted action based on a cooperative spirit.

If one section does not understand another section's work, no team work can be accomplished. This mutual understanding between different departments engaged in different work was all the more important in our navy due to the inferiority of communications facilities. To illustrate by one instance, when scouting planes started on their mission, the crew of one plane have to be thoroughly aware not only of the nature of the other airplanes' mission, but of the general ultimate purpose the entire unit has in view to attain. In spite of the great effort made to insure such a mutual understanding, the result has left very much to be desired. On the side of the Allies, complete harmony of actions was maintained and assured throughout the entire system. Their entire organization acted just like one man under the baton of one leader in spite of the infinite variety of ramifications. We could never do that, and our efficiency was always much lower.

Moreover, our plans and actions were alike nonscientific, very much of rule-of-thumb fashion. They lacked rigid system, which deplorable circumstances rendered everything very complicated, confusing and difficult of handling. It called for superhuman abilities to extract a unified, concentrated action out of such a mass of chaos. Hope and effort at last were given up, and everybody, every unit just shifted for itself. This subject from the broad, general standpoint has already been very much discussed, so here I will limit my discussion to what concerned the navy only.

[*Page 89:*]

1. In the period directly before the surrender, from about the beginning of July, the American task forces kept on giving punitive attacks all over the mainland of Japan, to which we replied only sporadically in the twilight and during the night. Sometimes we even completely missed the counterattacks by fighting planes or responses by the anti-aircraft. Was this due to the evaporation of the fighting spirit or the lack of ammunition?

In fact, against these breathless attacks by the American task forces, some of our air units, some of the commanders-in-chief of the naval bases and the Air Fleet, urged upon the commander-in-chief of the navy the wisdom and necessity of undertaking a counterattack. The commander-in-chief of the navy would not lend an ear to this suggestion. His attitude was adamant, imperturbable: "If we consumed our airplanes now, what could we do when the enemy commenced their landing operations on the mainland?" This was his idea. He meant to keep what still remained of the air force for the last supreme moment. He was never aware that peace talks had long since been going on and it had already been decided to accept an unconditional surrender. If he had only known this, he would have used without stinting all the air forces there were, as the enemy's landing operations were never to take place. The government was doing one thing, the Supreme Commander on the front line quite another. Between the two there was no communication, no understanding, no concerted action. Such is really inconceivable, but nevertheless quite true. American planes' ceaseless attacks had been nothing but a mute response to our appeal for surrender!

2. Now let me examine the navy's relation to the army, whose cooperation was absolutely needed in the amphibian defense operations when the enemy came landing.

[Page 90:]

Japanese amphibian operations continued to be modestly successful only for a short while, from 8 December 1941 to the spring months of 1942. In the amphibian operations, the navy's mission as we understood it, included the protection and piloting of the transports, covering the operation by barrage and so forth. The rest belonged to the army. Such an idea was, however, out of date, not up-to-date, not modern. In the incipient stages, our amphibian operations were successful, because the enemy had not been prepared. When, however, the Allies began to offer resistance after the summer of 1942, our structure built on sand readily crumbled. Our amphibian operations ended with the taking of Rabi on the southeastern extremity of New Guinea. At the battle of the Solomons, the worthlessness of our amphibian operation was proven beyond all dispute.

The indispensability of equipping both our army and navy just like the Allies, if we were to carry out the amphibian operations with any measure of success, dawned on our war leaders only this late. Thereupon the army and the navy started to build landing craft, but quite independently of each other. There was no idea of consultation. What was more amazing was that the army set about building submarine transports. Between the two departments of the national defense there was no concert even as regards such important issues. Besides, there were no serious, careful studies about the particular forces to man such boats and their equipment, let alone any positive plan to insure an efficient cooperation to such an end. Thus here also there was no unity of actions.

These hastily-built transports were used in October 1944 in actual fighting in the Philippines, but the result was far from satisfactory. We felt bitter disappointment. On the part of the Americans, they handled their task forces, amphibian forces, marine corps and land

[Page 91:]

forces with marvelous efficiency, enabling each unit to display the maximum of its power separately no less than as one unified organization. Here was food for thought. What makes for such a great difference? On our enemy's part, an organization of forces on such a great scale, incurring perfect dovetailing between each unit composing the whole, maintaining a concert of actions that left nothing to be desired, making possible the development of efficiency that absolutely defied comparison, where does this all come from? Our inferiority came home to us keenly. We feel like acquiescing in our defeat without a murmur.

THE REAL MERIT OF THE AMERICAN FIGHTING FORCES

When we first embarked on this war with the United States, we felt a very real fear of her enormous resources; nevertheless, we were quite confident of our fighting spirit, which we felt was indisputably superior. Our estimate of America's natural resources, however, was not based on accurate scientific calculation. It was just a vague general feeling. So we reckoned to beat America at the start, and this reckoning we based on the comparative number of the then readily available warcraft on the Pacific chessboard. After such an initial victory, we calculated to fight it through by sheer dint of superior fighting technique. With such a mental attitude we took a plunge. We were firmly confident in our allegedly superior fighting technique and fighting spirit. The initial victories in Pearl Harbor, Malay, the Philippines, Java and Sumatra only helped this self-confidence grow. The confidence became overconfidence, self-conceit and culminated in the awful mess of Midway.

Subsequently we met the Americans taking the offensive on a really grand scale beginning around the Solomons. When we started to lose one battle after another, we could not but fully admit, if reluctantly, that

[*Page 92:*]

the Americans' fighting technique and spirit were something we were entirely unprepared for. We were made to taste the full meed of it. When we experienced the misfortune of being a close witness of America's maximum efficiency displayed around the Marianas in the course of 1944, we just gave up all hopes of victory. The Pacific war has given Americans an opportunity to display their full fighting efficiency. Far across the immense space of the Pacific Ocean they have come, attacked, and brought Japan to her knees. They have accomplished an immortal exploit. The glory of American arms will shine on the pages of world history until the end of time. The ignominy of it for Japan, on the other hand! We have shamed our ancestors by our ignorance and folly!

This war may mark an end of the system of warfare based on heat emanation and machineries. If World War III should occur, it will perhaps be fought on an entirely different principle. We think we have correctly grasped the real essence of the American fighting power. It is its essence, her unsurpassed organizing power and ability to do teamwork on a scale vast beyond human imagination. It is human electricity to which her big navy, gigantic air forces, immense army, stupendous transportation, inexhaustible resources would be but wires, dynamos, plugs, and what not. In the last analysis, America's superior fighting power is only one expression of her superior manpower.

We had entertained a great error in the survey of the American racial character. We had thought that we could easily tackle them and that a race steeped in material comfort, seemingly absorbed in a hunt for pleasure, was spiritually degenerate. It was too late when we discovered the Americans, the true Americans. They stood up for the defense of liberty, and once they stood up for that great idea, no price was too

[*Page 93:*]

dear for them. They scorned life itself. They sacrificed their everything, all earthly pleasures, the intimate ties of family affection, even ostentatious sense of glory. Their ideal became everything for them. They fought desperately, furiously, fanatically, insensible to danger, forgetful of self. The Americans that appeared in "Gone with the Wind" appeared again absolutely unchanged in the present war. We have discovered that bravery and self-sacrifice is not the sole monopoly of the Japanese.

On 24 January 1942, when we attacked Balikpapan, in Borneo, four American destroyers charged into the midst of the Japanese transports lying at anchor in the harbor, and sank four of them and inflicted serious damage on a patrol boat. In those days our fleet was nothing like the thing it became towards the end of the war. It was well equipped, strong and all-powerful, a tough enemy to deal with. The American commander who dashed with small craft into the midst of the transports under convoy by such a powerful fleet did indeed challenge certain death. It is beyond all doubt that he and his men had taken a death-defying resolution.

On 12 November 1942, in the battles of Guadalcanal, the American fleet under Rear Admiral Callaghan's command encountered the "Tokyo Express" composed of the battleships *Hiei, Kirishima* and about ten other warships within the anchorage of Guadalcanal. This meant for him an almost hopeless adventure, because his fleet had suffered defeat at the hands of "Tokyo Express No. 1." Admiral Callaghan's mental attitude on that occasion must have been quite similar to that of Lieutenant Cushing in the American Civil War. By the way, it was a strange affinity of fate that on this occasion an American destroyer by the name of *Cushing* met its doom.

[*Page 94:*]

In the aerial fights also there should have been a great number of unknown heroes. Of those that came within the ken of our knowledge, we may name those that came to attack Tokyo under General Doolittle's command on 18 April 1942, and those that chased our fleet in the twilight hours of 20 June 1944, in the engagement of the Philippines. This was a really reckless adventure. It was in the twilight. The distance was almost a record one. The landing back on the carriers when they returned after dark and using up the fuel is an impossible feat. On this calculation we had not expected this. Our amazement surpassed bounds when we sighted them. This could not be done by mere spirit of adventure. Only the supreme sense of self-sacrifice could have inspired them to such a heroic deed!

Before the war we refused to attribute any practical value to the torpedo boat. But great was our surprise when the Americans employed this weapon against our "Tokyo Express." We had miscalculated when we judged this type of vessel as of no value. We had always depended upon the rough waves that rolled in the seas near Japan. Somehow we had imagined that war with America would be fought only in the seas near Japan Proper where the high waves would rob such small torpedo boats of any fighting capacity. As it actually turned out, our fond battle in the area that suited our convenience never occurred. The American navy used it with great effect in the South Seas, where the seas are quite smooth. "To err is human!" came home.

In the battle of Leyte, October of 1944, the Japanese fleet composed of the battleships *Yamashiro* and *Fuso* and other lighter craft fell victim to American torpedoes without inflicting any damages worth mention on the enemy. The operation of torpedoes requires supreme cour-

[*Page 95:*]

age, nerves of steel. Americans did the job with full credit to themselves.

Americans also acquitted themselves of the scouting activities in the most splendid manner. They spread their nets on the immense waste of the Pacific for the search of hostile elements. Nothing could escape their vigilance, not even a submarine periscope. The constant activities of their scouting planes, keeping up untiring efforts in successful pursuit of their objectives puts to shame some of our naval flying boats which were devoured by the American hunting dogs (destroyers) even before they took to the air. (At Tulagi, August 1942.) The American vigilance versus the Japanese torpor makes a striking contrast! The American destroyers caught our flying boats without giving them time to fly up!

All through the war, almost not once could our fleet escape the vigilance of the American navy. In the battle off Santa Cruz our Third Fleet was almost caught unawares by the enemy that was invisible. A single bomb dropped by an American plane gave us warning in time. We escaped by a hairbreadth falling in the snare that the American navy had prepared for us. We were given time to prepare, and the battle that followed resulted in our favor. For us it was a "bomb of salvation."

On 27 May 1944, our navy's anniversary day, the Allied Forces came to Biak Island to land there. Having the mission of transporting the reinforcement forces on that island, our fleet with the army forces aboard started from Davao in the Philippines and cruised towards the island. In no time the American patrol flying forces detected and compelled it to turn back. This was really an amazing feat because the American patrol planes came from the far-away (almost 1,000 miles) base of Hollandia, New Guinea.

[*Page 96:*]

The activities of the B29, flying all over Japan, night and day, rain or shine or wind, scouting bombing, dropping different kinds of mines in the Inland Sea which had hitherto been considered absolutely safe from aggression, in the waters around Japan North and South, East and West, causing sclerosis of the traffic arteries of the empire and working havoc in the economic life of the people and ultimately forcing the Japanese government to accept a surrender that was unconditional—well, these were the activities on the part of our enemies. They just compelled wonder and admiration in spite of ourselves. Their intrepid valor, untiring endurance, conquering whatever obstacles came their way, would defy all attempts at imitation by this race that is short of temper, gets soon hot and soon cold, impatient and unendurable, possessed of many a defect fatal to the accomplishment of a great scheme.

Let us indulge some introspection. We have done brave feats, self-sacrificing, exposing ourselves to all imaginable dangers, charging amid rains of shells, using our bodies as bombs and torpedoes, readily resigning to our fate in the unshakable faith that we were fighting for the emperor and the country, and in doing that we forgot every interest that was dear and precious to us, ties of family affection, comfort and flesh, longings for life, and such attitude we used to call the "Fighting

Spirit of Japan!'' But is such a spirit exclusive to this race? Is that Japan's monopoly? In the attitude towards death there is some difference in some cases: Sometimes we die for death's sake, making the attainment of the objective something like a by-product. Americans never do this. They never court death for the love of it, but when the attainment of an objective calls for defiance of death, they do not fear to die. They are just as fearless as we are. As far as the effect to the adversaries is concerned, there is absolutely no difference between our attitude and theirs.

[*Page 97:*]

Before the battle of the Marianas in June 1944 we had thought, felt dead certain that American forces could never venture across the most dangerous reef zones, but here also we were wrong. Their Underwater Demolition Corps just blasted the apparently insurmountable barriers and opened the path for the landing of their troops which followed just like gigantic breakers, wave after wave with a force and dash that was irresistibly overwhelming. They did all this in the face of our terrific fire and under showers of bombs from the air. They had, however, never demonstrated such a daredevil bravery before their mine-sweeping corps cleaned the sea areas of the mines we had thickly planted to block them. They had done everything humanly possible to minimize the danger, and then they came up with a fury that laughed death to scorn. They will not die any more than they can help. Theirs is a civilized man's warfare. When we had learned the precious lessons, the war was already over.

Their ''Guinea Pig System'' is an institution quite the same in spirit as our ''Special Attack Corps.'' The crew of the ''Guinea Pig'' drive their craft across the mined areas just to touch and cause the mines to blow up. Taking the risk on themselves, they make the route safe for their comrades that follow. This is certainly the most effective way to clean the path and remove the dangers. In such a case death must be braved. It is necessary to risk death. Then they just play with death. The spirit of America, nothing different from ours.

We had, however, not yet fully comprehended the true worth of the American soldiers. This chance came only after our surrender.

Following Japan's acceptance of the Potsdam Declaration on 15 August 1945, the Allied advance groups landed towards the end of that month at Atsugi, Yokosuka and adjacent districts, preparatory to receiving Japan's convoys for signing the surrender terms. Atsugi was

[*Page 98:*]

formerly our naval base where our air forces used to stay under a commander renowned for his peerless intrepidity. Among his subordinates there were quite a few who were at heart very indignant at the ignominy of surrender. These recalcitrant elements had been thoroughly eliminated before the arrival of the American representatives, so that those appointed to surrender at that base were all resigned to the inexorable fate. They were looking forward with great interest to this arrival of the American representatives. Meantime, they arrived.

On arrival they did not avail themselves of the various accommodations prepared by the Japanese for them. They did everything by their own hands with amazing deftness. We were witness to the perfect cooperation among all their personnel. From the commander to the lowest of the subordinates acted just like one man.

We have already watched every piece of action done by the Americans on this occasion, and the thought flashed on our minds: "Our defeat was no accident." There were more than enough convincing reasons for the American victory. Such an impression was not in Atsugi alone. It was the same at Yokosuka, Kanoya and at all other places where the Occupation Forces landed, the real worth of the American forces is not their material superiority. It is their brains that handled the materials.

CONCLUSION

I have written this booklet with a view to explaining why our navy with its thorough knowledge of America as a result of many years' ceaseless study should have assented to war with her. In Chapter I, I gave my opinion that the fatal decision was the result of an erroneous education that produced a confusion in the naval mind between the war and the battle. One bold decisive stroke in the pitted engagement between the two massed fleets was our navy's idea of the American-Japanese war.

[*Page 99:*]

In Chapter II, I dwelt on the errors, miscalculations, failures and losses that resulted from the original misconception. The ultimate defeat is the most eloquent witness of the blunders of which our naval authorities had been guilty. By way of further illustrations, I have cited many actual instances, showing the activities and the merits of the American forces, especially of their navy.

After all, my conclusion is: Our navy has lost the war by "battling" instead of "warring." This fatal confusion was due in my judgment to our erroneous education. To point out what should have been the right education is idle effort. Our navy is no more. The verdict was severe. In conclusion I wish to mention just one thing. And it is that education is important, really very important.

In 1907 Prince Higashi-Fushimi went to Europe. His suite included the late Admiral Kanji Kato who was then a commander, and the late Colonel Matsuishi who died rather young. It was about the time when our Naval College was established. One evening, Colonel Matsuishi called on Commander Kato and expressed his congratulation on the promotion of the Naval College, but in his congratulations he mixed his warning:

We (the army) have had the Military College already for some years. Major Meckel (German) has been directing the course of the education in the college as an advisor, and already he has brought his personal influence very much to bear on the spirit of the students. Unfortunately he has inspired the young brains with Machiavellian ideas, which is something very much to be bewailed. This is very dangerous, apt to mislead the young officers to undesirable consequences. You have just started the Naval College. It is fresh and clean. The beginning is very important. I hope and pray for its future that you will keep Machiavellianism outdoors by all means.

This is said to have been a warning given by an army officer forty years ago to the navy. Admiral Kato told us this episode one evening at a small party to which we invited him after his retirement from the

[*Page 100:*]

navy's active service. Our navy took this warning very seriously, kept away from politics, concentrated our attention to what strictly concerned the navy only. But we made a mistake of a different kind, a grave mistake that ultimately has proved the navy's undoing, just as the army has been poisoned by Machiavellianism and dug its grave. We conceived the war with America on a far too small scale, studied it as a battle. The idea of the Battle of Tsushima has prepossessed us, this fatal ''One Decisive Battle Idea.'' We never became aware of this mistake, much less outgrew it. We find ourselves done for!

INDEX

Map Used to Brief Emperor Hirohito on December 27, 1941

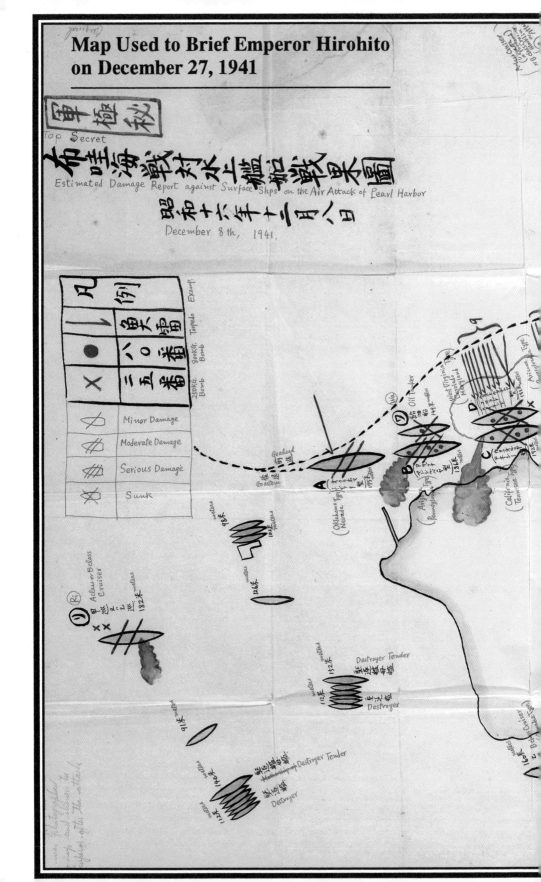